The Cherokee Diaspora

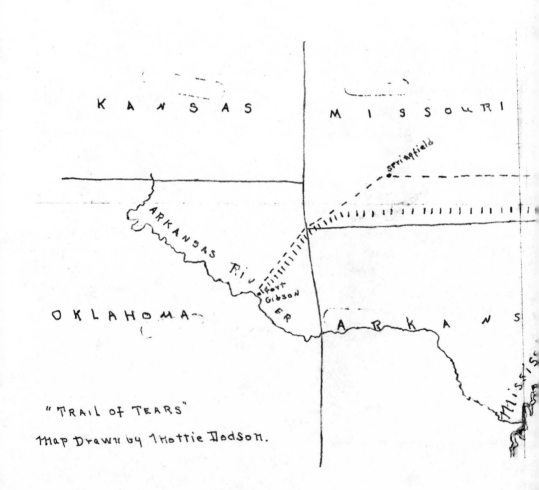

K A N S A S

M I S S O U R I

Springfield

ARKANSAS Riv

Fort
Gibson
ER

O K L A H O M A

A R K A N S

MISSISS

"TRAIL OF TEARS"

Map Drawn by Thottie Dodson.

GREGORY D. SMITHERS

The Cherokee Diaspora

An Indigenous History of Migration,
Resettlement, and Identity

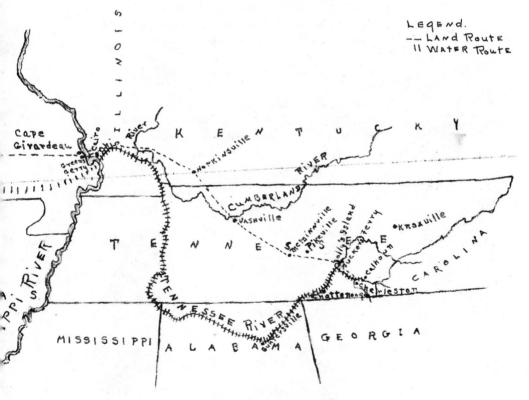

Yale UNIVERSITY PRESS/NEW HAVEN & LONDON

Map on pages ii and iii: Mottie Dodson's Map of the Trail of Tears, M1990.052, ca. 1830s, Oklahoma Historical Society, Research Division. At the end of the nineteenth century, the Dawes Commission recognized Dodson as Cherokee by blood, a legal designation that Cherokee officials disputed. Still, Dodson dedicated herself to preserving Cherokee history. The overland route shown in this map depicts the Northern Route (ignoring Benge's and Bell's routes), which ran south of the Northern Route, while the water route that Dodson attempted to portray in actuality took Cherokee exiles west along the Tennessee River, south down the Mississippi River, and west to Indian Territory along the Arkansas River. Dodson's cartographic imprecision is a poetic reminder of the uncertainties of life in the nineteenth-century Cherokee diaspora.

Yale University Press books may be purchased in quantity for educational, business, or promotional use. For information, please e-mail sales.press@yale.edu (U.S. office) or sales@yaleup.co.uk (U.K. office).

Set in Minion type by Newgen North America.
Printed in the United States of America.

ISBN 978-0-300-16960-7 (cloth : alk. paper)

Library of Congress Control Number: 2015933298

A catalogue record for this book is available from the British Library.

This paper meets the requirements of ANSI/NISO z39.48-1992 (Permanence of Paper).

10 9 8 7 6 5 4 3 2 1

For Brooke

Contents

Prologue

On a cold, bleak winter afternoon in July 2001, I sat in the reading room of the National Archives of Australia in Canberra, Australia's capital city. Cradled on the desk in front of me was immigration file A12513. On a single page, printed on both sides, was an application for residency, dated December 17, 1965. The document had an unmistakably musty smell, but its contents, both typed and handwritten, were clearly legible. The information in that file revealed to me that an American family wished to settle just outside of Brisbane, the capital city of Queensland, under the Commonwealth of Australia's "General assistance passage scheme." In its bureaucratic format there existed nothing exceptional about this application; that is, until I began reading the genealogical information attributed to the matriarch of the family—a family consisting of eleven people. Cherokee Meeks nee Taylor was her name. At first I thought nothing of it. I read on. Cherokee Meeks's mother, Georgia A. Taylor, was "White, English decent and Quarter Cherokee Indian."[1]

Cherokee Meeks was, to use a phrase that was still part of the racial lexicon in the United State and Australia during the 1960s, a "mixed-blood."[2] Hastily written annotations filled the margins around the blank space where a dutiful government bureaucrat had typed Cherokee Meeks's name. Her father, according to the anonymous individual who penned those notes, was Charles F. Taylor, "White, English descent." He claimed to be born in Summers, Arkansas. His wife, Georgia A. Taylor nee Rogers, was born at Fort Gibson in Indian Territory. Their daughter, Cherokee, was also born at Fort Gibson, on a crisp December day in 1921. As I gained a genealogical snapshot of Cherokee Meeks's heritage, myriad questions crossed my mind. Why did her parents name her Cherokee? Was her mother concerned that her own Indigenous identity had become so "diluted" by centuries of intermarriage and interracial sexual encounters that she wanted her daughter to have a constant reminder that she was not simply "white" but descended from the Cherokee people? Names, and the practice of naming, matter. They can tell us a great deal about social power relations, cultural values, and personal aspirations. In the year Cherokee was born, 1921, the law had more or less adopted the rhetoric of "blood quantum" and the practice of reducing Americans to a cold set of numbers—1/4; 1/2; 3/16; 5/16; 1/256 "blood"—that defined genealogy in racial terms.[3] Did Georgia worry that government demographers might define her daughter's Cherokee ancestry out of existence? In giving her daughter the name Cherokee, what values, historical images, and memories did Georgia Rogers have in mind? What did she think it meant to be "Cherokee"? More importantly, what did she want her daughter to think it meant to be Cherokee?

It is not clear who penned the genealogical notes on that 1965 application for residency. It might have been a faceless bureaucrat, or it could just as easily have been her husband, Fred Tucker Meeks. Fred Meeks was a white man. He met Cherokee sometime during the early 1940s. They married at Fort Smith, Arkansas, on December 20, 1945. Together, they had nine children—eight boys and one girl—ranging in age from eighteen to three at the time of their residency application. Fred and Cherokee clearly hoped to make a new life for their family in Queensland. It was a good choice; Fred had worked for a time as a rancher and as an electrician, and had experience in public service— in Denver, Colorado, and Tulsa, Oklahoma, respectively. Additionally, the family claimed to have financial resources at its disposal, declaring "Twenty five Hundred Dollars in Clothing and Ranching equipment, such as Saddles, Fifteen to Twenty Thousand Dollars in Currency, on

Arrival." The Meeks family was the kind of immigrants the Commonwealth of Australia wanted.

Still, Australia remained a deeply racist and color-conscious society in the mid 1960s. Its immigration laws reinforced the ideals popularly referred to as the "White Australia" policy. So why would a woman of Cherokee descent—a wife and mother of nine—want to relocate to such a country? Were Fred and Cherokee even aware of Australia's racial politics? Probably not; they had no reason to know, or care. Australian immigration officials did care, however. It was their assessment that Fred and Cherokee were "white Americans" and would "assimilate" into Australian society. Still, someone thought it important enough to make that notation about Cherokee's mother: "White, English decent and Quarter Cherokee Indian."

I was not in Australia that winter to conduct archival research on the Cherokees. I had other questions, and many, many, other sources to grapple with. So, immigration file A12513 sat in my external hard drive for the next five years. I was unable to forget about Fred and Cherokee, however. I often opened that file; when I did I returned to the questions that had swirled through my mind on the other side of the world that July afternoon in 2001. What on earth were Fred and Cherokee Meeks doing, thinking, feeling, in applying for residency in a country neither of them had ever been to, where they had no kin to help ease the transition to life in a foreign nation? And that issue of Cherokee Meeks's identity continued to raise questions in my mind. Did she feel comfortable being perceived as a "white American"? If so, why did her husband feel the need to provide details about her Cherokee genealogy? Would Cherokee have wanted Fred to divulge that information? Was it part of the family's history to openly and unflinchingly talk about such details? Perhaps this was exactly what Georgia A. Taylor intended. No matter where life took her daughter, Cherokee would never—indeed, could never—forget that little part of her history, her "blood," that was "Indian." Immigration file A12513 left me with more questions than answers.

Finding answers to the questions I had about Cherokee Meeks's identity, the motives behind her migrations, and the aspirations of her family to settle in a faraway land has not been easy. Colonial archives are often suspiciously silent on such matters. Indeed, historian Rose Strem-lau seemed to channel my own exasperation with the archives of settler colonial America when she observed that "before and after removal, the Cherokee diaspora largely went undocumented."[4] I began this project hoping to transcend these historical silences. Whether or not we are to inquire about the identities of Native Americans and the African and African American people whose lives intersected with the Cherokees during the eighteenth and nineteenth centuries, I was determined to squeeze out of the archives (and non-archival sources) answers to my questions about Cherokee concepts of "home," "blood," "tradition," "migration," and "identity."

Like the written archives of American colonialism, the cartography of settler colonialism—which would be incomplete without its maps of shrinking Native American landholdings and the coerced Atlantic crossings taken by African slaves to the New World—offers up decep-tively simplistic insights. Take, for example, Emma Willard's elementary school primer entitled *A Series of Maps* (1828). Released just two years before President Andrew Jackson signed the Indian Removal Act, Wil-lard's primer provided cartographic "proof" that the Cherokee Indians were a sedentary people with no history of migration.[5] One map was particularly striking for the way it portrayed the fixed geographical loca-tion of the Cherokee people. While the Shawnee, Delaware, Iroquois, Huron, Yamasee, and Lower Creek were all represented as having histo-ries of travel and migration, a large green oval superimposed on the map of Southeastern North America instructed students that the land within that color-coded oval had always been part of the Cherokee Nation.[6]

Despite Willard's prominence as an educational reformer, her map of the "Locations and Wanderings of the Aboriginal Tribes" proved a blunt educational tool.[7] It was not until the Smithsonian Institution's James Mooney conducted ethnological studies of the North Carolina Cherokees at the turn of the nineteenth and twentieth centuries that a more nuanced picture of Cherokee ethnohistory began to take shape.[8]

What, then, do we know about the Cherokee? Since the late nine-teenth century, historians, anthropologists, and archeologists have pieced together a historical narrative of the Cherokee past. That nar-

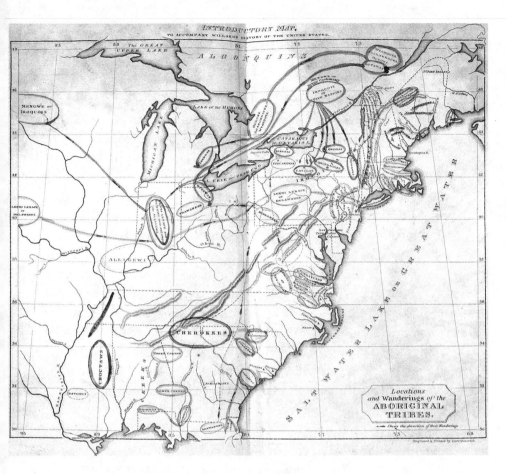

Figure 1: Emma Willard's "Locations and Wanderings of the Aboriginal Tribes." William L. Clements Library, University of Michigan, Ann Arbor.

rative routinely begins with scholars noting that the Cherokee are an Iroquoian-speaking people—possibly descended from a migratory group of northern Iroquois Indians—who settled in a vast and diverse area that included the modern-day states of Virginia, West Virginia, North and South Carolina, Georgia, Alabama, Tennessee, and Kentucky. By the time Europeans encountered Cherokees in the sixteenth century, Cherokee people knew this vast region as their homeland. In the woodland South, the Cherokee came to be known to Iroquoian-speaking people to their north, and Indigenous peoples throughout the South, as Cave People or Cave Dwellers. Cherokee oral tradition referred to

Cherokees as *Eshheeloarchie*, a Cherokee word meaning Keeper of the Sacred Fire.[9]

Contrary to Willard's 1828 insinuation that Cherokee history did not involve large-scale migrations and resettlements, archeologists and linguistics are now in general agreement that the Cherokee's ancient forebears migrated in a north-to-south trajectory and settled in the southern Appalachian Mountains almost 4,000 years ago. By the time the first Europeans encountered the Cherokees in the sixteenth century—the Spanish explorer Hernando de Soto led an expedition that saw him cross paths with the Cherokees in 1540—the Cherokee people lived in well-established towns. By the eighteenth century, the Cherokees placed great importance on their towns. The Cherokees defined a town as a group of people sharing the same ceremonial and council center. Typically, Cherokee people located these towns at the headwaters of rivers that flowed in an easterly and southerly direction. Cherokee townspeople spoke one of three regionally distinct dialects (the Lower, or *Elati* dialect; the Middle, or *Kituhwa* dialect; and the Western, or *Otali* dialect), and had well-established social conventions.[10] Cherokees understood that certain towns had specific functions and their chiefs had clearly defined roles. "Mother Towns," for instance, were sites of clan leadership, and the chiefs who presided over the town council were divided between red, or "war" chiefs, and white, or "peace" chiefs.

While town membership constituted a vital component of Cherokee corporate, or communal, identity, equally important was clan identity. One's clan identity gave both shape and meaning to cultural beliefs and practices. Exogamous marriage customs, the administration of justice, and the definition of gender roles were all influenced by clan membership.[11] Clan identity was characterized by a totemic system involving membership in one of seven matrilineal clans—*Aniwahya* (Wolf Clan); *Ani Tsiskwa* (Small Bird Clan); *Anikawi* (Deer Clan); *Anigilohi* (Twister Clan); *Anisahoni* (Blue Clan); *Anigatogewi* (Wild Potato Clan); *Aniwodi* (Red Paint Clan). Individuals lacking clan affiliation, such as captives of war or "strangers," stood outside the Cherokee system of reciprocity and mutual responsibility. Cherokees labeled captives *atsi-nahsa'i* (lacking kinship ties); they were, in essence, slaves, and as such lacked the protections that came with town and clan affiliation. However, unlike the racial slavery that characterized nineteenth-century American society, atsi-nahsa'i status did not necessarily entail a lifetime of bondage. The atsi-nahsa'i, who played a relatively minor role in the economic life of traditional Cherokee society, had a fluid identity that could just as easily involve adoption into a clan, or they could remain a slave and outside of clan obligations and protections.[12] The children of atsi-nahsa'i did not inherit the status of a slave.

Most histories of the Cherokees begin with this type of summary of "traditional" Cherokee life. An overwhelmingly large number of studies use this summary as the entry-point to frame the evolution of Cherokee political history toward a centralized form of government modeled on the American republic.[13] Historical narratives of the Cherokee routinely focus on the determined but ultimately failed attempts of a small mission-educated political elite to use the centralized Cherokee government to resist the federal government's forced removal of the Cherokees in 1838 and 1839.[14]

A small cohort of scholars has deepened our understanding of Cherokee history over the past generation by expanding the geographical and chronological scope of historical analysis. For example, John Finger's historical studies of the North Carolina Cherokees extended well into the twentieth century. More recent analysis by historian Rose Stremlau reveals how Cherokees in both North Carolina and Indian Territory grappled with economic, territorial, and political travails during the late nineteenth and early twentieth centuries while also striving to sustain kinship bonds and connections to community.[15] Historical research on Cherokee women has revealed the dynamism of Cherokee gender roles, relationships, and identities since the eighteenth century, while the groundbreaking scholarship of historian Theda Perdue on Cherokee slavery, race, and gender has provided readers with stunningly original insights and important syntheses regarding Cherokee history.[16]

This book builds on this prior scholarship. It does so with the aim of peeling back the layers of Cherokee history and revealing an even deeper, more complex, and richer past.[17] The following analysis focuses on three interconnected concepts: migration and resettlement, memory, and identity. I will elaborate on the theoretical dimensions of these concepts below. Suffice it to say, between the French and Indian War (the American theater of the Seven Years' War, 1756–63) and the Second World War (1939–1945), the experiences of migration and resettlement (be they forced or free), and the vagaries of memory, prompted innovations and changes in the way Cherokees understood identity. Cherokees traditionally defined identity in terms of the "Soul." Traditional Cherokee belief posits the existence of multiple souls. One is located in the head. This soul is a gift from the Creator, it is eternal, and it informs memory and consciousness. The second soul is located in the liver. It is responsible for the removal of yellow and black bile from the body. The third soul is located in the heart and circulates blood throughout the body. The fourth soul is found in the bones and underscores how men and women complement each other in Cherokee society.[18]

Settler colonialism changed the physical and cultural context in which Cherokees understood these multiple souls, and thereby altered who they imagined themselves to be as members of a communally oriented society. Frontier violence, trade with European colonizers, the arrival of Christian missionaries, and pressure from settler colonial authorities to cede Cherokee lands prompted Cherokees to give renewed meaning to old narratives. At the same time, the social dislocation and loss of knowledge that occurred following the arrival of Europeans, and the related outbreaks of disease during the sixteenth and seventeenth centuries, produced new traditions. Cherokees therefore engaged in the processes of cultural invention, reinvention, and renewal as many began to feel disconnected from their social structures, their cultural beliefs, and their ceremonial practices. By the end of the eighteenth and beginning of nineteenth century, some Cherokees grew to believe that the only means of preserving some semblance of Cherokee identity, or soul, involved migration.[19]

The chapters that follow focus on the years roughly between 1756 and 1945. During this period the Cherokees became a diasporic people. Unlike other diasporas—the Jewish, Armenian, Greek, Italian, African, Mormon, and even the Aztec—the Cherokee diaspora has earned scant attention from scholars of Cherokee history.[20] Thus, when I discovered that random 1965 file in the National Archives of Australia from a Cherokee family seeking permission to migrate and settle in Queensland, I had virtually no books or articles to help me explain how or why the

Cherokees became a traveling, diasporic people. I knew, for instance, that the Cherokee population in California grew from 258 in 1930 to 51, 394 by 1980, due in large part to intermarriage and the federal government's post-World War II policy of terminating tribal governments.[21] The Indian Relocation Act (1956) buttressed this policy. It encouraged Native American people to relocate from reservations and settle in urban centers like Los Angeles and Chicago. Still, I had no real answer to the "why" questions that I began asking in 2001. I needed to dig deeper, and farther back in time. Why did Cherokees migrate and settle in California? Why did some attempt to migrate and resettle in Australia, half a world away? This book seeks to answer these questions and to provide a better understanding of the origins of the Cherokee diaspora.

The following analysis is structured in a largely chronological fashion. However, while I am conscious of the importance of chronology in narrating continuity and/or change over time, I am also cognizant of the fact that human beings do not live their lives in the neatly packaged book chapters or historiographical boundaries constructed by historians. In fact, while eighteenth-, nineteenth-, and early twentieth-century racial nomenclature labeled people as "full-bloods" and "half-breeds" (and sometimes "mixed breeds"), the panoply of human experiences and identities that emerged in the Cherokee diaspora defies easy characterization. I have tried to remain true to the racial language used to describe Cherokees, and used by Cherokees to describe themselves, between the mid-eighteenth century and the early twentieth century. Whereas some scholars prefer to refer to "half-breeds" as "biracial" Cherokees, readers will quickly discern from the genealogies presented in this book that this more contemporary label is no more or less accurate (or offensive) than the former. I have therefore chosen to use the term "multiracial" throughout my analysis, a term that is somewhat awkward and imperfect to be sure, but which to my mind more accurately captures both the awkwardness and the tense mediation that accompanied diplomatic, trade, and cross-cultural encounters between Native Americans and Europeans after the sixteenth century. Moreover, the term "multiracial" moves us beyond the simplistic tendency in Anglo-American culture to refer to people of mixed racial and cultural ancestry as "biracial" or "bicultural" (and more offensive terms such as "half-breed" and "mixed-blood"), thus focusing our attention on the multiple generations of biological mixing and deep cultural layers that became one of the hallmarks of the Cherokee diaspora between the late eighteenth century and early twentieth.[22]

If these warnings about racial nomenclature and the articulation of artificial cultural binaries clarify anything it is that the chapters in this book are intended to reveal the untidiness, uncertainty, and anxiety that accompanied different forms of travel and migration, historically significant events, and new relationships—be they of a racial, political, economic, or cultural nature. To try to recover that level of complexity, it is sometimes necessary for the historian to think laterally, to appreciate the ways in which human lives, events, and ideas so often overlap, intersect, and make a mockery of our categorization of the world and its human history.

People of Cherokee descent had been engaged in such interpretive processes long before Europeans began arriving in the Americas during the sixteenth century. Like other woodland tribes who resided in what became the North American South—a vast geographical region extending from the Mississippi River to the Gulf of Mexico, and east to the James River and Chesapeake Bay—the Cherokees never had a static culture and identity, nor were they geographically fixed to a large yet ill-defined region on Western maps.[23] Having developed both innovative and adaptive cultural beliefs and social structures, the Cherokee people engaged in a process that anthropologists call "cycling" in an effort to maintain a collective identity and a sense of distinctiveness. Archeological evidence suggests that the process of cycling had existed in native North America long before the arrival of European colonizers. Cycling made possible the "recurrent process of the emergence, expansion, and fragmentation of complex chiefdoms amid a regional backdrop of simple chiefdoms." The existence of cycling during the chiefdom period (ca. 700 CE to 1650 CE) meant that centers of political power constantly shifted—a process anthropologists and archeologists call "fissioning" and "coalescence"—as chiefdoms declined and fell from power, while others rose to take their place.[24] It also meant that the Indigenous people of North America were not a static people, stuck in time or place—they lived in and nurtured dynamic cultures and, when necessary, migrated to a new "home."

Archeological evidence suggests that these processes led to the creation of the *Aniyaunwiya* (The Principal People), by 1,000 CE. This dates the origins of the people who became known as the Cherokee (or *Tsa-la-gi*) as a politically and culturally identifiable group to the beginning of the Mississippian era.[25] The Mississippian era became characterized by the processes of cycling, fissioning, and coalescence. By the fifteenth and early sixteenth century, these interlocking processes gave rise to macro-regional, clan-based societies.[26] These societies extended over a much larger geographic region than the chiefdoms that preceded them. Moreover, the political structure of Native American towns after the 1500s tended to be less centralized in nature, with power diffused among townspeople. These changes had a profound impact on the social and cultural development of life among the Cherokee people. We see these processes in action when we focus on the names that Cherokee people gave to their towns. Anthropologist Christopher Rodning argues that Cherokee town names such as Chota and Tallassee had Muskogean, rather than Iroquoian etymologies. Other town names do indicate an Iroquoian etymology, such as Seneca and Kituwah (or Keetoowah)— Kituwah being one of the seven original Mother Towns, situated along the Tuckasegee River, from which all other Cherokee towns grew— while others blended Cherokee, Catawban, and Muskogean elements. Rodning contends that such linguistic blending in town names reflects generations of human movement, resulting in the naming and renaming of the landscape and social environment in which Cherokees lived.[27] Cherokee town and village names could refer to time, such as Old Estatoe, or to local environmental features, such as the town of Keowee, which referred to the abundance of mulberries.[28]

By the eighteenth century, the history of cycling and coalescence was reflected in Cherokee cultural, social, and political institutions. On a practical level, a complex series of paths connected Cherokee traders, diplomats, hunters, and warriors to other Native American societies. And where people traveled, they took with them their cultural ideals, their economic objectives, and their political philosophies.[29] Some Cherokees forged trade and diplomatic alliances with other Indigenous people or with people of European descent, typically through commerce, intermarriage, or a combination of both. Significantly, intermarriage did not

Figure 2: The Kituwah Mound, site of one of the Seven Mother Towns, is considered by Cherokee people to be a sacred site. Photograph by the author.

automatically result in non-Cherokees' being adopted into a Cherokee clan—that privilege had to be earned and was often linked to elaborate ceremonies and rituals that Europeans found difficult to comprehend.[30] Travel and human movement, however, did not always involve intimate human relationships; they could simply involve a form of exchange, as was the case for Cherokee traders who sold items such as pipes made of steatite (or "soaprock") to European settlers. Alternatively, Cherokee prophets traveled as far away as modern-day Indiana in an effort to forge Pan-Indian unity against the expansion of the settler frontier; while Cherokee chiefs from towns such as Echota traveled along the Great War Path—a path that cut through both Creek and Cherokee towns, and provided a clear route to the colony of Virginia—to engage in diplomacy or, in the case of Cherokee delegations in the 1730s and 1760s, journey across the Atlantic to London as ambassadors for the Cherokee people.[31]

Students peering at Willard's map in search of clues about Chero-kee society and culture would not see the dynamism of these different forms of human movement, much less the feelings of belonging that came from a clear sense of geography, town life, and clan membership. Instead, Willard's map provided students with a Europeanized name on a map. That oval-shaped figure that was meant to highlight for students the boundaries of Cherokee Country looked authoritative, fixed in print and presumably since time immemorial. However, the history of so-cial and political instability that defined the Mississippian chiefdoms, the fissioning and coalescent societies that followed, and the paths and navigable rivers and streams that connected Indigenous towns were all suggestive of a much more dynamic past. Against this more intercon-nected, politically contested, and historically contingent backdrop, it is possible for us to begin to see how Cherokee identity developed its multi-dimensional and diasporic qualities during the late eighteenth, nineteenth, and early twentieth centuries.[32]

Understanding the Origins of the Cherokee Diaspora

By the outbreak of the Seven Years' War (1756), Cherokee traditions of oral storytelling were well developed. Oral narratives served a variety of functions, from the medicinal to the mystical. Many of these narra-tives contained clues about the importance of travel and migration in Cherokee culture. One version of Cherokee oral tradition posits that the Cherokees (or *Tsalagi*) are the Keepers of the Sacred Fire (*Esh-he-el-o-archie*). According to the early twentieth-century Cherokee author Wil-liam Eubanks, the god Nel-ho-nu-hi placed the Cherokee in *Ah-ma-ye-li* (the midst of the waters) "when the earth was divided."[33] One version of this narrative insists that the Cherokee forefathers did not traverse any water, while other interpretations claim that Cherokee ancestors crossed a "great bridge that later sank to the bottom of the ocean."[34]

As I outline in chapter 1 of this book, the Cherokees have a number oral traditions that seek to make sense of their historical origins and of travel and migration. Perhaps the most famous Cherokee oral narrative is that of Selu (Corn Mother) and Kana'ti (The Lucky Hunter).[35] The

legend of Selu and Kana'ti provides insight into the gendered logic behind the matrilineal clan system in traditional Cherokee culture. In the
course of his ethnological work among the North Carolina Cherokee,
James Mooney collected a number of versions of the Selu and Kana'ti
narrative. One of these versions relates that shortly after the world was
made, Selu and Kana'ti, the original woman and man, lived at Pilot
Knob, a small town by a river. Here Selu and Kana'ti lived a peaceful
and harmonious life with their only child, a son, until the arrival of the
Wild Boy, or I'nage-utasun'hi (He-who-grew-up-wild), led to disrup-
tions to the supply of corn, beans, and wild game, and the boys killed
Selu on suspicion that she was a witch.[36]

The story of Selu and Kana'ti is well known, but it contains a
moral that is often underappreciated. It is that portion of the Selu and
Kana'ti narrative that reveals the importance of travel, direction, and
color in Cherokee culture. Kana'ti, who became angry after discovering
that his sons had murdered Selu, travels to visit the Wolf clan, where he
asks the chief if the Wolves would kill the two boys for their crime. The
Wild Boy, who possesses the ability to transform himself into "a tuft of
down," sits atop Kana'ti's shoulder as he details his request to the Wolf
chief. Thanks to the Wild Boy's transmogrification, the boys are able to
prepare for the Wolves and ultimately kill all but two or three of their
intended executioners.

Kana'ti, who does not expect his sons to survive, does not return
to his home. Instead, he travels farther afield. After the brothers beat off
the Wolves, they begin to wonder where their father has gone. The Wild
Boy tries to narrow their search by taking a "gaming wheel" and rolling
"it toward the Darkening Land." When the wheel returns, the brothers
know that Kana'ti did not travel west. Repeating this procedure to the
South and then to the North, the brothers discover that their father had
not traveled in either of those directions. When the boys roll the wheel
toward the "Sun Land"—the East—and it fails to return, they know
where their father is to be found.[37]

The brothers promptly travel eastward and eventually catch up
with their father. Kana'ti expresses surprise at seeing them, but man-
ages to induce the boys to travel with him. Kana'ti leads the boys to a

swamp, where danger is known to lurk. Kana'ti then travels ahead, leaving the dangerous swamp, and the boys, behind. On investigation, the boys discover a panther living in the swamp. Both boys attempt to kill the panther but their arrows prove ineffective, prompting them to flee the swamp and hurry to rejoin their father.

Thereafter the brothers have to evade a tribe of cannibals before once again catching up to their father. But Kana'ti again moves ahead of the boys, traveling so far in fact that he comes to the "end of the world, where the sun comes out." When the brothers once again rejoin Kana'ti, they are surprised to find him sitting with Selu, and together Kana'ti and Selu instruct their sons that they must go and "live where the sun goes down." After staying with their parents seven days, the boys travel into the Darkening Land. They come to be called Ansga'ya Tsunsdi' (The Little Men), "and when they talk to each other we hear a low rolling thunder in the west." The Thunder Boys, as they are also known in some versions of this narrative, are able to travel back to the east, but they always return to the "darkening land" after their journey.[38]

This aspect of the Selu and Kana'ti narrative provides insight into the color-coding that Cherokees associated with their sense of geography and direction. It also provides us with clues that Cherokees associated travel with certain types of emotions. In traditional Cherokee culture, the color red represented the East, the North was blue, the South was white (and also associated with warmth), and black represented the West (and death).[39]

Travel westward was therefore marked by uncertainty and much anxiety. Indeed, in the context of the federal government's increasing pressure on the Cherokee to leave what early nineteenth-century Cherokees called their "ancient soil"—a phrase that connoted a sense of history and tradition, and that gave Cherokee identity its sense of geographical rootedness—in the Southeast, anxieties about the "Darkening Land" became acute.[40] This proved especially true after the Indian Removal Act was passed into law in 1830. For example, The *Cherokee Phoenix* newspaper, the first Native American newspaper in the United States, printed warnings urging Cherokees to remain committed to the ancient soil of their forebears and not to migrate into the West because "there have been many instances of Indians having irrecoverably lost their eye sight while attempting to cross the great western prairie reaching towards the Rocky mountains [sic]."[41] Thus, travel, depending on the direction one headed, could be hazardous, even deadly.

The study of Cherokee travel and migration brings into focus the manner in which Cherokee people interpreted narratives about their origins, understood their relationships to other human beings, and re-imagined their cultural beliefs and kinship practices in new places. As the anthropologist Raymond Fogelson observes, Cherokee identity has never been monolithic.[42] Indeed, Cherokee identity can be understood as a multi-dimensional, multi-sited concept. Cherokee identity is therefore rooted in the Cherokee concept of multiple interconnected souls, guided by the harmony ethic, and embodied by Cherokee people who have for centuries nurtured what it meant (and means) to be Cherokee in multiple places, in different narrative forms, and in the context of changing human relationships.

For Cherokees, the pressures of eighteenth-century colonialism played a major role in reshaping the purpose of travel and the nature of Cherokee politics and diplomacy. Prior to the 1760s, Cherokees traveled east to London in England, and west to the base of the Rocky Mountains. With the exception of a legend about the "Lost Cherokees" living at the foot of the Rocky Mountains, Cherokees knew that travel usually concluded with a return journey home.[43] By the late eighteenth century, this changed. A small but steadily increasing number of Cherokees began migrating westward, seeing migration and resettlement as the best way to avoid Euroamerican violence and political interference, while maintaining what they imagined was a traditional Cherokee way of life.

Historians typically understand Cherokee travel, migration, and resettlement from the vantage point of the nation-state framework and in the context of forced removal in 1838 and 1839. The Cherokees did, as I detail in chapters one and two of this book, both adopt a nation-state model that mirrored that of the American republic, and articulate requirements for citizenship in the Cherokee Nation.[44] The important, and much cited, work of historian William McLoughlin, and subsequent scholarship by Andrew Denson, has proven vitally important to our historical understanding of Cherokee sovereignty and nationalism.[45]

The concept of a geographically discrete nation-state that dominates Cherokee historiography was, we should not forget, the product of European colonialism. Europeans embraced the nation-state framework of government over the course of the seventeenth and eighteenth centuries. European political theorists and philosophers imagined nation-states as the embodiments of modernity, a civilized expression of the people's will, a will that was increasingly being shaped by formal systems of education. By the eighteenth century, British colonial officials in North America endeavored to reduce the Cherokees' decentralized form of town and clan governance to that of a Cherokee "nation." Thus, by the time the Cherokees appropriated the nation-state framework in defense of their lands in the Southeast of North America, they had become well versed in the European brand of political modernity and "civilization."[46]

Eighteenth-century Cherokee chiefs and headmen recognized the importance of European political rhetoric in their diplomacy with British colonial officials. Once the British cemented their military and political power over North America, following their triumph in the Seven Years' War, Cherokee chiefs recognized that it had become a diplomatic necessity to appropriate various forms of Western political discourse if they hoped to be understood by colonial officials (and later officials of the United States) and effectively protect their towns, landholdings, and livelihoods.

Settler pressures on Cherokee landholdings culminated with a series of removal crises in 1806 and 1809, in 1817, 1828, and 1829. The Cherokees responded to these crises by promulgating their own written constitution in 1827. That document declared to the world that the Cherokee people did in fact constitute a sovereign nation-state whose "body politic" was indeed "civilized." There were further removal crises to come, however. These crises eventually resulted in most of the Cherokee population being forced from their homes by the United States military and becoming exiles from the homeland they had fought so hard to retain.[47]

The time and space in which social, cultural, and political structures are "secured," preserved, or, in the case of the Cherokee Nation in the Southeast, created, are important to understanding the collective identity that people construct for themselves.[48] When the Cherokees formed their nation in the early nineteenth century, they did so with two objectives in mind: to preserve the communal traditions that informed Cherokee conceptions of balance and harmony in the world, and to use a diplomatic language that was understandable to Europeans and Euroamericans so they could effectively defend the Cherokee "homeland."[49] In these ways, Cherokee leaders hoped to keep their ancient fires burning in the woodland South.

Out of the Cherokee nation-state model would eventually flow clearer and more precisely prescribed definitions of citizenship, a form of collective identity that Cherokee politicians and lawyers worked hard to define and defend over the course of the nineteenth century. At the same time, Cherokee emigrants traveled into, and out of, the Cherokee Nation with increasing regularity. With a fixed geographical and political understanding of Cherokee nationhood taking shape during the early nineteenth century, so too did diasporic Cherokee communities and families emerge as they traveled outside of the Cherokee Nation and became settlers in faraway lands.

This brings me to the three interconnected concepts that frame this book: migration and resettlement, memory, and identity. Since the groundbreaking analysis of Erik Erikson in the 1950s and 1960s, social scientists have understood identity in relational terms.[50] Social interactions are thus key to the way scholars understand identity. Identity is also bound up in other relationships, such as the relationship of an individual (or group of people) to a particular history and geography, and particular politics, social customs, and cultural mores. Through these lenses, identity is defined through self-perceptions, or translated into prescribed categories—such as legal concepts of citizenship, or racial and gender identities. In other words, identities can originate from within a person and they can be imposed from above, just as governments attempt to do when they articulate laws or citizenship restrictions.[51] Identity formation therefore constitutes a mediated sense of selfhood and collective belonging, communicated through language—be it written or verbal—and recognized through the sanction it receives in either informal cultural forms and practices, or formalized institutional definitions.[52]

A small but growing number of Cherokee migrations into the trans-Mississippi West during the late eighteenth and early nineteenth century contributed to significant changes in how Cherokee identity was expressed, and from where it was articulated. Like other human societies, Cherokees understood migration in spiritual or theological terms, as well as seeing it as the product of strategic decisions. During the early nineteenth century, the actor John Howard Payne recorded Cherokee stories about travel and migration. As the following chapters make clear, Payne's record of Cherokee beliefs revealed the syncretic nature of early nineteenth-century Cherokee epistemologies, with narratives of ancient floods, exodus, and migration punctuating Cherokee oral traditions.[53]

Narratives of migration, both mythic and historical, reflect how the movement of human beings across land and water are among the central facts of the human experience. Travel and migration constitutes a physical as well as spiritual reality that shapes and reshapes a sense of self (or "soul" in traditional Cherokee philosophies) and community both in the mind of the individual and in the stories a community nurtures to explain the motives behind the cycles of migration, relocation, and settlement.[54]

For the vanguard of the Cherokee diaspora—those late eighteenth- and early nineteenth-century migrants who set off westward and settled in the trans-Mississippi West prior to forced removal in 1838 and 1839— migration must surely have evoked feelings of anxiety, apprehension, and anticipation. These emotions were conditioned by historical context and mediated, as all human actions and events are, through the social ecology and geopolitical context that gave rise to those migrations. When, for example, migration is the product of violence or political coercion, the "trauma of exile" penetrates deep into the soul of the individual and the community, informing the exiled group's perception of the past, and its relation to the present, in ways that structure multigenerational and emotionally powerful conceptions of group identity. For the vast body of the Cherokees, exiled in the trans-Mississippi West by the coercive actions of federal and state governments in the late 1830s, relocation to a foreign land far from their ancestral homeland brought into focus the contested meanings of history, memory, and identity. Was

it possible to hold on to a "pure," "traditional," or "authentic" Cherokee identity once thrust into diaspora? What did such an identity look,
act, and sound like? Would anyone know? Could anyone *remember*?[55]

Diaspora scholars have for many years emphasized how diasporic
peoples feel a sense of exile from their homeland. A homeland can represent something tangible, such as a geopolitical nation-state. It can
also occupy a part of one's imagination, thereby producing a less tangible, but no less real, sense of connection to something, somewhere.
As the Cherokee diaspora developed over the course of the eighteenth
and nineteenth centuries, both concepts of homeland developed. By
the midpoint of the nineteenth century, Cherokees could locate two
"homelands"—a political homeland, that of the Cherokee Nation in Indian Territory, and a homeland in the Great Smoky Mountains of western North Carolina that Cherokees—especially those who remained
in the Southeast after removal at the end of the 1830s—*imagined* as
their ancestral, or ancient, homeland. For some, the imagined ancestral homeland located in the Great Smoky Mountains constituted both
an ancestral and political "home." For Cherokees living in diaspora—
say in New York or California—the continued existence of Cherokee
communities in the Southeast provided tangible reminders of Cherokee
tenacity and endurance, while the forging of a political homeland in
Indian Territory after removal in the 1830s not only constituted a visible,
political form of Cherokee identity, but also represented the determination of Cherokees to thrive and prosper no matter where they lived.

Built upon European and Euroamerican concepts of nationhood
and political sovereignty, the malleable concept of "home," or a "homeland," gave meaning to the identities of diaspora Cherokees. Wherever
Cherokees traveled, migrated, or settled, they carried with them an understanding of this connection. They also travelled with an understanding of how colonialism had affected, and continued to affect, the lives
of Cherokee people. The incorporation of Cherokee histories involving
encounters with settlers and the economic, social, and political structures that shaped settler colonial societies in North America added new
layers of meaning to Cherokee oral traditions. Cherokees thus wedded
their oral traditions to memories of specific historical events, not simply reciting the "facts" of such encounters, but using imagination and

creativity to convey a complex set of meanings.[56] In doing so, Cherokees fostered patterns of remembering, oral storytelling, and increasingly, written forms of historical narration that contributed to the renewal and clarification of what it meant to be a Cherokee living in diaspora.[57]

Memory was therefore critically important to Cherokee historical consciousness between 1756 and 1945. The act of remembering, narrating memories, and commemorating historical events, places, or people, has long played a significant role in shaping both individual and collective understandings of identity in societies throughout the world. Literary scholars and psychologists have endeavored to understand the significance of memory and commemoration by focusing on the individual, or the self, concepts alien to traditional Cherokee culture. In contrast, anthropologist and folklorists, sociologists and political scientists, and historians have all endeavored to understand the socially constructed nature of memory and how narratives of the past become institutionalized to produce sanctioned, or what seem like "common sense," understandings of history and collective identity.[58]

If there exists a collective memory of migration in relation to the Cherokee people in the vernacular history of the United States, it is of a people who were forced to leave their ancestral homeland against their will in the 1830s and who suffered great hardships and loss as a result. With the benefit of hindsight—and thus a sense of exculpatory detachment from history's wrongs—most Americans agree that the era of removal was characterized by injustice and oppressive federal government policies toward Native Americans.[59] But as this book demonstrates, as important as forced removal became—and remains—to Cherokee identities, and to the way history is used and memories structured to give meaning to American history, Cherokees did engage in other forms of travel, migration, and memory creation. That people of Cherokee descent came to contextualize these different forms of human movement with reference to the forced removals of 1838–1839 reveals much about the evolution of a historically informed Cherokee identity by the late nineteenth and early twentieth centuries.[60]

Territorial displacement therefore became a critically important facet of Cherokee collective memory and oral narratives. The repeated narration of such memories—which occurred in both oral and written

form over the course of the nineteenth and early twentieth centuries—
embedded traumatic historical events in Cherokee culture in ways that
shaped and defined Cherokee identities.[61] Indeed, social scientists have
detailed how Indigenous people in settler societies from the United
States to Australia and the Southwest Pacific have experienced, and continue to experience, feelings of victimhood, economic discrimination,
fractured kin relations, and social marginalization grounded in a lived
history—that is, in a present that is directly connected to the wrongs of
the past. Native American studies scholar Nancy Mithlo refers to these
phenomena as Indigenous "blood memories," or the collective memory
of Native America's historical encounters with colonialism that give
meaning to native genealogies and past wrongs.[62]

Prior to the federal government's forced removal of the Cherokees
and other Southeastern Native Americans in the 1830s, Cherokees began
migrating westward. Historians have long known of these Cherokees
as the "Old Settlers," or Western Cherokees—a people from whom a
number of the modern-day members of the United Keetoowah Band of
Cherokee Indians in Oklahoma, one of three federally recognized Cherokee Bands, claim to be descended. There were other western migrations
of Cherokees prior to the 1830s, most notably the migration of a small
band of Cherokees to Texas under the leadership of Duwali (Chief John
Bowles).[63] In the following chapters I argue that these Cherokee migrants constituted the vanguard of the Cherokee diaspora. Their travels
were different from all previously known journeys involving Cherokees
into the trans-Mississippi West. They were not simply hunters or warriors, but entire kin networks migrating west and searching for a new
place to settle and call home.[64] To preserve what they understood of
Cherokee identity and a Cherokee way of life, or because their leaders signed treaties with the federal government that ceded land to the
United States, the Cherokees who followed their chiefs into the trans-
Mississippi invariably left kith and kin behind in the cis-Mississippi, or
the region between the trans-Appalachia and Mississippi River. In the
1820s and 1830s those remaining in the Southeast fought political battles
to preserve what remained of the Cherokee homelands without their
trans-Mississippi cousins.[65]

The Cherokee diaspora was thus forged in a changing settler colonial context, as the territory Cherokees had come to know as their ancient homeland in the cis-Mississippi became caught in the crosshairs of imperial warfare, encroaching settler frontiers, and the transition from British colonial government to the settler colonial rule of the United States.[66] The term diaspora, derived from the ancient Greek term *diasperien, dia* meaning "across," and *sperien* meaning "to sow or scatter seed," is an apt way to describe changes in Cherokee life, culture, and politics over the course of the late eighteenth, nineteenth, and early twentieth centuries.[67] In diaspora, the Cherokee people became settlers and were forced to re-imagine their nation, their identities, and the nature of their homeland.[68] What slowly emerged, as I noted above, were two types of homelands.

These homelands helped to give diasporic Cherokees a "multi-sited" sense of identity. As much at home in white communities as they were in the Cherokee Nation of Indian Territory or the Qualla Boundary Reservation in North Carolina, many Cherokees continued to travel and migrate throughout the United States and into the central and southwest Pacific islands during the nineteenth and twentieth centuries. This human movement had various motives, but as Cherokees moved through the diaspora they tried to nurture their Cherokee identity, expressing who they imagined themselves to be and where they belonged in the world by carefully considering their actions, thoughts, and words—both spoken and written, in English and in Cherokee.[69]

The chapters that follow explore these themes in more detail. My analysis is divided into two parts. Part I, chapters 1–4, explores the significance of Cherokee narratives about human creation and migration, and the impact that frontier and borderland violence had on Cherokee communities in the cis-Mississippi (and ultimately in the trans-Mississippi West), and reveals the complexities of different types of migration between the 1750s and 1850s.[70] These migrations raised questions about the political and social structures of Cherokee communities, the significance of race and gender identities, and the importance of geographical residence to one's feelings about being Cherokee.

Part II, chapters 5–8, focuses on the nuances of Cherokee identity during the American Civil War, the tumultuous decades of

Reconstruction, and the rise of the allotment, assimilation, and termination era between 1880s and the Second World War. As these chapters demonstrate, the American Civil War ushered in a new era of uncertainty and anxiety for many Cherokees. It was a period in Cherokee history that was filled with renewed challenges, to the Cherokees' political sovereignty, to Cherokee culture, and to the genealogical and racial sense of what "blood" meant to Cherokee identity.

This book, then, tells a story that is both uniquely Cherokee and commonly human. It is a story of love and hate, of heartfelt compassion and vile racism, of cultural retention and reinvention. It is, in other words, a story that runs the gamut of human experiences and emotions. Above all, it is a story of how the Cherokees became a diasporic people, and continued to be Cherokee.

Part 1
Origins

The Origins of the Cherokee Diaspora

Uring the latter half of the eighteenth century, the Cherokee people experienced an unprecedented series of challenges to their established modes of life. The matrilineal
and matrilocal social structures that gave Cherokee life
its meaning and purpose were increasingly exposed to an overlapping
series of imperial political, commercial, military, and cultural pressures.[1] When American forces swept through Cherokee Country during the Revolutionary War (ca. 1775–1783), they exacted vengeance
on the Cherokees for their leaders' allying with the British. American
troops destroyed scores of Cherokee towns, the demographic centers
of eighteenth-century Cherokee life. Once the war ended, Cherokee
people began the task of rebuilding their lives, although they did so on
communal farmsteads that sprawled along rivers and creeks.

Major social and political changes also reshaped Cherokee life
during the latter third of the eighteenth century.[2] Established centers of
political power shifted, both geographically and in terms of who held
power, with an increasingly influential generation of "mixed-blood"
Western-educated Cherokee leaders shaping the future of Cherokee
politics. All of these changes occurred as a growing number of Cherokee
townspeople became refugees and migrants within the cis-Mississippi.
Elders struggled to recall a time when such a significant movement of

people had occurred. While most Cherokees migrated to different sections of Cherokee Country in the Southeast, reluctantly parting from the land and rivers that anchored communal life in the southeastern portion of North America, a small number of Cherokees began seeking refuge from the ravages of colonial warfare and aggressive settlers by looking farther afield, and to lands beyond the western banks of the Mississippi River.

For the Cherokee, as for other Indigenous peoples in the American South, the latter half of the eighteenth century was both a traumatic and a transformative epoch in their collective histories. Whether they chose to relocate in different parts of Cherokee Country, rebuilding their towns or clearing land for farmsteads, or trekked beyond the Mississippi and to Missouri, Arkansas, Texas, or colonial Mexico, Cherokees continued to nurture kinship relations. Holding on to old memories and remembering kinship ties was no easy task during a time of colonial warfare, shifting settler frontiers and borderlands, and an increasingly mobile, migratory existence for many hundreds (and ultimately thousands) of Cherokee people. The cumulative impact of colonial encounters with Spanish, French, and British settlers, traders, and colonial officials therefore opened a new chapter in Cherokee history. In a sense, the Cherokee both became victims of aggressively expansive settler societies, and became Indigenous agents of settlement and re-settlement themselves. This unnerving epoch magnified the significance of intratribal rivalries, led to political and military conflicts with other Indian tribal leaders and warriors, and placed the regenerative qualities of Cherokee social structures and cultural beliefs under intense pressure.[3]

In the decades between the French and Indian War (1754–1763) and the Treaty of Washington in 1819, when Eastern Cherokee leaders declared their determination to resist further cessions of land and remain in the Southeast, the Cherokee diaspora was born. During these tumultuous decades Cherokee chiefs ceded 58,555,280 acres of land in Virginia, Georgia, Tennessee, Alabama, and North Carolina either to British colonial governments in North America or to the federal government of the United States. For a people whose homeland once included portions of present-day southwestern Virginia, West Virginia, Kentucky, Tennessee, Georgia, the Carolinas, and Alabama, the loss of land and loss of access to the rivers and streams that sustained Cherokee towns and farms was life altering. How Cherokees responded to the challenges of the eighteenth century spoke volumes for the resilience and innovative qualities of the Cherokee people and their leaders. As the following chapter reveals, the Cherokee were becoming a dispersed people during the latter half of the eighteenth century and this dispersal was occurring on a geographical scale that seemed unprecedented to them. The language of nationalism therefore became a useful rhetorical device that enabled an increasingly diasporic population to locate a cultural and political "home," helping Cherokee people to keep their sacred fires burning and imagine an identity that was deeply rooted in history, language, tradition.

Prelude to Dispersal

Cherokee Country covered over 40,000 square miles and included seven matrilineal clans. As I outlined in the introduction, these clans structured social and cultural life, administered justice, established red (war) and white (peace) chiefs, and helped regulate communal agricultural and economic activity.[4] While matrilineal clans and matrilocal kinship systems played a critical role in structuring eighteenth-century Cherokee life, towns and the development of regional identities proved equally important to Cherokee political and sacred life. Archeologists observe that Cherokee towns were scattered through one of three geographically and linguistically distinct locations: the Lower Towns in what became the states of North Carolina and Georgia; the Upper, or Overhill, Towns in Tennessee and northwest North Carolina; and the Middle Towns along the Tennessee River and western North Carolina. Within these geo-linguistic divisions, Cherokee scholars also identify the Valley Towns that extended from southwest North Carolina to northeastern Georgia.[5]

Recent archeological, anthropological, and historical research highlights the importance of town and regional identities among the eighteenth-century Cherokees. Scholars observe that following the decline and gradual abandonment of the Mississippian era chiefdoms from the fifteenth century, Indigenous people experienced a period of

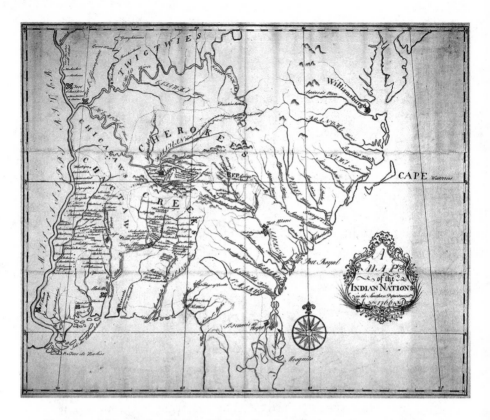

Figure 3: Map of the Indian Nations in the Southern Department, 1766.
William L. Clements Library, University of Michigan, Ann Arbor.

social instability and migration. This movement of people, which coincided with environmental changes associated with the Little Ice Age
between the sixteenth and early nineteenth centuries, and with the initial waves of European colonists and traders entering North America,
culminated in what archeologists and anthropologists refer to as "coalescent societies."[6]

Archeologist Christopher Rodning has studied the complexities
of early eighteenth-century Cherokee town life and constructed a vivid
picture of the macro-regional coalescent societies among the Cherokee.
Rodning's analysis indicates that after two centuries of migration, linguistic blending, and the overlapping of social structures, an identifiable
Cherokee identity came into focus. Rodning contends that this was an
identity composed of "multiethnic congeries."[7] Evidence of multiethnic

Cherokee populations can be seen, for example, in the way some Natchez Indians were integrated into Overhill Cherokee towns during the seventeenth and eighteenth centuries.[8] This type of assimilation reflected the importance of adoption in the formation and renewal of Cherokee town and clan identities. Non-indigenous observers recorded other forms of multiethnic life among eighteenth-century Indians. For instance, Israel Shreve, the farmer turned colonel in the Second New Jersey Regiment during the Revolutionary War, spent much of his service in and around New Madrid, along the Mississippi River, and in the Ohio Valley. He observed the enduring strength of multiethnic Indigenous towns, noting in his diary on March 13, 1789, that the Delawares, Shawnees, Cherokees, Chickasaws, and French settlers lived peaceably in close proximity to one another at Lance La Grasse. At a time of war, Shreve recorded being greeted by as many as fifty-eight Delaware, Cherokee, and Chickasaw men, and "a Number of Women both on foot and horseback."[9]

Shreve may well have exaggerated the degree to which people of different ethnic backgrounds intermixed; after all, rumors of Cherokees scalping and "Destroying & Massacuring Several Families" in settler townships along the western frontier, in the mid-Atlantic, and on Virginia's western border had highlighted feelings of anxiety among whites since the late 1750s.[10] Nonetheless, geography and gender did play an important role both in binding people together in a community, and in differentiating social identities. Where Cherokee men engaged in diplomacy, flexed their warrior muscles and used their martial skills to protect Cherokee towns from violent settlers, Indigenous women also used their diplomatic savvy and acted as mediators between whites and American Indians. The Cherokee *Ghighau* (Beloved Woman, or Most Honored Woman) Nanyihi (Nancy Ward) played an active diplomatic role. Nanyihi acted as head of the Cherokee Women's Council and sat with peace and war chiefs during council meetings. Nanyihi used her position as Ghighau to attempt to preserve peace and harmony between Cherokees and whites. In other instances, intermarriages were designed to mediate Cherokee–white political and economic relations, with the white male spouse being incorporated into the Cherokee's matrilineal and matrilocal kinship system.[11]

Cherokee towns were structured around clearly defined social roles and political obligations. Sociologist Duane Champagne has argued that these structures revolved around "symbolic structure," or a "society-wide institution of roles and relations based on respect, [and] charisma tradition."[12] In turn, these structures, institutions, and relations gave meaning to regional identities, as well as clan affiliations. Built into this clan- and town-based system was a certain degree of social and cultural adaptability. Within Cherokee towns, for example, leadership roles were regularly contested, and dwellings and public structures were invested with specific social significance—mounds, for instance, were sites of ceremonial significance, while structures such as menstrual huts designated a space with a clearly defined gendered function.[13] Additionally, a combination of cultural and linguistic continuity was blended with innovativeness to renew and keep meaningful social relations and clan identity. For instance, the sacred fire that occupied an important ceremonial place in chiefdom-era culture continued to be incorporated into ceremonial culture in eighteenth-century Cherokee towns. Indeed, to the eighteenth-century Cherokees fire represented warmth, life, and the light of home.[14]

Eighteenth-century Cherokee towns became important sites of political decision-making. These towns produced strong and charismatic chiefs, such as Wrosetasetow (Mankiller) of Great Tellico; Moytoy, or Amo-adawehi (whom the Scottish adventurer Alexander Cuming titled "Emperor of the Cherokee"), an Overhill chief who succeeded Wrosetasetow in prominence; and Old Hop (Kanagatoga) of Chota. But Cherokee towns were more than sites of colorful regional politics; they also anchored a deeply felt attachment to the land at a time of increasing contact with non-indigenous traders and colonizers. Historian Dixie Ray Haggard notes of this period, "Each Cherokee village had a binary governmental structure which blended religious and civil matters together. This system consisted of a red, or war structure and a white, or peace structure."[15] Furthermore, towns were comprised of "households" that included members from each of the seven matrilineal clans. While eighteenth-century Cherokee towns were politically autonomous, clan kinship proved critical to binding Cherokee people from different towns and regions together, providing them with a coherent, if malleable, sense of common political identity.[16]

Given that Cherokee towns anchored Cherokee identity and politics to specific geographical spaces by the early eighteenth century, travel beyond the safety of the local township, if it occurred at all, was usually conducted for temporary purposes. For example, warriors, hunters, and diplomats traveled as far west as the base of the "Mexican Mountains" (what we know today as the Rocky Mountains), while Cherokee diplomats journeyed across the Atlantic Ocean at least twice during the eighteenth century on diplomatic trips to England. These transatlantic diplomats – who included Attakullakulla (Little Carpenter), Oukah-Ulah, Clogoittah, Kallannah, Tahtowe, Kittagusta, and Ounaconoa in 1730, and the "Emissaries of Peace" Outacite (or Ostenaco, also known as Man-Killer), Woyi, and Cunne-Shote in 1762 – were as much objects of the English public's curiosity as they were emissaries for their towns and clans.[17] Surviving evidence suggests that travel westward or across the Atlantic Ocean was almost exclusively the province of males. Significantly, no oral or written evidence survives to suggest that these various journeys resulted in the permanent settlement of Cherokees in foreign lands. However, by the middle decades of the eighteenth century, some Cherokee travelers did indeed become emigrants, rekindling their sacred fires in new locations and settling on lands unknown to their ancestors, altering the town and clan basis for Cherokee identity, and prompting what historian Wilma Dunaway calls "ethnic reorganizations" among the Cherokee.[18]

The social, cultural, and political changes that gave rise to the Cherokee diaspora thus began dispersing Cherokees throughout the cis-Mississippi and even farther afield during the latter half of the eighteenth century. These changes were set in motion by an interrelated set of factors. Cherokees adapted to the pressure of settler colonialism—be it in the form of warfare; connections to transatlantic systems of trade (in slaves, guns, and myriad other commodities); or disease transfer, as occurred in 1766 with a devastating disease outbreak.[19] In particular, Cherokee economic activity narrowed, with men focusing their hunting expeditions on surplus hunting for trade purposes. In politics, the gradual centralization of Cherokee leadership, and the eventual adoption of laws and a written constitution modeled on that of the United States, proved to be innovations that ultimately transformed the socio-political structure of Cherokee life.[20]

It is important to keep in mind, however, that while the decades between the French and Indian War and the emergence of the American republic bore witness to social dislocation and territorial displacement, most Cherokee people continued to live on land between the Appalachian Ridge and the eastern banks of the Mississippi. Here Cherokee town and farm life was punctuated by growing waves of aggressive settlers. At the outbreak of the French and Indian War, a Lower Town Cherokee Headman allegedly exclaimed that his people "look on all the White people to be the same as themselves as they tred [sic] on the same ground."[21] By the time of the signing of the Treaty of Long Island in July 1777, the violence and bloodshed of the previous two decades had fundamentally altered such cordial perceptions. For instance, Onitossitah (Corn Tassel), an Upper Town Cherokee peace chief, upbraided the white colonists for the way in which "you marched into our towns; . . . killed a few scattered and defenseless individuals; spread fire and desolation wherever you pleased; and returned again to your own habitations."[22] Just one year after the American colonists declared their independence from the British Crown, Onitossitah thus issued his own declaration, announcing his disapproval for the aggressiveness of the Americans, and insisting that "We are a separate people!"[23]

An important, albeit understudied, way in which Cherokee people nurtured a distinctive sense of themselves in the cauldron of colonial politics, trade, disease transfer, and warfare, was through the articulation of migration narratives. Cherokee migration narratives served three broad functions: first, they explained where the Cherokee people came from and why their towns were structured in the ways that they were by the eighteenth century. Second, migration narratives reminded Cherokees that no matter how far they traveled from the bright light of their town's sacred fire, they would remain connected to the Cherokee people through the clan kinship system. Indeed, rekindling sacred fires in new towns or, increasingly after the Revolutionary War, on farmsteads, provided Cherokees with both a sense of continuity of identity and a feeling of being part of a community they could call home. Finally, Cherokee migration narratives used human movement to emphasize the spiritual significance of the land and nearby rivers or streams to a person's role, and thus identity, in Cherokee society. For example, these narratives portrayed men as engaging in the work of hunting or acting as protectors by assuming the role of warrior. For such men, travel was both a regular part of their life and integral to Cherokee understandings of masculinity. But the travels these men embarked on were never migratory; they were not geared towards the establishment of new and permanent communities far from the game they hunted, the fields that the women of their clan cultivated, and the towns in which their wives and daughters played pivotal roles by manufacturing basketry, preparing meals, and overseeing clan adoption ceremonies.[24]

Migration and origin narratives therefore helped to revivify the social and spiritual meaning of Cherokee identity. Like the stories told by other Southeastern Indians, Cherokee origin narratives were part of an oral tradition that explained the origins of humanity and its spiritual qualities, narrated the cosmological significance of land and water, and emphasized the importance of migration.[25] To eighteenth- and nineteenth-century ethnologists and linguists, the study of these narratives provided clues to understanding Cherokee perceptions of the world. For the Cherokees, migration narratives helped to give meaning to a world filled with spiritual powers—both good and evil in nature—that required periodic renewal. From this perspective we can begin to appreciate why Cherokee elders used their *ulanigvgv*, or personal and spiritual power, to emphasize the overlapping significance of migration and renewal (or cleansing) that appeared to be needed in the late eighteenth century.[26]

Cherokee migration narratives also provide us with fresh insights into the adaptive and innovative ways in which Cherokees understood "traditional" concepts of balance and harmony. For eighteenth-century Cherokees, living on the land in a state of *tohi* required town and clan members to live in good health, balance, and peace. Cherokee people also endeavored to live on a given tract of land in *osi*, a state of neutrality and balance.[27] These concepts remained the cornerstones of Cherokee social and spiritual identities during the late eighteenth and early nineteenth centuries. They were both a form of spirituality and a historical epistemology that connected the past to the present. Cherokees referred to this as *kanohesgi*, a word used for history and for story. These precepts reminded Cherokees that according to Cherokee legend, their ancestors had their origins in the eastern portion of North America and had migrated when it became necessary to ensure the maintenance of tohi and osi.[28]

In the eighteenth century, various European and Euroamerican traders, colonial officials, and settlers attempted to decipher the meaning of Cherokee origin stories. Migration narratives were of particular interest to amateur ethnologists. Alexander Long, a Carolina trader, recorded a version of the Cherokee migration story in 1717. According to Long's account, the Cherokee were not a migrating people in the hunter-gatherer sense of the term, but migrated in search of lands to settle, sustain them, and multiply their numbers. Land was important to the Cherokee because they could move over it, settle "vacant" lands and build towns, and thereby ensure harmony between the natural environment and the multiplying Cherokee populations.[29]

European and Euroamerican observers recorded variants of this and other Cherokee origin and migration narratives over the ensuing century. Cherokee informants shared their archive of oral tradition with non-indigenous people in ways that reflected the social status, age, and/or gender through which such narratives were filtered. Such was the case with the naturalist William Bartram and his informants, who included both Indigenous and non-indigenous people. Unperturbed by, or unaware of, the interpretive challenges posed by a diverse array of informants, Bartram claimed that the Southeastern tribes migrated from the West, crossing the Mississippi and moving eastward.[30] Of the Cherokee, Bartram claimed "they are altogether a separate nation from the Muscoges, of much antientier [sic] establishment in those regions they inhabited." He admitted to making no explicit effort to ascertain the origins and trajectory of Cherokee migrations, writing only, "I understood they came from the West, or Sun setting."[31]

Over the course of the late eighteenth and early nineteenth century, missionaries and amateur ethnologists continued to investigate the migration narratives and spiritual beliefs of the Cherokee people. While the authors of these accounts often bemoaned the difficulty of acquiring "authentic" Indian informants, their reports provide insight into the cultural and religious syncretism that was reshaping Cherokee identity. In the late eighteenth century Cherokee informants often emphasized the more immediate imperial pressures that were inspiring new waves of Cherokee migration. For example, the Overhill peace Chief Scholanuetta (also spelled Squollecuttah, and known to the whites as Hanging Maw), wrote to Secretary Daniel Smith in June 1793 to inform him that Anglo-Cherokee violence had resulted not in the eradication of Cherokee towns, but only in their dispersal and resettlement. Scholanuetta, who had been attacked by "some bad white men" in 1792, and struggled to find the white path of peace, declared, "blood has been spilt at both our houses."[32] Turn-of-the-century violence was thus woven into Cherokee memories of the early American republic. Onitossitah (Chief Corn Tassel), for example, often recalled the violence and outbreaks of disease that afflicted Cherokee people and precipitated the dispersal of many towns and the reestablishment of Cherokee communities on farmsteads after the Revolutionary War. However, Onitossitah contrasted these upheavals with his understanding of what he imagined life to be like among the ancient Cherokee, stating:

> In travelling through the wilderness, the *A qui uh a* took the lead. Each tribe marched by itself and camped separately. Also, each clan kept distinct, without intermingling with other clans of the same tribe. The clans were distinguished by having feathers of different colors fastened to the rim of their ears. Each clan was composed of the descendents of one family, and, being blood connections, the members were forbidden to intermarry. . . . The Cherokees, and the Creeks also, had seven sides to their respective Council Houses,—each clan occupying its own appropriate division; the men sitting on one end of the seats, and the women on the other. Each clan was viewed in all respects as one family.[33]

Stories of Cherokee migration and dispersal acquired renewed significance during an era in which pressures from Anglo-American settlers forced the Cherokees to relocate their homes to lands west of their mythical origins. According to the geographer and ethnologist Henry Schoolcraft, the nineteenth-century Cherokee leader Stand Watie was fond of retelling a story he heard as a boy. Watie claimed that Cherokee elders taught "a tradition of their [the Cherokees'] crossing a large water, apparently a river, which was done by tying grape vines together, and making a sort of vine-bridge, over which they walked."[34] Cherokees often told ethnographers about how the ancient Cherokee migrated from the west and settled on lands east of the Mississippi. During the early decades of the American republic, then, the growing pressure from white settlers and political leaders for Cherokee removal prompted many Cherokee elders to defend their people's land rights by reciting stories about their origins and the heroic migrations made by their forebears before settling in what became the American South. The process of storytelling, or *kanohesgi*, involved the reading of a text or the examining of objects and people to narrate connections between the past and present.[35]

Cherokees in Transition

During the latter half of the eighteenth century, Cherokees encountered grave challenges to their existence as a people, challenges posed by an imperial context changing at lightning speed. From Florida to the Mississippi, Cherokees engaged in a self-conscious struggle—a struggle that was both cultural and martial in nature—to maintain a recognizable sense of Cherokee identity rooted in traditional town and matrilineal kinship ties. Keeping the sacred fire burning in these towns proved a difficult task, given the social dislocations caused by mortality from disease transfer, and the Cherokees' fragile and at times violent relations with Spanish, French, British, and ultimately Anglo-American imperial powers. Adding to the volatility of a colonial milieu in flux were both the increasing numbers of African and African American slaves in the cis-Mississippi and rising waves of Native American refuges—such as the Delaware, Shawnee, and Osage—displaced by settler colonial pressures in the Ohio Valley and upper Mississippi. Indeed, political and social instability was becoming a new reality for Cherokees everywhere, as for all Indigenous Americans.

A new age of warfare defined the opening chapters of the Cherokee's diasporic history. Several decades of intense fighting, starting with Cherokee warriors traveling north and engaging the "French Indians" in warfare in the years immediately preceding the French and Indian War, ultimately changed the global dynamics of imperial politics and set the Cherokee on a path to becoming a diasporic people.[36] While Cherokee chiefs such as Kanagatoga (known to the English as Old Hop), the *uku* (fire king) from the Mother Town of Chota, were not averse to courting French trade into the 1750s, for much of the eighteenth century the Cherokees remained a solid British ally in North America.[37] When war broke out in 1756, there was no suggestion that the Cherokee-British alliance was about to fracture. That it did break down reflected two significant developments. First, wartime violence and instability highlighted the continuing significance of regional identities among the Cherokee. In October 1757, for example, Willinawa, who was from the Overhill Town of Toqua, informed the English that "The people of Tellico have lately been Rogues."[38] English officials learned that the chiefs of this important Overhill Town had made contact with the French and their Indian allies, thus compromising an important imperial buffer zone in English wartime strategizing. From a Cherokee perspective, however, Willinawa's accusations might be interpreted as an example of the enduring significance of town-based rivalries among Cherokee chiefs. While a desire to acquire prestige among fellow town members may have continued to shape the chief's words and actions, given the broader imperial context in which Willinawa's remarks were made it is also possible to view his speech as a call for Cherokee unity against foreign enemies. Thus, Willinawa informed the English that "The Tellico people have lately talked good, and promised, not to hearken any more to the Savannah," and, to promise their loyalty, kill "some of them."[39]

This regional jockeying for political authority and influence among fellow Cherokees was compounded by a second development: the growing influence of Cherokee war (red) chiefs. Centered in the

Lower Towns, a new generation of warrior chiefs refused to suffer the aggression of non-indigenous settlers. Lower Town war chiefs became particularly incensed that settlers began occupying larger portions of what they considered ancient Cherokee hunting grounds. As the British saw things, the Cherokee presence along the Virginia-Pennsylvania borderland, and reported incidents of Cherokee war chiefs having "slain divers of his majesty's good subjects," put settlers and colonial officials on edge.[40] British efforts to mollify the already inflamed Cherokee war chiefs and prevent them from "picking up the hatchet" came to naught, especially after white frontiersmen continued to take an aggressive posture and engage in unprovoked attacks against Cherokee war chiefs and warriors throughout the 1750s. Thus, as the French and Indian War raged on, the Anglo-Cherokee War broke out in 1758. Under the leadership of war chiefs such as Oconostota, the Cherokee displayed impressive fighting prowess.[41] They were, however, defeated. While terms of peace were agreed to in 1761, that peace was achieved against a backdrop of "Indian rogues," giving rise to anxieties among whites about the fate of "their frontier plantations." There were calls from frontier settlers to put "all the Cherokees to death," and British troops burned over one thousand acres of Cherokee crops as a means to induce the Cherokee to sue for peace.[42] The peace agreement of 1761 led to a significant loss of hunting lands and accelerated the dislocating effects of settler colonial expansion on Cherokee clans and towns.[43]

Thousands of Cherokees now found themselves displaced from the only homes they had ever known. The ceding of thousands of square miles of Cherokee land in the years immediately after the French and Indian War forced Cherokee people to reestablish life in new townships and increasingly on new farmsteads, often southwest of their original homeland.[44] As this transition got underway, the cultural and biological fabric of Cherokee life changed. In particular, interracial liaisons and intermarriage between Cherokee men and European women, and more commonly between European men (most often traders) and Cherokee women, which had been occurring from the Appalachian Mountains to the Mississippi for much of the seventeenth and eighteenth century, attracted much greater cultural and political attention from both Cherokees and the colonial Americans during the latter half of the eighteenth century. The intermarriages that Cherokee women sometimes entered into with white men were designed to seal diplomatic and trade relations, relationships defined by mutual obligations. The transnational significance of such marriages was underscored during the late eighteenth century when Cherokee women struggled to ensure that their white husbands conformed to Cherokee principles of reciprocity in a matrilineal system, while white men tried to impose their own gendered ideals on these unions, thus adding to a growing atmosphere of distrust between the Cherokee people and white Americans.[45]

At a politically tumultuous and militarily unstable period in Cherokee history, an assertive generation of war chiefs, unwilling to heed the advice of the peace chiefs, continued to rise in stature. With memories of the French and Indian War and the Anglo-Cherokee War still burning brightly in the minds of Cherokees, the outbreak of the Revolutionary War in 1776 presented the war chiefs with an opportunity to extract revenge on Anglo-American settlers for the loss of Cherokee hunting grounds and for the settlers' refusal to conform to the reciprocal responsibilities associated with marriage and adoption in Cherokee clan life. While the American Revolution was, in the words of historian Edward Countryman, "a disaster" for American Indians, the conflagrations in which Cherokee war chiefs and warriors became embroiled highlighted the messy entanglement of their people with the rapidly expanding and increasingly powerful Anglo-American frontier. To Cherokee chiefs such as Onitossitah (Old Tassel), the issue was clear: the Anglo-Americans were talking about living in "friendship and amity," but were in fact taking Cherokee land.[46] In a 1784 address to Alexander Martin, the governor of North Carolina, Onitossitah made this point when he complained that "Your people are always rangeing [sic] through our Country, and marking our lands." Onitossitah hoped for a peaceful solution to the violence that these encroachments on Cherokee land had caused but worried that the governor "have throwed [sic] us away."[47] War chiefs such as Doublehead and Tallantusky were all too aware of the pressures enunciated by Onitossitah. Initially, Doublehead and Tallantusky believed the only appropriate response to white aggression was war. Young Cherokee warriors agreed. They wanted to visit a bloody form of retribution on white settlements during the 1780s and

1790s.[48] By 1805, however, when they signed the second Treaty of Tellico, Cherokee war chiefs had altered their views and saw in migration toward the setting sun the best hope of keeping their sacred fires burning and securing a life of balance and harmony for the Cherokee.[49]

The Revolutionary War may have been "a disaster" for American Indians, but for the Cherokee in the decades after the war it also clarified the urgent need for sociological, ideological, and institutional adjustments. The Cherokee thus emerged from the era of Revolution with a clearer sense of themselves as a separate people, under constant siege from non-indigenous outsiders. The best means of expressing this sense of collective identity was another matter. War chiefs, particularly Lower Town chiefs like Doublehead and Tallantusky, believed they had the answer. They helped Cherokee people relocate their townships and reestablish life as, in their eyes, a sovereign people distinct from the invading white settlements. If Cherokee warriors' "taking up the hatchet" was not enough to dissuade aggressive white settlers from entering Cherokee lands, then the war chiefs would assert their masculinity and leadership by bravely leading Cherokee people along a path that led to the founding of new towns and farmsteads far from the intrusiveness of whites. As notions of separateness and sovereignty became entrenched in Cherokee political rhetoric, centralized Cherokee institutions came to be seen as vital to the effective governance and political identity of a dispersing people.[50]

The task of reordering Cherokee political institutions, and thus, political affiliations, proved difficult. Some scholars suggest that Cherokee women, for example, appeared to demonstrate better adaptive skills, or a greater willingness to incorporate changes in economic and culture life into their daily routines. This adaptability was in part a legacy of intermarriage with white men, some of whom became fathers to biracial children and could on occasion make a genuine effort to raise a family with knowledge of both the Cherokee and white worlds. In the decade after the Revolution, intermarriages often involved British loyalists and Cherokee women. These types of marriages, along with the presence of a growing army of missionaries inculcating in Cherokee children the ideals of Christianity and Western thinking, led to gradual changes in Cherokee social and cultural life.[51] However, for Cherokee men such as

Doublehead and the younger chiefs, who were not yet ready to accept the level of cultural adaptation that some Cherokees were being exposed to, such change was too much too fast. To these men, the Treaties of Hopewell (1785) and Holston (1791), which sought to regulate trade with the Cherokee and reform the traditional dispensation of justice, undermined nascent Cherokee concepts of autonomy and collective identity. If the Cherokee were going to reorganize their political structures—from autonomous towns to a centralized form of government in the East, and emigrant communities in the West with their own written laws—they were going to do it on their own terms, and at a pace agreed to by all Cherokee people.

In the 1790s, then, the political divisions between peace chiefs such as Onitossitah in the Upper Towns, and Lower Town war chiefs such as John Watts, Doublehead, Little Turkey, and Tallantusky, sharpened. In a rapidly changing Cherokee world, those Upper Town Cherokee men who shared the conviction that change was occurring too quickly joined Lower Town Cherokee allies. The coalition of chiefs that emerged in the Lower Towns strove for an alliance with the Spanish to counterbalance the United States' growing influence. At the same time, Cherokee warriors persisted in their belief that they must fight to push settlers back, lest their traditional folkways be erased forever. And fight they did—with the Americans, among themselves, and against other American Indian warriors.[52] But they seemed to be fighting a losing battle. While they, like most Cherokee people, justifiably viewed the federal government's Indian policy of "civilization with honor" with suspicion, the Cherokee religious ceremonies, economic practices, and social values that they clung to were fast losing cultural currency among an increasingly dispersed Cherokee people.[53]

The Upper Town peace chiefs saw the impact of this change unfolding before their eyes. They recognized that American power was growing and came to realize that continued land cessions would further erode the value of the traditional warrior and hunter as a marker of Cherokee identity, not to mention Cherokee manhood. A growing appreciation for Anglo-American racial ideology crystallized this issue for prominent Upper and Valley Town families, particularly the expanding group of mission-educated, slave owning, "mixed-bloods." Exposed to the teachings of committed missionaries and to Yankee cultural ideals in parts of the Cherokee diaspora such as Connecticut, these multiracial Cherokees would, over the course of the 1790s and into the nineteenth century, recognize the significance that Anglo-Americans placed on Cherokee travel and migration.[54] To Anglo-Americans, displaced Cherokees became examples of the wandering Indian savage. In contrast, white frontiersmen and their families were not portrayed as aimless wanderers, but imbued with bravery and the frontier spirit.[55] Such stereotypes were not idle matters. They informed Indian policy and ultimately shaped the "democratization" of American politics in Jacksonian America, resulting in a shift in federal Indian policy from "civilization with honor" to the forced removal of the Southeastern Indians.

But all this lay in the future. At the turn of the century, land cessions in Virginia and what became the state of Tennessee, and in the western portions of North and South Carolina, saw young Cherokee warriors take up arms against imperial interlopers and rival Indigenous tribes. The Chickamauga (sometimes spelled Chickammoggy in colonial records), led Cherokee resistance efforts by engaging in guerilla war in Tennessee. Under the leadership of Dragging Canoe and Doublehead, they also established the five Lower Towns of the Chickamauga— Lookout Mountain Town, Nickajack, Running Water, Long Island Village, and Crow Town.[56] White frontiersmen reported that Chickamauga warriors were fierce combatants who sometimes engaged in "savage" and "unprovoked outrages" against peaceful European and Anglo-American settlements.[57] In the minds of many Chickamauga, however, military strikes against settler communities reflected their determination to resist the unwelcome territorial encroachments of white Americans as fellow Cherokees struggled to reestablish what they understood as a traditional way of life. The Chickamauga thus sent a message to both the Cherokee people and white Americans: they did not have to adapt to the sociocultural ideals of the American republic and they were determined to fight to keep the sacred fire burning on their land.[58]

However, Chickamauga tactics proved ineffective at a time when the United States was dealing with the Cherokee as a sovereign nation. The Americans chose to negotiate with Little Turkey (the "First Beloved Man") and other chiefs as though they were representatives of what American leaders perceived as a centrally governed Cherokee nation.[59] By taking such a diplomatic position, American officials contributed to a widening of the political gulf between Upper and Lower Town Cherokees in the early republic. While this gulf was real enough, such neat geographical distinctions do not fully convey the fluidity of Cherokee social, cultural, and political identifications during the early nineteenth century.[60] Indeed, the dispersal and attempted reformation of Cherokee townships and farmsteads—both in the South and farther west—underscored just how uncertain these times were for the Cherokee people.

The Cherokee political landscape was literally and figuratively changing. Chickamauga warriors and the diplomatic tactics of American officials were not the only factors fueling this change. Mission-educated "mixed-blood" Cherokee men began acquiring ever more economic and political power, adapting the language of the nation-state to Cherokee politics, and assuming to speak for all Cherokees during the early nineteenth century. John Ross (or Cooweescoowee), whose mother was Cherokee and father and maternal grandfather were Scottish, and who went on to become the Principal Chief of the Cherokee Nation in 1828, imbibed the lessons of missionaries as a child. Early in his life, Ross came under the influence of the Reverend Gideon Blackburn in Tennessee.[61] Like many biracial, mission-educated Cherokees, Ross traveled extensively as a young man, acquiring the polish deemed necessary for a future leader of his people and developing along the way an outlook on whites that saw him distinguish among "bandits"—those of little means who aggressively attempted to dispossess the Cherokee of their land—whites who expressed sympathy for the Cherokee—such as missionaries and others who demonstrated a willingness to negotiate with Cherokee leaders but whose trustworthiness was questionable—and federally appointed Indian Agents and state and federal politicians generally.[62] From the perspective of some non-indigenous observers, educated "mixed-bloods" were as worthy as any white men of the label "civilized." The travel writer Thomas Nuttal gave voice to these sentiments when he praised Chief John Jolly (or Oolootekea) and his brother Tallantusky. Nuttal noted, "I should scarcely have distinguished [Tallantusky] from an American, except by his language. He was very plain, prudent, and

Figure 4: Chief John Jolly (also known as Oolootekea, Jol-lee, Col-lee; or by his Cherokee name, Ahuludegi), ca. 1834. Smithsonian American Art Museum and the Renwick Gallery, gift of Mrs. Joseph Harrison, Jr.

unassuming in his dress and manners; a Franklin among his countrymen, and affectionately called the beloved father."[63]

White Americans often commented on the physical appearance and dress of people they referred to as "half-blood" and "full-blood" Cherokees. Cherokee men stood on average 5'6" in height, while Cherokee women averaged 5'3 1/2" in height. Cherokee women and girls reportedly "copied from the whites" the latest fashions. Cherokee men wore a "short gown, generally called hunting shirt; . . . [and] a beaded belt, (especially in winter), is worn around the waste." Additionally, Cherokee men wore "homespun pantaloons," although some of the older men wore "dear-skin leggings." In footwear, little separated

Cherokee men and women, most wearing moccasins, although early-nineteenth-century observers noted the increased use of shoes and the incorporation of a cloak resembling "the highland plaid of Scotland."[64] For the Cherokee, clothing was a way to express a sense of individual identification within a communal setting. However, Cherokee fashions also revealed a culture in transition, something that was indicated by the sharing of female styles, the specificity of Cherokee male dress, and the generational differences in clothing choice.

White Americans held well-dressed multiracial men like Tallan-tusky in high regard. Indian agents, missionaries, and elected officials in Washington increasingly turned to educated, mixed-race Cherokee men to negotiate treaties.[65] For instance, Chief Tallantusky—"a half Indian, and dressed as a white man"[66]—infamously put his signature to the Second Treaty of Tellico, an agreement that ceded over 5.1 million acres of Cherokee land in Kentucky and Tennessee to the United States. Tallantusky, along with Chief Doublehead, led Lower Town chiefs in signing over to the United States more than nine million acres of land. As the Americans saw things, as much as the Lower Towns were sites of Chickamauga resistance, they were also ripe for manipulation. Thus, in return for their signatures, Tallantusky and Doublehead each received the promise of land in Arkansas Territory. The Arkansas Territory constituted a strategically important part of the Arkansas River Valley, a region defined by a web of Native exchange and diplomatic networks that connected indigenous groups throughout the region, farther west, and in the Southeast. Doublehead failed to collect on the federal government's promise of land in this vibrant borderland region and remained in the east.[67] However, when Cherokees learned of such deals being struck opinions usually diverged. While economic opportunism and martial resistance often coexisted, dividing families and communities on the sale and exchange of land, Tallantusky and other like-minded chiefs believed that by agreeing to migrate west and establishing Cherokee towns far from intruding whites they might once again live in a state of tohi and osi.

In the Valley and Upper Towns, a talented and ambitious group of young and educated leaders saw an opportunity to capitalize on growing

Cherokee anxiety over land cessions and frontier violence. The "full-blood" and mixed-race chiefs among this rising generation of Cherokee leaders claimed their political authority from their mothers—an authority, ironically, that they eventually exploited in an attempt to transition the Cherokee Nation into a patriarchal society—and included notable figures such as The Ridge (later known as Major Ridge), the wealthy slave owner James Vann, and Charles Hicks.[68] While countervailing forces remained and worked against them for decades to come, these men eventually oversaw the concentration of political power into the hands of a multiracial Cherokee elite in Georgia. The men who formed this nascent political elite syncretized Cherokee political principles and American republican political ideals, thereby producing a rhetoric that accused Tallantusky, Doublehead and other Chickamauga chiefs, in ceding land to the Americans, of not conducting themselves in a manner that would ensure balance among the spirit world, maintain public order, and reinforce their commitment to clan and community.

Indeed, Pathkiller (or Nunna-tihi), the Cherokee Principal Chief between 1808 and 1809, rejected talk of migration among his fellow Lower Town chiefs and urged Tallantusky and his people to return "home" so as to prevent further violence between whites and Cherokees who had migrated to Arkansas.[69] Pathkiller was no doubt also aware of the simmering tensions among the Cherokee over the ceding of land to the Americans. For example, The Ridge and his allies accused a number of prominent Lower Town chiefs of destabilizing Cherokee society; they must stop ceding land to the Americans, lest The Ridge and his allies see fit to visit "blood law" upon them for the unauthorized sale of communal property—a fate that ultimately befell Doublehead when The Ridge shot him through the jaw, and an accomplice, Alex Saunders, took an ax to Doublehead's skull and ended his life in August 1807.[70] The Ridge and the rising generation of multiracial Cherokee leaders from the Upper Towns therefore tied their politics to land in unprecedented ways. They opposed selling Cherokee communal lands, as Chickamauga chiefs like Doublehead had done, because The Ridge and his allies envisioned a Cherokee future in which Cherokee spirituality, migration, and land use patterns were framed within a politico-legal framework immediately recognizable to Europeans: the nation, which in Cherokee is phonetically pronounced *A ye li u do tiv sv*.

In response to the type of intratribal violence that cost Doublehead his life and unrelenting American pressure on Cherokee landholdings, a number of prominent Lower Town Cherokees and their chiefs began choosing migration over ongoing conflict, initially heading for Missouri and Arkansas. United States officials speculated that between 5,000 and 6,000 Cherokees migrated and resettled west of the Mississippi prior to the Treaty of 1817.[71] These estimates were wildly inflated. Recent scholars estimate that approximately 5,000 settlers entered the Arkansas Valley during the early republic. The Cherokee were a significant proportion of these settlers, but by no means the majority. Nonetheless, emigration of Cherokees to the Arkansas Valley continued the westward movement of Cherokee people, which began to accelerate after the French and Indian War. Treaties that the Cherokee signed with the British, Virginia, and Carolina governments from 1768 contributed to a sudden contraction in Cherokee landholdings, thus providing the stimulus for the westward migration of Cherokee people. These migrations began in earnest during the 1780s and 1790s, continued through the first Treaty of Tellico in 1804, and through two removal crises, the first between 1806 and 1809, the second between 1817 and 1819.[72]

Historian William McLoughlin argues that Cherokee nationalism was born during the first removal crisis. Certainly, an increasingly wealthy Cherokee elite using nationalistic rhetoric can be traced to this period.[73] Though the Cherokees were an increasingly dispersed people, the language of nationalism helped to reinforce the idea—among Cherokees and especially among whites—that the Cherokee people were united and would not lose their distinctive sense of identity no matter where they traveled. We see this among the Cherokee during the late eighteenth and early nineteenth centuries. In the decades prior to President Thomas Jefferson's famous 1808 letter to "My Children, the Chiefs of the Upper Cherokees," urging them to migrate west, small parties of Cherokees squatted on land around Fayetteville in northwest Arkansas.[74] The earlier Cherokee travelers to cross the Mississippi were largely men, most pursuing a traditional hunting lifestyle, or engaging

claim to the ideology of paternalism that the Southern slaveholding gentry routinely emphasized.[82] The existence of a growing population of elite Cherokee men like Tom Graves suggests that as the Arkansas Cherokees incorporated racial slavery and American economic and political ideals, the cultural mechanisms through which social relationships were experienced and then defined began to alter to meet the demands of life along the Western frontier of the Cherokee diaspora.

As Cherokee communities began dispersing, a redrawing of Cherokee blood, gender, and political boundaries slowly began to unfold in an increasingly systematic and prescribed fashion. The Arkansas Cherokees faced numerous challenges as they began this process. These included violent encounters with a number of groups of Osage warriors; an imperial political situation in flux, with the Louisiana Territory shifting from Spanish, to French, to Anglo-American governance in quick succession; and the westward migration of both Shawnee and Delaware refugees from the Ohio River Valley and Anglo-American settlers.[83] While the Arkansas Cherokees had long wished that they could live in peace with non-Cherokees "from the sun-rise to the sun-set," the pressures on them during the 1790s and into the early nineteenth century were immense and multifaceted.[84]

The chiefs of the Arkansas Cherokees therefore recognized the importance of social innovation and cultural adaptation to survival.[85] They transplanted families and bands from east to west, and cultivated affectionate familial bonds in a strange and hostile land. While the Arkansas Cherokees might be viewed as victims of Anglo-American settler colonial expansion and the losers in a battle for political control of the emerging Cherokee Nation in the east, such a perspective obscures the active—and thus critical—ways in which Cherokee emigrants to the Arkansas Valley helped to create one version of a multidimensional, multi-regional Cherokee identity.[86]

We can gain an insight into how this identity was fast becoming an important feature of the nascent Cherokee diaspora by examining one of the most famous Cherokees to migrate to Arkansas, Connetoo. To white Americans, Connetoo was known as John Hill. At first glance, Connetoo embodied the qualities of the Cherokee frontiersman. Of mixed racial ancestry—although some Americans speculated that he was a white man adopted by the Cherokee—he served as a middleman in the trade conducted between Cherokee settlers and Europeans at Arkansas Post, a bustling trade center established by the French in 1686 along the Arkansas River.[87] Like other mixed-race Arkansas Cherokees, Connetoo also owned land and slaves. His motives for migrating to Arkansas and engaging in these various trade, social, and economic practices were no doubt complex, as all human motivations are. But family appears to have been at the core of Connetoo's motivations. Caught in the crosshairs of shifting power dynamics in Cherokee politics and an aggressively expanding American republic, Connetoo led his family and a small band of followers west. Arriving in Arkansas in 1796, Connetoo's family and band of followers established a small settlement about 50 miles from the St. Francis River in Arkansas. According to US officials in Arkansas at the time, Connetoo claimed that he and ten other Cherokee families had forged a new settlement for themselves. By the end of the first decade of the nineteenth century, Connetoo was reportedly complaining that his quiet little township had grown to about six hundred Cherokees.[88]

There's no way of verifying Connetoo's population estimates with any degree of certainty. His migration and resettlement, however, indicates that Cherokees migrating to Arkansas during the late eighteenth and early nineteenth centuries were not all single men. On the contrary, they included family units and larger bands of Cherokees who hoped to re-create the types of homes and farmsteads they remembered in the east. Prior to the New Madrid earthquakes in 1811 and 1812, these Cherokee townships dotted the landscape along the St. Francis.[89] After the earthquakes, most Arkansas Cherokees migrated farther west, settling along the White and Arkansas Rivers. Having dispersed toward the setting sun because of both manmade and natural forces, the vanguard of the Cherokee diaspora worked once again to establish permanent, secure, and prosperous Cherokee towns and farmsteads. Seen in this light, the Cherokees' violent clashes with Osage men, their involvement in trade networks, their adoption of racial slavery, their willingness to migrate in search of their own version of tohi and osi, and their nurturing

of the type of patriarchal family structures that Cherokee elites were beginning to encourage back east, represent a number of the important
connective threads in the diasporic life of Cherokee people.

In a letter to Cherokee Indian Agent Return Meigs, Connetoo
spelled out these objectives for the United States government. Conne-
too wrote, "Sir I Wish to inform you this fourteen years Since I have
Crossed the Mississippi. Come to the Country Called the Lusiana When
I first Came hear I had Warr all Raised me But now I had firm pease and
Was making good times."[90] Connetoo was by no means the only leader
among the Arkansas Cherokees to think in this way. Others, such as
Unacata (White Man Killer), the métis trader William Webber, George
Duvall, and Moses Price (Wohsi) shared similar opinions.[91] They hoped
to live in peace with the Indigenous and non-indigenous peoples
around them, forge a balance between the natural environment and the
spiritual and material needs of the people, and to govern their version
of Cherokee society as patriarchs and protectors of stable family units.
These Cherokee leaders took the sacred fire with them as they and their
followers marched toward the setting sun and began nurturing Cherokee settler communities in the trans-Mississippi West.[92]

The manner in which the Western Cherokees, as they came to
be known, acquired land west of the Mississippi, and developed their
own written laws, drove a political wedge between them and the Cherokees who remained east of the Mississippi, causing a conflict that ultimately boiled over in Indian Territory following the Trail of Tears. In
other words, pressure from increasing waves of white settlers and federal government efforts to force a westward pattern of migration on all
Southeastern Indians exacerbated a Cherokee dichotomy: the quest for
tohi and osi that inspired some Cherokees to migrate into the trans-
Mississippi West, and the reality of Cherokee factionalism that followed
Cherokees wherever they migrated and settled. Despite this, or perhaps
because of it, Cherokees continued to migrate westward and southward.
For example, under the leadership of Duwali, a small group of Cherokees
established permanent settlements in east Texas during 1819–1820.[93]

The Texas Cherokees migrated west from Cherokee Country in the
east, first settling in Missouri, then Arkansas, and finally in Mexican-

Figure 6: "The Bowl," also known as Chief John Bowl (or Bowles) or by his Cherokee name, Duwali. Courtesy of the Texas State Library and Archives Commission, #1/102−661.

controlled Texas.[94] They traveled with hopes of living peaceful, prosperous lives. They faced innumerable pressures. From the east, Anglo-Americans had set their sights on the land where the Texas Cherokees were establishing homes and farms, between the Angelina and Neches Rivers. To the west of this region, the warlike Comanches threatened Cherokee settlements with constant warfare and raiding. In addition, the Texas Cherokee settlements were ethnically diverse. Shawnees, Kickapoos, and representatives from several other tribes lived in and around Cherokee settlements. According to the Anglo-American press, the Texas Cherokees and their associated bands were "fugitive bands" who migrated west and were in essence "intruders" on Texas territory.[95] The Cherokees' attempts at countering such perceptions, by engaging in what became a fractured diplomacy with Mexican and Anglo-Texas officials, underscored the precariousness of life for Cherokees living in diaspora during the 1820s and early 1830s.

The latter half of the eighteenth century was a period of warfare, political uncertainty, social change, territorial loss, and unprecedented levels of migration for Cherokee people, both within the Southeast and into the trans-Mississippi West. As the following chapter reveals in greater detail, a new generation of Cherokee leaders emerged in the early nineteenth century and tried to make sense of all of these changes. Their task would not be easy. The extension of Southern slave society, the socioeconomic changes wrought by the "market revolution" and the democratization (for white men) of American politics during the Jacksonian Era, and the spread of evangelical Christianity (know to historians as the Second Great Awakening), all muddled a Cherokee world already in flux.

Nonetheless, Cherokee people responded to the changes occurring around them in creative ways. Some joined the Western Cherokees in the trans-Mississippi, though increasing numbers of Cherokees threw their support behind chiefs who expressed a determination to resist further land cessions and removal from the ancient soil upon which their homes were built. And the Cherokee Beloved Women, whose political influence was being steadily eroded by the introduction of patriarchal laws and the centralization of Cherokee government, adapted nationalistic and Christian language to redefine their identity and defend Cherokee land rights.[96] Like their male counterparts, Cherokee women blended Cherokee traditions with foreign beliefs—such as Christianity—and political concepts—like nationalism—that in time proved critical to the formation of a diasporic Cherokee identity.

In the late eighteenth century Cherokee townships and farmsteads on both sides of the Mississippi were fluid territorial spaces. This fluidity, however, did not bespeak a randomness in Cherokee travel and migration; on the contrary, Cherokee movement was calculated and rational. As we shall see, further migrations occurred during the early nineteenth century, culminating in the forced removal known as the Trail of Tears. This latter movement of Cherokee people highlighted how the eliminationist rhetoric encoded in American attitudes toward Indigenous people came to define the federal government's treaty-making efforts during the early nineteenth century.[97] In this settler colonial context, a new generation of Cherokee leaders solidified their political power and attempted to marry the traditional concepts of tohi and osi with

Christian and nationalistic modes of thinking. They did this in an effort both to define Cherokee politico-legal opposition to removal, and to geographically and culturally re-map a coherent sense of what it meant to be Cherokee.[98] According to some Cherokees, the history of their people was just beginning.

Colonialism, Christianity, and Cherokee Identity

At the opening of the nineteenth century, the Cherokees continued the struggle to rebuild their communities amid the devastation caused by the Revolutionary War. Wave after wave of settlers encroached on their lands—with removal crises between 1806 and 1809, in 1817, 1828, and 1829 resulting in the cession of 6,689,280 acres of Cherokee land, in addition to the 14,068,000 acres of Cherokee land ceded to the United States between the 1780s and the beginning of the nineteenth century. In this context the Cherokee people, as historian William McLoughlin has observed, experienced a level of social instability and "anomie" that few could remember from previous times. The decades of the early American republic— roughly between 1789 and the 1820s—were a troubled time in the Native South.[1]

For the Cherokees, the stakes of diplomacy with the United States were high. As the Anglo-American frontier drew nearer from the North and East, Cherokee leaders recognized all that was at stake: the lands that they and the people they represented considered their ancient soil, in addition to the rivers and streams that helped to make that soil fertile and provide a geographical sense of rootedness. In Cherokee Country, the late eighteenth and early nineteenth century was an era of human movement, the likes of which had not been seen in living memory. To make sense of this movement, Cherokees turned to their oral traditions. They drew especially from stories about ancient migrations and didactic tales of the spirit world. And the Cherokees innovated, eventually expressing their belief systems and sense of uniqueness in written form, thereby providing a permanent inventory of the Cherokee past. From this written and oral catalog of Cherokee history and philosophy, future generations might draw wisdom, and craft new and innovative strategies for negotiating with the United States government.

Well might the Cherokees innovate. During the American Revolution and the decades immediately following the republic's formation, Cherokee people strove to nurture long-held connections to the land and the water that filled rivers and streams. They did so, however, against a backdrop of towns and villages destroyed by war, amid hunger and destitution, and with kinship ties fragmented by disease and the losses suffered during wartime. The era of the early republic had the potential to be a period of ruin for the Cherokees; it was not. Phoenix-like, the Cherokee people picked themselves up, sought out new town sites, and rebuilt homes on farmsteads that provided material comfort and spiritual sustenance. Most Cherokees revived kin ties, establishing new farmsteads by migrating and resettling within the loosely defined borders of Cherokee Country, especially in modern-day Tennessee, Georgia, and Alabama. A small number, though, saw no future in Cherokee Country. As the previous chapter outlined, these Cherokees migrated beyond the western banks of the Mississippi River and settled in Missouri, Arkansas, or Texas. Historians came to refer to these Cherokee migrants as the Western Cherokees, or Old Settlers. Such labels do not do justice to their legacy, for they truly were the vanguard of an emerging Cherokee diaspora, a vanguard that underscored the idea that there were many paths that Cherokee people could travel to nurture distinctive feelings of Cherokeeness.[2]

During the decades of the early American republic, it was hard to identify a unified Cherokee identity. But a remapped Cherokee identity was indeed being sketched out by Cherokees. Focusing on the rise of a small Cherokee elite—well-educated, wealthy, slave-owning, and multiracial—historians William McLoughlin, Theda Perdue, Michael Green, and Andrew Denson have all argued that Cherokee leaders used nationalistic language to transform the Cherokee political system. Cherokee men such as Charles Hicks, John Ridge, Elias Boudinot, and John Ross played pivotal roles in debating, and ultimately prescribing, the political and cultural meaning of "tribal nationalism."[3] And as the sociologist Duane Champagne argues, the rapidity of these political changes was made possible by a long tradition among the Cherokees of separating religious from political authority.[4]

A careful analysis of early nineteenth-century Cherokee political and social discourse reveals that tribal nationalism was deeply influenced by the teachings of Christian missionaries. Indeed, just as missionaries worked during this time to remake the Cherokees into a "civilized" people, a small, multiracial Cherokee elite gained a firm hold on Cherokee political power and attempted to prescribe their own definitions of a "civilized" Cherokee identity. In this chapter we begin to see how the Cherokee people wrestled with the possible uses and limitations of both Christianity and nationalism in their quest to define Cherokee identity in terms recognizable to themselves, and to Euroamericans. These efforts also highlight how influential Cherokee leaders viewed education and literacy, and trade and economic prosperity, as crucial building blocks to the articulation of Cherokee identity. Complicating these efforts was migration and the unpredictability of human movement in a colonial context in flux. In fact, answering the deceptively simple question, "Who am I?" proved a difficult task for all Cherokees, but particularly for their leaders, in the decades prior to forced migration at the end of the 1830s.

Religion, Literacy, and Cherokee Identity

Of all the external forces that challenged established modes of life among the Cherokees, Christianity proved the most pervasive. Christian missionaries exhibited a keen interest in the spiritual welfare of the Cherokee people during the eighteenth and nineteenth centuries. This was especially true of Moravian and Quaker missionaries.[5] As early as 1740, for example, the Moravians proposed a mission in Cherokee Country. The Moravian missionaries, like the Congregationalists who followed them into the South, established "settled mission enclaves" among the region's Native American populations. Missionaries insisted that these enclaves would operate as models of settled life. Teachers delivered lessons in both Cherokee and English, giving Indigenous people the best possible opportunity to receive and recognize the "virtues" of Christianity and the material benefits associated with commercial agriculture and modern forms of trade.[6] While the Cherokee did not grant the Moravian Church permission to establish a mission among them until 1800, the Moravians claimed their first Cherokee converts as early as the 1770s. By the early nineteenth century, Moravian missionaries could point to Cherokee leaders such as Charles Hicks, a baptized member of the Moravian Church, as evidence of their success.[7]

Baptist and Methodist missionaries also proselytized among the Cherokee during the early nineteenth century. Unlike the Moravians, the Baptists and Methodists did not establish "settled mission enclaves." Instead, they channeled their evangelical energies into itinerant missionizing. Baptist and Methodist missionaries believed that this type of activity would prove the most effective in saving Cherokee souls. Over the course of the first three decades of the nineteenth century, both Methodist and Baptist missionaries among the Cherokees also adopted an anti-removal stance and some became distinctly antislavery in their politics. These intersecting political positions did not always complement one another. Congregational missionaries, for example, tended to mute their abolitionism in the company of Cherokee slaveholders. Similarly, Methodists preachers in the South were generally acknowledged to harbor supportive views on the westward extension of slavery.[8] As with all Christian denominations, Methodists and Baptists expressed a variety of viewpoints on slavery, perspectives that gave rise to schisms within these Christian denominations.[9] However, an observer from the Methodist Episcopal Church, writing in the *St. Louis Christian Advocate*, charged that throughout the South "Methodist preachers themselves are, to a large extent, involved in the iniquity [of slavery], not simply of winking at the evil, but by actually owning and breeding slaves."[10] The issue of racial slavery proved a particularly emotional and politically divisive one for Christian preachers and missionaries. As the

Cherokees acquired their own class of wealthy slave owners during the early republic, they too expressed divergent views on the issue of racial slavery.

On other prominent social issues, such as temperance and marriage, missionaries from different Christian denominations were more consistent. For example, both Methodist and Baptist missionaries regularly emphasized the importance of sobriety and patriarchal forms of monogamy. Methodist missionaries believed the message of Christian conversion and personal morality was winning Cherokee supporters. In 1822, just one year after establishing a mission to the Cherokees, the Methodists insisted that they had procured over one hundred converts.[11] Baptist missionaries also laid claim to considerable success in converting Cherokees. Strikingly, their success was largely among "conservative" Cherokees, or men and women who continued to hold on to traditional Cherokee cultural practices and beliefs, and who looked forward to the day when racial slavery would be abolished. The Baptists' most significant coup occurred when the prominent Cherokee political leader Jesse Bushyhead converted to the Baptist faith and became a vocal advocate for temperance.[12]

During the early republic, missionaries from all Christian denominations grappled with the merits of bilingualism, debated pedagogy, and questioned whether or not to adopt an itinerant or settled form of missionizing.[13] All agreed, however, that conversion to Christianity and the extension of American civilization were not mutually exclusive. Missionaries thus recognized that they had an important role to play as imperial agents in fostering the growth of Anglo-American settler "civilization." In fact, missionaries tended to see themselves as social engineers working to produce a particular type of Christian and "civilized" Indian population.[14] They believed that no group understood the practical implications of biblical narratives about life, death, and resurrection better than the Cherokees.

Few organizations attempted to implement this brand of Christian "humanitarianism" as rigorously as the American Board of Commissioners for Foreign Missions (ABCFM). Founded in 1810, the ABCFM was the first organized missionary society in the United States. From its very beginning, the American Board had an international focus—

missionizing to Indigenous people in the United States and abroad—and an interdenominational membership. However, Congregationalists and members of Reformed Churches comprised the core of its membership.[15] In taking its message to the Cherokees, the American Board aimed to "set the lamp of life in the forest of Cherokeera."[16] The "separatist" origins and independent ethos of the American Board's Congregationalist missionaries, coupled with its unwavering opposition to the removal of the Cherokees from their Southeastern homeland, resonated with many ordinary Cherokee people who were determined to hold on to their farms and practice their traditions free of central government interference. For these Cherokees, their identity—their souls—remained tied to the land of their forebears and to maintaining balance and harmony among the different forces in Cherokee society. The land sustained them, helped to define relationships with other human beings, and connected Cherokee people to a history that gave the present its deep meaning. Cherokees thus viewed American Board missionaries as useful allies in their fight to remain an autonomous people so they might keep their sacred fires alight throughout their Southern homeland.[17]

The Cherokees sought to interpret the lessons imparted by American Board missionaries in an active, and—to the discomfort of some missionaries—critical way. Although the missionaries often disapproved of the way Cherokees interpreted biblical lessons, in fact these interpretations displayed how Cherokees actively incorporated Christian philosophies into their own belief structures.[18] One such "superstition" that the Cherokee people spoke of during the early nineteenth century was *Ani Hyuntikwalaski*, or how the Cherokees acquired fire. The story overlapped with the Cherokees' questioning about the white man's power, with regard to his ancestors' ability to "catch lightening" and acquire fire in the manner that the Cherokees believed their forebears had acquired fire. According to the narrative of Ani Hyuntikwalaski, the Thunderers, who inhabited darkened lands in the West, and the Water Spider were the sons of Kana'ti and Selu—the Lucky Hunter and the Corn Mother of the Cherokees. The Thunderers set fire to a sycamore tree, which was located on a faraway island. Various birds and snakes tried unsuccessfully to collect the fire. It was the ingenious Water Spider who ultimately succeeded in collecting the fire by spinning a small bowl (*tusti*), fastening it to his back, and returning with a burning coal. Hereafter, the narrative explains, "man has had fire."[19]

Such stories were the cultural soil from which Cherokee questions about Christianity sprang. These questions mixed Cherokee beliefs with curiosity about the significance of the Christian stories that missionaries relayed to Cherokee people. In other words, the Cherokees engaged in a type of "spiritual miscegenation," to borrow historian John Smolenski's provocative phrase, that did not sit well with prominent missionaries.[20] Smolenski's phrase helps to focus our attention not only on the amalgamation of Cherokee and Christian belief structures, but also on the racial differences that missionaries and their settler allies imagined between themselves and Native Americans. The comingling of people from very different geocultural backgrounds thus held the potential to foment some explosively violent colonial encounters and to discourage sincerity among Cherokee converts. Aware of this, missionaries were eager to prevent such violence, to preach against the blending of Christian and Cherokee beliefs, and thus to "save" the Cherokee's soul as quickly as possible.[21]

For growing numbers of Cherokee people, cultural and religious syncretism was as much a survival strategy as it was a means to rearticulate Cherokee spirituality in a rapidly changing world. However, leading American Board missionaries were not prepared to accept such syncretism because they feared it was a gateway to atavism—or the reversion to traditional "heathen" beliefs and practices following public (and presumably false) declarations of Christian conversion. Missionaries therefore worked hard to stamp out the influences of traditional culture. This process began with the removal of Cherokee children, in particular "the children of half breeds and of the leading men of the nation," from their native parents.[22] This was the approach of missionary Cyrus Kingsbury, who used pecuniary logic to extract Cherokee children from their parents. He planned to tell Cherokee parents that "we would take their children and teach them freely, without money."[23] Kingsbury insisted that the purpose of removing children from their parents was to "teach them their duty toward their parents, to their fellow relatives and to the Great Spirit, the great father of us all."[24] Moreover, by removing Cherokee children from the "society of the natives" and the "influence of their heathen parents," American Board missionaries believed that they could remake Cherokee families into patriarchal models of Christian virtue.[25] One missionary went so far as to inform American Board officials in Boston that he had the support of Principal Chief John Ross to create just such a Christian mission among the Texas Cherokees.[26]

Of the Cherokees who availed themselves of a missionary education, few were more prominent than John Ridge and his cousins, Stand OoWatie (or Waite) and Buck OoWatie (better known as Elias Boudinot). These young men were exactly the type of pupils that missionaries envisioned would lead the Indian race into a "civilized" future. They were bright, possessed mixed racial ancestry (although all three insisted they were "full-blood" Cherokees), and descended from "leading men of the nation." Boudinot, as we'll see below, became an outspoken model for how a "modern" Cherokee should think and act. Missionaries touted his brother, Stand Watie, and his cousin, John Ridge, as exemplars of what a Christianized, civilized, and highly educated American Indian was capable of becoming.

The Ridge-Boudinot-Watie family story is sometimes portrayed as a "Cherokee tragedy."[27] On the contrary, it can also be seen as a story of the Cherokee diaspora in the making—a story of renewal and reinvention that was every bit Cherokee as it was Christian. Take, for instance, the early life of Stand Watie (Degadoga). He was born in 1806 at Oothcaloga (modern-day Calhoun), a Valley Town located in what became western Georgia. His father, David OoWatie, was a full-blood Cherokee, his mother a so-called half-breed. He received his formal education from the American Board's Brainerd Mission, located near present-day Chattanooga, Tennessee. This training prepared Watie for his future life as a leader of the Cherokee people. Not unlike the cosmopolitan white elites of colonial and Revolutionary-era America, he became comfortable with travel, slipping effortlessly between white and Cherokee society. Watie also became both a civic and economic leader, returning to Georgia after he completed his studies in Tennessee and taking a position as a clerk at the Cherokee Supreme Court, serving as speaker of the

Cherokee National Council, and rising to become a prominent Cherokee slaveholder.[28]

Watie's cousin, John Ridge, enjoyed a similarly stunning rise to political and economic prominence during the 1810s and 1820s. John Ridge
(Skahtlelohskee) was also born in Oothcaloga in 1803. His "full-blood"
father, Major Ridge (Kahmungdaclageh) was a successful proprietor
and prominent political leader. His mother, Susanna Wickett Ridge
(Sehoya), a multiracial Cherokee woman, was described by contemporaries as a "handsome and sensible" woman who possessed "an excellent character."[29] Indeed, Major Ridge and his wife, whom he married in
1790, had themselves come of age in an era when the cultural influences
of missionaries and white settlers began to set Cherokee society on its
transition from a matriarchal to a patriarchal system of governance and
inheritance. John Ridge, then, was born into this transitional era. His
parents were determined that young John would thrive in the new world
they were helping to make. He therefore attended the Moravian's mission school at Spring Place, Georgia; was a pupil at the American Board's
Brainard mission school in Tennessee; and subsequently entered an
academy in Knoxville, Tennessee, before transferring to the American
Board's school in Cornwall, Connecticut.[30] John Ridge emerged from
his studies a refined and educated man. Sam Houston, the former Tennessee governor, future Texas president, and adopted Cherokee son of
Chief John Jolly, observed that the young John Ridge was the equal of
the finest white man.[31] More than this, though, Ridge acquired an intimate knowledge of white America's highest intellectual and cultural
ideals, traveled throughout North America, and developed an ability to
move easily between the white and Cherokee worlds—a quality that
was fast becoming one of the hallmarks of the Cherokee elite's diasporic
sense of identity.

One of John Ridge's more noted siblings, Sarah Ridge, also embodied these qualities. Sarah Ridge was well educated and equally well
traveled. In many ways, Sarah was a daughter of the nascent Cherokee
diaspora, albeit in ways that her parents and missionaries deemed appropriate to her family "pedigree" and gender. Sarah was born in 1804.
Like her famous brother, she received a missionary education before

Figure 7: Portrait of John Ridge, ca. 1838. Library of Congress Prints and Photographs Division, Washington, DC.

attending a Moravian seminary in Winston-Salem, North Carolina and the Female Academy in Huntsville, Alabama. In North Carolina, Sarah Ridge, along with Mary Watie, Elias Boudinot's sister, reportedly became "deeply awakened" to her love for the "divine Providence" and the eternal welfare of her soul.[32] She also grew to become a beautiful young woman, attracting both Cherokee and white suitors. Above all, Sarah Ridge displayed great determination, once riding a horse for hours until it was broken.[33] As a member of a leading Cherokee family and role model for future generations of diasporic Cherokee women, Sarah Ridge needed all of the emotional and physical determination she could muster during the tumultuous decades of the 1820s and 1830s.

The missionaries earmarked the Ridge-Boudinot-Watie youths and other "children of half breeds and of the leading men of the nation" as the models for what was fast becoming a geographically dispersed and racially diverse Cherokee population. The early nineteenth-century Cherokee diaspora was an intercultural and interracial world, something that missionaries and Indian Agents understood, and they worked hard to control, manage, and engineer it in ways that they believed would make the Cherokees a more "civilized" race. That said, it is important to note that the educational and social networks to which the missionaries introduced Cherokee children played a significant role in fostering interconnections with other leading Cherokee families and influential whites. American Board missionaries thus supported intermarriage between whites and Cherokees, believing that such unions had a positive moral affect on the Cherokees—engendering in Cherokee women a "solemn, submissive" demeanor, and in Cherokee men a motive to take their patriarchal responsibilities seriously. Moreover, both missionaries and leading Cherokee families believed that a well managed mingling of "blood" (through the agency of patriarchal marriage), and cultures (under the guidance of Christian missionaries), would eventually cement a mutual dependence between American settlers and Native Americans.[34]

Talk of interracial marriage and intercultural exchange led to the articulation of anxieties among literate Cherokees about the "character" of the Cherokee people. An anonymous writer using the nom-de-plume "Socrates" emphasized what he or she believed was the fragility of human "character" in the context of interracial marriage. Scholars have long puzzled over the identity of the Cherokee "Socrates," but the anonymous author's anxiety about the impact of marriage between white men and Cherokee women was clear for all to read in the pages of the *Cherokee Phoenix* newspaper. In a series of open letters in 1828, Socrates tied the character of the Cherokee Nation to its "exercise of sovereignty" and the ability (and willingness) of its citizens to forego individual desires in preference for the common good. Socrates thus urged Cherokee parents to instruct their children on the importance of carefully selecting a marriage partner. Socrates did not specifically address the issue of interracial sex, but instead remained focused on intermarriage, warning readers of the *Cherokee Phoenix* about the potential dangers posed by white men. As the character of the Cherokee citizen was not guaranteed for time immemorial, much less citizenship assured for life, Cherokee people must remain vigilant and guard against "the thief, the robber, the vagabond and the tippler, and adulterer."[35]

Socrates' warnings about the perils of intermarriage with whites came at a time when the Ridge-Boudinot-Watie family was extending their kinship connections to the white world. These connections did raise suspicions among Cherokees. Just as white Americans expressed serious reservations about the efficacy of racial "amalgamation," so too did Cherokees worry about their social and cultural institutions in a world where cultural distinctions were blurred by intermarriage.[36]

Like the Ridge-Boudinot-Watie family, the Ross family was all too aware of such suspicions. John Ross was well connected in white America thanks to his business dealings and diplomatic travels on behalf of the Cherokee Nation. On the issue of intermarriage, though, he expressed reservations—especially when a Cherokee man married a white woman, thus raising uncertainty about the matrilineal clan membership of the "issue" produced in the marriage.[37] Ross eventually overcame his concerns. His second wife, Mary Stapler, was a white woman. The Ross family forged connections in both the white and Cherokee worlds not simply through marriage, but also through educational and business connections. Bound to both the Cherokee and colonial worlds of the Atlantic basin by ties of blood, culture, and commerce, the Rosses became one of the leading Cherokee families of the nineteenth century.

William Potter Ross, John Ross's nephew, rose to political prominence by mid-century, but his formative years reveal much about the diasporic world that many multiracial Cherokee elites occupied. William Ross was born into a leading mixed-race Cherokee family in Tennessee on August 28, 1820. He received his education from a Presbyterian Mission school in Will's Valley, Alabama, and the Greenville Academy in eastern Tennessee. Subsequently, Ross attended Hamil's preparatory school in New Jersey, and eventually entered Princeton College, where he graduated with honors in 1842. His racial lineage, his travels, and his educational pedigree helped Ross cement the connections—in both the Cherokee and Euroamerican worlds—that would serve him well through the remainder of his adult life.[38]

At a time when debate about Cherokee removal was intensifying, the young William Ross was becoming well traveled and cultured, like

Figure 8: Portrait of John Ross, ca. 1843. Library of Congress Prints and Photographs Division, Washington, DC.

other Cherokees of his class, education, and racial standing. During the late 1820s and early 1830s, William Ross devoted a minimum of six to seven hours each day to his studies, which included lessons in Greek and Latin. He also allotted time to expand his cultural horizons, traveling to Philadelphia to take in that city's finest theatrical productions. However, Ross's educational and cultural pursuits did not blind him to the political pressures being placed on the Cherokees by white Americans and the nature of the expanding diaspora in the American West. In an 1837 letter to John Ross, William wrote that he was filled with anxiety after learning that one of his uncles was planning to migrate to Arkansas. William Ross elaborated on the rationality of these feelings, explaining, "it's very sickly at the west."[39]

William Ross's assessment of the "society" and health of the West, an area many Cherokees were traveling to and settling in, was shared by other Cherokees of his class. For example, William Shorey Coodey, John Ross's Princeton-educated nephew, spoke of "our brother Cherokees in that country" whose migration into frontier Arkansas had transformed these settlers into "rude and uncivilized" Indians. Connected by the "tie of blood" to these Western Cherokees, men of Coodey's lineage and social breeding assumed that they constituted a class of leaders respon-sible for one day re-integrating these degraded frontier Cherokees into the Cherokee Nation.[40] Looking to the future, young men like William Ross and William S. Coodey imagined that they would eventually lead the Cherokee people toward a more "evolved" state of "civilization" by turning them away from "intemperance and fornication," and "their heathenish practices."[41]

The missionaries who contributed to Ross and Coodey's educa-tion recognized the need for constant vigilance in order for such ideals to take hold among the Cherokees. The tale of Nancy Man was a case in point. In the early 1830s, Man availed herself of the American Board's missionary and religious services. She appeared devout, and eventually submitted to a patriarchal marriage. However, missionaries discovered that she professed her devotion to Christ "as a cloak for her desires," for she married a white man who turned out to be "a depraved drunken fel-low altogether her inferior."[42] The power of the missionary to engineer a race of "civilized" Cherokee people clearly had its limits.

Nancy Man's marriage was the type of relationship that missionaries and their Cherokee allies wanted to discourage. The model for Cherokee intermarriage was instead embodied in the life stories of multiracial elites like John Ridge. While a student in Cornwall, Connecticut, Ridge met and fell in love with a fourteen-year-old girl by the name of Sarah Bird Northrup. At a time when discussion of racial "amalgamation" among white Americans was producing anxious questions about the future complexion of the American population, the Ridge-Northrup marriage scandalized the white residents of Cornwall, Connecticut.[43] Distressed by reports of interracial courtships at Cornwell, the Reverend Herman Dag-gett, the Superintendent at the Cornwell Mission School, sent an urgent message to Jeremiah Evarts in April 1823. The message read:

> I wish to call your attention to a subject which appears nearly connected to the welfare of the FMS. The Steward has gener-ally had a girl, or young woman, as cook in his family, who is of course much in the company of the scholars, when they go to their meals, work about the house, or occasionally visit the kitchen at other times. Two years ago a case occurred of

improper intimacy between the hired girl and one or two of the colored boys, which gave us a great deal of trouble, and resulted in the necessity of sending the girl away. We have now another case of this kind, which I fear may be of very serious consequences to one of our most promising Indian scholars, and indeed the reputation of the school.[44]

In the face of these concerns, John Ridge and Sarah Northrup continued their courtship and married on January 27, 1824.[45] Sarah Northrup's decision to marry Ridge attracted the disapproval of Cornwall's white residents, one of whom, Emily Fox, expressed her displeasure in the form of poetry. Fox lamented:

> She was blest with beauty bright and fair
> There were few with her could compare.
> O, 'tis hard for her to relate the truth,
> She fell in love with an Indian youth!
> "Now Sarah is gone—her we ne'er shall view—
> She's gone, and to her love proves true,
> O yes, she's gone, and her Indian too—
> Now Sarah we will bid adieu.[46]

When news of the interracial marriage between Ridge and Northrup traveled outside of the town of Cornwall, Connecticut, it caused a similar level of controversy. Writing in the *American Eagle* newspaper, Isaiah Bunce expressed his disgust by declaring "that girl [Northrup] should be whipped, her husband hanged and her mother drowned."[47]

While American Board missionaries worried about the potential damage that commentaries like Bunce's could do to the Cornwell School, many also felt that the Ridge-Northrup marriage had the potential to set an example for Cherokee people. Certainly Ridge thought so. In 1826, he wrote, "Mutability is stamped in every thing that walks the Earth. Even now we are forced by natural causes to a Channel that will mingle the blood of our race with the white."[48]

For missionaries, the Ridge-Northrup marriage served as an example of how interracial marriage exercised a positive moral influence on the multiracial children of those unions and produced a culturally "civilized" people. Missionaries therefore defended specific examples of Indigenous-white marriages, insisting that by choosing marriage over illicit sex, couples like Ridge and Northrup elevated the moral tenor of Cherokee communities to such an extent that "the rays of the sun of righteousness," as missionaries were wont to exclaim, would penetrate "the gloom of heathenism and superstition."[49]

The Ridge-Northrup marriage also put a new spin on the history of interracial exogamy among Cherokees in the early nineteenth century. The existence of interracial marriages between white men and Cherokee women was well known and commonly recognized (if not accepted) by early nineteenth-century Americans. However, inverting the gendered makeup of such marriages posed a challenge both to white racial sensibilities and to Cherokee matrilineal and matrilocal clan membership and kinship relationships. While Cherokees and white Americans struggled to come to terms with the cultural implications of Indian men marrying white women, those who defended such marriages emphasized how couples like Ridge and Northrup contributed to the growth of Cherokee commerce, prosperity, and "civilization." As evidence of this, American Board missionaries claimed that marriages between "mixed-blood" elite men and white women saw couples living in relative comfort, most reportedly possessing "a farm from which it draws on support."[50] Additionally, missionaries reported that so-called half-breeds and their families lived in homes that were kept "in good order, much more cleanly than those of their white neighbors." Most importantly, the homes of these Cherokee "half-breeds" were, according to missionaries, a vast improvement on the filth, intemperance, gambling, and prostitution that prevailed in Cherokee communities where traditional notions of communalism prevailed.[51]

The American Board's binary between "civilized" and "traditional" Cherokees was simplistic and overdrawn. However, the aspirations of the rising multiracial Cherokee elite were well served by this binary, with its members exploiting it to their socioeconomic and political advantage. Prominent Cherokee families took seriously their responsibility of setting a "civilized" example for all Cherokees to follow. They encouraged missionaries to remain among the Cherokees and continue their holy labors. For example, missionaries reported that John Ross envisioned a Cherokee "reservation" where Indigenous children might receive lessons in "civilized" practices from devoted missionaries. Ross's thinking on education in the Cherokee Nation evolved substantially during the early nineteenth century, and he eventually became convinced that Cherokee-run and operated boarding schools would best serve the educational needs of Cherokee children.[52] Other educational proposals were more explicitly race-based. For example, David Vann, a prominent Cherokee slaveholder, actively sought the American Board's support for a mission to "half-breed" Cherokees. According to John Ridge, Vann's vision centered on mixed-race Cherokees who, while they spoke fluent English, were "in other respects deficient in education." If a new breed of Cherokees was to emerge and play a leading role in prescribing a renewed sense of Cherokee identity, men such as Ross and Vann felt that they would lead by strengthening Cherokee ties to white American blood, education, religion, and commerce.[53]

By the beginning of the nineteenth century, then, the leading Cherokee families in the Southeast had allied themselves with the religious and cultural values prescribed by missionaries. The children of these leading families ultimately became the most influential political and economic figures in Cherokee society during the 1820s and 1830s. However, the apparent complicity of missionaries and prominent Cherokee families in shunning "traditional" folkways in preference for an acculturated Euro-Cherokee identity based on Christianity, patriarchy, race, and nationalism was not quite so simple.[54]

Those Cherokees who availed themselves of a missionary education, converted to Christianity, and entered the arenas of politics and trade were not simply pawns of American imperialism who inadvertently contributed to their peoples' elimination. The Cherokee people, whether educated in North Carolina, Georgia, Tennessee, Alabama, New Jersey, or Connecticut, actively interpreted the lessons imparted to them. Some saw an opportunity to profit economically and politically, while others sought the rhetorical skills to rearticulate the significance of traditional beliefs and customs. Most, at least in the early nineteenth century, chose to mix together what they perceived to be the best qualities of Euroamerican and Cherokee culture.[55] Their object was not simply survival, economic self-sufficiency, or the articulation of a nationalist identity—although it was all these things at times—it was to interpret the changing world around them and renew their sense of Cherokee identity in ways that would help all Cherokee people meet the challenges posed by American imperialism, religious syncretism, and Cherokee migrations.[56] All people engage in processes of cultural renewal, more often than not unwittingly. For the early-nineteenth-century Cherokees, however, the remaking of a collective sense of identity was both conscious and wrenching.[57]

Just how unsettling this process was can be seen in the "nativist" backlash of the late 1820s. In 1824, Nunna-tsune-ga (White Path), an illiterate chief with reported links to the ancient Cherokee priesthood of the Ani-Kutani, began to raise his voice against the processes of acculturation and Christianization.[58] Nunna-tsune-ga, born in 1761 in what became northeastern Georgia, was devoted to what he understood to be traditional Cherokee cultural beliefs and practices. Nunna-tsune-ga had attracted a considerable Cherokee following for his opposition to the multiracial, mission-educated, and slave-owning elites. Nunna-tsune-ga was not opposed to all forms of Cherokee acculturation and political change, but he did want non-indigenous people to show greater respect for Cherokee cultural beliefs and practices.

Nunna-tsune-ga was particularly concerned about the way mission-educated Cherokees appeared to be eschewing important components of Cherokee belief systems. As Nunna-tsune-ga understood the cultural changes taking place around him, the mission-educated mixed-bloods were contributing to the erasure of fundamental aspects of Cherokee identity. For example, the Cherokee purification customs were seriously challenged by changes in Cherokee marriage laws and practices.[59] With missionary encouragement, a Cherokee woman's control over her reproductive choices and the prohibitions that once existed on marriage within a clan were eroded by a new set of written Cherokee laws.

Nunna-tsune-ga's opposition to such changes had been building for some time. In 1825, he was expelled from the Cherokee National Council for his vigorous opposition to written laws that he believed undermined traditional Cherokee social and cultural practices. Unperturbed, Nunna-tsune-ga continued his opposition. Most famously, he rejected the first written Cherokee constitution in 1827, seeing it as another example of the mixed-race Cherokee elite's aping of the white man's ways. "White Path's rebellion" therefore represented a "conservative" response to the fast rising, and increasingly powerful, mixed-blood and educated elites.[60] Sadly for Nunna-tsune-ga and his supporters, his time (and political influence) had passed. At the level of the National Council, those illiterate chiefs who held "traditional" beliefs were increasingly reduced to the status of politically impotent figureheads. By 1817, the Standing Committee of the National Council—the institution that wielded real power over Cherokee politics—was dominated almost exclusively by mission-educated mixed-bloods. And after 1819, the president of the National Council and principal chief (from 1828) of the Cherokee Nation, John Ross, saw himself as the leader who spoke for all Cherokee people. Although Ross insisted that his power to speak for the Cherokee people was rooted in the coming together of all Cherokees in National Council, Nunna-tsune-ga and his supporters viewed the rise of Ross and other singularly powerful multiracial Cherokee elites as further evidence of the erosion of traditional communal politics.[61]

Many Cherokees shared Nunna-tsune-ga's anxiety about traditional Cherokee beliefs and practices being swept away by Euroamerican culture and political forms. Cherokees expressed this anxiety in a number of ways. The Booger Dance was one of the more robust and comical ways in which Cherokees made known their feelings about whites. The Booger Dance was performed during the Winter Ceremony. Male dancers disguised with masks and gourds performed absurd sexual pantomimes and were given names by audience members such as Black Buttocks, Big Testicles, and Sooty Anus.[62] The Booger Dancers thus portrayed both black and white outsiders as lewd, ridiculous, and menacing. Such performances made the Cherokee peoples' feelings about the changes occurring around them abundantly clear.

A Syllabary for a Diasporic People

Despite such performative displays of defiance, by the 1820s the world that traditionalists like Nunna-tsune-ga and the Booger Dancers once knew not only seemed tainted by outside influences, but seemed to be on the verge of disappearing forever. Over the next century, "traditionalist" cultural revivals continued to punctuate social and cultural life throughout the Cherokee diaspora. In his own time, however, Nunna-tsune-ga was not alone in lifting his voice in opposition to American imperialism and what he saw as the Cherokee elite's sycophantic embrace of acculturation. One Cherokee, Sequoyah, was particularly determined not only to resist American imperialism but to show to the world the genius of his people.

John Howard Payne, an actor turned author turned amateur ethnologist, collected one of the most detailed narratives of Sequoyah's life.[63] In the 1830s, Principal Chief John Ross granted Payne permission to compile a history of the Cherokee people's culture and customs. At the time, this work earned Payne the suspicion of both federal and Georgia authorities. Officials feared that Payne's ethnological endeavors were a cover for his agitation against the federal government's efforts to remove Cherokee people from the region that comprised their southeastern homeland. With this cloud of suspicion hanging over him, Payne nevertheless persisted. On one October evening in 1835, he sat in a room "full of Indians" and listened to an account of the life of George Gist (or Guess), better known as Sequoyah.[64]

Payne was in Cherokee Country that October to attend a session of the Cherokee National Council. During the proceedings, Payne witnessed the communalism that endured—and that Cherokee "traditionalists" like Nunna-tsune-ga believed was on the decline—in Cherokee politics. Payne was spellbound as he sat and listened to incredibly detailed stories about George Gist. Payne later synthesized the accounts he heard that night, transforming the various stories of Gist's life into a coherent narrative of a Cherokee hero. Payne's narrative began with a chronicle of Sequoyah's early life. It quickly progressed to tall tales of a Cherokee hero, a hero who gave to the Cherokee people the greatest gift of all: the Cherokee syllabary.[65]

The Cherokee syllabary was an example of cultural syncretism. It was also a Cherokee response to the creeping cultural hegemony of Euroamerican settler society.[66] Where English literacy provided the increasingly powerful, but numerically small, multiracial Cherokee elite with the ability to communicate and transact business with Cherokees and non-Cherokees living far from their own townships or farmsteads, the syllabary reportedly gave ordinary Cherokee people a feeling of cultural empowerment and connectedness. The Cherokee National Council recognized just how important Sequoyah's "transcendent invention" was when it agreed to strike a medal in his honor in 1824. In 1832, when Sequoyah finally received his medal, Chief Charles H. Vann celebrated Sequoyah's genius, praising Sequoyah for giving the Cherokee people the ability to communicate over vast distances, transact business, record legal proceedings, and preserve Cherokee history in writing. In Vann's words, the "old and young find no difficulty in learning to read and write in their native language and to correspond with their distant friends with the same facility that the whites do."[67]

Who was this Cherokee genius? In travel narratives, government documents, and personal correspondence, his name was recorded variously as Sequoyah, George Guess, and George Gist. Over the course of the nineteenth century, he became a Cherokee folk hero known to thousands as Sequoyah. Born in the early 1770s, Sequoyah was the son of a white man and a Cherokee woman. Sequoyah was raised by his mother, his father having abandoned mother and child shortly after Sequoyah's birth. Sequoyah grew up among the Overhill Cherokees in what became the state of Tennessee, where his mother taught him to milk cows, herd livestock, harvest the family's seven to eight acres of cornfields, and skillfully ride a horse. Sequoyah's birth and upbringing thus took place in two worlds in transition. The world of the Euroamerican settlers was expanding and growing increasingly powerful, and the settlers were becoming impatient with the natives, seeing them as impediments to American civilization's westward expansion. Life in the Cherokee world was also changing, altered by trade, colonial politics, disease, and warfare. The Cherokee people struggled to keep their sacred fires burning and to maintain some semblance of balance and harmony in a world that appeared to be on the verge of splintering into unrecognizable fragments.[68]

That Sequoyah's life came to represent something more than another episode in colonial exploitation was a testimony to the adaptive skills of Sequoyah's mother and the strong sense of Cherokee identity she imparted to her son. Rather than being swept away by Euroameri-

Figure 9: Sequoyah, "Inventor of the Cherokee Alphabet," n.d. Library of Congress Prints and Photographs Division, Washington, DC.

can settler colonialism, Sequoyah and his mother became active participants in the changing world around them. They sold, sometimes on credit, "a variety of small articles of goods" to hunters and itinerant traders passing their home.[69] As Sequoyah grew into a young man, his entrepreneurial instincts led him to diversify his economic activities. He capitalized on the Cherokee fashion for ornamenting the body with silver "ear-rings, nose bobs, armlets, bracelets, gorgets & fine chains" by manufacturing and selling these items. The ornaments that Sequoyah made and sold were not your run-of-the-mill consumer items. Using his considerable artistic talents, Sequoyah learned to engrave his name, in English, on these items. In so doing, Sequoyah cemented for himself a position of increasing visibility in Cherokee social and economic life.[70]

Sequoyah then channeled his various skills into the invention of a Cherokee system of writing. According to an elderly Cherokee man named The Bark, Sequoyah became incensed by the wonder with which many Cherokee people held the "white man's" ability to communicate without talking. Seeing "nothing in it [the white man's literacy] so very wonderful & difficult," "one day he [Sequoyah] went so far as to declare that he was of opinion that he could find out a way by which the Cherokee could detain and communicate their ideas just as well as the white people could." The Bark explained that Sequoyah drew inspiration from the biblical stories of Moses, stories he had learned from Christian missionaries. Determined to become the literary Moses of his people, leading them to a promised land in which Cherokee people had the power to communicate their ideas, beliefs, and experiences in writing, Sequoyah set to work placing Cherokee "marks in the stone."[71]

Just as the biblical Moses was a heroic figure to Judeo-Christian people throughout the world, so Sequoyah through his invention became a hero to Cherokee people everywhere. The choice of heroes tells us much about a culture. For the Cherokee, increasingly under assault from the American republic's expansionism, Sequoyah represented Cherokee defiance, adaptability, and ingenuity. While the average Cherokee marveled at the ability of the white man to communicate without speaking, Sequoyah resisted such awe. "The white man is no magician," Sequoyah allegedly exclaimed to a small group of his friends. He continued, "It is said that in ancient times when writing first began, a man named Moses made marks upon a stone." Sequoyah scratched some marks on a stone to prove to his Cherokee friends that he too had the power to communicate without speaking. Thus began the Cherokee hero's quest to create a form of writing that could unite all Cherokees.[72]

Like all historical heroes, Sequoyah ignored the doubters. He toiled selflessly to create a Cherokee system of writing, and through his "long and silent study," he devised what became the Cherokee syllabary.[73] Once his "alphabet" was complete, Sequoyah gradually introduced his invention to Cherokee legal practitioners, leading politicians, children, and adults. The turbaned Cherokee genius slowly won approval for his system of written communication from all sections of Cherokee society. And so his legend began to grow. Sequoyah, the man who gave the Cherokee people their own written language, was now said to have descended from a family of high rank on his mother's side.

The legend of Sequoyah thus emphasized the maternal inheritance of the hero's genius. Additionally, and in keeping with traditional Cherokee conceptions of gender roles and inheritance, the campfire storytellers who helped to embed the legend of Sequoyah in Cherokee culture also recognized the traditional concept of leadership imparted to the hero by two of his famous uncles, Tallantusky and Corn Tassel (who was also known as Rayetaeh, Kaellahnor, Udsidasata, Onitossitah, Old Tassel, Old Corn Tassel, and Kahn-yah-tah-hee). Tallantusky was the warrior chief who counseled warfare against the encroaching settler frontier at the turn of the century, and who eventually joined with other Lower Town chiefs to lead the Cherokee in establishing new settlements west of the Mississippi River. Corn Tassel was the brother of Sequoyah's mother and the principal chief of Old Echota, a town famed among the Cherokees as a place of refuge. Both were reputed to be influential figures in Sequoyah's formative years.[74]

This genealogical detail suggested that Sequoyah was exposed to two distinctly different examples of how one might lead a Cherokee life. One possibility would be to migrate and resettle on land west of the Mississippi, while retaining a clear sense of self and community as Cherokee. An alternative might be to relocate to a Cherokee farmstead in the South, as scores of Valley and Overhill Cherokees did prior to the Trail of Tears, and assert a strong Cherokee identity based on a sense of connection to the territory of one's ancestors. In his own lifetime, Sequoyah absorbed these various influences and approaches to the re-articulation of Cherokee identity. He was no stranger to travel, but at the same time he recognized the political and economic value of a strong sense of territoriality. Sequoyah ultimately mediated these two approaches to Cherokee identity by channeling his energies into the creation of the Cherokee syllabary.

Unlike the multiracial mission-educated elites of the Valley Townships, Sequoyah ultimately took refuge from the rising tide of white settlers in Cherokee Country by joining the Old Settlers and relocating to

Arkansas Territory. Far from being in a desperate state of impoverish-
ment or living solely "traditional" lives, as their Cherokee cousins in the
east often claimed, the Arkansas Cherokees were a highly articulate and
culturally self-confident wave of diasporic emigrants. In 1817 Sequoyah
signed a removal treaty and joined a party of 331 Cherokees who "voluntarily" set out for Arkansas. Sequoyah took his syllabary with him.
Whether in Georgia, or North Carolina, or Arkansas, or even Mexico
among the fragments of Texas Cherokees who chose to migrate south
and settle among the Kickapoo Indians following the rise of the Republic of Texas, Sequoyah's "gift to his people" provided Cherokees with the
ability to communicate with other Cherokees, and over vast distances,
without talking.[75]

Race, Sex, and Diaspora

Language had always been important to the Cherokee people. Sequoyah
understood this. As John Howard Payne's narrative of the Cherokee
hero's life suggests, Sequoyah was determined that the Cherokee language should transcend time and place, existing as a permanent reminder
of Cherokee life and ideas. In essence, the Cherokee language became
both a verbal and written marker of Cherokee identity, fixing a porous
set of cultural ideals to the meaning of Cherokeeness. For Cherokees,
especially those who became migrants and settlers on the western side
of the Mississippi prior to forced removals in the late 1830s, the prospect
of a bilingual culture coincided with a period of unprecedented movement and sociocultural uncertainty. Sequoyah was acutely aware of the
colonial pressures that were creating this dispersal. Nonetheless, right
up until his death while visiting Cherokee relatives in Mexico in 1843,
he remained committed to the idea that his syllabary could—indeed,
would—ensure that a uniquely Cherokee identity burned brightly, irrespective of where Cherokee people lived.[76]

Sequoyah's life and his transformation into a figure of mythologi-
cal proportions underscore the importance of invention, interpretation,
and synergism in early nineteenth-century articulations of Cherokee
identity. While literate Cherokees borrowed from Euroamerican society,
culture, and politics, they did so not to become imitations of the white

man, but to assert their own particular understanding of Cherokee history and sense of political unity. Elias Boudinot, John Ridge's cousin,
played a significant role in articulating a reimagined sense of Cherokee
identity during the 1820s and early 1830s.

Boudinot was born sometime around 1804 (dates vary from 1802
to 1804) in Cherokee Country (or what whites saw as northwestern
Georgia). He grew up in Oothcaloga, a region famed for its "single-
family homesteads," and spent his formative years under the influence
of his Cherokee father, OoWatie, (also known as David Watie).[77] During his youth, Boudinot went by a number of different names, some
documents listing him as Buck OoWatie, Buck Watie, and his birth
name Galagina ("The Buck"). He appears to have taken the name Elias
Boudinot between 1818 and 1820 in honor of the Revolutionary-era sol-
ider, statesman, and philanthropist Elias Boudinot. Galagina's choice of
name reflected how his diasporic travels—from his native Oothcaloga
to New England—shaped his intellectual development.[78] Indeed, at the
American Board's school in Cornwall, Connecticut, Boudinot received
the Western educational polish that his father's formative lessons had set
in motion.

At Cornwall, Boudinot shared lessons with Malay, Maori, Hawaiian, Choctaw, Oneida, and fellow Cherokee students.[79] Missionary
teachers taught the young Boudinot the moral and ethical importance
of Christianity, the value of "civilized" agricultural methods, the efficacy of American-style government and legal procedures, and significantly, the social and spiritual value of Western patriarchal marriage
practices. During the early 1820s, Boudinot's understanding of how
these aspects of "civilized" life might be applied to Cherokee culture
became increasingly sophisticated. He spoke openly about the importance of embracing the Christian God, and he expressed an ardent desire to spread the Christian faith among his people as a crucial step in
their "advancement."[80] Above all, Boudinot contended that the "spread
of knowledge and religion" among the Cherokees was fundamental to
"obstruct[ing] their way to oblivion" and ensuring their future progress
as a "people."[81]

The full range of Boudinot's vision for the Cherokee people found
its expression in his presentation to an audience of sympathetic white

Figure 10: Elias Boudinot, or Buck OoWatie. Public Domain.

Americans at the First Presbyterian Church in Philadelphia on May 26, 1826.[82] Fresh-faced, mission-educated, and politically ambitious, the twenty-two-year-old Boudinot delivered a deeply thoughtful and nuanced speech. It was at once a defense of Cherokee land rights, a blueprint for a diasporic Cherokee identity, and the first sustained critique of American racism by a Cherokee Indian.[83] "An Address to the Whites," as Boudinot's 1826 speech was entitled, came at a moment when debate over Cherokee territorial removal was intensifying, making his address as much a political argument about government-sponsored removal as it was a statement on race and Indigenous identity.[84]

   Boudinot's "Address" was delivered at a time when the Cherokees in the Southeast were under increasing pressure to relocate to the trans-Mississippi West, and during a period when diplomacy between the Western Cherokees and the United States government was intensifying.[85] In his outline for a future Cherokee identity, Boudinot's message was visionary, perhaps too visionary for many of his people. While convinced that the United States should respect Cherokee land rights, Boudinot contended that Cherokee identity was not dependent on a specific place, that the Cherokee people did not need a particular tract of land to retain a clear sense of what it meant to be Cherokee. This was an argument that challenged white Northeastern supporters of Cherokee land rights to think about Cherokee identity and land in less romantic terms. And it also challenged the Cherokee people, especially traditionalists, to feel confident that they would endure as a people irrespective of where they established their towns and farmsteads.

Boudinot's vision, then, was of an evolving Cherokee people. In the context of removal politics in the 1820s, his use of ethnological stage theory—positing the Cherokee people as an example of how human societies improve step-by-step in the scale of "civilization"[86]—certainly had implications for the defense of Cherokee land rights in the Southeast. However, the importance of Boudinot's argument ultimately transcended the context in which it was delivered. One of the more poignant passages from his 1826 address declared, "You here behold an *Indian*. My kindred are *Indians*, and my fathers sleeping in the wilderness grave—they too were *Indians*. But I am not as my fathers were—broader means and nobler influences Have fallen upon me," proved, in time, to be truer than most Cherokee and Euroamerican people realized in 1826.[87]

So what was the content, the meaning, behind Boudinot's typically "civilized" Cherokee? In answering this question, Boudinot was acutely aware of the political and territorial uncertainty faced by the Cherokee people. He recognized that such feelings fanned the flames of speculation about his people's future. Most disturbingly, this speculation fueled theories that the Cherokee were a race doomed to extinction. Boudinot countered such dire predictions by positing a Cherokee version of linear, historical, time. Cherokee history, as Boudinot presented it, combined the threads of an ancient Cherokee past—articulated as "time immemorial"[88]—with a "modern," "civilized," Cherokee way of life. Boudinot's chronology was designed to counter the way Euroamericans racialized time by presenting Cherokees (and other Indigenous Americans) as stuck in a "primitive" stage of development.[89] Just as Euroamerican colonialism had transformed the American landscape, so too were Cherokee people agents of historical change. In other words, Boudinot argued that neither the land nor its Indigenous inhabitants were being erased because of their supposedly static natures; instead, Cherokees were evolving, improving, and reinventing themselves in meaningful ways.

In the 1820s, Boudinot's linear historical framework served his commitment to defend Cherokee land rights. During the 1820s, the Committee and Council of the Cherokee Nation shared Boudinot's determination to defend the Cherokees' homeland in the Southeast. Cherokee leaders consistently resisted talk of emigration beyond the western banks of the Mississippi. Many feared that "if we are compelled to leave our country [in Georgia], we see nothing but ruin before us. The country west of the Arkansas territory is unknown to us."[90] Boudinot's 1826 argument in Philadelphia echoed the Cherokee Committee and Council's commitment to Cherokee land rights in the cis-Mississippi. It did so by outlining the Cherokee people's historical "advancements." To support this argument, Boudinot highlighted how educational, linguistic, political, and economic developments during the first two decades of the nineteenth century showed how Cherokees had given up their superstitions and hunter-gatherer ways in preference for a more civilized life.[91]

Educational and economic accomplishments provided Boudinot with a framework on which to structure Cherokee history. He insisted on the importance of a collective Cherokee history that was grounded in both the ancient traditions of the Cherokee ancestors and the modern linear history being made as a result of the interconnections of Euroamericans and Cherokees in nineteenth-century America.[92] Boudinot was attempting a delicate rhetorical balancing act. In Philadelphia that spring evening in 1826, he tried to achieve this balance by appealing to the historical imagination and evangelical zeal of his white audience. Boudinot posited that the ancient "Cherokees have had no established religion of their own." Missionaries had brought the light of "established religion"—specifically Christianity—to the Cherokees. It was through the intellectual agency of the Cherokee people that Christianity received its deep historical meaning in Cherokee culture. As Boudinot explained, the ancient Cherokees "believe[d] in a Supreme Being, the Creator of all, the God of the white, the red, and the black man."[93] It was this monotheism, Boudinot contended, that gave the Cherokee people a foundation upon which they could identify with, adapt to, and co-opt the ideals of Christianity, and Anglo-American commerce and politics, to meet the needs of their lives.

Where the so-called ancient Cherokees once lived by the chase and relied on oral tradition to give meaning to life, the modern Cherokees had empowered themselves by acquiring learning, literacy, and "modern" legal and economic structures. This before-and-after framework prompted Boudinot to declare that in time the Cherokees' "modern civilization" would be celebrated, and their "savage" history, replete with "the mangled bodies of women and children," consigned to a long-since-concluded chapter. Boudinot's famous words, "You here behold an *Indian*," therefore represented less a war cry than an assertion of Cherokee identity reinvented.[94] As Boudinot would go on to argue in the years following his 1826 "Address," the Cherokee were not simply a "body politic"—a nation of citizens bounded by laws and arbitrarily drawn borders on maps—but were a "people in a body" whose accomplishments were carried from New York to California by agents of the *Cherokee Phoenix* newspaper, Cherokee writers, and a growing epistolary culture.[95]

For all the celebrated advances in Cherokee learning and economy, the change that truly seemed to mark the Cherokees as a "civilized" nation was the adoption of written laws and organized forms of government. Among the Eastern Cherokees, evidence of written laws dates to 1808, while the first known written laws among the Western Cherokee are dated 1820. In the East, the recording of written laws was accompanied by the centralization of Cherokee government, a development that took political power out of the hands of Cherokee women and away from local town councils. In the cis-Mississippi, the Cherokee National Committee was formed in 1817, and in 1827, an official (written) Cherokee Constitution was enacted.[96] The bulk of these early written laws focused on ensuring balance and harmony in Cherokee communities. Issues such as theft of property, land and water rights, intoxication, and restrictions on the freedom of movement for "negroes" dominated the law books of the Cherokees in the East during the first third of the nineteenth century.[97]

Cherokee laws and the formation of a centralized form of governance in the cis- and trans-Mississippi served two interrelated purposes:

they demonstrated to Euroamericans the extent to which Cherokees were a "civilized" people, and they restricted and reshaped political life among the Cherokees. Elias Boudinot recognized these developments in his 1826 "Address" and in his subsequent writings. In 1826, he described Cherokee government as "well suited to the condition of the inhabitants."[98] As the Cherokees "rise in information and refinement," Boudinot hypothesized, "changes in it [government] must follow, until they arrive at that state of advancement, when I trust they will be admitted into the privileges of the American family." This was an extraordinary statement (one that John Ross also proffered in 1834).[99] Statements of this nature have prompted some historians to posit that Boudinot was a "tragic figure" torn between two worldviews—the "savage" and the "civilized."[100] Boudinot certainly expressed Eurocentric views, but to present him as a "tragic figure" torn between two opposing cultural poles oversimplifies how cultures unfold, develop, and are taken by individuals and adapted to meet the perceived needs of their present reality. In an era when Cherokee leaders regularly referred to the president of the United States as the "Great Father," and were at pains to emphasize just how "civilized" they had themselves become, Boudinot's words should be understood as political pragmatism, an assertion of Cherokee social and cultural evolution, and a vision for the Cherokee future, all at the same time.[101]

Significantly, Boudinot's political pragmatism and evolutionary theorizing coalesced into his insistence on racial equality between whites and Cherokees—an insistence that did not, at least publicly, extend to people of African ancestry. According to the 1835 Census, there existed 201 interracial marriages between whites and Cherokees living east of the Mississippi.[102] These intermarriages were the most intimate indication of how the worlds of the Euroamerican colonists and the Cherokees were overlapping and becoming increasingly intertwined. In his 1826 "Address," and in his subsequent writings, the idea of marriage between Cherokees and whites provided Boudinot with an opportunity to underscore how the Cherokees were far from a race on the verge of extinction; they were the equals of any white Americans. As Boudinot's cousin, John Ridge, famously quipped, Cherokee and white blood will inevitably intermingle and "win[d] its course in beings of fair complexions, who will read that their ancient ancestors became civilized under the frowns of misfortune."[103]

In Boudinot's mind, no "civilized" belief or behavior demonstrated the degree to which the Cherokee were embracing "civilization" more than the practice of monogamous interracial marriage between Cherokees and whites. In a literal and metaphorical sense, Boudinot posited interracial marriage between Cherokees and whites, and the reproduction of multiracial and multicultural children that ensued, as a means of ensuring the future of the Cherokee race. In the early nineteenth-century, Cherokee marriage laws were altered to reflect the growing power of the mixed-race elite. These multiracial leaders believed that patriarchal marriages were crucial indicators of a modern form of Cherokee identity.[104] As historian Fay Yarbrough argues, "Cherokee lawmakers . . . [conflated] race and status, shifting towards an understanding of race as signifying condition and vice versa."[105]

Boudinot's public statements on marriage (and his personal choices) moved increasingly in this racially conscious direction. With a growing number of Cherokees incorporating racial slavery as an important part of Cherokee social and economic life, and with Cherokee lawmakers busy seeking out more efficient legal mechanisms with which to prevent African Americans from marrying Cherokees or acquiring the rights and protections of Cherokee citizenship, Boudinot announced in his 1826 "Address" that "Polygamy is abolished" among the Cherokee. What's more, he claimed that "Female chastity and honor are protected by the law."[106] What Euroamericans once saw as markers of Cherokee racial inferiority were now, in Boudinot's version of Cherokee history, remnants of a dark chapter.[107] And just as white children were ideally raised in nuclear, God-fearing, patriarchal families, so too were future generations of "civilized" Cherokee children to be reproduced and "bred" in similarly nurturing environments.

In this area of his own life, Boudinot strove to practice what he preached. He asserted his civilized Cherokee identity in a very public way when he married a white woman, Harriet Gold. Gold, a missionary teacher, met Boudinot in Connecticut, the "land of intermarriages."[108] News of the Boudinot-Gold marriage, however, did not sit well with the bride's relatives. Family members labeled the relationship a "calamity" that bore all the hallmarks of "criminality." Gold's brother-in-law, Daniel Brinsmade, dismissed the relationship as a product of "animal feeling" and predicted that the union would produce "black young one's and a train of evils."[109]

Implicit in these remarks was the assumption that Harriet Gold had crossed a racial boundary that should not have been breached. Cornwall's white residents certainly made their feelings clear on this issue. Gold's friends and relatives burned her in effigy after hearing news of the impending nuptials. Gold's brother, Herman Vaill, also expressed his disgust in a letter to his sister. "Dear sister Harriet R. Gold," Vaill began, "whose Gold shall shortly become dim."[110] Boudinot also encountered public condemnation. Prior to the couple's wedding, Boudinot received vile threats of violence. In one letter, the anonymous correspondent made his or her intentions perfectly clear by including a drawing of a gallows.[111]

In the face of family condemnation and threats of violence, Gold and Boudinot endured and started a family of their own. Boudinot viewed his little family as the embodiment of a modern and civilized Cherokee household. Monogamously married, devoutly Christian, Boudinot wrote lovingly about his family. He described the "Indian black eyes" of daughter Mary, and added a touch of sardonic humor when he referred to his wife as "my squaw."[112]

Elias Boudinot possessed a keen wit and penetrating intellect. In his 1826 "Address," in his editorials for the *Cherokee Phoenix*, and in his private correspondence, Boudinot's focus was on imagining a better future for the Cherokee people. This work bespoke a cerebral leader, perhaps too cerebral (and visionary) for his fellow Cherokees at a time of great stress. But Boudinot was not simply a man who led with his mind and his pen. He attempted to lead by example. In marrying Harriet Gold and starting an interracial family, Boudinot, like his cousin John Ridge, demonstrated that, in a very real sense, the future of the Cherokee people was intertwined with white Americans. When Harriet died in August 1836 after giving birth to the couple's seventh child, Boudinot took time to grieve his loss and eventually remarried. In this area of his own life, Boudinot continued to lead by example. His new wife, Delight Sergeant, was also a white woman with important connections in New England society.[113] While Boudinot used intermarriage to draw Cherokees and whites closer together, other of his actions revealed a concomitant resolve to distance Cherokees from blacks. In both word and deed, then, Boudinot provides us with a window into the growing antipathy that Cherokees had for African American people, and how he envisioned the future of a diasporic Cherokee people intertwined with white Americans.

Boudinot's marriages may well have been companionate matches based on romantic love. Indeed, historian Ann McGrath observes that the romanticism of early nineteenth-century literature influenced the tenor of Boudinot's correspondence with both Gold and Sergeant.[114] But love is not, nor has it ever been, a transhistorical emotion; like anger, envy, greed, and myriad other human emotions, feelings of love are influenced by, and mediated through, the social and cultural context in which they are "felt." Perhaps, then, Boudinot remained hopeful that his interracial marriages would set an example to other Cherokees and help to augment the Cherokee population in the Southeast. Or perhaps Boudinot saw his marriages in political terms, as alliances with the white world that might serve to protect Cherokee land rights. Historians are uncomfortable with speculation, but in this case we have only speculation to go on. More to the point, all of the above scenarios are possible explanations for Boudinot's decision making and actions.

What is certain is that following the Indian Removal Act (1830), Boudinot ceased his fight for Cherokee land rights in the Southeast and instead redirected all of his energies into preserving the Cherokee as a people, irrespective of their geographical "home." When he placed his signature on the Treaty of New Echota (1835), an agreement that the federal government cited as evidence that Cherokee leaders were agreeing to relocate west, he knew he had signed his death warrant. Signing away Cherokee communal lands to whites without the consent of all Cherokees breached both Cherokee written law and "blood law."

Like Boudinot, his fellow Treaty Party members Major Ridge and John Ridge were fully aware that their signing of the Treaty of New

Echota ran afoul of "blood law." Still, they persisted in the uncertain course they had now embarked on, and attempted to rebuild their lives and their fortunes in diaspora. For Boudinot, the prospect of a life exiled from the ancient soil of the Cherokee's Southeastern homeland focused his attention on the meaning of Cherokee identity. We saw this focus in his 1826 "Address," and it was a concern that remained in subsequent editorials for the *Cherokee Phoenix*, where he explored the same types of questions that Principal Chief John Ross dared contemplate only in private prior to forced removal in the late 1830s. Had John Ross and Elias Boudinot sat down together at some point in the 1830s to discuss their differences and formulate an answer to the question of "Who are we?" they might have emphasized the success of Cherokees in absorbing Christianity on terms agreeable to their "ancient" traditions; the educational accomplishments of Cherokee people; and the Cherokees' ingenuity, both in terms of Sequoyah's "invention" and in the entrepreneurial initiative displayed by their people in forging a diversified economy. They also would no doubt have taken pride in the "modern" legal and political institutions that Cherokees had created.

Still, nagging questions would have remained. Was it really possible to unite the two branches—Eastern and Western—of the "Cherokee family" that were emerging during the early nineteenth century?[115] And would the Cherokee people be able to declare with any certainty that they and their kin had a "homeland"? These were difficult questions to answer in the early 1830s. They became even more vexing during the forced removals of the late 1830s and in the decades that followed.[116]

T·H·R·E·E

Removal, Reunion, and Diaspora

N
o event changed the course of nineteenth-century Cherokee history more profoundly than the forced migration in
the 1830s. Beginning in 1838, the United States government
and army compelled thousands of Cherokees to leave
their homes, townships, and farmsteads.[1] In preparation for the journey into the West, Cherokee people were forced to huddle around military establishments such as Fort Butler in North Carolina. Located on
a prominent hill overlooking the Hiwassee River, the newly completed
Fort Butler was one of six forts in North Carolina. These forts became
important gathering places for Cherokees as they prepared themselves
for the journey into the trans-Mississippi West, a journey few of them
wanted to make.[2]

Much has been written about the forced migration of the Cherokees from their Southeastern homeland during 1838 and 1839. This ig-
noble chapter in American history is well known to American school
children and the reading public. It is a history characterized by the greed
of white Southerners, the racism of a president and his administration,
and the political divisions that crystallized among the Cherokees during
the debates over relocation in the early nineteenth century. Historians
typically place this history, and the history of Cherokee politics, in the
framework of a nation-state and the Cherokees' nascent "nationalism."[3]

Most historians agree that by the early 1830s political loyalties in the Cherokee Nation had become bifurcated. On one hand, historians characterize the Ross Party, led by Principal Chief John Ross, as patient and determined diplomats who steadfastly defended the Cherokee people's land rights. In contrast, the Treaty Party, led by John Ridge, Stand Watie, and Elias Boudinot, plays the role of the villain in the historical narrative of removal. History has remembered the Treaty Party as being willing, for a price, to sign over to the United States the land that the vast majority of early nineteenth-century Cherokees believed was the ancient soil of their forebears.[4]

This chapter expands on the above narrative of Cherokee removal by placing the politics of removal in the larger context of Cherokee diasporic politics between the 1817 treaty—in which the Cherokees ceded 651, 520 acres of land in Georgia and Tennessee to the United States—and the opening of the 1840s, when the vast majority of Cherokees resided in the trans-Mississippi West.[5] In both the cis-Mississippi and the trans-Mississippi West, innovative groups of Cherokee migrants reestablished political affiliations, and also gave new meaning to family and kinship relations. Whether Cherokees chose or were forced to live in diaspora during this period, the maintenance of Cherokee identity rested on efforts to sustain kinship relations, remember traditional cultural practices, and give renewed meaning to Cherokee oral traditions. Increasingly, how Cherokees imagined their identity also rested on their ability to recognize written representations of that identity. In this sense, Sequoyah's syllabary was rightly hailed as a "gift to the Cherokees." However, it was not Sequoyah's syllabary that emerged as the lingua franca of the Cherokee diaspora; instead, English became the dominant form of written communication in the Cherokee diaspora during the early nineteenth century. English literacy skills were the medium through which Cherokee leaders developed laws. These laws resembled those of the American republic, but were designed with the protection of Cherokees in mind. Perhaps most importantly, the English language gave growing numbers of Cherokees the ability to "think" and communicate in English, thereby providing a new outlet for imagining and expressing Cherokee philosophies.

As the following discussion details, prior to the forced removals that became known as the "Trail of Tears," a growing number of Cherokee people made the decision—strategic or otherwise—to settle in Arkansas Territory, Indian Territory, or the Cherokee Neutral Lands in Kansas. And a small number of Texas Cherokees tried to play off Mexican and Anglo colonists in the hope of carving out a colony for themselves in East Texas. Some of these Texas Cherokees remained in East Texas after the Texas Republic was proclaimed, while others migrated south, settled in Nacimiento, Mexico, and intermarried with the Kickapoo Indians.[6] The movement and migration of Cherokees thus created new challenges for Cherokee leaders, searching desperately for ways to prescribe Cherokee identity in an increasingly diasporic context. Forced removal at the end of the 1830s presented the greatest challenge of all. Significantly, the psychological and physical pain associated with removal, and the anxieties that accompanied Cherokee efforts to rekindle their sacred fires in diaspora, did not go undocumented. In written and oral form, Cherokee people began amassing a new archive of knowledge that helped them define what it meant to be a diasporic Cherokee.

The Politics of Diaspora

The vanguard of the Cherokee diaspora—the Western Cherokees, and the followers of Duwali in Texas—added new geopolitical dimensions to Cherokee politics during the first three decades of the nineteenth century. While the Western Cherokees worked hard to reestablish kinship communities and socioeconomic structures, they also earned a reputation for being, as historian Rennard Strickland observes, "notoriously independent."[7] Their independence reflected the fact that the Western Cherokees were, collectively, an educated, articulate, politically and economically savvy, and well-traveled group of people whose origins traced back primarily to the Upper Towns. The leading men of the Western Cherokees made regular visits to major American cities, including New Orleans, Philadelphia, and Washington, DC, to engage in trade, be entertained in America's finest theaters, or to lobby for the people they represented. While some of the Western Cherokees clung to many aspects of "traditional" culture—namely hunting and warrior pursuits—they never considered themselves completely exiled from white American culture, nor did they perceive themselves to be isolated from their "brothers" among the Eastern Cherokee.[8]

The Western Cherokees' written laws reflected both their independence and the anxieties associated with the establishment of new Cherokee settlements. The Western Cherokees enacted their first laws in 1820, combining a commitment to the Cherokee ideals of balance and harmony with Western forms of constitutionalism and law making. Under Chief John Jolly, the Western Cherokees established a system of government in which three chiefs shared equal executive powers, although the power of these chiefs was limited by the Western Cherokees' committee and council. Initially, the government of the Western Cherokees focused primarily on passing laws designed to promote peace and harmony. Particular attention was paid to the establishment of a "Light-Horse company," its stated "duty" being "to preserve peace and good order among the Cherokees on Arkansas."[9]

As with other settler communities—be they Native American or Euroamerican—violence and larceny plagued Western Cherokee communities, especially those whose members had migrated with their slaves and sought to reestablish their life as influential planters. Warfare with the local Osage Indians or harassment from poor whites seeking opportunity in the West did not sit well with the Western Cherokee's leading men. As a consequence, the Western Cherokees in Arkansas tried to maintain lines of communication with their Cherokee "brothers" in the East to ensure the resolution of political and social problems as they arose.

As the principal chief of the Cherokee Nation East, John Ross was the recipient of many letters from the Arkansas Cherokee leaders. Ross lent a sympathetic ear to the plight of the emigrant Cherokees in the West. Cherokees everywhere, Ross acknowledged, struggled to protect and preserve their communities in the face of challenges from corrupt American politicians, treaties and laws that the white man failed to uphold, and the constant threat to hearth and home posed by aggressive white settlers, especially poor whites—whom Ross and other Cherokee leaders likened to "a disease."Ross also saw a threat from unscrupulous Cherokee leaders, such as Treaty Party members.[10]

Prior to the forced migrations of 1838–1839, however, one of the key issues in the letters exchanged between Ross and his Western "brothers" was the apportionment of the Cherokee annuity to the Arkansas Cherokees. According to the Treaty of 1819, the emigrant Cherokees were entitled to one-third of the federal government's annuity payments to the Cherokees. This stipulation became a growing source of tension between Eastern and Western Cherokee leaders over the course of the 1820s. The Western chiefs, who made regular trips back to the Cherokee Nation East to express their political views, saw the annuity as vital to the peace, prosperity, and security of Cherokees in the West. Increasingly, though, a growing number of their eastern brethren objected to this distribution of resources, some insisting that the Western Cherokees chose to separate themselves from the nation and were therefore entitled to nothing from the Cherokee Nation in the East.[11]

Disagreements over the allocation of the Cherokee annuity evolved into vigorous political disputes among the chiefs of the "Cherokee family," which later spilled over into the politics of reunification in Indian Territory during the late 1830s and early 1840s. But in the decade and a half before removal, these geopolitical disagreements also highlighted the significant and growing power of the Cherokee government under John Ross. The centralizing of Cherokee governance began in the late eighteenth century and quickened during the early nineteenth century. In the years following the publication of the first written Cherokee laws in 1808, the educated multiracial elites assumed and solidified their political power. They began the work of delineating the powers of the executive, legislative, and judicial branches of Cherokee government. Their model was the United States, and their efforts culminated in a written constitution in 1827. Despite protests from Cherokee traditionalists such as Nunna-Tsune-ga, the 1827 constitution represented the systematic efforts of Cherokee elites to prescribe the political parameters of Cherokee identity and to show to white Americans that they were a civilized race whose land rights ought to be respected. The opening preamble of the Cherokee constitution reveals the intellectual and

leaders made repeated trips to Washington, DC, in hopes of alleviating some of this diplomatic pressure, but nevertheless most Cherokees remained distrustful of Andrew Jackson. When the Indian Removal Act finally passed in 1830, John Ross attempted to strike a defiant diplomatic pose, echoing the sentiments of the Cherokee people by recommitting the National Council to the defense of the Cherokee Nation. Cherokee distrust for the United States government, and the Jackson administration in particular, ran deep. In expressing the Cherokee peoples' determination not to be removed from their ancient homeland, Ross insisted that the United States government had "duped" the Cherokee people and was now attempting to force them to settle "on land to be assigned them beyond the Mississippi."[22]

Politically and territorially, the nascent Cherokee diaspora was under great stress from the expanding United States. This was the case in the trans-Mississippi as well as in the cis-Mississippi. In the westernmost reaches of the diaspora, the Texas Cherokees also encountered the growing military and political force of the Anglo-Americans. After originally establishing multi-ethnic and multi-tribal communities in Spanish Texas in 1820, the Texas Cherokees dreamed of forging communities characterized by traditional concepts of balance and harmony in the Southwest. Now they saw their dream thwarted by the aggressiveness of the settlers and traders who comprised the expanding Anglo-American frontier. Under the leadership of war chief Duwali and the peace chief Gatun-wali (Big Mush or Hard Mush), the Texas Cherokees sought a land grant from the newly formed Mexican government (1821), hoping that such a grant would provide them with legal protections against the Anglo-Americans who might migrate to, and settle in, Texas. According to nineteenth-century topographer George Bonnell, "The [Texas] Cherokees and their twelve associate bands are all tribes from the United States. They consist of Cherokees, Shawnees, Delawares, Kickapoos, Quapaus, Choctaws, Boluxies, Iawanies, Alabamas, Cooshattas, Caddoes, Tahookatookies, and Unataquas."[23]

The Cherokee and their "associate bands" in Mexican Texas, under the diplomatic leadership of Richard Fields, began negotiations with the Mexican government in an attempt to acquire legal protections over the lands they occupied in East Texas.[24] What they actually received from the Mexican government was the legal status of "colonist," a status that did not carry the rights of Mexican citizenship.[25] This was a meager concession that displeased the Texas Cherokees, divided their leaders, and left them legally unprotected from Comanche warriors and exposed to legal and military challenges from wave after wave of land-hungry Anglo-Americans. As the leaders of the Texas Cherokees saw things, they had earned the right to this land now coveted by Anglo-Americans because they "were not intruders on the whites, for they were there first."[26]

The Texas Cherokees found themselves caught in the vice-like grip of imperial politics. Indeed, they soon recognized that they would become collateral damage in the imperial battle for possession and control of Texas if they did not engage in savvy diplomacy. By the early 1820s, however, the diplomatic writing was on the wall for the Texas Cherokees. Spanish colonialism in North America was in serious retreat, the Mexican government was indifferent to Cherokee concerns, and the hostile racial views of Anglo-Texans did not bode well for the future of the Cherokees in Texas. This diplomatic and social pressure took its toll on the Texas Cherokees, and political tensions soon became societal fractures. Duwali, for example, was reportedly hired by the Mexicans to assassinate fellow Cherokee negotiators John Dunn Hunter and Chief Fields.[27] This ill-conceived attempt on the part of the Mexicans to co-opt segments of the Cherokee leadership in Texas served only to further destabilize the Texas Cherokees and make their unified resistance to Anglo-Texas colonialism ever more fragile.

Ultimately it was not Mexican deception that most galled the Texas Cherokees, but the apparent duplicity of a man the Cherokee considered one of their own: Sam Houston. Duwali and other Texas Cherokee leaders trusted Houston, who was the adopted Cherokee son of Oolootekea (John Jolly). Duwali therefore felt comfortable negotiating a land deal with Houston that he believed would ensure their future peace and prosperity. Houston, conscious of the anti-Indian views held by Anglo-Texans, became a key player in this land agreement, which the Texas Cherokees initially greeted with howls of protest. In a letter to Duwali, "My friend," dated November 22, 1835, Houston reassured

Figure 11: Sam Houston (image created ca. 1904). Library of Congress Prints and Photographs Division, Washington, DC.

the elderly chief, insisting that "all that I promised to you at our talk in Nacogdoches has been done, and your land is secured to you! So soon as it is possible you will find Commissioners sent to you, to hold a treaty and fix your lines, that no bad men will go inside them without leave." Houston added, "I want you to be happy and I will go to see you soon as I can. Tell all the chiefs and people, that I will hold them by the hand always. Your friend and brother."[28]

This was diplomatic correspondence, sent to the Cherokee on behalf of the Texans. This letter can also be interpreted as an example of Houston's affection for the Cherokees and concern for their wellbeing. Houston was thus instrumental in bringing about an agreement with the Texas Cherokees at San Felipe de Austin on November 13, 1835, which proclaimed the "sincere desire" of all Texans to live in peace with the Cherokees and their associated bands, and to protect their lands.[29]

However, less than a year after the 1835 agreement, Houston wrote to the *Niles' Weekly Register* to report that "our situation is unsafe: some Cherokees with the native Castillians, have returned to the Cherokee village of Matamoras, and say that the Indians of the Prairie and a Mexican force are about to attack this portion of Texas."[30] Was Houston facing up to the political and military realities that he believed Anglo-Texans faced? Perhaps. During 1836 and 1837, Anglo-American and Anglo-Texan opinion turned sharply against the Texas Cherokees. Duwali and his people came to be seen as dangerous enemies, and thus, the Anglo-Texans refused to recognize Houston's 1835 treaty, which was signed by the respective parties in February 1836, when Texas declared its independence in 1837. To Cherokee leaders such as Duwali, the issue was uncomplicated: Houston had betrayed the Cherokees. But Houston's apparent change of heart regarding the Cherokees also reflected the tenuousness of his own identity as an adopted Cherokee.[31] If ever there existed a man "caught between two fires" in the early nineteenth century, it was Sam Houston.

Houston appeared truly pained when he witnessed the intensifying conflict between the Anglo-Texans and Cherokees. Many Cherokees arrived in Texas with resentment toward Anglo-Americans, the memory of recent struggles with whites over land rights in the cis-Mississippi fanning the flames of distrust. At the same time, the Cherokees maintained a sense of themselves as a dignified people; they refused to trade, for example, with the white "ruffians" who peddled all manner of items on the western fringes of the Cherokee diaspora. These two factors— the white hunger for land and violent "ruffians" eager to "lick" some Cherokees—made for a military and political powder keg. The result was the removal of the Cherokees from Texas in 1839 and 1840, a removal that coincided with the forced removal of Cherokees from the cis-Mississippi. Feeling utterly betrayed, the Texas Cherokees retreated to the Red River, burning bridges and destroying their farms as they were forced to migrate north into Indian Territory.[32]

In December 1839 Houston penned some thoughts on the removal of the Texas Cherokees in which he commented that they "had cause to hate the white people."[33] Perhaps Houston was feeling remorse for what Duwali saw as his treachery. Whatever his motives for making these comments, he remained as convinced in 1839 as he had been in 1835 that "the Cherokee claim to this land was a valid one."[34]

Historians generally assume that the history of the Texas Cherokees ends with their removal at the end of the 1830s and the rise of the steads, the state of Georgia sought to expedite the process of divesting the Cherokee people of their lands. The state passed a series of laws stripping the Cherokees of their rights to sovereignty, distributing Cherokee lands to settlers by way of a lottery and incorporating Cherokee lands into state counties.[47] Cherokees responded to Georgia's legal maneuvering and the passage of the Indian Removal Act with unvarnished criticism. In an open letter to the *Cherokee Phoenix* in 1830, the Cherokee "Socrates" declared, "When the states tyrannically and compulsively throw their laws into this nation without our consent . . . and consign to ruin all the fruit of our labor for the years past, at whose door does the sin of consequence lie?"[48] The members of the Cherokee National Council believed that the "sin of consequence" lay with the state of Georgia. Thus, Cherokee leaders and their supporters famously challenged Georgia's legal maneuvering in two landmark cases, *Cherokee Nation v. Georgia* in 1831, and *Worcester v. Georgia* in 1832.[49]

The case of *Cherokee Nation v. Georgia* centered on the Cherokees' request that the United States Supreme Court prevent Georgia from imposing its laws in Cherokee territory. However, the Supreme Court insisted that the Cherokee Nation was not a "foreign state" and refused to hear the case. Chief Justice Marshall did declare the Cherokee Nation to be a "distinct political society," but its status was that of "domestic dependent nations."[50] This disappointing ruling did not deter the Cherokees and their supporters. The following year, the case of missionary Samuel Worcester's arrest and expulsion from the Cherokee Nation by Georgia officials appeared before the Supreme Court. Worcester was sentenced to four years imprisonment with hard labor by Georgia officials for residing in the Cherokee Nation without the permission of state authorities. The Supreme Court overturned the state's decision, declaring Georgia's law in this case to be unconstitutional. The Court reiterated its ruling in *Cherokee Nation v. Georgia* regarding the Cherokee Nation's "distinct political" status, implicitly acknowledging the Cherokees' territorial sovereignty, a sovereignty that the state of Georgia had no legal grounds for breaching. The Court also added that the federal government possessed the sole responsibility for administering Indian affairs.[51]

These cases failed to halt growing political pressures for the forced relocation of the Cherokee people.[52] Indeed, President Jackson took solace in the Supreme Court's inability to enforce its ruling in *Worcester*, observing that "the decision of the supreme court has fell still born, and they find they cannot coerce Georgia to yield to its mandate."[53] The Jackson administration thus proved itself unrelenting in pushing for Cherokee removal. This prompted Cherokee leaders to express their anxieties about being forced to migrate to a land "unknown to us." Cherokees insisted that it would be "cruel . . . to send helpless old men, women, and children" west of the Mississippi River where the land was a "barren inhospitable desert."[54] John Ridge was fully aware of such sentiments, and the ideologies that informed calls for Indian removal. Immediately following the passage of the Indian Removal Act, Ridge lamented that "the mountains of prejudice entertained against us by the Anglo Americans" meant that the Cherokee people "are fated to be wretched."[55]

As the most prominent member of the Treaty Party, Ridge slowly grew to believe that emigration west might be the only means of preserving the Cherokee people's future. According to the federal government's census of the Eastern Cherokee in 1835 (known as the Henderson Roll), the Eastern Cherokees numbered 16, 542. Their Western brethren numbered about 5,000, a figure that did not include Texas Cherokees.[56] Despite the growing prosperity, increased rates of literacy, and organized legal and political institutions of the Cherokee Nation, pressure for removal of the Eastern Cherokees proved unending. Ridge and his Treaty Party colleagues recognized American racism for what it was and saw the diplomatic writing on the wall—removal was imminent. Thus, Ridge, Boudinot, and other prominent Treaty Party men began a concerted effort to convince fellow Cherokees that their only future as a people lay in the West. This position inflamed Cherokee traditionalists and "anti-treaty party" Cherokees, who jealously guarded their Southeastern homeland from dispossession.[57] Traditionalists attempted to keep the sacred fire burning during this uncertain time in Cherokee history, operating both as the protectors of ancient traditions and "as a mutual-protection organization against threats to Cherokee treaty and land rights."[58]

On December 29, 1835, at the town of New Echota in Georgia, United States Indian Agents met with a delegation of Cherokees led by John Ridge, Elias Boudinot, Archilla Smith, S. W. Bell, John West, William A. Davis, and Ezekiel West. By signing the Treaty of New Echota, these men agreed to the sale of Cherokee land in the East in return for land in the trans-Mississippi West.[59] As I noted in the previous chapter, this disposal of Cherokee communal lands by a small, unrepresentative minority of Cherokees went against traditional notions of Cherokee law, which prohibited individual Cherokees from selling communally held territory. It also flew in the face of the "modern" Cherokee Constitution, a document that outlawed the sale of communal land to non-Cherokees and mandated the death penalty for those who broke the law. Why, given such strict cultural and legal guidelines, did the members of the Treaty Party agree to the New Echota Treaty? Boudinot and Ridge certainly knew how vile, violent, and bloodthirsty whites could become. They had experienced such hostility in Cornwell, Connecticut. Those experiences, combined with the knowledge that the federal government refused to enforce the *Worcester* decision, may have sown the seeds of distrust for white people and ultimately convinced the Treaty Party members that the only way the Cherokees could rid themselves of the frontier violence and avoid the degradation of forced displacement was to choose exile on terms at least partially of their choosing. As Boudinot explained his decision to sign the Treaty of New Echota, "Instead of contending uselessly against a superior power, the only course left, was, to yield to circumstances over which . . . [the Cherokees] had no control."[60] In the West, Boudinot hoped, the Cherokees might again take control of their lives and their collective destiny.

That fateful decision by Treaty Party members appeared to be vindicated in the ensuing years, as the white proponents of forced migration became more insistent on the removal of the Cherokees from the Southeast. For example, Indian Agent John G. Wool presented the Cherokees with a dire warning in March 1837: "The people of Georgia, of North Carolina, of Tennessee, and of Alabama have decreed it. Your fate is decided; and if you do not voluntarily get ready and go by the time fixed in the treaty you will then be forced from this country by the soldiers of the United States." Failure to accept the federal government's assistance to migrate west would thus plunge the Cherokee into a "deplorable" condition.[61]

Following the signing of the Treaty of New Echota, members of the Treaty Party began preparing to migrate west. Most Cherokee people, still clinging to the hope that John Ross could preserve their land rights, tried to continue living their lives in the cis-Mississippi.[62] The prospect of being relocated to a distant land far from the towns, homes, and farmsteads they had known for generations was too terrible a fate for them to even contemplate. The National Council did confront forced emigration, and the treaty purporting to represent the Cherokee people's legal sanction for removal. Under the leadership of John Ross, the Council labeled the Treaty of New Echota a "fraudulent and invalid instrument." Moreover, Ross and his supporters described the Cherokees who had signed that document as "parties unauthorized to represent and to bind our nation," and claimed that the document itself served only to defraud the Cherokee people of their ancient homeland in the cis-Mississippi.[63]

In the years after the Indian Removal Act became law, Ross had considered a number of ideas that might enable the Cherokees to continue living on the "land of our fathers." During the first half of the 1830s, Ross insisted that removal to the West would "result in disaster" and destroy the Cherokee as a people.[64] It would, Ross argued, "denationalize" the Cherokee, resulting in a loss of political identity and group cohesion.[65] Ross made scores of written pleas to the Jackson administration in which he laid out these concerns. He also outlined the history of treaty-making between the United States government and the Cherokee Nation, hoping this history would underscore the legal right of the Cherokee people to remain in the South.[66] But Cherokee lobbying in Washington, DC, was falling on deaf ears, and Ross knew it. In one desperate attempt to preserve Cherokee land rights in the East, Ross proposed that the Cherokee might become United States citizens if the federal government would agree to protect their rights by treaty to remain on what Cherokees considered their ancient soil.[67]

None of Ross's efforts bore political fruit. However, in the years after 1835 chiefs and headmen from throughout the Cherokee diaspora joined Ross in challenging the legality of the New Echota Treaty. In March 1837, for example, a delegation of Cherokee leaders from different geographical and political factions descended on Washington, DC, to lodge just such a protest. This diasporic delegation, led by John Ross and John Looney (Western Cherokees), referred to the New Echota Treaty as a "spurious compact." Further criticism of the agreement reflected the enduring significance of communalism in Cherokee social and political life. According to the delegates' statement, "not more than three hundred" people, "Indians and negroes," assembled at New Echota in 1835. This passage was by no means insignificant. Claiming that a small and unrepresentative group of Indians and a collection of "negroes"—who by this time were marked by Cherokee law as racial outsiders and considered by most Cherokees to be fit only to labor as slaves on Cherokee plantations—the delegates emphasized that the Treaty Party had no legitimate authority to call a council into session. Indeed, those assembled at New Echota were so small in number (and some of a perceived inferior racial standing in Cherokee society) as to be utterly unrepresentative of the entire Cherokee population. Put simply, the treaty was not a true reflection of the will of the Cherokee people.[68]

The "Great Emigration"

Relocation into the West may not have been the will of the Eastern Cherokee people, but it became their reality in 1838–1839.[69] Like the Texas Cherokees, who began arriving in Indian Territory in 1839 and 1840, Eastern Cherokees under John Ross's leadership joined the Old Settlers, and Treaty Party members in the trans-Mississippi West. For the Old Settlers, the vanguard of the Cherokee diaspora, the convergence of these groups in Indian Territory posed serious challenges to their political autonomy and territorial sovereignty. They had begun migrating to Indian Territory in significant numbers in the 1820s, and in 1828, the Arkansas Cherokees agreed to terms with the United States government to resettle permanently in Indian Territory. The treaty of 1828 promised the Arkansas Cherokees 7, 000, 000 acres of land, in addition to a western "outlet," in Indian Territory.[70] Over the course of the early 1830s, the Arkansas Cherokees continued the process of migrating into these lands. After the signing of the Treaty of New Echota in 1835, they were also joined by approximately 1, 500 Cherokees belonging to the Treaty Party, many of whom were wealthy plantation owners who had traveled west with their slaves. Thus, the 1830s was an important decade in Cherokee history, a time when different migratory threads of the nascent Cherokee diaspora converged in what became a new "home-land" in Indian Territory. Together these reluctant and mostly unwilling migrants debated their differences and worked to reestablish family life, stimulate agricultural production, and set up a system of government that they hoped would promote peace, good order, and keep the sacred fires—now exiled in the trans-Mississippi West—alight. Then, in 1838, the first great wave of Cherokee migrants associated with the forced removal from the cis-Mississippi began arriving. Over the following two years, the federal government engaged in what historian Alfred Cave describes as a gross abuse of presidential power and illegal activity to strip between 12, 000 to 15, 000 Cherokees of their property, thereby forcing them to make the journey to Indian Territory.[71]

Some Cherokees, however, did remain in the cis-Mississippi. They kept the Cherokees' sacred fires burning on the ancient soil of the Great Smoky Mountains. Of the approximately 1, 100 Cherokees who remained in the Southeast, the most famous was Tsali.[72] What Tsali did, or was reputed to have done, during the removal process quickly became the stuff of legend. To many Cherokees, Tsali's story of exile and self-sacrifice served as an example of resistance to federal government power. Drawn from sources that include reports from U.S. army officers, the federal Indian agent to the Cherokees, the anthropological analysis of the Smithsonian Institution's James Mooney, and Cherokee oral histories, Tsali's story became a part of Cherokee (and to a lesser extent, American) collective memory.

So what did Tsali do to earn such a storied place in Cherokee history? In general terms, as related by the above sources, Tsali used violence in retaliation against federal army officers, a number of whom were alleged to be drunk, when they prodded his wife, Wilani, with a bayonet to make her walk faster. According to General Winfield Scott's account of the incident, the attack on Wilani was an "unprovoked outrage."[73] After taking his revenge on the inebriated U.S. army officers, allegedly killing two of them, Tsali fled to a mountain refuge. There he remained, until fellow Cherokees convinced him, at the behest of the American military, to surrender. The legend of Tsali emphasizes how he ultimately sacrificed his own life so that his people could remain free to live as they had always lived in the mountains of western North Carolina.[74] Tsali the hero, the self-sacrificing father and husband, the man who resisted American settler colonial expansion and chose to die in the Cherokee's ancient homeland, ultimately became the inspiration for what the historian Catherine Albanese calls "a new myth of origins."[75]

In the uncertain years between 1838 and 1840, the North Carolina Cherokees tried to endure the crushing poverty that engulfed their villages as thousands of their fellow Cherokees made the unhappy journey into the trans-Mississippi West. In return for not having the United States military pursue them and remove them to Indian Territory, the North Carolina Cherokees relinquished their legal identities as Cherokees. They became citizens of North Carolina, individual members of a state who, under terms of an 1819 treaty, were given a 640-acre reservation at Qualla in western North Carolina.[76] For the time being, the ability to remain on ancestral Cherokee soil seemed like a pyrrhic victory indeed.

For the vast majority of Cherokee people who called the cis-Mississippi home, the events of 1838 and 1839 meant leaving the only homeland they had ever known. Most Cherokees who endured the forced migration to Indian Territory experienced a deep sense of loss, isolation, and disconnection from the sounds, smells, and sights of home. For those Cherokee emigrants who clung to traditional beliefs, and viewed the Cherokee "homeland" as eternally connected to lands on the eastern side of the Mississippi, removal to an unknown western territory traditionally associated with death had profound psychological effects.[77] So profound was the trauma associated with forced migration that the memories of removal became an integral part of a diasporic Cherokee history and identity in the decades after 1838–1839.[78]

The Cherokee people structured removal narratives around several important themes. For example, feelings of powerlessness and fear often went hand-in-hand with physical pain and suffering. John Burnett, a private in the United States Army, witnessed the early stages of the removal process in 1838. His notes highlight the relentless mix of psychological and physical suffering experienced by Cherokees. "I saw helpless Cherokees arrested and dragged from their homes, and driven by bayonet into the stockades. And in the chill of a drizzle rain on an

October morning I saw them loaded like cattle or sheep into six hundred and forty-five wagons and started toward the west."[79]

Cherokees who survived the journey west echoed Burnett's description. A common theme emphasized by survivors was that of trudging grimly through harsh weather conditions and unforgiving terrain. In freezing temperatures, the very young and the very old were remembered as being especially vulnerable, likely to sicken and die.[80] The tragedy of losing loved ones was compounded by the fact that the elderly Cherokees took "the ancient customs" of their people with them to their graves.[81] As one emigrant recalled: "The trail of exiles was a trail of death."[82]

If death—understood in both its literal and metaphorical senses —hung over the "trail of exiles," so too did hunger. Hunger, a sensation with the power to manifest itself both physically and emotionally, followed the Cherokee emigrants all the way to Indian Territory. Rations were limited at best, and what sustenance the army provided quickly diminished, depleting both body and spirit of energy. As one emigrant recalled, the "people got so tired of eating salt meat."[83] Much as the specter of death chipped away at the human spirit, so did hunger reduce Cherokees physically, leaving them clinging to life, bereft of a meaningful existence.[84] Along with the effects of exposure, the ravages of dysentery and dehydration, whooping cough, and unpredictable acts of violence, as one scholar observes, "exacted a terrible toll on the people of the Cherokee Nation" during the forced migration westward.[85]

The imagery of Native American "exiles" being forcibly led down a "trail of death" speaks forcefully to the evolving historical consciousness of the Cherokee diaspora.[86] If the Cherokee diaspora had begun with the emigration of a few thousand Cherokees to Arkansas Territory and Texas during the late eighteenth and early nineteenth centuries, it was now coming into full focus as the creation and by-product of an aggressive and disruptive form of settler colonialism. Unjustly (indeed, illegally) exiled from their cis-Mississippi homeland, forced to travel by land and water routes to Indian Territory, many Cherokees did indeed die on the journey west. Many others experienced a different sort of death, a social death in which the human spirit—the soul—was suddenly displaced from its "home." For most Cherokees, the sense of exile and loss was deeply felt. While the wounds of exile never fully healed, the sense of spiritual and psychic loss would in time be nurtured back to good health.[87]

The arrival of John Ross and the Eastern Cherokees in the trans-Mississippi West remains one of the most significant events in United States history. For the Cherokees, this forced migration was transformative. It changed the geographical, political, and sociocultural tenor of Cherokee life. Added to the Old Settlers, or Western Cherokees, there were 12, 000 to 13, 000 Eastern Cherokees, forced into exile in 1838 and 1839. As the 1840s opened, most Cherokees now lived west of the Mississippi River. The Cherokee diaspora had truly become a diaspora of exiles.

But would the experiences of exile dominate what it meant to be Cherokee into the 1840s and beyond? More immediately, who should have the political power to govern this diaspora of exiles? And where would the Cherokee diaspora's "homeland" be located? Surely what the vast majority of Cherokees perceived as their ancient soil, their Southeastern homeland in the cis-Mississippi, would always remain "home"? These were incredibly difficult questions for the Cherokee people to answer in the two decades before the American Civil War.

If John Ross and the Cherokees who had been forced to migrate to Indian Territory wanted the pre-removal trans-Mississippi Cherokee settlers to "*join* them" in a common political union—as he in fact did—Ross would have to convince the Western Cherokee that he and his supporters were not simply trying to "assume a power over" them. Any attempt to assume power, the leaders of the Western Cherokee maintained, would represent an "unwarrantable and unreasonable" extension of the Ross Party's self-serving objectives for the future.[88] In the 1840s, these political battles constituted more than a struggle for control of the Cherokee Nation in Indian Territory; they were aimed at finding some sort of common ground upon which a collective sense of Cherokee identity might be articulated. They also serve as an entry point for understanding broader social and cultural changes in mid-nineteenth-century Cherokee life. As the Cherokees entered the 1840s, the future seemed uncertain on so many levels.

F • O • U • R

Uncertain Futures

In May 1840, John Love, a Virginia-born soldier stationed at Fort Gibson in the Cherokee Nation, wrote to "My dear father" with the intention of informing him of events in the West. With news of the removal and resettlement of the Cherokees and other Southeastern Indians trickling back east by way of newspaper reports, personal correspondence, and daily gossip, Love's letter to his father painted a picture of the newly resettled Cherokees that went against the grain of dire stories of death, violence, and political instability.[1] Love reported, "There is a great deal of *polished society* in the Cherokee natives as different from all conception I had ever formed of the Indian character as black from white, and the baleful spirit of party intrigue and unfriend[ly] beings I hope will be soon banished from the nation."[2]

Love's assertion that the Cherokee possessed a "polished society" in the West made a lie of broad-brush racial generalizations of Native Americans as a savage and, at best, "uncivilized" race.[3] According to Love, such racial stereotypes did not accurately describe the Cherokee communities taking root in Indian Territory. As Love saw things, Cherokee society in Indian Territory resembled white society back east—orderly, structured, and law-abiding. Despite the traumatic circumstances under which the Cherokees found themselves living in the trans-Mississippi West, a "polished," civil society was quickly emerging in Indian Territory. Men like Love were surprised to see that although this was an Indigenous society, it was a "civilized" society nonetheless.

If any group of Indians was going to succeed in reestablishing their "modern" social and political structures in the West in the 1840s, it was the Cherokees. Or so thought white observers like John Love. Throughout the Anglo-Atlantic World, sympathetic whites listened attentively to stories of the Cherokee people lifting themselves up from the despair that followed them on the journey into the West. In 1839, for example, London attendees at the Society of Friends annual meeting heard how the Cherokees were forced to leave their Southeastern homeland due to the "unrighteous mandate of the Federal Government," but had quickly begun the work of reinstituting their own civil government, agricultural practices, and "the mechanic arts."[4] Cherokee society was led by multiracial political and economic elites, whose prominent members were presumed to possess the same traits that characterized the very best white men. The Cherokees—at least their economic and political elites—did not appear to harbor "a spirit of hostility" toward the white man.[5] They were too busy for that. Indeed, Cherokee leaders were busy drafting new laws, refining political institutions so that they met the demands of the West, operating slave plantations, and establishing public schools and seminaries of higher learning. Some even oversaw evangelical Christian efforts to missionize to fellow Cherokees, promote temperance, and espouse the benefits of patriarchal monogamy as the key to a "happy home."[6] To some whites as well as Cherokees, it seemed that the only thing standing in the way of the Cherokees' enjoying the fruits of "civilized" life was the partisan politics—"the baleful spirit of party intrigue"—that characterized political and social life in Indian Territory in the late 1830s and early 1840s.

The Cherokee peoples in the trans-Mississippi West therefore worked hard to overcome the trauma of being separated from what they saw as their ancient homeland in the Southeast of the American republic by forging a political homeland in Indian Territory. While the creation of this political homeland did not mitigate the trauma associated with the "great emigration," it did provide an increasingly diasporic people with a political focal point on which to fix their allegiance. This new political homeland played a major role in structuring Cherokee movement and keeping kinship ties alive, while also becoming an important symbol, reminding Cherokees living throughout North America and the Pacific that there was a geographical refuge from the settler colonial world, occupied and governed by fellow Cherokees. The North Carolina Cherokees, following the forced emigration of 1838–1839 and a subsequent failed attempt by the federal government to force the remainder of the North Carolina Cherokees into Indian Territory between 1841 and 1844, looked with pride to the political homeland that their kin were helping to forge in Indian Territory, while at the same time being mindful of the important spiritual connection they were charged with keeping alive in the ancient homeland.[7]

Forging a New "Homeland"

As the 1830s gave way to the 1840s, the future of the Cherokee people remained uncertain. A number of interrelated factors fueled this uncertainty. Most significant were the trauma associated with forced emigration; the resentment felt by the Old Settlers, or Western Cherokees, toward the "multitudes" of new Cherokee emigrants; and deep-seated factionalism that threatened to explode into a Cherokee civil war.[8] As one delegation of Cherokee chiefs observed, "On the arrival of the Eastern Cherokees at their newly assigned settlements various difficulties presented themselves to a complete and cordial amalgamation of the different portions of the Nation."[9]

Much has been written about these tensions, but rarely have scholars tried to understand them from the perspective of the intersecting settler colonial, migratory, and diasporic contexts in which they occurred.[10] Indeed, the seething tension between the Treaty Party and Ross Party that began in the Southeast during the internal debate over removal manifested itself in violence and tense political maneuverings in the late 1830s and early 1840s. In June 1839, for example, John Ridge and Stand Watie, leading Treaty Party members, joined the Old Settlers in opposition to John Ross and his supporters. Amid a cacophony of calls for peace and harmony, unity, and good order, the Old Settlers expressed bemusement, believing that union already existed among Cherokees in the West. The chiefs among the Old Settlers insisted that

Cherokee communities on the western frontier of diaspora had for decades cultivated a sense of political connection through allusions to "brotherhood," "union," and the articulation of laws. If discord existed among the Cherokees, it was because of the disorder and violence that the new emigrants had introduced to Indian Territory and the political agitation of Eastern Cherokees under John Ross's leadership.[11]

Political disagreements among Cherokees were not the only causes of social disorder and bloodshed in the trans-Mississippi West. The forced migration of a number of non-Cherokee tribal nations and confederacies from East to West tested the limits of traditional adoption practices. For instance, several bands of Seminoles squatted on land in the Cherokee Nation in the early 1840s.[12] Additionally, reports that Choctaw men looked to Cherokee women as potential marriage partners quickly circulated among Cherokee communities. According to the British social activist and Quaker William Tallack, Choctaw men reportedly saw Cherokee women as ideal mates. Tallack alleged that the "young Choctaws eagerly seek matrimonial alliances with the Cherokee ladies, many of whom are well dowered both with wealth and education, and have adopted crinolines and pianos."[13]

Ross and his allies were determined to assert political control and restore peace to Cherokee society in Indian Territory. While Ross shared the general conviction that political union among Cherokees was necessary to securing the future welfare of the Cherokee people, he emphasized that the Old Settlers had no formal written constitution, and he dismissed the idea that unity already existed among Old Settlers and those recently arrived from the cis-Mississippi.[14] Ross, who increasingly blamed the Treaty Party and the Old Settlers for political discord, insisted that the Cherokees were a "house divided," and a house divided "cannot stand."[15]

The year 1839 proved to be particularly eventful for the Cherokee people. In that year, Treaty Party leaders met the fate many had foreseen for themselves when they signed the Treaty of New Echota in 1835. Most famously, Major Ridge, his son John Ridge, and Elias Boudinot all lost their lives in a bloody spree of violence that some contemporaries insisted was Cherokee "blood law" in action.[16] Blood law was traditionally practiced in Cherokee society to ensure balance and harmony, and typically involved the clan members of a homicide victim exacting vengeance (usually death) on the murderer, or on a member of the murderer's clan. This system of justice, which Cherokees believed to be sacred, restored balance to the world and prevented large-scale feuds.[17]

Contrary to the ancient traditions of clan justice, the blood law deaths of prominent Treaty Party members in 1839 did not bring about balance and harmony among the Cherokee factions. Instead, the violent manner in which these prominent Cherokee leaders met their deaths cast a cloud of suspicion and mistrust over that summer's council meetings. Boudinot's brother, Stand Watie, a prominent Treaty Party figure who managed to evade would-be assassins, was convinced that the assassins were Ross Party men. Watie therefore vowed not to rest until he had extracted his revenge. John Rollin Ridge, John Ridge's son, harbored similar feelings. Ridge dreamed of the day when he could avenge his father's murder by stabbing John Ross to death.[18]

Feelings of distrust, suspicion, and a desire for vengeance thus pervaded Cherokee public life in Indian Territory. That summer, council meetings proved contentious affairs as the chiefs of the Old Settlers and their Treaty Party allies questioned the authority of the newly arrived Eastern chiefs to legitimately represent the Cherokee people. Ross and his supporters refused to shrink from these challenges, accusing the Western chiefs of being obtuse and stubborn on key questions. In particular, Ross Party representatives accused their political opponents of deliberately working against the formation of a Cherokee political union. While Western Cherokees such as Sequoyah shared with the chiefs of the new emigrants a desire for "peace and brotherhood," the Old Settlers and their Treaty Party allies were generally unwilling to take a back seat in defining the future of "the great Cherokee family."[19]

Questions about how, where, and by whom the Cherokee people should be governed were critical to the reformation of Cherokee nationalism, and thus critical to the creation of a political focal point for the loyalty of Cherokees living in diaspora.[20] Ross's political skills, his eloquence, and the force of his personality increasingly dominated and shaped this debate. He "invited" the chiefs of the Old Settlers— John Looney, Sequoyah, Tobacco Will, John Drew, and William S. Coodey—to participate in reunification talks.[21] In private, Ross believed that the demands being made by the Old Settlers for a prominent place in a new Cherokee government were outrageous; in public, he promised all factions that they stood on "equal ground" in all negotiations.[22] Amid the violence and tense political standoffs that characterized the summer of 1839, Ross and chiefs from both the Eastern and Western Cherokees eventually signed their names (or placed their mark) on a document that vested political power in "the Cherokee people" and declared: "The interests of the red men are the same. Let us always be friends and for ever hold each other firmly by the hand."[23] In an act of political theater, John Ross joined Sequoyah and George Lowrey to confirm their shared desire for "good order" by signing their names to a document promising to end frontier violence.[24]

Ross continued to court support for his version of unity during 1839 and 1840. In convention on July 23, 1839, he instructed Sequoyah, Richard Taylor, John Martin, Jesse Bushyhead, John Drew, Charles Coodey, and other delegates, that "We are one people. Our interests, our hopes, our dangers are the same."[25] Ross's message of unity for the "whole Cherokee family" was accompanied by assurances to Old Settlers that the recently arrived Cherokee emigrants had "no desire or intention to trespass upon the rights of others."[26] Moreover, Ross maintained that the Old Settlers should not look upon the new emigrants as "strangers or intruders in this country," but as "brothers." All Cherokees, Ross concluded, possessed the "agency" needed to brighten the light of the council fire, reconstitute kinship ties severed by the tyranny of distance, and forge a unified Cherokee Nation that would become a beacon of peace and prosperity for all members of the "Cherokee family."[27]

However, the issues dividing the "Cherokee family" exiled to Indian Territory were not inconsequential. Even after the Cherokees adopted a new constitution in September 1839 and designated Tahlequah as the capital of the Cherokee Nation, many sources of tension remained.[28] While political elites squabbled over leadership roles, the bulk of the Cherokee people lived with daily reminders of the uncertainty that life in diaspora so often imposed upon them. The Cherokee tradition of adapting, innovating, and getting on with being Cherokee was being severely tested in Indian Territory.[29]

The Cherokee people were exiled to a parcel of land in Indian Territory that Congress had set aside for them in 1834. When the vast majority of Cherokees began arriving in Indian Territory during 1838 and 1839, large sections of the country they encountered there were like nothing they had seen before. In other places, however, the landscapes were strikingly similar to those they remembered in the cis-Mississippi. The land allocated to the Cherokee Nation in Indian Territory included prairies, dry and arid landscapes, well-timbered bottomlands, and mountains that reminded some of the Great Smoky Mountains.[30] Would Cherokees nurture this diverse territory according to traditional ideals of balance and harmony? Would the land be owned communally, or purchased by individuals in fee-simple? And how would these and other questions be determined if Cherokee factionalism continued unabated?[31]

Ross wanted answers to these questions. He more than most recognized that it was not just Cherokee factionalism impeding a satisfactory resolution of such questions, but also the perceived hostility of the federal government toward the Cherokees in exile. "How long the Cherokees will still have to combat with the unrelenting party in power," Ross wrote of Martin Van Buren's Democratic administration in December 1840. Just as he had in the Southeast before the forced emigrations, Ross now spoke of unifying Cherokee people so that pressure could be placed on the federal government to negotiate with the National Council and clarify for the Cherokee people "their rights."[32]

Ross genuinely felt that he was duty-bound to unite Cherokee people throughout the diaspora, including those still living in homelands in the cis-Mississippi. He displayed this commitment when he attempted to acquire information on the number and condition of the Cherokee population remaining in the pre-removal homeland of the Southeast. On the eastern side of the Mississippi, Cherokees still remained in Tennessee, Georgia, Alabama, and North Carolina. Ross also welcomed information on the condition of Cherokees living in diaspora. Shortly after arriving in Indian Territory, Ross received information that remnants of the Texas Cherokees were still living near the town of Rusk, Texas. These Cherokees had somehow evaded the forced emigration order imposed on them by the Republic of Texas, but they now expressed a desire to come "home." The "home" they envisioned returning to was a product of removal and a political creation of the Cherokee government led by Ross in the Cherokee Nation West. The Texas Cherokees, long separated from kin in North America's Southeast and from those recently forced to relocate to the trans-Mississippi West, could never have imagined when they began their journey westward that they would someday call a previously unknown pocket of land in Indian Territory "home."

Nonetheless, according to reports received by Ross, these Texas Cherokees longed to be reunited with fellow Cherokees. One report stated that the "remnant" Texas Cherokees "were comfortably situated," but had assumed that fellow Cherokees had forgotten about them. The Texas Cherokees were understandably astounded, therefore, when they encountered people who spoke their language. In correspondence with Ross, James M. Payne wrote that the Texas Cherokees "rejoiced . . . that we had come, to take them to their own country that they once more should see their relatives, which they had despaired of enjoying the social and kindred ties, of their all, peace, & happiness." The small party of Texas Cherokees who eventually migrated north to Indian Territory consisted of four women and eight children—all of whom were likely born in Texas—and had all reportedly expressed an eagerness to make the journey along the Red River and into the Cherokee Nation in Indian Territory. On arrival in the Cherokee Nation, this small party of Texas Cherokees looked forward to restoring the kinship ties that had long been broken by migration and isolation. They would have to do so amid political factionalism and the ever-present threat of frontier violence.[33]

The boldest political attempt to end Cherokee factionalism, establish some form of law enforcement in frontier communities, and nurture "tranquility," occurred at Tahlequah in early June 1843.[34] That June, the International Indian Council convened in the Cherokee Nation. The International Council was a massive political and cultural event. Invitations—which included wampum—were sent to leaders from thirty-six tribes, of which seventeen ultimately accepted.[35] At Tahlequah, an estimated 3,000 to 4,000 Native American people, eight interpreters, an unknown number of missionaries, and scores of curious white onlookers joined the invited chiefs. For four weeks, Council delegates made speeches, socialized, danced, and engaged in "ball-play."[36]

Despite the emphasis that the delegates at the International Council placed on the importance of peace and "tranquility," factionalism among the Cherokees continued to threaten the fragile new communities taking root in Indian Territory. While the Cherokee Nation adopted a new constitution in 1839, the rumblings of factional discontent had not subsided by the mid 1840s. In 1845, some forty-five Old Settlers and Treaty Party members left the new political homeland of the Cherokee people. Thoroughly disenchanted with the state of Cherokee politics, and harboring deep feelings of antipathy toward John Ross, this small party of Cherokees migrated south, eventually settling and building new homes in Texas.[37]

What most rankled Old Settlers and Treaty Party supporters was the manner in which John Ross aired Cherokee political disputes on a national and international stage. In the spring of 1846, for instance, Ross presented a "Memorial" to the United States Congress in which he reaffirmed his conviction that he was the rightful leader of the Cherokee Nation in Indian Territory. According to Ross, the Cherokees were a "once powerful, but now feeble, and already much injured people." Only he and his supporters were capable of preserving the "very existence of their country and people."[38] Contrary to the views of his political foes, Ross contended that if dissent existed among the exiled Cherokees in Indian Territory, it was the product of the Western Cherokees and the Treaty Party, whom Ross labeled "a desperate gang of banditti, [and] half breeds, notorious in the nation as wanton murderers, house-burners, and horse-stealers."[39]

The factionalism within Cherokee politics was shaped by the colonial context in which those divisions were formed. Similarly, the American colonial context gave rise to the "banditti," "half breeds," and murderers whom Ross referred to. One issue, however, had especially profound effects on the political landscape of the nascent Cherokee homeland: racial slavery. When the Cherokee incorporated white America's version of racial slavery in the Southeast during the late eighteenth and early nineteenth centuries, it altered traditional systems of captivity, adoption, and kinship. During this period, racial slavery gave rise to a small but powerful slave-holding faction in Cherokee society. Along with a wealthy merchant class, early nineteenth-century Cherokee slaveholders were determined to protect their economic interests and preserve their social status. It was such anxieties that prompted a number of Treaty Party members to sign the Treaty of New Echota in the hope that they might preserve their socioeconomic status in diaspora.[40]

The significance of racial slavery in the Cherokee diaspora needs to be understood in its early nineteenth-century context. By the mid-point of the 1830s, fewer than 3 percent of the Cherokee population owned slaves. According to the federal government, the Cherokee slave population increased from 583 in 1809 to 1,592 by 1835, constituting 10 to 15 percent of the Cherokee population.[41] While slave owners represented a small portion of the total Cherokee population, their political influence was significant, with names such as Vann, Ridge, and Ross dominating Cherokee politics. When these slave owners were forced to migrate west, they took their slaves, and their political anxieties, with them.

Racial attitudes helped shape these anxieties and give meaning to their identities as Cherokee slaveowners.[42] James Vann, whom one historian observes was "far-famed, little loved, and greatly feared," became one of the wealthiest Cherokee slave owners in the antebellum South. Vann oversaw the operation of a well-ordered plantation complete with a "two-story red brick mansion with fireplaces at each end and elegant 'porticos' at the front and rear."[43] The economic, racial, and social value of slavery among the Cherokees was of the utmost importance to a new generation of elites who defined the Nation's power structure. Principal Chief John Ross, for example, owned enough slaves to work five fields under the direction of overseers.[44] And John Martin, the first Chief Justice of the Cherokee Nation's Supreme Court, "reportedly owned 100 black slaves."[45]

The total number of slaves that Cherokees took with them into the trans-Mississippi West is difficult to ascertain.[46] We do know that by 1860 the slave population of the Cherokee Nation in Indian Territory stood at approximately 2,511.[47] The Cherokee slave population was maintained by both natural increase and the purchase of slaves. A regular trade in slaves and agricultural commodities connected Cherokee slave owners to regional markets, particularly those in Arkansas and Texas. Newspapers advertised the buying and selling of slaves, and alerted literate Cherokees of slave runaways or revolts.[48] Indeed, racial slavery was so interwoven into Cherokee life in Indian Territory in the two decades before the Civil War that an entire infrastructure used to support the Cherokee slave economy was later transformed and used for other purposes. For example, the slave quarters formerly occupied by Lewis Ross's slaves were eventually converted into dormitories for the Cherokee Orphan Asylum, which was founded in 1871.[49]

Prominent Cherokee slave owners built grand plantation homes on sprawling estates and tried to perpetuate their wealth by selecting the best and most productive lands in Indian Territory.[50] Joseph Vann, for example, built an estate in Indian Territory that approximated the grandeur that was synonymous with the Vann family back east.[51] White Southerners admired these men, and the estates that slavery helped them build. For instance, George Butler, a rabid state's rights advocate and one-time agent to the Cherokees in Indian Territory, attributed the material progress of the Cherokees in their new homeland to the existence of racial slavery.[52]

Racial slavery had other, more unexpected, effects on Cherokees living in diaspora. Along the American South's western frontier and in the Southwestern borderlands, individual Cherokees encountered slavery in ways previously undocumented by historians. Scattered archival evidence suggests that slave-holding Texans contracted Delaware, Shawnee, Choctaw, and Chickasaw Indians to hunt down and steal slaves from the Comanche. The Comanche had long been a major source of anxiety for the Anglo-Texans. Euroamericans believed that striking at the Comanche's captive populations and disrupting their trade in slaves would be an efficient way to diminish their influence in the Southwest borderlands. But destroying the influence of slave-holding and slave-raiding Comanches—and Navajo and Apache slave raiders and traders in the Southwest—proved easier said than done, a fact borne out by the continuation of such raiding and trading in the Southwest into the late nineteenth century.[53] Among the many challenges to any effort to undermine Comanche slave raiding was the complex web of intertribal relationships, relationships that Anglo-Texans found hard to comprehend. These relationships involved race mixing, trade, and migration on a scale difficult for any colonial regime to monitor and control.

The example of Lucinda Edwards, a "half-breed Creek girl," and her brother-in-law, Jesse Chisholm, "a half-breed Cherokee," makes this point.[54] At some point in the late 1830s, at about the time that Southeastern Indians were arriving en masse in Indian Territory, Edwards came into possession of "two negro boys," Manuel and Aaron. It is unclear how old these children actually were—and indeed, if they were actually children or grown men—but at some point a Mr. Robertson of Texas had allegedly owned them. By some "complex exchange" between a slave trader and Jesse Chisholm, at least one of the slaves was sold to Chisholm. In 1839 Chisholm acquired the other slave from a Comanche slave trader. Chisholm then tried to bargain with the Comanche for other slaves. The Comanche refused to transact further business with Chisholm, presumably because the enslaved children Chisholm wanted to acquire were "white children" whom the Comanche "would not sell." Surviving historical documentation does not allow us to make definitive conclusions about why the Comanche refused to trade these "white children." Given the violence that punctuated colonial relations and the frontier exchange economy between the Comanche and Anglo-Texans in the Southwest, it is not unreasonable to assume that these particular Comanche traders decided it might be prudent to retain these children for future, more contentious, exchanges.[55]

At this point the trade between Chisholm and the Comanche broke down and both parties went their separate ways. Chisholm traveled with his two slaves throughout the Southwest, ultimately stopping for a period in Mexico, where a small Cherokee community, which included Sequoyah's kin, had settled following the rise of the Texas republic. Chisholm did not stay long, however, and by January 1841 returned to Indian Territory. Arriving at Fort Holmes in the Creek Nation on January 24, Chisholm sold the younger slave to his sister-in-law for $400. Among those who knew him, Chisholm was considered a "man of integrity." This may explain why informants from the Choctaw Nation regularly sent word to Chisholm that "Mr. Robertson" was coming after his two slaves. Whatever the actual motives for this type of intertribal cooperation, this affair highlighted the depth to which American colonial expansion had produced some unlikely alliances, much to the chagrin of Anglo-Americans.

If slaves were brought by their Cherokee masters into the trans-Mississippi West, so too did antislavery sentiment travel West with non-slave-owning Cherokees. Just as antislavery and abolitionist ideologies among white Americans sprang from a variety of cultural, intellectual, and political positions, so too was Cherokee opposition to slavery a product of diverse motives. Ranging from anti-black racism to antipathy for the "mixed-blood" slave holding elites and a desire to return to "traditional" forms of captivity and adoption, Cherokee antislavery sentiment defies easy characterization. Baptist missionary Evan Jones helped organize antislavery groups among the Cherokees, with the Keetoowah Society being the most notable. The Keetoowahs, whom Jones helped to organize in a "secret society," brought people with Christian (particularly Baptist) beliefs and "traditional" Cherokee values together.[56] The exact origins of the Keetoowah Society remain shrouded in mystery. Theories abound, such as early twentieth-century speculation that the Keetoowah traced their ancestry to ancient Egypt.[57] Whatever the Keetoowah's actual origins, the Society's growing prominence in the two decades before the Civil War, like that of other "secret societies" among the Cherokees, was based in part on opposition to racial slavery and to the self-interested politics of slave-owning elites.[58]

Other societies, such as the Cherokee chapters of the Knights of the Golden Circle, defended the interests of slaveholders against "the ravages of [the] abolitionists." The Knights' members included many prominent Cherokee leaders, such as Stand Watie, John Rollin Ridge, and William Penn Adair. When the Civil War finally broke out, Cherokee members of the Knights formed the core of the Southern Rights Party in the Cherokee Nation.[59]

Long before the American Civil War began, slave-owning Cherokees looked to their immediate future with uncertainty. Anxieties about "negro" conspiracies and reports of slave uprisings haunted Cherokee slaveowners.[60] For example, the infamous slave revolt in the Cherokee Nation in 1842 sent shockwaves through Cherokee communities, especially those with a direct connection to the slave economy.[61] In this instance, the prophesied "ravages of [the] abolitionists" melted into the political background as slave owners and Cherokee political leaders grappled with the very real impact of the slave revolt.[62] The National Council's response was swift, with Captain John Drew placed in command of a company of one hundred men "to pursue, arrest, and deliver over said Negroes to the commanding officer at Fort Gibson for safe keeping." That they did, as the "revolt" was quickly extinguished.[63]

North Carolina Cherokees

There were no longer any prominent slave owners or wealthy merchants among the North Carolina Cherokee during the 1840s and 1850s. In fact, only about 1,000 Cherokees remained, with Joel Poinsett, the Secretary of War, receiving information that approximately 500 Cherokees expressed "regret [that] they did not emigrate with their brethren."[64]

The expression of such feelings was likely a product of the hardscrabble existence that most North Carolina Cherokees endured. Impoverished, largely illiterate, socially fragmented, the so-called remnant Cherokees in the Great Smoky Mountains relied on one of their adopted kin for leadership. William H. Thomas, a white man adopted in his youth by Chief Yonaguska (Drowning Bear), worked tirelessly in the decades after removal on behalf of the North Carolina Cherokees, seeking to further their political and legal claims with the federal government. His task was immense. An 1840 census of the North Carolina Cherokees revealed the extent to which Cherokee towns, farms, and matrilineal family structures had been damaged—though, importantly, not completely destroyed—by United States colonialism and the removal process. The census highlighted the death of Cherokee children, loved ones, or spouses during the removal process. With the emergence of "orphans" in Cherokee communities, people struggled to adapt what they understood as traditional Cherokee concepts of education and adoption to the new social environment. Still, the great Chief Yonuguska urged fellow Cherokees not to "forsake their mountains," but to help one another rebuild Cherokee towns, farms, and social networks.[65]

And rebuild the Cherokee did. The Cherokee towns and farms that reemerged after removal, and that kept the sacred fires burning on the ancient soil of their Great Smoky Mountain homeland, constituted something more than simply rebuilt "traditional" Cherokee communities. True to the Cherokees' history of cultural innovation and social dynamism, Cherokee communities in western North Carolina embodied the cosmopolitanism that was fast becoming a hallmark of life in their mountainous homeland, as throughout the Cherokee diaspora. On the ancient lands of the Great Smoky Mountains where the North Carolina Cherokees believed the bones of their ancestors lay, Cherokees of the 1840s nurtured kinship communities that were racially and ethnically diverse. The Cherokee towns of western North Carolina attracted Cherokees from Georgia and Tennessee, and also bore witness to interracial and interethnic encounters and marriages. Catawba Indians, for example, lived with the North Carolina Cherokees, albeit at the fringes of their towns, and census data reveals that people from a diverse array of ethnic and racial backgrounds added to the texture of these communities and intermarried with the Cherokees, often in "common law" marriages.[66] One such marriage involved a blind Cherokee woman who lived with a white man.[67] Another involved Polly Murphy, a white woman, and her "Indian for a husband."[68]

While Cherokee families showed tremendous resilience in the face of immense hardship during the early 1840s, some Cherokees decided to leave North Carolina and migrate to Indian Territory. John Trimson, whom the 1840 census listed as the head of a family of 10, expressed his willingness to relocate his family from its Peach Tree home to the Cherokee diaspora's new political homeland in the trans-Mississippi West.[69]

Not all migration followed an east-to-west trajectory. Take for instance the life and travels of Mason Rackley. In 1835 Rackley lived with his mother, Polly Murphy, in North Carolina. By 1840, Rackley spent "part of his time" in Tennessee with his wife, and the remainder of his time with his mother's family at "Cherokee City" in North Carolina. Rackley thus divided his time between two worlds. He spent part of his life in the white world of the colonizer, presumably making enough money in Tennessee to support his wife and his mother back in Cherokee City.[70] When Rackley's wife died suddenly, he apparently decided to return permanently to Cherokee City.[71]

Mason Rackley's personal history highlights one of the ways that Cherokees worked actively to reinvigorate kin and social ties frayed by American colonialism. Not all of these efforts, however, related to the immediate support of family. More than a few Cherokees looked to the future and traveled in pursuit of educational opportunity, among them George Bushyhead. In 1851, Bushyhead left the familiarity of western North Carolina and set out for Baltimore in hope of furthering his education. His aim was to spend at least three months out of each year in Baltimore to continue his education.[72]

Bushyhead's journey in pursuit of an education also provided him with opportunities to access legal representation for the pursuit of land titles and the collection of delinquent payments from the federal government for the sale of land. For example, Bushyhead hired attorney David Siler to draw up "several powers of attorney" on his behalf, outlining Bushyhead's rightful claim to remuneration for land in Georgia, reportedly near "Elijah Town." Siler, however, "went dead" at Richmond, Virginia, while en route to Baltimore. Once in Baltimore, Bushyhead thus sought out new council to represent him and help him collect the money he felt was owed to him.[73]

The legal battles of Cherokees in the cis-Mississippi, to obtain title to reserved land or to have the federal government make good on its treaty promises to pay annuities and compensation for improvements to land lost during the removal era, continued a process begun in the 1830s.[74] Following the forced migrations of 1838–1839, the federal government agreed to terms that allowed some Cherokees to remain on land east of the Mississippi if they became citizens of the state they resided in.[75] In reality, most Cherokees in the cis-Mississippi were essentially refugees, exiles in their own land who remained in a legal limbo until 1842. In 1842, the North Carolina Cherokees received permission from the federal government to remain on lands set apart for them at the Qualla Reservation.[76]

The formal organization of the Qualla Reservation coincided with the failure of the federal government's second Cherokee removal. This second removal, which historian John Finger aptly characterizes as a "second rate sideshow," aimed to remove the Cherokees who had remained in the East and reunite them with the main body of Cherokees living in Indian Territory.[77] The failure of the second removal left federal politicians groping for answers to what they saw as the Cherokee "problem" in the East. Then, on February 1, 1844, the United States Senate passed a resolution demanding to know "if there be any Indians of the Cherokee Tribe remaining East of the Mississippi now, and if so, why they were not removed with that tribe in 1837 and 1838."[78] Additionally, senators wanted to know if granting citizenship to these "Indians" in the state of North Carolina was the reason the Cherokees had not been rounded up and forced to migrate west. With regard to the issue of Cherokee land grants in the cis-Mississippi, historical amnesia proved politically expedient for American lawmakers.

By the end of 1844, US officials believed that there remained two types of Cherokees in the cis-Mississippi. One group, after agreeing to live under the jurisdiction of state laws, had citizenship in their states of residence and were, from a legal perspective, not "Indians." The other group belonged to a band of Cherokees led by Chief Oochilla, who had been granted a tract of land and the right to stay in North Carolina as a reward for helping US officials track down Tsali and his sons when they fled into the Smoky Mountains after killing federal soldiers during the family's march to Fort Lindsay.[79] Still, the Cherokees in North Carolina were legally and territorially vulnerable. With the Qualla Reservation acting as the main population center for North Carolina Cherokees, in 1846 William H. Thomas assumed the responsibility of representing the legal, political, and economic interests of the North Carolina Cherokees to Washington lawmakers.

Thomas worked to protect the Cherokee reservations in North Carolina and to combat racist perceptions of the North Carolina Cherokees as "backward." He believed United States citizenship would accomplish both of these objectives.[80] In 1848, Congress made provision for a subsistence fund "to alleviate poverty among North Carolina Cherokees."[81] Through the 1850s the struggles of the North Carolina Cherokees continued, and efforts to extract payments from the federal government remained an ongoing challenge. While a small but growing number of Cherokees became relatively prosperous in North Carolina, poverty continued to define the realities of everyday life for most North Carolina Cherokees during the 1850s.[82]

By the 1850s another pattern emerged, with North Carolina Cherokees traveling to visit kin in Indian Territory. Cherokee agent James Taylor observed in 1857 that "Within the last two years, several of the

Cherokees in North Carolina, visited their relatives and friends in the Nation West." Taylor reported that the North Carolina Cherokees found the Indian Territory to be in a prosperous, tranquil state, and received "a kind reception" from "relatives and friends." Taylor concluded that the Eastern Cherokees "enjoyed their Nationality" among fellow Cherokees in the West, but typically returned to their ancient homeland after six months abroad.[83]

The exact number of North Carolina Cherokees who made the round trip journey across the Mississippi to visit family and friends is unclear. However, Taylor, himself a multiracial Cherokee, contended that "a portion of" the Eastern Cherokee were eager to "remove and join the tribe west of the Mississippi," but were unable to do so without financial assistance from the federal government.[84] Pulled West by the prospect of being with family and friends, Cherokees were also spurred to migrate toward the setting sun during the 1850s by the poverty of western North Carolina. Many calculations go into an individual or family's decision to migrate to a new land, and the North Carolina Cherokees were no exception to this rule. Indeed, Cherokees throughout the diaspora traveled for a variety of reasons, but for many Cherokees in North Carolina the physical and psychological comfort of being surrounded by family and friends seemed particularly alluring. For them "home" was both a physical place in the ancient homeland of the Southeast, and a relational concept defined by the warmth and re-affirmation of identity derived from family and friends.

Living in Diaspora

For a growing number of people of Cherokee descent during the 1840s and 1850s, travel and migration had the potential either to sever any remaining ties to Cherokee communities in the trans- or cis-Mississippi, or to reaffirm one's identification with the Cherokee people. In the decade and a half before the American Civil War, the Cherokee Nation in Indian Territory enjoyed what some historians call its "golden age." Political stability was finally achieved, paving the way for the relative economic prosperity that Cherokee traders and slave owners longed for. Additionally, the establishment of public schools and seminaries allowed for educational advancements, and a judicial system was created to oversee the administration of law and order within the Cherokee Nation. Not all Cherokees, however, enjoyed the fruits of this "golden age."[85] For some, the future remained clouded with uncertainty.

During the 1840s and 1850s, the American settler frontier continued to spread westward. With the annexation of Texas and the acquisition of Oregon in the mid 1840s, the sectional politics of slavery, and slavery's connection to the territorial expansion of the United States, intensified. Cherokees throughout the diaspora paid close attention to the social and political developments in the United States. In time, divisions over slavery would drive Cherokees apart just as they divided the citizens of the American republic. But in the 1840s and 1850s, such divisions remained in the background as Cherokees began enjoying an era of relative political stability and economic prosperity. Perhaps it was the enjoyment of these prosperous and somewhat optimistic times that gave people of Cherokee descent the confidence to travel and even settle throughout North America and the Pacific, knowing that back "home" the trauma of removal and political factionalism had given way to balance and harmony. These travelers set out from the Cherokee Nation for a variety of reasons. Some traveled to California with dreams of striking it rich after the discovery of gold in 1848. Others traveled beyond the California coastline and into the Central Pacific, while still other Cherokees turned to the classrooms of the Northeast or set their sights on the politics of "Washington City" in hopes of representing the Cherokee people's interests to the federal government.

In 1849 approximately 80,000 people traveled to California in search of gold. Among these treasure-seekers were Cherokees. Some of them were well-known in their communities, such as Dennis and Edward Bushyhead, the sons of the temperance crusader Reverend Jesse Bushyhead. The Bushyheads, born in Tennessee, initially migrated west and re-established their family in the borderland town of Breadtown, located along the Arkansas-Indian Territory border. It was at this location, later known as Baptist Mission, that Reverend Jesse Bushyhead served as chief justice and co-edited the newspaper the *Cherokee Messenger* along with the Baptist missionary Evan Jones. Through the *Cherokee Messenger*, Jones and Bushyhead tended to the spiritual needs and physical wellbeing of the Cherokee people. Their version of Christianity contained a message of sober living directed at Cherokees in the trans-Mississippi West. Their message also traveled eastward with a network of Atlantic World missionaries, who received the *Messenger* in cities as distant as Boston and London.[86]

News of the discovery of gold in California, however, inspired Dennis and Edward Bushyhead to try their luck in California.[87] Other Cherokees joined them. Martin Scrimsher, who was born in Tennessee in 1806 (and who could trace his family's genealogy back to Cherokee and English forebears in the Virginia colony), made the journey to the California goldfields. In some instances, white women traveled from the Cherokee Nation in Indian Territory to California with their Cherokee family members. This was the case for Barbara Hildebrand, a white woman who traveled from the Delaware District in the Cherokee Nation and settled for a time in California with her Cherokee husband William Longknife. In California, fellow Cherokees such as George Brewer, James Vann, John Hildebrand, and Richard R. Keys, to name just four, joined Barbara and William Longknife in diaspora.[88] What most of these gold seekers had in common was their marital status: the vast majority were single men. Once in California they joined a cosmopolitan mix of other single men, including men from the Northeastern United States, Mormons from Utah Territory, members of the Jewish diaspora, and Chileans, Mexicans, Hawaiian, and Chinese migrants in search of their own version of El Dorado.[89]

The Cherokee men who set out for California's goldfields typically began their journey in the Cherokee Nation in Indian Territory. From there they traveled west along the Cherokee Trail, or Old California Road—a road that Arkansas residents encouraged the Cherokees to build following the discovery of gold in California—and traversed the Rocky Mountains before making their way to California.[90] When gold was discovered in the British colonies of Australia in 1851, some Americans boarded steamers in San Francisco bound for Sydney or Melbourne. Both black and white Americans were part of this transnational exchange of fortune seekers, and colonial Australians speculated that Cherokees were also among these temporary migrants.[91] Most

Figure 12: The California Trail that took Cherokees over the Rocky Mountains and on to California. Library of Congress Prints and Photographs Division, Washington, DC.

Cherokees, however, ended their westward travels in California during the 1850s, the vast majority taking an overland route that took up to 161 days to complete.[92]

The alternative to this overland route was a paddle steamer or sailing ship, which traveled via ports in Panama, Nicaragua, or Cape Horn before docking in San Francisco Bay.[93] Most Cherokees stayed in California for only a few years. Some Cherokees did stay longer, like the Bushyheads, who remained in California for two decades. Irrespective of the length of their stay, very few Cherokee gold seekers found their fortunes in California, most leaving the goldfields empty-handed and eventually returning "home," usually to the Cherokee Nation in Indian Territory.

The experience, however, was not inconsequential. For Cherokees living in diaspora, California became a symbol of hope, prosperity, and sanctuary. Back in Indian Territory, Cherokees received news of life in

California through correspondence and in the tales of adventure that Cherokees brought back with them when they returned to Indian Territory. The Cherokee Nation in Indian Territory may have experienced its "golden age" between 1846 and 1861, but the "golden state" was clearly having an impact on the Cherokee's previous associations of the West with death, illness, and "blackness." Indeed, some ten miles from the tiny Cherokee town of Nowata, located along the St. Louis, Iron Mountain and Southern Railway, Cherokees founded the town of California, thereby creating a permanent reminder of the growing importance of the Pacific in Cherokee imagination.[94] Living diasporic lives created new opportunities for Cherokees and facilitated new experiences and new memories, memories that to some Cherokees were significant enough to be celebrated by this name etched into the landscape of their political homeland.

By mid-century, the Cherokee Nation in Indian Territory had become a political homeland. For Cherokees who lived diasporic lives outside that homeland and away from their ancient soil in western North Carolina, literacy skills and a keen understanding of the history of the early nineteenth century helped to give meaning to their Cherokee "blood." Cherokees who felt rooted to the land of the Great Smoky Mountains, or who lived diasporic lives during this time, made calculated personal and family decisions about the risks and benefits of migration and resettlement outside of the respective homelands. Above all, the diasporic lives of Cherokees outside of either the trans-or cis-Mississippi homelands reflected how so many of them had become by the 1840s and 1850s a "cultured," well-educated, and widely traveled people. For Cherokees living in California, Hawaii, or along the eastern seaboard of the United States, personal and professional connections to non-Cherokees in various walks of American life often far exceeded those of the average white American, most of whom remained anchored to a small town or local community.

Few Cherokees wrote or spoke more eloquently about life in diaspora, specifically in California, and its relation to Cherokee history than John Rollin Ridge (Chees-quat-a-law-ny, or Yellow Bird). Born in Georgia on March 19, 1827, John Rollin was the son of John Ridge and Sarah Ridge nee Northrup. While John Rollin was still a young boy, his father placed his signature on the infamous Treaty of New Echota, a fateful act narrated in the previous chapter of this book. The Ridge family subsequently migrated west, eventually settling at Honey Creek, a small frontier town along the Indian Territory-Missouri border.[95] The ensuing years, though, were anything but peaceful; in fact, they were deeply traumatic for the Ridge family. At just twelve years of age, John Rollin lost his father to Cherokee executioners who carried out the death sentence demanded by Cherokee "blood law" for John Ridge's part in signing away Cherokee communal lands in the Treaty of New Echota. The Ridge family remained at Honey Creek for one week following John Ridge's murder. In fear, the family then relocated to Fayetteville, Arkansas, where other Treaty Party families also re-established their homes.[96]

The decision to relocate to Arkansas was not an uncommon one for Cherokee families who owned slaves or who had connections to the Treaty Party. In fact, it proved such a popular place for Cherokee settlement that the white settler populations of Arkansas feared that Cherokee factionalism would spill over the border and engulf white communities in bloody political feuds.[97] As one historian observes, "so many Cherokees came into Arkansas that the people of Washington County [in Arkansas] petitioned the Governor to have the militant ones, at least, removed."[98] For John Rollin Ridge, the move to Arkansas changed the course of his life. It was in Arkansas that he got into an argument over a horse with a man named David Kell, who was assumed to be a Ross Party supporter. The argument between Ridge and Kell escalated into violence, and finally resulted in Ridge killing the man. If Ridge did not already feel that his life was defined by feelings of exile and uncertainty, he would from this time forward.[99]

John Rollin fled with his wife to northern California where he found sanctuary from the death that awaited him if he returned to either the Cherokee Nation in Indian Territory or Arkansas. Exiled from his extended family, Ross apparently found peace of mind harder to come by in California than he had anticipated. The same year that he killed Kell, Ridge published a history of "The Cherokees" in the *Northern Standard*, a Texas publication out of Clarkesville. Written perhaps as an attempt to understand his place in the Cherokee world Ridge so recently had fled, the article described Cherokee history as "noble and thrilling," although the "iron arm of cold state policy" had made the recent past "tragic." Ridge constructed a linear history of the Cherokees, charting the transition from "their savage customs and traditions" to the "condition of civilized life."[100] Despite the "evolution" of Cherokee "civilization," the Southern states "unjustly" made claims to Cherokee lands that "every intelligent man" knew were fraudulent. And yet, the federal government ultimately bowed to Southern demands and forcibly removed the Cherokee people from the land of their ancestors.[101]

Ridge's history of the Cherokees was thus punctuated with uncompromising critiques of the United States' brand of colonialism. It also contained a pointed account of the partisanship that divided Cherokee society during the early nineteenth century. For example, Ridge wrote that the members of the Ross Party—whom he blamed and never forgave for the killing of his father—were filled with "bitter animosity" for the Treaty Party. According to Ridge, the fate that befell his father and other prominent Treaty Party men had enabled John Ross to secure power and rule with a "vindictive" spirit. As Ridge reflected on events from his Marysville, California, home, this was the real tragedy of Cherokee history. It was a history in which "this suffering minority" of "patriotic" Cherokees and the "best and purest intellects of the nation" endured abuse and suffered death at the hands of duplicitous Ross Party members.[102]

During the 1850s, Ridge did his best to maintain a regular correspondence with his Cherokee kin back in Indian Territory and Arkansas. This correspondence covered a wide range of issues, such as his plight as an impoverished writer, requests for money from family members to help in the establishment of a press, and the recent political history of the Cherokee Nation. Writing to "Cousin Stand" [Watie], Ridge confided in a September 1853 letter that he missed his relatives and "my beautiful home in the Cherokee Nation." At the same time, Ridge revealed his racial attitudes and the depths to which his life had fallen when he characterized his diasporic predicament as worse than the life of exploitation endured by the slaves that he and his father had once owned. Ridge claimed to have worked "harder than any slave I have ever owned, or my father either," because "a series of bad luck" had left him virtually impoverished. "I have tried the mines, I have tried trading,

I have tried everything, but with no avail, always making a living but nothing more," Ridge confided in Watie.[103]

From a financial and psychological perspective Ridge appeared discouraged by his diasporic life.[104] His concerns about money, however, paled in comparison to the intensity of his feelings of isolation, loneliness, and longing to be among kin in Arkansas and Indian Territory. Ridge revealed to Watie that he felt "tormented so by the folks at home whenever I talk of going back to the nation." Fearing for his safety if he returned, Ridge explained that his kin "urge me in their letters so much not to venture to stay even in Arkansas with any family." With the bonds of kinship loosened by vast distances, Ridge overcame feelings of melancholy "by providing for my family in this country so as to place them above all want; and then I will be at liberty to follow the bent of my mind which leads me back to my own people and to my own country."[105]

In diaspora, Ridge's Cherokee identity was defined and strengthened by his absence from the homes of kin in Arkansas and Indian Territory. Unable to nurture family bonds through daily encounters and conversations, Ridge found his Cherokee identity in his memories and in his imagination. And because of Ridge's geographical isolation, his mind worked overtime to continually remind him of his loyalty to both his blood relatives and the Cherokee Nation. Ridge expressed these feelings like any other tormented writer: with words. But like any writer, he needed a venue in which to share his ideas. For this reason Ridge wrote to "Cousin Stand" in 1855 with a proposition. He asked Watie, "Don't you believe it would be a good plan to establish a paper somewhere in Arkansas, or some place where it will be safe from the commotion of Cherokee affairs and devote it to the interests of the Indian race? It is my opinion that it would pay well, and it would certainly do a great deal of good."[106]

Ridge's aspirations were motivated by financial concerns and a desire for influence.[107] However, they were also inspired by his self-professed patriotism and a longing to feel connected to other diaspora Cherokees. Thus motivated, Ridge tried to convince "Cousin Stand" of the efficacy of his proposed scheme by insisting, "I assure you this is no idle talk. If there ever was a man upon earth that loved his people . . . I am that man." Separated from the Cherokee homeland in Indian Territory, Ridge reiterated that his proposed newspaper was a product of his devotion to the Cherokee people, an affection that distance could not extinguish. "I don't care if I can get back into the Nation right away or not," Ridge claimed, "The paper will do just as well, and better, in the state."[108]

Ridge envisioned his newspaper not only as a means of connecting widely scattered Cherokees, but also as a vehicle for chronicling the history of "Indian rights and interests" throughout the United States. In an October 1855 letter to his mother, John Rollin outlined his desire to use his proposed newspaper as a forum for Cherokee politics. He explained that such a newspaper will "make it [the Cherokee Nation] feared and respected." With the memory of removal and the death of his father still burning in his thoughts, Ridge claimed that "Men, government, will be *afraid* to trample upon the rights of defenseless Indian tribes, when there is a power to note up their deeds."[109]

According to a 1904 biographical essay on John Rollin, Californians remembered him as a fine journalist and a "gifted representative of the Cherokee nation."[110] His literary career, which began in Arkansas, reached its zenith with the publication of his novel *The Life and Adventures of Joaquin Murieta, the Celebrated California Bandit* (1854).[111] According to literary scholar Sean Teuton, *Joaquin Murieta* allowed Ridge to "carve out creative space" in which he could explore the abuses that came with colonialism.[112] *Joaquin Murieta* also allowed Ridge to explore the panoply of emotions connected to the "deep-seated principle of Revenge," a principle that had shaped his own life following his father's brutal death.[113] But there was something more in the writing of *Joaquin Murieta* than simply a tale of vengeance; it was the belief that space—defined as both a location and the freedom to reflect on one's identity and relationship to the rest of the world—helped John Rollin explore the contours of his own identity. In California, thousands of miles from his place of birth, his closest relatives in Arkansas, and the political homeland of the Cherokee diaspora in Indian Territory, Ridge discovered the meaning of his Cherokee identity. His was an identity built on a foundation of past wrongs, a desire for vengeance, and the inventive layers of memory shaped and reshaped by time, space, and

deeply personal events that remained lodged in his historical consciousness until the day he died.[114]

John Rollin Ridge was arguably the most famous Cherokee living
in diaspora during the nineteenth century. He was not, however, the
only well-known Cherokee living a diasporic life. Elias Cornelius Boudinot, born in Georgia in 1835, also spent much of his life in diaspora.
The son of Elias Boudinot and Harriet Gold, Elias Cornelius grew to
manhood with the knowledge that his father also had been executed
for placing his signature on the Treaty of New Echota. Elias Cornelius
was too young to recall the graphic details of his father's brutal death in
1839. Indeed, his childhood memories were of an entirely different character than those of John Rollin Ridge. The young Elias Cornelius was
not raised in the trans-Mississippi West, but among his mother's family
in New England. From infancy, he was surrounded by white people. A
bright young man, he went on to study law and eventually "returned" to
his kin in Arkansas, where he spent time working as a newspaper editor
and eventually entered politics as a member of the Democratic Party.[115]

Where John Rollin Ridge found meaning in his life through writing, Elias Cornelius Boudinot found his calling in the law and as a representative of the Cherokee people. A man of the diaspora who was equally
at ease in Tahlequah and in New York, Elias Cornelius represented the
legal claims of the Cherokee people to the federal government from
residences in Arkansas, New York, and Washington, DC. Like John Rollin Ridge, Elias Cornelius Boudinot was well traveled, highly educated,
and committed to the Cherokee people. Unlike Ridge, Boudinot did
not perceive his identity through the prism of self-imposed exile; Boudinot's identity lay in the practice of law and his life-long commitment
to the preservation of the Cherokee Nation's territorial sovereignty in
the trans-Mississippi West. Due to his work as a lawyer on behalf of the
Cherokee Nation, Boudinot remained a prominent figure in Cherokee
legal and political affairs until well into the late nineteenth century.

There were other Cherokees traveling and living in the trans-
Mississippi diaspora who were not as famous as John Rollin Ridge or
Elias Cornelius Boudinot. Some, as mentioned above, journeyed to
California in search of gold. Others traveled across the Plains, over the
Rockies, and on to California for other reasons. While their motives for

doing so are unclear, members of at least one Cherokee family boarded a steamer in San Francisco Bay and set off for Hawaii. It was not uncommon for ships from San Francisco to stop in Hawaii en route to the gold fields of Australia in the 1850s. For one diasporic Cherokee woman, Mary Jane Longknife, Hawaii was her final destination.

Like the lives of many other diasporic Cherokees outside of the public or political spotlight, Longknife's life, her travels, and her struggles highlight the impact of American colonialism on Native American people in the mid nineteenth century. She was born in Utah Territory in 1851, or so federal census takers guessed.[116] Her parents, William Longknife, who was Cherokee, and Barbara Longknife, who was white, were both born in Tennessee, in the years 1830 and 1829 respectively.[117] There are few surviving records that would allow us to determine precisely why William and Barbara Longknife decided to leave Tennessee and head west. There are a number of plausible scenarios, such as a desire to flee the cis-Mississippi as pressure for Cherokee removal intensified. Alternatively, the family may have been unable to secure a reliable livelihood on the basis of small-scale farming. The Longknifes certainly would not have been the first Cherokee family to travel toward the setting sun and beyond the Mississippi River in hopes of creating a peaceful, self-sustaining life. Their destination could just as easily have been Utah Territory, where Mary was born, or Mexico, or Arizona Territory.[118] However, in 1850, with gold fever still in the air, the Longknife family set off with the Cherokee Argonauts for California in search of their "golden fleece."

The Longknife family's journey westward began in the late 1830s when they relocated from Tennessee to what became the Delaware District of the Cherokee Nation. By the end of the 1840s, the family had apparently made the decision to continue farther west, presumably in hopes of finding gold. The Longknifes were in good company. Among the seventy-five people in their caravan for California were James S. Vann, George Brewer, John W. Candy, Richard R. Keys, and the onetime Cherokee Indian Agent Return J. Meigs. The caravan began at the Verdigris, a tributary of the Arkansas River, and headed northwest along the Cherokee Road, or Old California Road. It was on this journey that Mary Jane Longknife was born. Mary Jane's sibling, Anna Diane

Longknife, was born in 1859, several years after the family had settled in California. For reasons that remain unclear, the Longknife sisters emigrated to the Hawaiian island of Oahu, where they received their formal schooling at the Sacred Heart School in Honolulu, a convent school opened—over the objections of local Congregationalists—by Belgian and French nuns in 1859.[119]

Between the 1820s and 1860s, Hawaii became the stage for some fierce competition among Christian missionaries. Whether the Longknife sisters were aware of the religious politics of the island chain remains unclear. What is certain is that they entered a colonial environment in which Catholics were more-often-than-not unwelcome, and in which the teachers and disciplinarians who operated missionary schools became important colonizing agents. Congregationalists under the auspices of the American Board of Commissioners for Foreign Missions, Episcopalians, Reformed Catholics, and Mormons were among the more conspicuous Christian groups to travel to the Central Pacific in hope of saving souls and educating Indigenous converts.[120]

At the Sacred Heart Convent School the Longknife sisters encountered Indigenous peoples from throughout the Hawaiian Islands and the Pacific Rim. Like the Cornwall School in Connecticut, Sacred Heart educated a cross section of Indigenous children, teaching basic literacy in addition to bourgeois ideals about sexuality and a woman's role in a patriarchal society.[121] At Sacred Heart, the Longknife sisters would have received the general education deemed appropriate to Indigenous children at mid-century, and also gender-specific skills such as needlework and cooking.[122]

We know much less about Mary Jane Longknife and her sense of Cherokee identity than we do about John Rollin Ridge and Elias Cornelius Boudinot. Unlike Ridge and Boudinot, Longknife lived her life out of the public eye and far from both the political and ancestral homelands of the Cherokee diaspora. Like thousands of other Cherokees living in diaspora during the nineteenth century, Longknife lived a quiet, dignified life. Unlike the vast majority of those fellow Cherokees, she chose to live that life in the Central Pacific. We have only slivers of information to imagine what her life as a diasporic Cherokee woman in the Central Pacific might have been like. That she remained attached to her Cherokee identity we can infer from the effort she and her family members made to enroll as Cherokees on the Guion Miller Roll of 1906–1909. Surviving records allow us to assume that Longknife married—she went by the name Mary Jane Woodward at the time she enrolled as a Cherokee—and lived the remaining years of her life in Oahu. She breathed her final breath of tropical air in 1906. She is buried in a Honolulu cemetery.

For Cherokees like John Rollin Ridge, Elias Cornelius Boudinot, and Mary Jane Woodward, the personal decision to live a life in diaspora was influenced by larger historical, social, and political factors. The calculations involved in Cherokees' decisions to migrate and settle outside of either the trans-or cis-Mississippi homelands could involve the search for economic independence, a desire for political influence, the need for a safe haven from political violence, and/or a desire to reinvent how the world perceived them. Significantly, life in diaspora, whether freely chosen or reluctantly accepted, opened new perspectives on what it meant to be Cherokee during the 1840s and 1850s. For most Cherokees living in the newly formed political homeland in Indian Territory, what it meant to be Cherokee remained tied to the memory of forced removal. In the Cherokee Nation in Indian Territory, tribal factionalism, frontier violence, and a new era of economic prosperity and cultural self-confidence shaded memories of the past with experiences lived in the present. Filtered through the initial uncertainties of life in frontier and borderland towns, the political disputes and social cleavages that defined the Cherokee Nation in the late 1830s and early 1840s would be revisited and rewritten in the 1860s to meet a new set of challenges. When the American Civil War broke out in 1861, the "golden age" of the Cherokee Nation in Indian Territory was destined to come to a bloody end.

When the American Civil War eventually erupted in the West, virtually every Cherokee family and community was touched by some of the most ghastly violence of the war. Their cis-Mississippi cousins, especially those in western North Carolina, also experienced crushing hardship during the Civil War. As the guns of war began thundering across battlefields all over the South, the North Carolina Cherokees remained locked in a struggle against poverty while also trying to nurture the ethic of harmony that had for centuries characterized Cherokee town life. For Cherokees throughout the diaspora, then, the American Civil War posed new challenges to Cherokee identity and reminded diaspora Cherokees of the uncertainty that had shadowed them on a daily basis at the end of the 1830s.

Part 2

Diaspora

War, Division, and Refugees

To the citizens of the Cherokee Nation in Indian Territory, the American Civil War was a foreign war.[1] As members of a sovereign Indian nation, the Cherokee people and their leaders viewed the potential impact of the war from a variety of perspectives. Most Cherokees considered the prospect of a large-scale war in the trans-Mississippi West as a threat to the future wellbeing of the diaspora's political homeland. Others, especially wealthier Cherokees and Cherokee slave owners, believed they shared a social and economic stake in the fate of the Confederacy. However, as the guns of war sounded just beyond the borders of the Cherokee Nation, virtually every Cherokee citizen recognized that it was all well and good to sympathize with either of the combatants, but it was quite another to become involved in a violent struggle barely a generation after removal.

A little over two decades had passed since the United States army forced 12,000 to 13,000 Cherokees to relocate from their homeland in the Southeast and create a new homeland—an invention of nineteenth-century colonialism, politics, and legal thinking—in Indian Territory. To the east, the outbreak of war posed equally immediate threats to the communities of the "remnant" Cherokee population living in western North Carolina. The North Carolina Cherokees occupied reservation lands that were in the heart of the Confederacy in Appalachia.[2] The land on which the Eastern Cherokees eked out their subsistence livelihoods was geographically and politically vulnerable to the fortunes of the war. As historian John Finger observes, William Thomas, who had played an instrumental role in pressing the land claims of the North Carolina Cherokees with the United States government, recognized that the fate of these lands, and the Cherokee people, was less than clear.[3]

Whether the Cherokee liked it or not, both their trans-Mississippi political homeland and what had come to be seen as their cis-Mississippi ancestral homeland eventually became embroiled in the American Civil War. For Cherokees residing in these respective homelands, the war threatened their social, economic, and political existence. For those Cherokees living in diaspora—in, for example, Arkansas, Texas, and California in the trans-Mississippi; Connecticut, Virginia and the District of Columbia in the East—just as for those Cherokees living on lands long imagined to be the Cherokee homeland, in the region encompassing Tennessee, Georgia, and the Carolinas in the Southeast— the Civil War held the potential not simply to unsettle established political and cultural modes of life, but to result in the complete erasure of a recognizable Cherokee identity, much less an identifiable political or ancestral homeland.

The Civil War was an uncertain, anxious time for all Americans, but especially for Cherokee people. In the darkest hours of war, any thought of the future gave way to the basic quest for survival. In those dark hours, the Civil War not only opened old political wounds and exposed Cherokee warriors to combat, but it gave rise to tens of thousands of Cherokee refugees. Between 1861 and 1865, a new chapter was opened in the Cherokee story of "home" and exile, the legacy of which posed challenges for Cherokee and United States officials well into the twentieth century.

The Diaspora Divided

The Civil War divided American families, towns, and regions. This was no less true for Cherokees than it was for white Americans. In North Carolina, William Thomas worried that the Cherokee people were now at risk of being "over run by deserters and renegades."[4] In the trans-

Mississippi West, the prospects for the Cherokee Nation appeared equally dire. Indeed, the Civil War became an economic, social, and legal calamity for the Cherokee Nation. Certainly this was the view of Principal Chief John Ross and missionary Evan Jones, the reputed founder of the Keetoowah Society.[5]

Many Keetoowahs had links to the anti-slavery Pin Indians, although the strength of these connections remains unclear. While a number of Cherokees remembered the Pins as a loose coalition of traditionalists, determined to execute "blood law" on the signers of the New Echota Treaty and terrorize slaveholding families,[6] the term "Pin Indians" became a catch-all phrase to describe Cherokees opposed to the Confederacy who engaged in guerrilla-style fighting and raiding activities. The name referred to the insignia of crossed pins that members wore on their lapels.[7]

Although the extent of the political and paramilitary connection between the Keetoowahs and the Pins remains unclear, what is clear is that John Ross's political opponents in the Cherokee Nation went out of their way to link the Ross Party to the Keetoowahs and Pin Indian "terrorism."[8] For example, William Walker recalled that his father "took mother over into Arkansas, to get out of danger" while the war raged and violence threatened the safety of Cherokee families like the Walkers in Indian Territory. As a result, Walker was born in Arkansas, a child of war and of the Cherokee diaspora.[9] While the violence that led to the refugee migrations like that of Walker's parents was real enough, most Keetoowah members do not appear to have been as radical as their pro-slavery opponents portrayed them. In fact, the Keetoowahs were a fairly conservative organization. During the war Evan Jones and the Keetoowahs shared Ross's focus on preserving Cherokee sovereignty and protecting Cherokee people from the ravages of war.[10] Ross received regular reports from officials and relatives that indicated just how precarious the Cherokee Nation's future had become. In November 1863, his nephew William Potter Ross informed the principal chief of "the loss of property they [the Cherokees] have sustained, the sufferings they have endured, and the ravages of death in their midst."[11] The Civil War transformed the political homeland of the Cherokee diaspora, reducing the Cherokee Nation from a "numerous, intelligent, wealthy tribe" to a body politic "robbed, plundered and murdered; their homes have been burned, their fields laid waste, their property seized and destroyed."[12]

In early 1861, no one in the Cherokee Nation could foretell just how extensive this plunder and murder would be. However, the specter of a foreign war certainly worried Principal Chief Ross and many other Cherokees. Uppermost in their minds were fears that the Civil War could provide a pretext for one, or even both, of the warring parties to disregard Cherokee sovereignty, seize their land and slaves, and force the Cherokee people into yet another traumatic emigration experience.

At the outbreak of the war, Cherokee identity was defined in different legal ways in different parts of the diaspora. For those living in Indian Territory, citizenship in the Cherokee Nation constituted the most common legal identity. The cultural and social meaning of that identity varied, but so long as Cherokees resided within the territorial boundaries of the Cherokee Nation (even if they spent part of their time in Arkansas, or Missouri, or Texas, on business or temporarily living with friends and family), the Cherokee Constitution prescribed their rights and legal protections. This legal status also meant that if war did break out between the North and the South, citizens of the Cherokee Nation were under no obligation to take up arms and fight for either side.

East of the Mississippi, Cherokees living in Tennessee, Georgia, Kentucky, Alabama, and especially North Carolina, faced a less certain legal existence. The law defined Cherokees living in any one of these states as citizens of the state in which they permanently resided.[13] Unless they were motivated by legal compulsion to define their racial identity, it is difficult to accurately identify Cherokees still living in the Southeast between 1840 and 1861. Like Choctaws, Creeks, or Chickasaws remaining in the Southeast after removal, these Cherokees were often ignored by government officials, leaving the historian with an uneven or absent archival paper trail from which to reconstruct their respective histories. Moreover, Indigenous people living in the cis-Mississippi after removal tried to keep to themselves.[14] This was certainly the case for the North Carolina Cherokees. Their visibility to the historian, limited as it is, is largely a product of William Holland Thomas's patronage. As citizens of North Carolina, the Eastern Cherokees under Thomas's leadership became members of a Confederate state when North Carolina seceded from the Union in May 1861.

In the trans-Mississippi West, the legal and political status of the Cherokee was somewhat clearer, even if the immediate future was no less certain. As the leader of a sovereign tribal nation, Principal Chief John Ross received news of the outbreak of the Civil War with one overarching objective in mind: preserving the sovereignty of the Cherokee Nation. Ross initially believed that a neutral position would best serve that objective. He may have been attempting to buy time and observe the course that the war took before declaring Cherokee support for one side or the other. On May 17, 1861, Ross issued a neutrality proclamation. He reminded the Cherokees of their obligations to the United States government and warned against partisanship.[15] Recognizing Ross's strategy, the Confederacy sent Albert Pike, a Little Rock attorney, and Benjamin McCulloch, to negotiate a treaty with Cherokee leaders in May 1861. Pike understood the challenge before him, commenting that Ross "is very shrewd. If I fail with him it will not be my fault."[16]

Over the following months, negotiations between the Confederate agents and Ross unfolded. If Ross had entered these negotiations determined to preserve the sovereignty of the Cherokee Nation in Indian Territory, then Pike and McCulloch needed to find a way to convince Ross that aligning with the South would in fact preserve that sovereignty. With these negotiations ongoing, Ross simultaneously assured the federal government that the Cherokee Nation remained bound to the United States in "amity and reciprocal rights and obligations" by treaties.[17] The Cherokee Nation, with its borderlands with Arkansas, Missouri, Kansas, the Creek Nation, and to the south, the Choctaw Nation, was vital to military success in the trans-Mississippi. With the Lincoln administration withdrawing Union troops from Indian Territory at the beginning of the war, Pike, McCulloch, and the Commissioner of Indian Affairs David Hubbard insisted that "Neutrality will scarcely be possible" in this critical part of the trans-Mississippi West.[18]

Ross, however, was a tough negotiator. He remained steadfast in his commitment to preserve Cherokee sovereignty, even after Confederate negotiators turned up the pressure by opening talks with sympathetic "mixed-bloods." Slowly, however, Ross's public position on the war changed. This shift was due in part to the intensification of Confederate negotiations, and in part to events within the Cherokee Nation. In early July, for instance, Ross received reports of violence, rampant drunkenness, and efforts to raise the Confederate flag at Webbers Falls.[19] Commissioner of Indian Affairs Hubbard, recognizing Ross's long-held belief that the strength of a nation derives from the unity of its people, emphasized the likelihood of Southern success because

> [W]e are daily gaining friends among the powers of Europe & our people are arming with unanimity scarcely ever seen in the world before. Your laws, your slaves, and your separate nationality are secured, and made perpetual, and in addition, nearly all your debts are in Southern Bonds, and these we will also secure. If the North succeeds you will most certainly lose all. First your slaves, they will take them from you, that is one object of the war, to enable them to abolish slavery in such manner.[20]

Such rhetoric had its desired effect. At a national council attended by 4,000 Cherokee men in August 1861, Ross reiterated his commitment to Cherokee sovereignty, but concluded with remarks that underscored the impact Confederate negotiators were having on his thinking. He insisted that the time had come "to adopt preliminary steps for an alliance with the Confederate States upon terms honorable and advantageous to the Cherokee Nation."[21]

Following Ross's speech, the Cherokees voted to officially align with the Confederacy in "the conflict between the whites."[22] On October 7, 1861, the neutrality of the Cherokee Nation in Indian Territory officially ended. In a treaty with the Confederate States of America, the Cherokee Nation agreed to "an alliance offensive and defensive, between the Confederate States of America and all of their States and people, and the Cherokee Nation and all the people thereof."[23] In return for Cherokee support of the Southern war effort, the Confederacy agreed to protect the territorial boundaries of the Cherokee Nation and the Cherokee citizens residing therein, and to uphold a variety of other provisions, such as Cherokee access to "navigable streams" in the Confederacy.[24] For the Cherokee who signed the 1861 treaty, the agreement with the Confederacy represented both a means of protecting their economic interest in racial slavery and a way of preserving the sovereignty of the Cherokee Nation in Indian Territory.

In an address to the Cherokee people on October 9, 1861, Ross justified the Cherokee alliance with the Confederacy. "The United States have been dissolved and two great governments now exist," Ross explained. He insisted that the "unanimity" that bound the Confederate states together "must sooner or later secure their success." In the current situation, the preservation of Cherokee sovereignty and the socioeconomic influence of Cherokee slave owners within that nation demanded that the position of neutrality be abandoned. Geography, culture, and institutional similarities meant that an alliance with the South was not only logical but also expedient.[25] In the American South, arguments in favor of secession were buttressed by the interlocking arguments for "states' rights" and a desire to perpetuate slavery and the internal slave trade. Just as Southern political leaders could not (indeed, refused to) separate the political ideology of states' rights from the economic and social significance of racial slavery, so too did Ross find it impossible to uncouple questions about Cherokee sovereignty from the issue of racial slavery within the Cherokee Nation in Indian Territory. In Ross's words,

> [the Civil War] is a war of Northern cupidity and fanaticism against the institution of African servitude; against the commercial freedom of the South, and against the political freedom of the States, and its objects are to annihilate the sovereignty of those States and utterly change the nature of the General Government.[26]

It seemed "natural," therefore, that the Cherokees should align themselves with the white South, given that the "Cherokee people had its origins in the South; its institutions are similar to those of the Southern States, and their interests identical with theirs."[27] In a decision that reflected the strength (and nepotism) of Cherokee kinship bonds in a time of war, Ross placed his nephew-by-marriage, John Drew, in charge of raising an army to fight to defend the Cherokee Nation's borders. To the chagrin of Stand Watie, who believed he had formed the first mounted rifle regiment in the Cherokee Nation, Drew's army became known as the First Cherokee Mounted Rifles and was comprised predominantly of "full bloods."[28]

The Cherokee Nation's decision to officially enter the war on the side of the Confederacy was not, however, as popular among Cherokee citizens as Ross made it seem.[29] Most Cherokees cared little for the Confederacy's cause, and cared even less about the economic and social interests of slaveholders. Indeed, many Cherokees felt a sense of loyalty to the Union. These self-proclaimed "Loyal Cherokees" sometimes worked as scouts for the Union Army, or enlisted in active service with federal troops. The Loyal Cherokees served in Missouri and Kansas, and, after federal troops reentered the Cherokee Nation in June 1862, returned to the Cherokee Nation where they served in defense of the Nation's borders.[30]

The Pin Indians were by far the most visible examples of Cherokee resistance to the Confederacy's cause in the trans-Mississippi West. As noted above, Confederate Cherokees charged that the Pins were allied with the Ross Party and the Keetoowahs, a collective political force whose true object was suspected to be the abolition of racial slavery. The Standuaitie Party, as Stand Watie's pro-Confederate Cherokees were sometimes called, felt that Ross never truly supported the Confederacy's cause. The Standuaities thus played an important role in spreading rumors about the Ross party's links with the Pins and Keetoowahs.[31]

The Keetoowahs and Pin Indians did indeed form the nucleus of the Loyal League.[32] On the other side, pro-Confederate Cherokees who occupied positions of political leadership and economic influence prior to the war were joined by pro-slavery organizations like the Knights of the Golden Circle. The Knights publicly accused Pin Indians of scalping the Confederate war dead.[33] According to the Standuaities, the Pin Indians were joining forces with runaway slaves and "levying black-mail indiscriminately upon the inhabitants [of the Cherokee Nation], and murdering right and left with habitual brutality."[34]

Since the early twentieth century, historians have referred to pro-Confederate Cherokees as "mixed-bloods" or "white Indians."[35] While some of these Cherokees were of biologically mixed descent, the term "mixed-blood" more accurately describes the socioeconomic and cultural identities of the pro-Confederate Cherokees. Many owned slaves, had accumulated great wealth, and maintained connections with Cherokees and whites in Arkansas, Texas, and throughout the slave owning Southeast.[36]

It was to one of these slaveholders, Stand Watie, that Arkansas officials turned to lead a Cherokee regiment. Slaveholding Cherokees had long feared the social impact of abolitionists and their radical political allies. In defending their "rights," wealthy slaveholding Cherokees issued public statements denouncing the "secret abolition" and claimed to have acquired "unmistakable evidence" that proved the fanatical abolitionists had "imperiled" the Cherokee Nation.[37] Pro-slavery Cherokees therefore bristled at the thought that abolition might gain support in their nation, with one group of slaveholding Cherokees declaring that "The Constitution and Laws of our Country recognize the institution of African slavery & we will oppose any change in that Constitution & those Laws in this respect by abolition influence."[38]

This type of rhetoric earned Watie and other slaveholding Cherokees praise from white Southerners. Just as whites in the South were proud of the slave societies they were part of, so Cherokee slave-owners shared that sense of pride. White Southerners thus celebrated Watie's politics, calling him a patriot of "the true Southern party," and emphasizing his mixed-blood identity—a racialized identity that Watie himself had never laid claim to. In contrast, Confederates labeled Ross and the Pin Indians as "Full-bloods," a designation meant to discredit those Cherokees who were unsympathetic to the Southern cause.[39]

Even after Ross agreed to treaty terms with the Confederacy, Southern suspicions about Cherokee loyalty lingered. These perceptions say as much about the anxiety of Southern political leaders as they do about the intensely factionalized nature of Cherokee politics. Throughout the diaspora, Cherokee leaders expressed a variety of views about the war and the alliances Cherokees entered into. Ross supporters, for example, referred to the men who comprised Stand Watie's regiment as "the most desperate characters."[40] And as far away as California, John Rollin Ridge expressed his suspicions of Ross's political motives by linking the principal chief to what he saw as the disastrous policies of the Lincoln administration. According to Ridge, the Lincoln administration had overseen nothing but "disaster and ruin" since it came to office. [41]

A combination of territorial and economic motives, in addition to deeply felt historical and cultural perceptions of the world around them, served to divide Cherokee loyalties during the Civil War. A complex social psychology buttressed many of these divisions. In 1860, census records indicate that Native Americans owned 7,367 black slaves. Of this number, an estimated 2,511 slaves were owned by Cherokees.[42] But Cherokee loyalties during the Civil War did not simply fall along lines of class, or according to who did or did not own slaves. Racism proved an important factor in shaping wartime allegiances in that they presaged what a post-war world should look like. For instance, Cherokees could be against slavery, but they could also be against blacks remaining in the Cherokee Nation. As historian William McLoughlin observes, "the Loyal Cherokees shared the views of most northern whites at the time. They were willing to end the institution of slavery but unwilling to allow civil or social equality to former slaves, and they were not eager to have them living in their vicinity."[43]

When the Cherokee Nation finally became drawn into the trans-Mississippi theater of war, their world suddenly, and dramatically, changed. The Battle of Pea Ridge in Missouri, which took place between March 6 and 8, 1862, was one of the most significant events in the Cherokee contribution to the war. A coalition of Cherokee forces including Colonel Stand Watie's Cherokee Mounted Volunteers fought for the Confederate cause under the leadership of General Pike.[44] The Battle of Pea Ridge involved the first large-scale use of Cherokee troops outside of the Cherokee Nation in Indian Territory. The deployment of Cherokee troops in this fashion was in direct violation of the treaty agreement John Ross had signed with the Confederacy. However, with the battle to control the trans-Mississippi West intensifying, Confederate strategists believed it was essential that Cherokee soldiers serve outside the Cherokee Nation's borders.

The fighting at Pea Ridge was bloody and intense, and produced numerous captives of war. Union soldier William S. Burns, who spent one evening during the campaign huddled under a table with a comrade from New York, wrote to his brother, Charles Burns, "I have a bright, active 'contraband' who takes good care of me, and mine. I *captured* him at the Battle of Pea Ridge."[46] The Battle of Pea Ridge was, as one soldier wrote in a letter to his sister, a "big Battle," a fact that may explain his boastful tone in describing an effort that "whipped them out badly."[47]

The Confederates' defeat at Pea Ridge not only foretold the fate of their cause in the trans-Mississippi, it also exposed the Confederacy's military leaders in the West to harsh criticism.[48] When news of Pea Ridge reached Southeastern newspapers, it confirmed the beliefs of many white Southerners that American Indians, like African Americans, lacked the requisite physical and mental qualities to perform with discipline and honor in battle. White Americans in both the North and South harbored suspicions that Native Americans were ill-disciplined and predisposed to acts of savagery. These perceptions appeared to be confirmed when reports began to surface of Indian warriors indiscriminately taking scalps from dead soldiers. The *New York Tribune* accused General Pike, for instance, of leading an "Aboriginal Corps of Tomahawkers and Scalpers."[49] According to one historian, however, the "small amount of scalping in the battle" was committed by soldiers in the First Mounted Cherokee Regiment, a command under the direction of John Ross's (reportedly pro-Union) brother-in-law James Drew.[50] Regardless of who was responsible for the alleged scalpings, reporting of such acts fanned the flames of anti-Indian racism in the trans-Mississippi theater. One Union soldier spoke for many white Northerners (and Southerners, for that matter), when he recalled the capture of two of the "infernal Indians . . . We have seen one that was killed. I wish it had been the last of that race."[51]

The residents of the trans-Mississippi West immediately recognized the importance of Pea Ridge. Local commemorations became commonplace, and continued during the ensuing years even as fighting for control of the trans-Mississippi West intensified.[52] The First Battle of Newtonia in September 1862, for example, was a bloody confrontation that saw American Indians fighting for both the Union and Confederate armies.[53] Further violence and bloodshed followed Newtonia, with the Battle of Locust Grove, just north of Tahlequah, bringing the battlefront to the doorstep of the Cherokee Nation's capital.[54]

Guerrilla fighting, frontier skirmishes, and acts of outright terrorism also punctuated the Civil War experience for American Indians, blacks, and whites in the trans-Mississippi West.[55] Such violence was not new to the American frontier, but in Arkansas, Iowa, Kansas, Missouri, and Indian Territory during the Civil War, the violence served to magnify white racial suspicions about Indian savagery.[56] For example, in northern Iowa, so-called Indian troubles resulted in reports of "a fight between two soldiers and eight or ten Indians, near Peterson, Clay County, Iowa."[57] Such incidents were not official battles, but they were part of the Civil War's contribution to a long American tradition of conflict between American Indians and people of European descent.

However, such violence was not confined to confrontations between whites and Native Americans. Pin Indians and Standuaitie Party members brutalized each other during the Civil War. The intensity of this violence reflected deeply held political divisions that had existed since the removal era. One eyewitness, T. J. Mackey, offered a graphic report on the nature of the violence perpetrated by Cherokees. Mackay's account was a vernacular rendering of nineteenth-century narratives about Indigenous savagery, declaring: "The Indians of the Cherokee nation that adhered to the government of the United States were termed Pin Indians; those that adhered to the south were termed the Standuaitie party. When they take each other prisoners in battle they invariably subject them to torture, to the dislocation of limbs, the cutting of the joints, commencing with the fingers and toes, until the body is dismembered. That was practiced by the full-bloods, not by the mixed-bloods."[58]

Formal battles within Indian Territory were no less intense. Major battles occurred in all the tribal nations, with the largest occurring at Honey Springs in the Creek Nation, some twenty-five miles south of Fort Gibson, on July 17, 1863. The Battle of Honey Springs was the largest Civil War battle to take place in Indian Territory. The Union troops, led by Major General James G. Blunt, comprised a tri-racial force of whites, blacks, and American Indians totaling 3,500. Fighting against the 6,000 Confederate soldiers was intense and resulted in the destruc-

Table 1: Major Civil War Battles in Indian Territory

Tribal Nation / District	Battle & Year of Battle
Cherokee Nation	Caving Banks, 1861
	Cowskin Prairie, 1862
	Fort Wayne, 1862
	Locust Grove, 1862
	Webbers Falls, 1863
	Cabin Creek, 1st, 1863
	Cabin Creek, 2nd, 1864
Cherokee Outlet	Chustenahlah, 1861
Creek Nation	Fort Davis, 1862
	Honey Springs, 1863
Choctaw Nation	Backbone Mountain, 1863
	Perryville, 1863
	Muddy Boggy, 1864
	Boggy Depot, 1863
Leased District	Tonkawa Massacre, 1862

Source: Clarissa W. Confer, *The Cherokee Nation in the Civil War* (Norman: University of Oklahoma Press, 2007).

tion of the Texas Road Bridge, on a vital artery used by both whites and Cherokees traveling between the Cherokee Nation and Texas prior to the war. In the wake of such damage to infrastructure and extensive loss of lives, Union forces achieved a stirring victory. The Confederate forces did endeavor to regroup, but the war was slipping out of their control in the trans-Mississippi. Starting in September 1863, a string of Confederate Indian surrenders opened a new, even more dangerous phase in the war as organized military campaigns were superseded by guerrilla warfare and raiding.[59]

While the Battle of Honey Springs proved to be the turning point in the Civil War in Indian Territory, the people of the Cherokee Nation also witnessed a significant number of battles between 1861 and 1865, as table 1 indicates.[60] In large part, the frequency of battles in the Cherokee Nation was a product of its geography. Bordering Arkansas to its east, the Choctaw Nation to its South, and Missouri and Kansas to the north, the Cherokee Nation was an important crossroads in the trans-Mississippi theater of war. By the end of the war, the strategic value of the Cherokee Nation was evident in the massive destruction of property. Of all the great homes owned by wealthy Cherokees, and whites married to Cherokees, prior to the war, only the home of George Murrell remained standing in 1865.

Few Cherokees could ignore the potential for such destruction by the time fighting broke out at Webbers Falls in 1863. Webbers Falls was in the heart of Cherokee slaveholding country in the southern portion of the Nation. That battle, a crushing defeat for the Confederacy, prompted Cherokee slaves who had not yet absconded from their bondage to seek refuge behind Union lines.[61] It also resulted in a flurry of political maneuvering among those old political rivals, the pro-South Treaty Party faction and the Ross Party supporters. Indeed, John Ross, who had been arrested by Union troops and quickly paroled, recognized the magnitude of the situation. As early as September 1862, long before the disastrous Battle of Webbers Falls, Ross visited Washington and emphasized the loyalty of the vast majority of Cherokees.[62] He hoped that by underscoring the Cherokee people's allegiance to the Union, he would induce President Lincoln to authorize aid to the Cherokee Nation.[63]

Ross spent much of the war with his wife and her white family in Philadelphia. From the safety of his wartime residence, Ross worked to reassure Lincoln of the Cherokee people's support for the Union. Ross's transformation from neutrality, to Confederate ally, to Union loyalist was not simply an open acknowledgement of the Cherokee Nation's vulnerable political and economic position; it reflected Ross's clear recognition that the Civil War threatened the very survival of the Cherokee people and their political homeland in Indian Territory. As the war continued in the trans-Mississippi West, Cherokee properties were looted and destroyed, crops and arable farmland pillaged, and thousands of Cherokee refugees were displaced from their homes, forced to cling to life in one of the many putrid refugee camps that dotted the Missouri and Kansas landscape. These wartime refugees gave rise to what Cherokee leaders later called the "refugee business," a crisis that threatened to destroy any collective sense of Cherokee identity in the trans-Mississippi West.

Wartime Refugees

The Civil War devastated Cherokee communities. As many as 10,000 people, or one-fifth of the Indian Territory's population, died during the Civil War because of disease or starvation. Of the approximately 1,018 American Indians who enlisted and fought for the Union, three-quarters lost their lives due to disease. And the Western Cherokee population, which was approximately 21,000 at the beginning of the war, fell to between 13,500 and 14,000 by war's end.[64] In the face of such losses, reconnecting the bonds of kinship in American Indian communities would not be easy. Just how difficult this process would be was evident in the large orphan population that emerged among the Cherokees following the war. This troubling demographic development drew attention to the seriousness of the challenges associated with refugees.[65] So physically distressed were Cherokee refugees—and all American Indian refugees of war, for that matter—that Colonel William A. Phillips, the Union's Commanding officer for Indian Territory and Western Arizona, noted as much in his official correspondence. Phillips, a Scottish immigrant who had settled in Kansas, was more than familiar with privation on the American frontier. He was not prepared, however, for what he witnessed among Cherokee refugees. In a letter to the Secretary of the Interior in May 1861, Phillips implored the federal government to assist the refugees, insisting that relief efforts on behalf of "Cherokee women and children by agents and superintendents, are entirely inadequate."[66]

During the Civil War there were refugees throughout the United States, many of them in its trans-Mississippi territories. In Indian Territory, the first large-scale group of refugees coalesced under the leadership of the "loyal Creek," Opothleyohola. Opothleyohola attracted Creek, Seminole, Cherokee, and black refugees to his movement. Confederate officials characterized this movement as "pro-Union," although Opothleyohola and his followers seemed more concerned with finding refuge from the war in 1861 and 1862.[67] Pursued by Confederate troops under the command of Colonels James McQueen McIntosh and Douglas H. Cooper, Opothleyohola did attract Indian warriors to his cause, but the overriding hope of his followers was that they might escape the violence.[68]

Among Opothleyohola's followers were runaway slaves. During the war slaves ran away from plantations and farms owned by whites, Cherokees, Creeks, Choctaws, and Seminoles. One former Cherokee slave recalled that "a whole lot of Cherokee slaves run off at once."[69] Some followed charismatic leaders like Opothleyohola, others sought sanctuary behind Union lines, while still others failed to find the safety they longed for and returned to the plantations where they had once been enslaved.[70]

The emergence of large populations of orphans, refugees, and runaway slaves reflected the destructive effects of the Civil War on the social as well as the physical landscape of Indian Territory and the Cherokee Nation. Cherokee people scattered throughout the West in a desperate search for refuge from the violence, bloodshed, disease that warfare produced, and in the case of slaves, an escape from the enslavement that oppressed and circumscribed their lives. Official reports pointed out, however, that the Indian refugees hoped to return to their homes after the war.[71] Federal officials could ill afford to get ahead of themselves, though, because there were so many refugees that provisioning these populations prior to their return "home" would prove a massive undertaking. According to the Cherokee Agent of Indian Affairs: "There are many [Cherokees] who do not apply for provisions at all. And still a great many more, who live near the lines of Missouri and Arkansas, who have been robbed of every animal upon which to travel, and of their clothing, so that they have neither horses to ride, nor clothing to wear, while coming here to get provisions."[72]

The wartime refugee experience was fraught with difficulties.[73] During 1862, so-called "loyal Cherokees" sought refuge from guerrilla attacks by hastily migrating north. In towns such as Drywood, Kansas, and Neosho, Missouri, refugee camps sprang up.[74] In Kansas alone, the refugee population—Indian, white, and black—was reported to be as many as 15,000 to 17,000.[75] The Third Cherokee Home Guard, a regiment supported by John Ross, administered the camps and oversaw a famous council meeting at Cowskin Prairie in 1863 that abrogated the Cherokee Nation's treaty with the Confederacy.[76] The Cowskin Prairie meeting also refocused attention on the political divisions between Ross and Watie. Confederate Cherokees were deposed, and Ross and acting chief Thomas Pegg received confirmation as the leaders of the Cherokee Nation.

Despite these developments, the Cherokee Nation and its border-lands with Kansas, Arkansas, and Missouri remained unstable. Some 8,000 to 10,000 refugees fled from their homes to those borderland zones in search of sanctuary from the violence that blighted Indian Territory.[77] In Kansas and Missouri, crowded refugee camps comprised Cherokees, former Cherokee slaves, and whites who had intermarried with Cherokees. Some of these refugees enlisted in Union regiments, served as Union scouts, and offered invaluable information about Confederate troop movements.[78] Many more, however, endured "extreme suffering" and became pawns in a dangerous political power game during 1863 and 1864 that included the federal government and the Confederate administration, the Republican and Democratic Parties, and the Ross and Watie factions among the Cherokee.[79] At stake was economic and political power. As the Union army worked to assure its military ascendency in the trans-Mississippi theater, Republican and Democratic politicians entered the presidential election year of 1864 batting around accusations of graft and corruption in the provision of supplies to refugees.[80]

An issue with great political significance for the future of the Cherokee Nation was who would exercise sovereignty over the Cherokee political homeland once the war ended.[81] In private correspondence sent from Quitman, Texas, in August 1863, W. J. Deupree, Stand Watie's surgeon, captured the fears of Cherokees of all political persuasions. Deupree worried that when the war ended there would exist no nation to govern the Cherokee people and exercise sovereignty on their behalf. He wrote, "Our land is lost[. R]efugees from every state. It does not require a philosopher to fore tell what deplorable future is in store for us, our wives & children. Woes, arrests, wretchedness & misery of every hue. Rapes, Rapine by the Feds & our negroes & every insult & disgrace that ever was offered a people we will have to bear."[82]

The future clearly looked bleak. Still, even as Union forces gained control of the trans-Mississippi, Watie and his supporters entered into both political and military battles against Ross men, Union soldiers, and Pin Indians. Watie's men sustained themselves by foraging, skirmishing, and seeking out booty.[83] The family and friends of Confederate Cherokees spent a significant part of the war as refugees. Unlike the poor and pro-Union Cherokees huddled in refugee camps in Kansas and Missouri, wealthy slave-owning Cherokee families often sought refuge in Arkansas or Texas. Prior to the war, many of these families had lived in the southern part of the Nation, or on the eastern edge of the Cherokee Nation along the border with Arkansas. A combination of entrepreneurship and the exploitation of slaves helped Cherokee families in these regions prosper. Samuel Harnage, for example, recalled that his father was a Texas Cherokee who migrated to the Cherokee Nation in 1839. Settling on the western bank of the Arkansas River, the Harnage family became prosperous cattle drovers and farmers, growing cotton, wheat, and corn.[84]

When the war came to Indian Territory, wealthy Cherokee families hoped to wait out the violence by temporarily lodging with friends and relatives with whom they had long had business or familial relationships in the Choctaw Nation, Arkansas, and Texas. Stung by their sudden loss of social and economic status, and feeling aggrieved at being exposed to "cold and hunger," the family members of Cherokee merchants, property owners, and slave holders migrated to Arkansas or Texas and waited eagerly for the war to end.[85]

From positions of economic and social privilege before the war, Confederate Cherokee families descended to the ignominy of refugee hardships during the Civil War.[86] Many, however, were spared the worst sufferings of the refugee camps and found safe havens in Texas, where family and friends provided temporary homes, and parents had the option of sending children to school if family finances allowed. Among the wealthy Cherokees who found refuge in Texas was Stand Watie's family. With her husband and eldest son, Saladin, engaged in active service, Watie's wife left behind a world of privilege in the southern portion of the Cherokee Nation and took their children to the relative safety of Texas.[87] The hardships experienced by the Watie family never

approached those endured by Cherokees and freed people in the refugee camps of Missouri and Kansas, but they did take their toll. In a letter
dated June 12, 1864, Mrs. Watie implored her husband to leave the service and return to the family. Stand and Saladin must, Mrs. Watie rea-
soned with her husband, forget about fighting and consider the needs
of their family. She concluded, "as for the Nation I believe it is bound
to go to the dogs and the more one does to save it the more blame they
will have to bear."[88]

Just as slave-owning whites in the Southeast struggled to come to
terms with the impact the war was having on their slave populations,
so wealthy Cherokees lamented their sudden loss of comfort and social
standing. Slave-owning Cherokees puzzled over the behavior of slaves
they had assumed were utterly devoted to them. Ella Coody Robinson,
whose wealthy family was the embodiment of a mobile, cultured, and
politically influential Cherokee elite, felt bewildered when slaves began
to run away from their masters. "The negroes had gone crazy and were
no help," Robinson recalled after a group of slaves absconded. Robinson's family had once been prominent members of Cherokee society at
Webbers Falls, but the war left them refugees. Embittered by her wartime displacement, Ella Robinson refused to return to Webbers Falls
after the war.[89] For Cherokees rich and poor, then, the Civil War seemed
to have ushered in the end of life as they knew it. The future did not look
promising.

Cherokees and the Civil War in the Southeast

When North Carolina seceded from the Union in May 1861, the North
Carolina Cherokees found themselves in an uncertain legal and political
position. They claimed, as one scholar points out, "to be Citizen Indians,
yet not having their person or lands protected under state and federal
laws."[90] Moreover, Cherokees in this impoverished pocket of what they
identified as their ancient homeland had long relied on the patronage
of Colonel William H. Thomas, an adopted Cherokee who now led the
North Carolina Cherokees into war. Given this background, the Civil
War raised serious questions about the future of Cherokee communities
in western North Carolina.

Thomas decided in May 1861 to form the "Junaluska Zoaves," named after the late Chief Junaluska. Junaluska had lived a diasporic life, traveling West as part of the forced emigration in 1838 and subsequently journeying back to his ancestral homeland in the cis-Mississippi. Thomas's Zoaves, which originally comprised two hundred warriors, were organized to protect the Cherokee homeland in the Great Smoky Mountains that Junaluska had been so determined to see again. The Confederate Cherokees who served in the Junaluska Zoaves therefore had little interest in the South's cause. They took up arms for the Confederacy out of loyalty to Thomas and a determination to protect their homeland.[91]

By 1862, however, the Confederate Cherokees in North Carolina were being drawn into the wider conflict of the Civil War. Thomas, whose political ambitions for elected office in Richmond, the Confederate capital, had faltered, formed "Thomas's Legion of Indians and Highlanders," a "mountaineer troop" of about 2,800 men that served primarily as a "home guard." Its ranks included whites and "every able-bodied man in the [Cherokee] tribe."[92] Not until April 1862, when the multiracial Cherokee George Washington Morgan mustered Cherokee warriors into three-year enlistments, did cis-Mississippi Cherokees officially take up arms for the Confederate cause. Among the noted Cherokees to serve in one of the two companies Morgan helped to form were Peter Greybeard; Astoogatogeh, Junaluska's grandson; Enola, a Methodist preacher and "all-purpose conjurer;" and Swimmer, who became a key informant for the Smithsonian Institution's James Mooney during the late nineteenth century.[93]

The Cherokee townships of western North Carolina that these fighting Cherokees hoped to protect were culturally syncretic and ethnically diverse, far more so than postbellum anthropologists like Mooney later assumed. As we have seen, this diversity was evident in the decades leading up to the Civil War. Once the war broke out, it was evident that Cherokee warriors found inspiration from their culturally syncretic backgrounds. Enola, for example, blended Methodism and traditional conjuring in preparation for battle. When James Mooney looked back on the Civil War era from the vantage point of the late nineteenth century he failed to see such syncretism. Instead he recorded evidence of cultural persistence during the Civil War. Mooney claimed:

> The war . . . brought out all the latent Indian in their nature. Before starting to the front every man consulted an oracle stone to learn whether or not he might hope to return safely. The start was celebrated with a grand old-time war dance at the townhouse on Soco, and the same dance was repeated at frequent intervals thereafter, the Indians being "painted and feathered in good old style."[94]

Mooney's characterization of Cherokee preparations for battle depicted Cherokee warriors seeking strength in the cultural and religious traditions that they believed had always been part of warrior culture.[95] Given the remote geography of the Cherokees living in and around Quallatown in North Carolina, ethnographers understood Indigenous traditions to be unchanging because of their perceived isolation from the outside world. In fact, this isolation was by no means complete. For over two centuries, Cherokees in this part of North America had actively adapted a myriad of external social and cultural influences in the hope of striking a balance between the continuity of traditions and the economic and political innovation they needed to survive in settler colonial America.

Irrespective of how the Junaluska Zoaves prepared for battle, what is clear is that they served in western North Carolina and parts of East Tennessee during the first year of the war. Thereafter Thomas's Legion marched to the Cumberland Gap where, in September 1862, they became part of Kirby Smith's Kentucky campaign. The Confederate Cherokees fought in the battles of Baptist Gap and Strawberry Plains. Like the Cherokees and other Indian warriors fighting in the trans-Mississippi theater, the "Indians belonging to a company of Cherokees," as they were described by one correspondent, allegedly engaged in scalping. Some sources suggested that as many as four hundred Union scalps were taken at Baptist Gap, a figure that likely owes more to the racial stereotypes that shaped the reporting on Indian warriors than to actual events. Nonetheless, in the immediate aftermath of the battle of Baptist

Gap, the Cherokee were ordered not to engage in such practices because "this was a christian [sic] war."[96]

Given the inconsistent nature of the evidence, it is unclear whether the Confederate Cherokees did actually engage in scalping at Baptist Gap. According to the unofficial chronicler of Thomas's Legion, William Stringfield, no instances of scalping ever occurred.[97] Springfield insisted that he "can truthfully declare that in all the Conduct of the Indians towards the Federals—or their families—they Were always humane and generous—no excesses of any Sort—even to those of ordinary white Soldiers."[98]

In the following year, the fortunes of Thomas's Legion followed the same trajectory as those of the Confederate war effort generally. At Gatlinsburg, Tennessee, December 1863, the Fifteenth Pennsylvania Cavalry, led by Colonel William Jackson Palmer, attacked Thomas's Legion, taking them utterly by surprise. One Cherokee soldier was captured and three wounded, while the remainder fled into the nearby mountains for protection. Thereafter, Thomas's Legion was on the defensive.[99] With great satisfaction, one Union soldier observed that the "skirmishes" with "the Squaws" at Gatlinsburg sent Thomas's Legion running, "scattering [them] over the ridges to the Great Smoky Mountains."[100]

Indeed, the fortunes of the Confederate Cherokees in the Southeast were rapidly declining. Substantial Cherokee losses at the Battle of Deep Creek confirmed this assessment. But if Thomas's Legion had looked forward to returning home to Quallatown, their spirits must surely have sunk even lower when they arrived to find a scene bordering on horrific. Women and children were starving at the Qualla Boundary Reservation. Most survived on weeds and bark. Some, like their Cherokee cousins in the trans-Mississippi West, had fled the starvation, traveling southward in the hope of finding shelter and, more urgently, food to sustain them and nourish their children.[101] Their plight touched the sympathies of Cherokees throughout the diaspora, included John Ross. In August 1864, Ross wrote to the Department of the Interior requesting aid to Cherokee refugees in the East, imploring the Secretary of the Interior to help these "unfortunate people."[102] No response was immediately forthcoming. These were harrowing times for North Carolina Cherokees.

For most Cherokees, the Civil War was both disruptive and devastating. Given that approximately 400 Eastern Cherokee men (out of a total population of roughly 1,000) saw active duty during the war, it is not unreasonable to assume that virtually every Cherokee family in North Carolina lost loved ones, or had family members flee as refugees.[103] The Civil War therefore put enormous strain on kinship networks, and the refugee experience for the North Carolina Cherokees produced discernible changes in social relationships and cultural patterns. For example, refugee slaves, now added to the families of Cherokees intermarried to either whites or blacks already living in Qualla townships, altered the complexion of Cherokee communities and forced kinship groups to innovate in the ways that traditional cultural beliefs and practices influenced the meaning and purpose of daily life.

Disease also had an impact on Cherokees living in North Carolina. In addition to seeing about 400 men go into military service during the war, the community lost approximately 300 members in a smallpox epidemic at the close of the war.[104] Thomas sought medical assistance for the Cherokees, but the vaccine brought to western North Carolina proved ineffective. Thus, when Cherokee refugees did begin to return home, they found townships in ruin, kinship ties severed due to death, in battle or from disease, and a general sense of confusion, anger, and frustration.[105] In the homeland in the Great Smoky Mountains, the American Civil War brought Cherokee society to its knees.

The multiple issues arising from wartime refugee experiences touched not only virtually every North Carolina Cherokee, but Cherokees throughout the diaspora. The social, cultural, and political issues that emerged among the Cherokees following the war were manifold. They included: loss of property; the desire to return "home;" the search for loved ones and kin; the destruction of basic infrastructure and agricultural land; the threat of death from illness and disease; and the need to care for children of different racial and ethnic backgrounds left orphaned and malnourished. With John Ross's death and burial in Delaware in 1866 (his body was later exhumed and relocated back to the Cherokee Nation in Indian Territory), the Cherokee people had to face these issues without the leader who had guided them for almost forty years.[106]

For Cherokees, whether they lived in western North Carolina, in the political homeland of the Cherokee Nation in Indian Territory, or in diaspora on either side of the Mississippi, the legacy of the Civil War lived on well after the war ended.[107] Civil War refugees, and the Cherokees who had lost kin during the war, posed one of the greatest challenges.[108] In the decades following the war, both Cherokee and federal officials worked to rebuild Cherokee towns and to reestablish the legal status of Cherokees, whites, and former slaves within Cherokee communities.

The "Refugee Business"

T he Civil War displaced millions of people. On both sides of the Mississippi River, whites, Native Americans, and African Americans found themselves thrust into uncertain futures. For black Americans, the unease was temporarily mollified by the thrill of winning their freedom with the passage of the Thirteenth Amendment in 1865. However, for tens of thousands of Native people, the Civil War represented the greatest threat to their existence as Indigenous Americans since the era of removal in the 1830s. Cherokee leaders understood this. They recognized that the post-war migrations of black and white Americans to the geographical center of the United States posed a serious demographic challenge to their nation, so recently vanquished in war. The Cherokee Nation was also significantly diminished in its territorial holdings—namely the Cherokee Strip and the Cherokee Neutral Lands in Kansas—due to the treaty terms that Cherokee leaders grudgingly agreed to with the United States in 1866.[1]

This loss of land was a critical blow to the political homeland of the Cherokee diaspora. Prior to the war, a relatively clear geographical pattern was emerging in the distribution of Cherokees living in diaspora. Politically, the center of Cherokee power shifted west, to the Cherokee Nation in Indian Territory. This became the political homeland, with Cherokees residing in Indian Territory and in the nearby states of Texas,

Arkansas, Missouri, and Kansas. Slightly farther afield, a smattering of Cherokees resided in the mountain West and western states and territories such as Arizona. East of the Mississippi, Cherokees lived in Georgia, Tennessee, Kentucky, and western North Carolina. Finally, long-distance migrations saw people of Cherokee descent travel vast distances during the nineteenth century and reside in, for example, Virginia, Washington, DC, Connecticut, and New York along the Atlantic seaboard of the United States, and in California and Hawaii to the west. For the well-educated, wealthy, and politically ambitious Cherokees living far from the political homeland of the Cherokee diaspora in Indian Territory and the pre-removal homeland in the Woodland South, mobility became one of the hallmarks of a diasporic Cherokee identity during the late nineteenth century. But with Cherokee landholdings, particularly those in Indian Territory, once again under attack from the colonial forces of the United States and its citizens, the stable physical basis for the concept of Cherokee political and ancestral homelands came into question. Cherokees throughout the diaspora and in the homelands in the cis-and trans-Mississippi found themselves caught between the trauma of the past and the uncertainty of the future.

In the West, Cherokee leaders greeted the post-Civil War developments with a mixture of hope and trepidation. Their anxiety was stirred by wave after wave of "homesteaders," "sooners," and "boomers," predominantly white migrants who carried aspirations of building a life for themselves and their families on the "Unassigned Lands" of Indian Territory. The Unassigned Lands became part of Oklahoma Territory and were located to the south of the Cherokee Strip. While Elias C. Boudinot, a Cherokee lawyer, brokered the terms upon which the Unassigned Lands became part of Oklahoma Territory, the catalyst for the westward migration of "homesteaders" had occurred while the American Civil War still raged.[2]

In 1862, President Abraham Lincoln signed the Homestead Act.[3] This federal legislation provided what most Americans saw as an invitation to settle the West. And settle they did, throughout the last four decades of the nineteenth century. A kaleidoscope of people—Northern and Southern whites, freedpeople, and wartime refuges of every race, religion, and ethnic background—went west after the Civil War. And the Cherokee Nation, the political homeland to a diasporic people, was right at the center of this movement of human beings. By 1885, 25, 000 white people called the Cherokee Nation "home." Five years later, that number had increased to 140, 000.[4] Cherokee officials thus felt their Nation was under siege.[5] It was in this context that Cherokee, African Cherokee, and African American refugees of war struggled to survive, return "home," and rebuild family and community networks torn asunder by the war. In the decades between the end of the Civil War and the passage of the Dawes and Curtis Acts, in 1887 and 1898 respectively, Cherokee leaders on both sides of the Mississippi found themselves struggling to determine who was and was not Cherokee. As detailed in this chapter (and the chapter to follow), the question of Cherokee identity was no small matter in the late nineteenth century, for it touched on the economics, politics, and cultural connectedness of Cherokee people throughout the diaspora and in their respective homelands. Indeed, racial concepts of "blood," social status, and migration all became intertwined in the political and legal battles to define Cherokee citizenship (and identity more broadly) during the late nineteenth century. In the immediate aftermath of the American Civil War the prominent Cherokee leader W. P. Adair gave questions related to identity, social status, "blood," and migration in the trans-Mississippi a name: "the refugee business."[6]

Post-War Realignments

Adair's pithy description of the enduring social and economic problems caused by wartime refugees in and around Indian Territory belied the complexity and scope of the problem confronting Cherokee officials. The post-war principal chiefs—William Potter Ross (1866–1867 and 1872–1875), Lewis Downing (1867–1872), Charles Thompson (1875–1879), Dennis Bushyhead (1879–1888), and Joel B. Mayes (1888–1891)—all found their administrations struggling to meet the challenges of the "refugee business" as they simultaneously worked to rally Cherokees around ideals of national unity and social harmony. With the "the havoc of war" fresh in every Cherokee's memory, Princeton-educated William Potter Ross urged Cherokees to once again "become one people."

However, with overlapping waves of white, black, and Native American refugees and migrants assailing the land and resources of the Cherokee Nation, such unity was going to prove difficult to achieve.[7]

Ross believed that it was vital for the Cherokee National Council to put aside old factional differences in order to effectively meet the challenges being posed to them in Indian Territory. These challenges included large refugee populations, aggressive railroad corporations— who were clamoring to slice rail lines through the Cherokee Nation, thereby opening it to more non-Cherokee "intruders"—and a diverse ethnic, racial, and socioeconomic mix of migrants heading west with dreams of starting a new life.[8] In their efforts to minister to the needs of wartime refugees, and to exclude "intruders" with no rights to settle on Cherokee lands, the National Council's first important task was to define the legal grounds upon which one might claim a Cherokee identity.

After the Civil War, post-war politics, the loss of land in the treaty of 1866, migration, re-settlement, intermarriage, and cultural exchange all complicated the "traditional" parameters for what it meant to be Cherokee.[9] Cherokee leaders were left with the challenge of finding the right formula of laws and public policy to ensure that anyone with a genuine claim to Cherokee identity would not be unfairly or arbitrarily excluded from the "Cherokee family." For example, how was the Cherokee National Council to understand Cherokee identity in the cis-Mississippi following the federal government's recognition of the Eastern Cherokees' separate tribal status in 1868 (and their subsequent legal efforts to clarify the basis for land title at the Qualla Reservation in 1894)?[10] Would Cherokee laws make it possible for people to travel and visit friends or kin in either the trans-Mississippi or cis-Mississippi worlds? How were Cherokees, many thousands made refugees by the Civil War, to reconstitute the frayed and, in some cases, severed, family and kinship ties that not only defined Cherokee identity but were also vital to the economic health of their communities? Was it even possible to repair kinship ties as Cherokees struggled just to sustain life in the refugee camps of southern Kansas and Missouri? At war's end, nothing was certain.

What was certain was that after the war the Cherokee remained a literate people. While English was the primary language for most Cherokees in the late nineteenth century—and the language of instruction in the Cherokee public schools and seminaries—Sequoyah's syllabary continued to instill a sense of cultural pride. Cherokee "traditionalists" in both North Carolina and Indian Territory kept the Cherokee language alive, just as they kept traditional cultural beliefs and practices meaningful in Cherokee life through contemporary interpretations. More importantly for a diasporic people, Cherokees maintained a connection to their Indigenous identity by developing a rich epistolary tradition and culture of written storytelling (*kanohesgi* or *kanohesginu*, which refers to historical storytelling). Writing became a means for Cherokees to record ancient traditions, define political identities, argue legal cases, craft their own histories, and maintain connections with Cherokee people throughout the diaspora. Writing from California, John Rollin Ridge observed that a "prodigious memory" went into Native storytelling, as evidenced by the fact that an Indian chief could recount "the history and main features of all the treaties, French, English, and American."[11]

In the wake of the Civil War, literacy and interpretive skills helped Cherokee political leaders to define Cherokee citizenship and defend the Cherokee Nation's sovereignty in Indian Territory. For individuals, literacy skills, a good grasp of Cherokee laws, and clear recollections of family genealogy all played an important part in nurturing family and kinship ties, and by extension, their Cherokee identity.

On both sides of the Mississippi, however, the years immediately after the war were characterized by disease, death, and displacement. These were not ideal circumstances in which to reconnect severed kinship ties or nurture Cherokee identities. Federal reports offer glimpses of just how bad the situation was for Cherokee and freedmen refugees when they tell of guerrilla fighters (or "bushwhackers"), Ku Klux Klansmen, and western outlaws adding to the social instability of Kansas, Missouri, Arkansas, Texas, and Indian Territory.[12] Despite a joint resolution passed by the United States Congress in April 1867 appropriating funds "to prevent starvation and extreme want" among vulnerable refugees in the South and Southwest, the federal government's response to the poverty among postwar refugees proved inadequate.[13] As a result, philanthropists such as the Quaker Elizabeth Comstock administered to the needs of African American and Native American refugees in the

West, while Cherokees in the cis-Mississippi were left to weigh the risks and benefits of remaining on their ancient homelands or heading west in the hope of reestablishing kinship bonds in the Cherokee Nation.[14]

Land was vitally important to Cherokees who hoped to rebuild their homes and provide for families, either at the Qualla Reservation in North Carolina or in the Cherokee Nation in Indian Territory. Holding onto that land, however, proved a difficult task in the postbellum decades. As a result, genealogy, or the rhetoric of "blood," became increasingly important to Cherokee identity.[15] In particular, "blood" and proof of a longstanding territorial connection to either the "Old Nation" prior to removal or the Cherokee Nation in Indian Territory became important factors in the official determination of the right to legally call oneself Cherokee.[16]

Legal claims to Cherokee citizenship occurred as old political factions in the Cherokee Nation began a series of political realignments following John Ross's death in 1866.[17] For example, the Downing (or "Union") Party attracted to its ranks a large constituency of "full-blood" subsistence farmers, who helped the party dominate Cherokee politics in the post-war decades. Its opponents, the National Party, included well-known Cherokees such as Dennis Bushyhead and William Potter Ross. Significantly, politics in the Cherokee Nation during the late nineteenth century was often punctuated with racial and cultural divisions between "full-bloods" (most gravitating toward the Downing Party) and "half-breeds," (the vast majority filling the ranks of the National Party).[18]

Lewis Downing (Lewi-za-wau-na-skie) understood the vital importance of political stability within the Cherokee Nation. He witnessed post-war political realignments from his position as principal chief of the Cherokee Nation in 1866 and between 1867 and 1872. Downing was born in eastern Tennessee in 1823, of mixed racial ancestry. His mother, Susan Daugherty, was the daughter of an Irish immigrant, Cornelius Daugherty, and a Cherokee mother. Lewis's father, Samuel Downing, was also a so-called mixed-blood, the son of Major John Downing and his Cherokee wife. Lewis Downing migrated west in 1839, accompanying the Baptist missionary Evan Jones and the Cherokee minister Jesse

Bushyhead. Downing eventually became a Baptist minister and maintained an active role in Cherokee social and political life in the decades leading up to the Civil War.[19] With the war over, and Downing occupying the position of principal chief, he knew better than most that wartime refugees, settlers, and Cherokees returning "home" would place enormous pressures on the Cherokee Nation's meager resources. He was also aware of the lurking threats just beyond the Cherokee Nation's borders, namely warfare across the Plains, the growth in white support for a territorial government in the western territories, and the movement of whites, African Americans, and non-Cherokee natives toward the Cherokee Nation.[20]

In a November 1868 letter to Anderson Sarcoxie, the assistant chief of the Delaware Indians, Downing warned that the Delaware should not attempt to migrate west of longitude 96 degrees. Even before their relocation beyond the Mississippi in 1838 and 1839, the Cherokee had a special relationship with the Delaware, seeing them as the "grandfathers of all the Indians."[21] Now, in the post-Civil War context, the Cherokee Nation had signed an agreement with the Delaware in 1867 in which the Cherokee Nation agreed to receive those Indians removed from Kansas by the federal government. While the relationship between the Delaware and Cherokee was often characterized by "bitterness," in the late 1860s Downing insisted that the Delaware and the Cherokee must focus their combined energy on creating a political sanctuary—a homeland—for all "Red people," not just Cherokees.[22] Reports that the federal army was committing atrocities against the Plains Indians—atrocities that included dismemberment and the use of hot irons "thrust through testicles or the anus"—certainly reached Native American leaders in Indian Territory during the late 1860s and 1870s, making Downing's concept of sanctuary all the more important.[23]

Similarly, Native leaders were conscious of the racial attitudes of men like James Farmer, who served in the US Army's Indian Service and wrote that "We on the frontier considered a dead Indian as a good Indian."[24] Downing, a brilliant and perceptive leader, did not turn a blind eye to the racist-inspired violence across the Plains and on the frontier.[25] As he explained to Sarcoxie:

> You see for yourself, that a fearful scene is being enacted in the destruction of the Red people of the Plains; and there is great prejudice existing in the minds of the whites against the Indians. The Indian Territory proper will, in all probability be the only Indian sanctuary that can be saved from the rapacity of the whites, and that only by the united efforts of the Indians themselves residing in it.[26]

Who should have access to, much less the protection of, Downing's imagined sanctuary in Indian Territory was not clear. In the northeastern corner of the Cherokee Nation, Miami, Ottawa, Shawnee, Quapaw, Poria, Modoc, Wyandotte, and Seneca-Cayuga Indians occupied tiny slivers of land in a borderland region that abutted the Kansas and Missouri borders, a borderland zone dotted by numerous refugee camps. To the northwest of the Nation and along the Cherokee Outlet, Osage, Pawnee, Otoe-Missouria, Ponca, Kaw, and Tonkawa Indians occupied a confusing borderland region where Cherokees struggled to maintain sovereignty amid growing waves of white settlers from the East.

Not only were the borders of the Cherokee Nation proving to be incredibly porous, the regions around those borders were unstable political and diplomatic terrain in the decades after the Civil War. And as Downing pointed out in his letter to Sarcoxie, violence across the Plains threatened Indigenous people no matter where they lived in the trans-Mississippi West. One detail that Downing left out of his letter to Sarcoxie was the role played by Cherokee warriors in the violence against Plains Indians. The famous Buffalo Soldiers, for example, included not only African American soldiers redeployed after the Civil War, but black Seminoles, Tonkawa Indian scouts, and Cherokees.[27]

John Benjamin Townsend became one of the most notorious—though now largely forgotten—Indian fighters of the post-Civil War decades. Born in Texas in 1835 to a white father and Cherokee mother, Townsend, known to friends and family as a "half-breed," grew to "hate" the Plains Indians. Townsend's hatred stemmed from a family tragedy—Comanche warriors had killed his parents while he was still a youth. After serving for a brief period in the Confederate Army, Townsend relocated to the Agua Fria Valley in Arizona in 1863, where he became a rancher. He took his hatred of Plains Indians with him and acquired a reputation among locals for being an expert "Indian exterminator." Drawing on newspaper reports from the early 1870s, one historian has argued that Townsend "killed more Apaches than most pioneers had ever seen."[28] However, Apache warriors had the last word on Townsend, shooting and killing him in September 1873. Townsend always traveled "well armed, and prepared to hunt and kill game or Indians," so his death came as a shock to those who knew him. In fact, his sudden demise brought genuine sorrow to the settler community in the Agua Fria Valley. At his death, Townsend was remembered as a "halfbreed" Cherokee, originally from Texas, who fought on behalf of the Confederacy's noble but ultimately lost cause. He was also remembered for killing "36 Indians" in "fair and open combat" during his life in Arizona.[29] Such a defender of "civilized" society was going to be missed.

Frontier violence thus both affected, and was perpetuated by, people of Cherokee descent after the Civil War. Still, non-Cherokee Natives perceived the Cherokee Nation as a place of refuge amid the bloodshed of Plains warfare. This is why, for example, the Delaware delegation was joined by Munsee, or Christian Indians from Kansas, in petitioning Chief Downing for sanctuary and the rights of adopted citizens in the Cherokee Nation in 1867. Acting on feelings of "humanity and a sincere desire to do good to all civilized Indians," Downing acceded to their request.[30] Similar requests came from farther afield, from the Cherokees' cis-Mississippi cousins: the Eastern Band of Cherokees.[31]

The Civil War left the North Carolina Cherokees wracked by displacement, disease, and destitution. Although few in number, and perceived by both whites and leading Cherokees in the West as "traditionalists" and "backward," North Carolina Cherokees were racially and culturally diverse. In 1866, the North Carolina General Assembly granted those Cherokees resident in their state the status of "permanent residents," but they remained, as historian John Finger observes, "anomalous" in a state divided by the racial binary of black and white.[32]

Although the Eastern Band of Cherokees did not organize their own form of government until 1889, local court records indicate that they did own property, and their leaders began debating a number of significant social and political issues in the decades between 1866 and

1889.[33] In 1868, for example, a tribal council of Eastern Cherokee leaders convened at Cheoah. Presided over by the Eastern Band's principal chief, George Bushyhead, the council discussed how the needs of the poor could be met, and how to adequately determine which of its residents had sufficient Cherokee "blood" to legitimately be considered members of the Eastern Band. Like the leaders of the Cherokee Nation in the trans-Mississippi West, the Eastern Band's chiefs understood the importance of differentiating between acculturated Cherokees in North Carolina, Tennessee, Georgia, and Alabama, and whites "playing Indian" or claiming the rights of adopted Cherokees by virtue of intermarriage. Thus, two issues, poverty and uncertainty about Cherokee identity, characterized the early post-Civil War years among the North Carolina Cherokees.[34]

According to the roll of Eastern Cherokees made by Silas Swetland during his travels through Alabama, Georgia, Tennessee, North Carolina, and South Carolina, there were 2, 335 Cherokees living east of the Mississippi.[35] Determining which of these people qualified for citizenship in the Cherokee Nation or enrollment as a member of the Eastern Band of Cherokees proved a painstaking task. However, many of the Eastern Cherokees did not petition for membership in the Eastern Band after the Civil War, but turned to the West and petitioned for adoption into the Cherokee Nation in Indian Territory, and the legal protections that came with citizenship. In addition to people claiming Cherokee ancestry, applicants for citizenship in the Cherokee Nation after the Civil War included Shawnee, Delaware, Munsee, Creek, Choctaw, and Natchez people.[36] Prior to the war, the National Council of the Cherokee Nation had toyed with the possibility that the Eastern Cherokees and some non-Cherokee Indians could acquire "all the rights & privileges of Cherokee Citizenship."[37] After the Civil War, Shawnee and Delaware Indians cited the 1866 treaty as legal justification for their assumed status as adopted Cherokee citizens. Eastern Cherokees therefore had good reason to believe that their petitions stood on even firmer legal ground. Political rhetoric emphasizing that the "two branches of the Cherokee family" were united by "blood" offered comfort to Eastern Cherokees that their Western kin had not forgotten them. In 1869, a Cherokee delegation to Washington, DC, "publically invited all who were of Cherokee blood, to come to our country and settle as citizens."[38] The Cherokee Act of Union (1874) subsequently declared that the Eastern and Western Cherokees were once more united as "one body politic."[39]

For Eastern Cherokees, the possibility of becoming transnational travelers with the ability to enter and leave the political homeland of the Cherokee diaspora proved something of a false hope.[40] With the "intruder" problem in Indian Territory worsening over the course of the late 1860s and 1870s, the National Council began backing away from previous statements of unity with the Eastern Cherokees. For example, Principal Chief Charles Thompson dismissed the 1869 statement, insisting that that Cherokee delegation did not represent the official views of the National Council. The Cherokee Nation had never invited all people of Cherokee "blood" to apply for citizenship. In fact, only the North Carolina Cherokees, Thompson wrote, "were invited by our National Council, conditionally, to come among us, and under this, they alone have a right to citizenship."[41]

The key word in Thompson's statement was "conditionally." By the 1870s no Cherokee had a "natural" right to enter and leave the Cherokee Nation at will. Members of the National Council wanted human movement and migration into and out of the Nation monitored. Calls for such monitoring were inspired by the growing suspicions of Council members that some of the applicants for Cherokee citizenship were not Shawnee or Delaware Indians, much less Eastern Cherokees, but were in fact white "intruders."[42] With such suspicions gathering momentum and shaping the tenor of Cherokee political debate over citizenship, Cherokee officials from all parties felt that action was needed. By the time the Cherokee Nation entered its postbellum "golden age" in the mid 1870s, it had become more difficult than ever to acquire citizenship rights, either through adoption or on the basis of "blood."[43]

For Cherokee leaders in Indian Territory, then, the bureaucratic and legal challenges associated with determining who was and who was not Cherokee needed to be addressed immediately. As the movement of people into, and across, the Cherokee Nation continued during the 1870s and 1880s, the National Council's policing of Cherokee citizenship and the capacity of the Cherokee Nation to absorb a large and ethnically diverse population of refugees, migrants, and settlers came under close scrutiny by its leaders. Cherokee officials worried about the types of migrants clamoring for Cherokee lands in the Cherokee Strip, a sliver of land running along the southern border of Kansas that Elias Cornelius Boudinot had worked to preserve for the Cherokees, and in the "Unassigned Lands" in Kansas (which many Cherokees blamed Boudinot for losing). They also worried about the migrants and refugees moving into the Cherokee Nation from Arkansas and Texas.[44]

The Cherokee Nation's territorial holdings and borders became unstable borderland zones after the Civil War. Federal legislation, such as the Homestead Act, nurtured this instability, as did the words of President Andrew Johnson who encouraged settlers to migrate to the Cherokee Strip, "settle it up, and make a country of it."[45] White Americans did "settle it up," at the same time as late nineteenth-century railroad monopolists were working to connect the region to markets throughout the United States.[46] As Cherokee leaders saw the changes unfolding before them, the opening of Indian Territory to the outside world posed a serious challenge to their nation's "racial sovereignty," to borrow Hawaiian scholar J. Kehaulani Kauanui's provocative phrase.[47] Therefore defining the demographic parameters of Cherokee citizenship assumed heightened importance, as Cherokee leaders sought out efficient bureaucratic and legal mechanisms to preserve the genealogical integrity of Cherokees and safeguard the land base of the Cherokee diaspora's political homeland.[48]

The National Council's concerns about the impact of migration on the demographic make-up of the Cherokee Nation meant that no one was above suspicion. Everyone claiming to possess Cherokee "blood," even people from famous Cherokee families, were required to gain the Cherokee Nation's approval of their claims to Cherokee citizenship. This was the case for the children of Elias Boudinot and Harriet Gold. Their most famous son, Elias Cornelius Boudinot, was himself an educated, cultured, and well-traveled son of diaspora, residing at various times in Arkansas, the Cherokee Nation in Indian Territory, Washington, DC, and New York. Eleanor Susan Boudinot lived for a time in Washington, Connecticut, where she worked as a school teacher; Mary Harriette Boudinot lived in Manchester, Vermont, and attended Mount Holyoke

Figure 13: "Historical Caricature of the Cherokee Nation" (1886). Library of Congress Prints and Photographs Division, Washington, DC.

College (the school that provided the model for the Cherokee Female Seminary); William Penn Boudinot received his education in the town that had so terrorized his parents during their courtship—Cornwell, Connecticut; Sarah Parkhill Boudinot died in New England, apparently from tuberculosis; and Frank Brinsmade Boudinot, the youngest child, lived with his father's second wife, Delight Sergeant, in Manchester, Vermont.[49] The Boudinots were an interracial family born of the Cherokee diaspora. Their identities stemmed from their paternal connection to the ancestral homeland in Georgia, maternal ties to New England, and political links to the Cherokee Nation in Indian Territory. In these ways, the Boudinot children exemplified the lives of diasporic Cherokees, buffeted by American colonialism but resilient nonetheless.

From the lessons of the past, Elias Cornelius and his brother, William Penn, found the spiritual strength and inspiration to claim their Cherokee citizenship and defend Cherokee land rights. William Penn, for example, praised the Cherokee tradition of communal land ownership in 1889.[50] In the wake of the Dawes Act (1887), the Boudinots lamented the "defective" forms of government embraced by the Americans, but they knew they could not stop "the white man's axe."[51]

Elias Cornelius espoused dual citizenship—in both the Cherokee Nation and the United States—as legal protection for a modern Cherokee identity. Many decades before the Society of American Indians began championing a similar position for all Native Americans, Cornelius insisted that the "only salvation for our people" was a legal system that recognized the right of Cherokee people to be citizens of both the Cherokee Nation and the United States, just as a white American could be a citizen of "Ohio and a citizen of the United States at the same time."[52] Given that many Cherokees had ties to white families, friends, and business associates, Boudinot believed dual citizenship was a perfect fit for the diasporic lives that many Cherokees lived.

Boudinot's position on Cherokee citizenship (or legal identity) had three major implications. First, by maintaining access to a land base—such as the Cherokee Nation in Indian Territory and the Cherokee Strip—Cherokees retained access to land that they could apply for title in and cultivate for the economic benefit of the Nation.[53] Second, dual US-Cherokee citizenship provided legal recognition of the indigenous status of the Cherokees in North America, safeguarding Cherokee identity in perpetuity (if only as a legal category), and providing legal protections for people of Cherokee descent irrespective of their place of birth or residence in the United States. The third major element of Boudinot's position reflected how Cherokees used their literacy skills to craft historical narratives designed to support Cherokee land rights.[54] In southeastern Kansas, for example, a morality tale was unfolding for those Cherokees who shared Boudinot's determination to prevent further losses of Cherokee landholdings. Not unlike the Cherokee Strip, the Cherokee Neutral Lands in Kansas appeared to be slipping out of Cherokee control. This tiny sliver of land had previously been in the possession of the Osage Indians, who ceded the land to the United States government in 1827. The government in turn assigned it as Cherokee Neutral Lands. Following the Treaty of New Echota (1835), the federal government envisioned using the Neutral Lands to re-settle Cherokee migrants. But times had changed. White settlers now coveted that land, prompting the federal government to act to facilitate white settlement.

In the wake of the Civil War, the forces of history appeared to be against Cherokee aspirations of retaining the Neutral Lands.[55]

The Cherokee Neutral Lands were important to the post-Civil War history of the Cherokee diaspora for another reason: they were a part of the Cherokee diaspora's land base very near the Civil War-era refugee camps between the Neosho and Verdigris Rivers. Thus, a transient population of American Indian and African American refugees, along with aggressive white settlers (the latter represented by the Cherokee Neutral Land League) all vied for a piece of what had become highly prized settler colonial real estate.[56] The treaty between the federal government and the Cherokee Nation in 1866 thus included a provision in which the Cherokee relinquished any legal claims to the Neutral Lands. Like the Osage before them, the Cherokees had been forced into a political corner, due in large part to the Cherokee Nation's official alliance with the now-vanquished Confederate South during the Civil War, and thus they were compelled to cede the Neutral Lands to the United States. Cherokee authorities subsequently looked to the destitute refugees and assertive frontier settlers on Kansas's Neutral Lands with growing alarm in the decade after the Civil War.[57]

This alarm was heightened by the myriad of "intruders" entering the Nation.[58] A complex set of treaty terms dictated the way the Cherokees policed intruders. For example, where the 1866 treaty had declared former Cherokee slaves free and eligible for citizenship in the Cherokee Nation, federal officials cited Article 5 of the treaty of 1835 as the legal basis for Cherokee authorities to legally exclude "intruders" from the Cherokee diaspora's political homeland.[59] So who was an "intruder"? Were white settlers intruders? Could people of Cherokee descent be intruders? And could a liberal definition of "intruder" be used to deny African Americans and African Cherokees citizenship rights?

The definition of an "intruder" was not a simple matter, and over the course of the 1870s and 1880s these questions were fiercely debated. Federal government officials observed that Cherokee authorities identified a number of different classes of intruders. These included "whites," "whites married to Cherokees," "people claiming Cherokee blood," and "those claiming citizenship under Article 9 of the 1866 treaty"—such as "freedmen" and all "free colored persons" who returned to the

Cherokee Nation within six months of the treaty's signing. Cherokee court and council authorities thus insisted that they had the right, as a sovereign nation, to determine the lineage (or degree of Cherokee "blood") of such people once they entered the Cherokee Nation and petitioned for citizenship. Cherokee authorities, however, did not determine the citizenship of applicants based simply on "blood" as "race," as understood in Euroamerican culture and law.[60] Certainly race and racism figured in the decision making of Cherokee officials, but so too did older, more traditional notions of genealogical connections in a clan group—although surviving records suggest that traditional matrilineal genealogies were not strictly adhered to by Cherokee citizenship applicants. Basing their decisions on empirical data (namely, population "rolls") and qualitative evidence (specifically, eyewitness testimonies), Cherokee officials sifted through thousands of applications for Cherokee citizenship. The content of these applications often reached far back in time, and into the recesses of both personal and collective memory. These memories, when coherently organized, comprised stories of migration, clan adoption, and intermarriage from the eighteenth and into the late nineteenth century.

The federal government experienced difficulty understanding Cherokee court and council deliberations on these matters. As far as the US government was concerned, the Cherokee National Council held the position that "all Cherokees who did not remove with the body of the nation immediately subsequent to the treaty of 1835, are barred the privileges of citizenship therein, being expatriated under their law, having its origin as they alleged, prior to the treaty of 1817."[61] This was only partly true. As the following cases demonstrate, there was far greater flexibility in Cherokee legal deliberations about citizenship than the federal government—and the Cherokee Nation for that matter—was willing or able to acknowledge publicly.

Who Is Cherokee?

On January 7, 1878, Principal Chief Thompson appointed members to a newly formed Cherokee Citizenship Commission.[62] The National Council had established the Commission to deal with the growing number of petitions for Cherokee citizenship after the Civil War. Thompson and the National Council no doubt felt justified in the decision to appoint commissioners when a report revealed that claims for citizenship had increased each year since the Civil War ended and showed no signs of abating. According to the report, which Thompson read to the National Council in November 1878, 320 claims had been lodged that year. Cherokee officials feared that that number would continue to grow and could eventually reach 1,600 per year if something was not done to stem the flow of refugees and the migration of whites and freedmen into the Cherokee Nation and nearby states and territories.[63]

The National Council originally conceived of the Cherokee Citizenship Commission (CCC) in 1868 to sort through the citizenship claims brought by freedpeople. When the commission began its work, however, commissioners found that the scope of their deliberations needed to be much broader than they had originally intended.[64] The CCC was, as Principal Chief Dennis Bushyhead informed the National Council in 1886, an expression of "this Nation's right of self-government."[65] As a self-governing nation with a diasporic population, the CCC was charged with determining who could and could not claim to be a legal citizen of the Cherokee Nation, and who could enter the nation without being labeled an "intruder." As one correspondent to the *Cherokee Advocate* argued in May 1884, the Cherokee Nation, like any sovereign nation, had the right to determine who was fit for citizenship and to exclude those "ratbags, bobtails, and pawsuckers, that come here to prove their rights and cannot."[66]

Cherokee officials certainly received their share of citizenship applications from "ratbags." Prospective citizens of the Cherokee Nation often insisted that they were entitled to the legal rights and protections of a Cherokee citizen because their parents or grandparents had told them that they were descended from Cherokees. Ellen Dean said as much in a letter to the Secretary of the Interior in 1886, explaining, "My mother always taught me that I was a Cherokee Indian and was Entitled to Rights in the Cherokee Nation that I am now ready to lay our case before any court of justice."[67] In the minds of Cherokee officials, oral testimony or assertions of this nature did not represent adequate evidence of a Cherokee genealogy. As a result, claims based on oral family histories, undocumented intermarriages, family separations because of travel or migration, or being a "descendent of the tribe left in East Tennessee," were judged insufficient by Cherokee leaders to admit an individual to the family of Cherokee citizens.[68]

Many Cherokee leaders and lawyers insisted on establishing physical criteria for Cherokee citizenship. The language of "blood" characterized such calls. "Blood" was a murky term in the 1870s. It existed at the intersection of race and genealogy, and represented a shift away from traditional understandings of what it meant to be Cherokee and toward a racialized understanding of identity, focused on the physicality of racial identification. A growing chorus of Cherokee political leaders called for a move away from "traditional" adoption practices in preference for racialized conceptions of "blood purity" and mixture. In 1878, for example, Cherokee leaders William Adair and William Potter Ross argued that applicants for Cherokee citizenship must be able to prove their Cherokee lineage if they hoped to successfully lay claim to Cherokee lands and the privileges of citizenship.[69] In this sense, "blood," or, more correctly, a clear knowledge (and proof) of genealogy, had become a powerful component of tribal connection that entitled those who possessed it to lay claim to a racially exclusive form of Cherokee identity.

When the CCC began investigating doubtful citizenship cases, its members established a number of patterns that had enduring consequences for the legal definition of Cherokee citizenship. The first and most obvious pattern to emerge was the onus that the Commission placed on applicants to present a detailed account of family genealogy. To validate a Cherokee genealogy, documentary proof was needed, usually in the form of character witnesses who could prove "beyond doubt" that the applicant and his or her family were of Cherokee lineage, or had Cherokee "blood."[70] According to the Cherokee Nation's constitution, that genealogy should at a minimum include a Cherokee father and any "free" woman, excepting "the African race."[71]

The second significant development was the formalization of the link between territoriality and citizenship. Beginning in 1877, the Commission listed the geographical origin of applications for Cherokee citizenship. This level of detail in CCC record keeping reveals the extent to which the Cherokee diaspora had expanded by the late nineteenth century. Applications were received, for example, from New York City; Baltimore, Maryland; Nashville, Tennessee; Marietta, Georgia; New Burnside, Illinois; Osage Mills, Arkansas; Fort Worth, Texas; Grass Valley, California; and throughout Indian Territory.[72]

In the 1880s, controversy over the allotment of tribal lands intensified, and in 1888 the Cherokee National Council declared that Cherokee citizenship required permanent residence within the Nation.[73] The specter of allotment had potentially grave implications for diasporic Cherokees and the political homeland in Indian Territory. In anticipation of allotment, and its potential ramifications for the legal parameters of Cherokee identity, by the end of the 1880s the National Council identified two classes of Cherokees: those who lived in the Nation and could prove that they possessed Cherokee "blood"—that is, "blood" as a marker of a genealogical connection to a Cherokee forebear—and were free of the "taint" of "African blood"; and those living in diaspora who self-identified as Cherokee, and were recognized by the National Council as Cherokee citizens because they could prove their Cherokee genealogy.[74]

In this way, the bureaucracy associated with Cherokee citizenship after the Civil War bore all the hallmarks of other modern bureaucracies in settler colonies—it relied, in short, on the establishment of legal categories. These categories included people claiming to be Cherokee by "blood;" former Cherokee slaves and the descendents of Cherokee freedpeople (as promulgated in the 1866 treaty)—many of whom claimed to have at least one Cherokee parent, usually a father; individuals adopted into a Cherokee family or kin group; and couples in compliance with Cherokee intermarriage laws. In his annual message to the Cherokee National Council in November 1879, Principal Chief Dennis Bushyhead revealed that over the course of almost two years, commissioners had reviewed 416 cases, of which 67 were granted Cherokee citizenship.[75]

The system seemed to be working. Fraudulent claims were assessed and summarily dismissed. Those with clear and reliable evidence of Cherokee "blood" were "readmitted" to the status of citizen. Still, the petitions for Cherokee citizenship kept coming, making the

Figure 14: Files contained in the offices of the Cherokee Citizenship Commission, Tahlequah, Indian Territory. Research Division of the Oklahoma Historical Society, Oklahoma City.

Commission's task a daunting and unrelenting bureaucratic burden. The applicant pool was diverse. It included wartime refugees, individuals claiming citizenship rights through marriage to a Cherokee citizen, Cherokees living in diaspora, and former slaves and their descendants. Some of these cases provide a fascinating glimpse into how the legal structures used by the Cherokee Nation to deal with citizenship claims overlaid older notions of clan adoption. For example, applications from Shawnee Indians used the era's legal jargon while also presenting commissioners with the logic of group membership based on traditional adoption customs.[76]

The ethnic and racial background of applicants also corresponded with geography. For instance, in the Canadian, Illinois, Snake, and Cooweeskoowee Districts of the Cherokee Nation, the vast majority of the petitions for Cherokee citizenship came from blacks, single white men, and white men married to Cherokee women. Principal Chief

Charles Thomson lodged his complaints about the latter two groups with the United States government, writing to Indian Agent S. W. Marston in 1877 that there were

> very many white men, believing that residence alone, will give them a title to land in the Nation, in the event of it becoming a U.S. Territory, yet [for] a citizen of the Nation to obtain a permit for them, to labor for a month or so, and may continue by labor for that month, but on the strength of that permit, they remain in the Nation, for several months, doing their own business independently of law, while it is even said, that some of them, pay a bonus for a permit, and do not work at all.[77]

Thompson gave voice to the concerns of many Cherokees, both those in public office and private citizens, who believed that white men were trying to use the Cherokee legal system to incrementally dispossess Cherokees of their land, and undermine the territorial sovereignty of the Cherokee Nation in the process. This was a strategy that threatened not only the Cherokee diaspora's homeland, but the Cherokee people's existence as a "body politic."

The threat of white "intruders" in the Cherokee Nation became one of the most significant issues in Cherokee politics during the postbellum decades. Cherokee leaders implored federal officials to send military personnel to help them protect their borders from white "intruders."[78] But the Nation's borders proved much too porous, and the federal government was largely indifferent to Cherokee demands that its sovereignty be protected.[79] When the federal government did insert itself into Cherokee politics it was usually because of perceived Cherokee treaty violations in relation to the National Council's treatment of freedpeople. African Cherokee refugees, and African Americans formerly enslaved by Cherokee masters, returned to the Cherokee Nation in the years after the war, just as other wartime refugees did. Freedmen refugees appear to have been attracted to the Cooweescoowee District, in the north and west of the Nation, since from this district an unusually large number of freedpeople petitioned the CCC for acknowledgement of their Cherokee citizenship (see chapter 7 for a detailed analysis of Cherokee freedpeople).[80]

That said, the CCC did receive applications from all corners of the Cherokee diaspora, and not always from wartime refugees. Some of the more emotionally fraught cases involved applicants who resided east of the Mississippi and in cis-Mississippi locations considered part of the ancestral homeland of the Cherokee people. In North Carolina, Georgia, and Tennessee, many individuals claimed a Cherokee lineage, insisting that they possessed Cherokee "blood." Witness testimonials were designed to "prove beyond a doubt" such assertions, but they also revealed that Cherokee "blood" had been mixing with white and black "blood" for generations. In North Carolina, the end of the Civil War revealed the racial and ethnic diversity of Cherokee communities, communities long assumed to be socially and culturally homogeneous.

As in so many rural communities in the two decades after the Civil War, life in western North Carolina became increasingly interconnected to the outside world. The economic depression of the 1870s underlined this interconnectedness. Even though the North Carolina Cherokees had an overwhelmingly rural economy, many tribal members found employment in the local lumber industry. When the Depression hit the American economy in 1873, Cherokee communities felt the full force of its impact, and thus the North Carolina Cherokees were among the many Southerners who migrated west during these troubled economic times. Caught up in an "exodus" out of the South—a movement of people that historian James Gregory refers to as the Southern diaspora, and that included whites and African Americans—some North Carolina Cherokees turned to the Cherokee Nation in the hope of finding a new "home" where they could make a living and nurture kin relations.[81]

As economic refugees caught the "Kansas fever" and headed west in the 1870s, several hundred North Carolina Cherokees found themselves caught up in the crosscurrents of white and African American movement toward the Midwest and West. Eventually, these North Carolina Cherokees and white and African American migrants spilled into Indian Territory, joining the remaining Civil War refugees as they too sought out both kin and economic opportunity in the Cherokee Nation.

These overlapping migrations heightened the anxiety of Cherokee officials regarding the demographic composition of their nation.[82]

Between 1866 and 1893, Cherokee officials recognized two "main branches of our people": those residing in Indian Territory, and those living permanently in western North Carolina.[83] While such definitions appeared to overlook Cherokees living in states such as Tennessee or Georgia, this geographical binary represented the two main population centers for the Cherokee diaspora. Since removal in the late 1830s, these two population nodes had exchanged both temporary and permanent Cherokee migrants. The federal government recognized this flow of people after the Civil War, with officials often reporting on the arrival of North Carolina Cherokees in Indian Territory.[84]

The path that North Carolina Cherokees took to the Cherokee Nation was not always a straight route; indeed, it was often a crooked and indirect journey. Some officials in the Cherokee Nation viewed that indirect path with suspicion. Cherokee leaders worried that these North Carolina Cherokees were not Cherokees at all, but white men "playing the Indian." Alternatively, some in Cherokee government began questioning the bonds of responsibility between the Cherokee Nation and the Eastern Band. In 1875, William Ross and W. P. Adair argued a case in which they insisted that the Cherokee Nation should not recognize the rights of the North Carolina Cherokees to federal annuity funds owed to the Nation. Ross and Adair claimed that after John Ross left the "ancient soil" of the East and re-settled in the West he had held on to an unrealistic desire in "his heart to have his people cling together, and together to seek to retrieve their losses in the new "Western home." This was a noble objective, but legally irrelevant and economically unsustainable in the Cherokee Nation's present condition. Legally, those individuals and/or families who had chosen to live in diaspora, among the Eastern Band or outside the Cherokee Nation in Indian Territory, lost their citizenship under post-war Cherokee law. Moreover, decades of migration and intermarriage meant that the diasporic Cherokee population was now much larger than it had been prior to removal, and according to Ross and Adair, could not realistically be supported by the Cherokee Nation. As Ross and Adair saw things, the Cherokee Nation in the West had become a distinct "body politic." The Eastern Cherokee were not a part of that body, and thus had no legal claim to federal funds owed or disbursed to the Cherokee Nation in Indian Territory.[85]

To protect this Cherokee "body politic" in the trans-Mississippi West, in 1869 the National Council agreed to a joint resolution relating to the North Carolina Cherokees, and in November 1870 passed an act based on that resolution, declaring:

> Be it enacted by the National Council, that all such Cher-okees as may heretofore move into the Cherokee Nation, and permanently, locate therein, as citizens thereof, shall be deemed as Cherokee citizens, *Provided,* said Cherokees shall enroll themselves before the Chief Justice of the Supreme Court within two months after their arrival in the Cherokee Nation, and make satisfactory showing to him of their being Cherokees.[86]

To spread the word of this new act among Eastern Band and diaspora Cherokees, the National Council had the *Cherokee Advocate* newspaper print the new act in both Cherokee and English. The Act—and subse-quent efforts to disseminate it among Cherokees—was aimed especially at North Carolina Cherokees. As Principal Chief Thompson stated, the Act of 1870 showed that the "*bonafide* Eastern Cherokees . . . are all wel-come to come 'home' as they will see from the act of the National Coun-cil, passed in 1870."[87] And as the Act made clear, those Cherokees who did come "home" must bind themselves to the sovereign land of the Cherokee Nation.

The bureaucratic process and legal jargon that the Cherokee Na-tion's politicians and lawyers placed in front of North Carolina Chero-kees was nothing short of a labyrinth. These high legal and political bar-riers are understandable in the context of unstable refugee populations, and the seeming lack of assistance from the United States government in preventing fraudulent claims for financial assistance in the Chero-kee Nation, especially with regard to the "intolerable evil" of the white "intruders."[88] With mounting pressure on the territorial and financial resources of the Cherokee Nation, the legal machinery of the Nation began to ramp up efforts to protect those who were legitimate citizens in the Cherokee Nation from fraud, and to establish a legal bulwark against the waves of intruders who coveted the Cherokee people's communally owned lands.[89]

The National Council had quite a legal balancing act to perform. Despite the grudging recognition that "a number of Cherokees [were] still remaining in Georgia, North Carolina, Tennessee, and Alabama" in the decades before the Civil War, and that it "would not look well to take advantage of our citizens misfortunes," suspicion toward all migrants to the Cherokee Nation grew more intense as intruders vied for land and resources within the Nation's borders during the post-war decades.[90] Over the course of the 1870s, North Carolina Cherokees who petitioned the Nation for citizenship struggled to differentiate themselves from the vast "intruder" populations. In fact, the North Carolina Cherokees had to overcome growing perceptions of fraud. The Cherokee Nation's lawyers, for example, referred to North Carolina Cherokees as "self-styled Eastern Cherokees," and claimed that their desire to draw on the Cherokee Nation's relief funds constituted a "pretended claim, set up by the North Carolina Cherokees," who in remaining in the East had become citizens of their state of residence. By questioning the North Carolina Cherokees' right to federal funds through the Cherokee Nation, the Nation's lawyers latched onto a strategy that raised serious questions about the citizenship status of Eastern Band Cherokees. As officials for the Cherokee Nation saw things by the latter half of the 1870s, there existed no legal "provisions for *fragments of a tribe*, who refuse to comply with the terms of their treaties, either for money or lands."[91]

By the late 1870s, then, the members of the National Council of the Cherokee Nation maintained that the Eastern Band Cherokees were an "impoverished people," with only a small fraction of them maintaining tribal government—that is, government separate from the state of North Carolina.[92] Moreover, by 1879 the Cherokee Nation's lawyers did not recognize the North Carolina Cherokees as being part of the Cherokee Nation in any way.[93] Applications for Cherokee citizenship originating from North Carolina were therefore viewed with intense scrutiny.[94] Cherokee lawyer William P. Ross was one of a number of prominent Cherokees who complained that part of the difficulty in determining who was and was not Cherokee lay in the absence of a clear legal definition of such an identity, and in the lack of adequate assistance from the US government to deal with the ongoing problem of intruders into Indian Territory.[95]

Once the Cherokee Citizenship Commission swung into action and began considering applications for Cherokee citizenship, it emphasized the importance of "blood" and empirical evidence (especially population "rolls" and residency status) to prove Cherokee genealogy. It also tied citizenship to a territorially fixed abode. Reiterating the National Council's commitment to Article 3, Section 5 of the Cherokee Nation's amended constitution (1866), the *Cherokee Advocate* printed the following statement in September 1877:

> All native born Cherokees, all Indians, and whites, legally members of the Nation by adoption, and freedmen who have been liberated by voluntary act of their former owners, or by law; as well as free colored persons who were in the country at the commencement of the rebellion therein, or who may return within six months from the 19th day of July, 1866; and their descendants who reside within the Cherokee Nation, shall be taken, and deemed to be citizens of the Cherokee Nation.[96]

In reprinting these constitutional amendments, designed to conform with Article 9 of the 1866 treaty, the National Council emphasized that "Here, as in all other cases, residence is held to be the essential qualification for citizenship."[97] Given these legal developments, any claim of Cherokee identity contingent on citizenship in the Cherokee Nation became particularly tenuous if an individual lived outside the nation.

In 1877, the *Cherokee Advocate* newspaper highlighted this tenuousness by declaring that citizenship in the Cherokee Nation was an exclusive legal identity. The "Cherokee include members of the Ross Party, the Treaty Party, Old Settlers or Western Cherokee," the *Advocate* editorialized. According to this logic, Cherokee identity, at least within the Cherokee Nation, was confined to those people descended from Cherokees who migrated west in the three decades prior to removal, and to those Cherokees forced to relocate during forced removal in the

1830s. Thus, "no other portion of the Cherokees, if any there were, are recognized" as legitimate representatives of the Cherokee people.[98]

The establishment of these links between migration, territoriality, and citizenship was an important legal development that was echoed in popular culture during the 1870s and 1880s. In fact, by the 1880s the notion that the only "real" Cherokees remaining in North America were those confined to Indian Territory pervaded popular perceptions. Belle K. Abbott mused in the *Atlanta Constitution* in November 1889, for example, that the Cherokee had been forced out of Georgia "only half a century" earlier, and yet "they have left no lasting trace behind them."[99] Such popularly accepted logic fit neatly with the Cherokee National Council's legal efforts to connect post-Civil War migration and the "intruder" population to specific moments of migration, "blood" quantum, and territorial residency. These were the connections that Principal Chief Dennis Bushyhead made during his time in office. Bushyhead, who had himself lived in diaspora at various points of his life, complained that North Carolina Cherokees were being "encouraged" by the Indian Office to migrate west and settle in Indian Territory. He argued that the Eastern Band, who, he insisted, were citizens of the state of North Carolina, were being aided by federal senators and encouraged to pursue citizenship claims in the Cherokee Nation that had no legal foundation. Bushyhead's comments may have sounded conspiratorial, but they reflected how the leaders of the Cherokee Nation felt, being under siege from one unrelenting wave of migrants after another. Faced with these challenges, the Nation's leaders and legal representatives began pulling away from their North Carolina cousins. Reiterating earlier legal opinions that Indian Territory "lands were secured to the Cherokee Nation as a body politic by patent," Bushyhead maintained that Eastern Band Cherokees were entitled to nothing in the Cherokee Nation.[100]

Coming Home?

Such opinions do not appear to have stopped North Carolina Cherokees from attempting to migrate to Indian Territory, settle, and petition for citizenship rights in the Cherokee Nation. James Obediah was one such applicant. Described by one witness as a "respectable man," Obediah applied for Cherokee citizenship, claiming, "I am a full blood Cherokee Indian I emigrated from North Carolina to the Cherokee Nation in the fall of 1871." Obediah claimed to be among 130 North Carolina Cherokees who migrated west in 1871. He added that on his journey westward, he was accompanied by his wife, Susey Wil-le-ge-stee, and her sister, Oonal-li, whom Obediah insisted was listed on the Murray Roll. Obediah's wife died suddenly in 1873, thus prompting his application for Cherokee citizenship in the hope that his estate would be legally protected and bequeathed to his sister-in-law upon his death.[101]

The case of James Obediah highlights one of the important motivating factors in citizenship petitions from North Carolina Cherokees—the desire to provide for members of an extended family after the death of the family patriarch. A similar set of kinship ties and sense of economic responsibility marked the citizenship petition of Charles S. Hubbard. Hubbard filed his petition for citizenship with his cousin, Ella Hubbard, of Knightstown, Indiana. Witness testimony suggested that Charles's father, Richard Hubbard, and his grandfather, Jeremiah Hubbard, were Cherokees by "blood." Additionally, Ella's father, Jacob Hubbard, was said to be Jeremiah's brother. This genealogical information was important because in 1772 or 1773, Joseph Hubbard and his wife left western North Carolina and resettled in Guilford County, in north-central North Carolina. Thereafter, the family name disappeared from rolls of Cherokee Indians. To counter the dearth of empirical evidence, eyewitness testimony reiterated the family's lineage and emphasized "a numerous company of relatives" prepared to relocate permanently to the Cherokee Nation. This final piece of testimony piqued the suspicions of Cherokee officials. Suspected of being a white man, Hubbard was deemed an "intruder" and his claim denied.[102]

North Carolina was by no means the only point of origin for citizenship petitions. Applications were filed from Tennessee, Georgia, Maryland, New York, Nebraska, Missouri, Illinois, Kansas, Arkansas, Texas, the Dakotas, and California. Applicants from the diaspora sometimes involved well-known Cherokee ancestors, such as those of the Ridge family in California, or Mary B. Boudinot, Elias Boudinot's daughter, who was "readmitted" from Washington, California.[103] Not all applicants, however, possessed detailed genealogical information, nor could they present eyewitnesses to testify that they were in fact descendants of a Cherokee lineage. An application from an "East Tennessee" man in August 1886 typified this type of petition. Claiming descent from a "remnant of the tribe left in the East Tennessee," the applicant testified to a racial affinity with Cherokees in the West, asserting: "I am Cherokee Indian by blood."[104] Cherokee officials generally found such applications to be wholly unsatisfactory. Simply claiming to be Cherokee "by blood" was not adequate proof for Cherokee officials to grant citizenship.

Citizenship Commissioners sifted through hundreds of cases from applicants claiming to have Cherokee, Shawnee, Delaware, Creek, Catawba, white, and black "blood."[105] The most common rationale for the rejection of such applications was that the petitioners presented inadequate evidence that they possessed Cherokee "blood." Cherokee officials routinely pointed out that such applicants did not have any Cherokee ancestors on the citizenship rolls from the years 1835, 1848, 1851, or 1852, or on the Old Settler roll of 1851. In some cases, commissioners viewed the absence of documentary proof of Cherokee "blood" as evidence of an attempt to commit fraud against the Cherokee Nation. The 1888 case of Mrs. Martha A. Payne versus the Cherokee Nation was one such case, in which Citizenship Commissioners suspected bribery and fraud on the part of citizenship applicants. Martha Payne was a widowed woman from Fort Smith, Arkansas, with an extended family of six to support. Cherokee Supreme Court records indicated that the Payne family received approval of their citizenship application in 1871. However, the Citizenship Commission later received new evidence that suggested "fraud and bribery" was involved in the 1871 application.[106]

In July 1887, the Citizenship Commission issued a summons for Martha Payne to appear before the commissioners and respond to the allegations of fraud. Other witnesses were also called to testify, including Sophia Pigeon and her sister Jennie. According to Sophia, Martha's grandfather was a man named Starling Gunter, one of Old John Gunter's sons. Old John Gunter was reportedly a white man who had lived with his Cherokee wife along the Tennessee River in the "Old Nation." Old John's son, Starling, allegedly had a daughter, Sarah L. Gunter, who was

Martha's mother. According to Sophia Pigeon's account, which was corroborated by another witness, Ann Hughs [sic], this made Martha Cherokee "by blood" by virtue of her Cherokee grandmother.[107]

This all seemed pretty cut-and-dried, that is, until Jennie Pigeon and Anne Big-Feather entered the story. Jennie Pigeon testified that she "had a *talk* with Anne Big-Feather," who claimed to have known the Gunter family in Tennessee. Big-Feather confirmed that Old John's children were born to a Cherokee mother, but that she died when the children were quite young. Shortly after his wife's death, Old John left the Cherokee community where he had long lived, and settled with his "white kin" in the United States. The children were raised as whites and remained separated from Cherokee culture and society until well into their adult lives. Old John's children and grandchildren had become "white," and when Martha reached adulthood she married and had children with a white man.

If evidence of cultural deracination was not damning enough, then the evidence of William P. Ross proved to be a dagger into the heart of Martha Payne's case. Ross, a "conspicuous man among the Cherokees," claimed that "he was well acquainted with the Gunters in the Old Nation." He knew of Old John, and his two sons, Starling and Charles, but was unaware of their Cherokee genealogy. In fact, Ross testified that Old John did take a Cherokee wife, Katy, when he entered the Old Nation but "from this marriage there was no issue." Ross insisted that Old John's sons were the "issue" of a marriage to a white woman, Maria.[108]

The Citizenship Commission heard additional testimony that suggested Martha Payne was all too aware of the fraudulent nature of her application when she originally applied for, and was granted, citizenship before the Cherokee Supreme Court in 1871. This new evidence post-dated Payne's original 1871 application and focused on the period between 1874 and 1876 when her attorney, George Johnson, stood for a seat in the Senate of the National Council from the Sequoyah District and attempted to bribe the Payne family in an effort to gain their vote. Johnson lost that election because some of the ballots cast were judged to be fraudulent. In a desperate bid to boost his electoral returns, he paid Jennie Pigeon to deliver false testimony claiming that the Payne family were in fact Cherokees, and that their votes in the senatorial election should stand. The conspiracy may well have worked, had Jennie Pigeon not been overheard standing "near the Capital doorway" bragging about a false "paper" she had signed. Within earshot of that conversation was none other than Dennis Bushyhead, the principal chief of the Cherokee Nation. The weight of Bushyhead's testimony, combined with that of William P. Ross, doomed the citizenship status of Martha Payne and her family. They had engaged in fraud and bribery on such a scale that the Citizenship Commission felt it had no option but to revoke the family's citizenship and declare them "intruders."[109]

The case of Martha Payne highlighted how politically contentious the issue of citizenship was in the Cherokee Nation in the decades after the American Civil War. During that period, old factional divisions gave way to a renewed grab for political power. There was much at stake—land, federal annuities, and power for power's sake. This was the very stuff of Gilded Age politics in the United States, and it was also what made Cherokee politics tick during the late nineteenth century. That said, this was also an era in which the Cherokee National Council lost territory through cessions of significant tracts of land, and struggled to deal with the violence and social instability caused by Civil War refugees and land hungry settlers—both black and white.

Long before DNA evidence entered the genealogical equation in charting one's ancestors, eyewitness testimony was critical to proving one's Cherokee "blood," or ancestry. Hearsay evidence was not enough to establish that genealogical connection to Cherokee forebears; rather, one needed witnesses who were in good social standing in the eyes of the Citizenship Commission. Being a "full-blood" Cherokee gave considerable weight to an eyewitness's testimony. The Citizenship Commission defined a "full-blood" not simply in terms of biological ancestry, but in relation to the language one spoke—preferably Cherokee—and the "traditional" cultural beliefs and practices that structured one's life. When a witness's language and culture combined with a clear knowledge of the applicant's Cherokee ancestry, the "purity" of that witness gave his or her testimony an authoritative, almost unimpeachable quality.[110]

However, Martha Payne's case highlighted the fact that no witness testimony was entirely unimpeachable. In addition, the Payne case revealed how multiple generations of travel and migration could cast doubt on the genealogical claims of a family. William Ross's testimony was crucial in underscoring the significance of migration and the "attenuation" of Cherokee "blood" that it was assumed to produce. Surviving records from the Cherokee Citizenship Commission highlight how migration and the mixing of "blood" had the potential to see one generation of an extended kin group stripped of citizenship, while an older generation might retain its citizenship. Similarly, members of a single family could be removed from citizenship rolls on the basis of migration and permanent residence, while other members of the same family may retain Cherokee citizenship.[111]

Not all cases involving questions of "blood' and migration hinged on suspicions of fraud, though. In some cases, the murky "facts" of a family's "blood" and migration history could play against them. This was the case for Martha Brown and her nephew Lafayette Teel. Martha W. Brown nee Fleetwood claimed that she was the granddaughter of Hosie Morgan. According to the evidence presented by Brown's attorney, Hosie Morgan "looked like an Indian," but did not speak the Cherokee language. According to one witness, Hosie left the Old Nation in 1839 but it was unclear if he was recognized as a Cherokee. He did, after all, have "curly, kinky or negro hair," and was also suspected of being a "Mexican or Spaniard."[112]

A number of other witnesses also brought into question the Cherokee "blood" of Hosie Morgan and his descendants. William Wilson testified that he "did not know of what blood" Martha Brown was, but that "she looked like a Negro." A Mr. B. W. Alberty echoed these sentiments. He alleged that the family had never applied for payment from the Old Settler fund and were in fact Catawba Indians who lived for a time in Kansas. Moreover, witnesses claimed that Martha had never married a man of "Cherokee blood" but was in fact married to a white man.[113]

The witness testimony in the case of Martha Brown and Lafayette Teel proved damning to their claim for Cherokee citizenship. After weighing all of the evidence, the Commission concluded that Brown and Teel had descended from Catawba and "Negro" ancestors, the latter being slaves. Despite the fact that they had lived continuously in the Cherokee Nation for many years, the intermixture of blood and the migrations of their ancestors (in addition to Brown and Teel's own travels) torpedoed their claim. They were denied citizenship and labeled "intruders upon the public domain of the Cherokee Nation."[114]

The Cherokee Citizenship Commission was designed to put bureaucratic processes in place to accurately, and transparently, determine a person's legal right to Cherokee citizenship. Applicants like Martha Brown and Lafayette Teel, and the many others who hoped to acquire Cherokee citizenship, needed to assemble witnesses known to be longtime residents of Cherokee communities, and to possess written evidence of Cherokee blood (usually in the form of the family name appearing on a federal Indian roll). The fact that oral testimony also carried great weight with Commissioners in certain cases reflected the enduring significance of oral traditions of knowledge among Cherokees in the trans-Mississippi West.

However, not all oral testimony carried the same evidentiary weight. Where lawyers might insist that a witness had "unimpeachable evidence," commissioners regularly determined claims to be false. In an era when Cherokee lawyers and politicians drew on the racialized rhetoric of "blood" to construct legal walls around the Cherokee Nation, evidence presented on behalf of people of African descent was all too often deemed insufficient. It is thus to questions about the legal status of Cherokee freedpeople (and freedpeople generally), mixed-race African Cherokees, and intermarried blacks that we now turn.

Cherokee Freedmen

On the eve of the American Civil War, approximately 15 percent of the Cherokee Nation's total population were slaves held by Cherokee slave owners. For some Cherokee slaves, life was defined by sadistic levels of cruelty, while others remembered relationships characterized by tenderness and genuine affection.[1] The American Civil War, however, was a watershed moment. Slaves seized the moment and fled the Cherokee plantations and homes that had once prescribed the parameters of daily life. Amid the chaos of wartime, Cherokee slaves joined thousands of other formerly enslaved people seeking temporary shelter in Kansas, Missouri, portions of Arkansas, or in isolated regions of northern Texas. In refugee camps, former Cherokee slaves waited for the war to end and their new life of freedom to begin.[2]

When the war did end, the 1866 treaty between the United States and Cherokee Nation confirmed the Cherokee Nation's Act of Emancipation (1863) and the Thirteenth Amendment to the US Constitution: slavery was no more. The abolition of slavery saw some Cherokee freedpeople—or "freedmen," to use the language of the era—make the decision to settle in townships and newly formed villages along, for example, the Neosho River in Kansas.[3] These settlements convinced some Cherokee leaders back in Indian Territory that Cherokee freedpeople had made the decision not to claim Cherokee citizenship under the provisions set forth in Article 9 of the 1866 treaty. Article 9 required freedpeople to return to the Cherokee Nation within six months of the 1866 treaty if they wished to claim their citizenship rights. That so many Cherokee freedpeople did not, or could not, return within that time frame prompted one Cherokee leader to declare in 1879, "The said colored people were held as slaves among the Cherokee prior to the Rebellion (1861). They were then freed and moved to Kansas."[4]

Such self-serving recollections helped to frame the legal grammar of Cherokee identity between 1866 and the beginning of the allotment era at the end of the 1880s. In the political homeland of the Cherokee diaspora, Cherokee officials implemented a legal system that was designed to exclude "intruders" from the Cherokee Nation. As the previous chapter noted, such efforts were both understandable and often justified. For many Cherokee freedpeople, however, returning to the Nation only to be labeled "intruders" and denied Cherokee citizenship was a cruel blow.[5] Cherokee freedpeople thus became ensnared in the politics of the "intruder" problem and the "refugee business," transforming their family histories of enslavement, overlapping migrations of Cherokee and African American people, and interracial marriage into legal and bureaucratic dramas.[6]

For most Cherokee leaders, especially former slave-owning Cherokees, the thought of sharing citizenship with people of African ancestry was appalling. Confederate Cherokees found the idea so distasteful that some proposed leaving the Cherokee Nation and establishing a separate nation-state.[7] Cherokee leaders knew that such a state was unlikely; they understood that they could not ignore questions about the legal status of Cherokee freedpeople and the social status of people possessing "African blood." Amid the legal and political debates about race, intermarriage, and residency within the Cherokee diaspora's political homeland, it was not easy being black and Cherokee during the late nineteenth century.

Policing Freedpeople in the Trans-Mississippi West

Articles 4, 9, and 10 of the treaty of 1866 established the legal foundation on which Cherokee freedpeople claimed citizenship in the Cherokee

Nation. That treaty also declared that Cherokee freedpeople returning to the Nation within six months of its signing were entitled to the "rights of native Cherokees" and could own property within the Cherokee Nation.[8] Thanks to Principal Chief Lewis Downing's broad multiethnic coalition—which included former abolitionists and "full-blood traditionalists"—the National Council passed legislation in 1871 that confirmed Cherokee freedpeople's right to citizenship, access to land within the Nation, and other legal protections.[9]

In theory, the treaty of 1866 and the National Council's 1871 legislation settled the legal status of Cherokee freedpeople. However, influential factions within the Cherokee Nation resisted the incorporation of freedpeople due to "economic factors."[10] Questions about land and political sovereignty, race and genealogy, shaped this resistance. The strains on the Cherokee Nation's financial and territorial resources prompted the National Council to act. In May 1883, Council members passed legislation restricting payments from the Nation's treasury to "citizens of the Cherokee Nation by Cherokee blood."[11] This decision angered those Delaware, Shawnee, and Creek Indians adopted as Cherokee citizens immediately after the Civil War; it also proved a serious blow to Cherokee freedpeople who were relying on the Nation's financial resources to help them re-establish life in what they felt was their homeland.[12] According to a federal official, only the Choctaw treated freedpeople as "arbitrarily and unjustly" as the Cherokee.[13]

Despite the federal government's criticisms, Cherokee leaders felt they had reason to be suspicious of freedpeople's claims. Indeed, the Bureau of Indian Affairs 1883 report enumerated 3,599 cases involving Cherokee freedpeople, substantially more than the entire population of people with "African blood" before the Civil War. The conclusion to that 1883 report seemed to bear out Cherokee suspicions, with 1,198 freedpeople being authenticated on Cherokee rolls and entitled to a share in the $100,000 set aside for former Cherokee slaves. This was not the end of the matter, however. An additional 1,243 freedpeople claimed to be owed a share of the freedman fund.[14]

Economics was certainly an issue in determining the identity of Cherokee freedpeople. But there was something more going on than just the jealous guarding of Cherokee finances. The question of extending citizenship to all of the freedpeople, Cherokees with "African blood," and African Americans who claimed to have married a person of Cherokee descent in the Cherokee diaspora's political homeland brought to the fore anxieties about the shrinking territory of the Cherokee Nation and the demographic nature of that homeland. The "multitude" of refugees and "pioneers" entering Indian Territory profoundly altered the demographic makeup of the Cherokee Nation, and the "irruption of negro freedmen" served only to heighten the fears of Cherokee leaders that the Cherokees were fast becoming a minority in their own homeland.

It was these fears that inspired the formation of the Cherokee Citizenship Commission (CCC). As the previous chapter detailed, the CCC was established to differentiate between "intruders" and those people with a legitimate right to Cherokee citizenship. Given that the number of people claiming to be Cherokee freedpeople was greater than the number of slaves held by Cherokees prior to the war, Cherokee officials viewed applications from people of African ancestry with skepticism. In 1876, for example, a year prior to the CCC's formation, the Cherokee Supreme Court reported that the Cooweescoowee District, named in honor of the late John Ross, was popular with African Cherokee migrants.[15] There was plenty of land in this large District for homesteading, and it was relatively isolated from the communities in which former Cherokee slave owners resided, such as the Tahlequah, Illinois, Canadian, Snake, Flint, and Sequoyah Districts. According to the Supreme Court's report, seventy "colored persons" entered the Cooweescoowee District in 1876, the vast majority deemed to have arrived too late to claim citizenship rights. Of all the "colored" applicants to claim citizenship rights from the Cooweescoowee District that year, only two succeeded.[16]

Given the Cooweescoowee District's close proximity to refugee settlements in Kansas, Cherokee leaders no doubt felt justified in taking a hard line against freedpeople in the north of the Nation. Similarly, migration through the borderland region with Arkansas posed challenges to the integrity of Cherokee sovereignty, with "gangs and cliques," the distillers of "moonshine whiskey," and freedpeople traveling over the Ozark Mountains and toward the Cherokee diaspora's political homeland.[17]

Members of the National Council generally agreed that the Nation needed more stringent citizenship laws. These laws made it increasingly difficult for freedpeople to successfully claim Cherokee citizenship. The official stance of the lawmakers was that the citizenship status of freedpeople was not a racial matter, but a matter of Cherokee sovereignty.[18] Thus, as the Nation rebuilt after the war, it emerged as a model of modern bureaucracy and empirical record keeping, in which the disinterested administration of the law masked the institutional racism of the Cherokee Nation.

Why, then, did so many freedpeople want Cherokee citizenship? Economic interests were only part of the answer. There was more to this question than simply money and land. To get at these deeper, more complex motivations, we must mine the letters, affidavits, and petitions written by, or prepared on behalf of, Cherokee freedpeople in their quest for citizenship rights in the Cherokee Nation. These documents contain clues about the emotional attachments Cherokee freedpeople and people of African descent felt for their Cherokee identity.

The "Blood" of a Diasporic People

Freedpeople and African Americans married to Cherokee citizens had to navigate a legal structure that established six categories of Cherokee citizens: "Cherokee by blood" (which included adopted Shawnees), "Minor Cherokees by blood," "Delaware Cherokees," "Intermarried Whites," "Cherokee Freedmen," and "Minor Cherokee Freedmen."[19]

For Cherokee freedpeople, successfully proving that they and their children belonged in the legal category of "Cherokee Freedmen" or "Minor Cherokee Freedmen" was no easy task.[20] The difficulties stemmed from the fact that Cherokees and people of African descent lived intersecting lives. These intersections were fraught with racial and sexual power dynamics that before the Civil War placed people of African descent in the category of chattel, and after the war continued to marginalize them throughout the Cherokee diaspora.[21]

This marginalization had begun with the Cherokees' adoption of racial slavery and the development of racially exclusionary laws. Developments in the nineteenth century reinforced Cherokee perceptions

Table 2: Colored Population of States and Territories Encircling
the Cherokee Nation and Indian Territory, 1860–1890§

State	Free Colored Population, 1860	Slave Population, 1860	Colored Population, 1870	Colored Population, 1880	Negro Population 1890
Arkansas	111,115	144	122,169	210,666	309,117
Missouri	114,931	3,572	118,071	143,350	150,184
Kansas*	625	2	17,108	43,107	49,710
Texas	182,566	355	253,475	393,384	488,171
Colorado**	N/A		456	2,435	6,215

Source: Historical Census Browser. University of Virginia, Geospatial and Statistical Data Center. Retrieved October 12, 2010, http://mapserver.lib.virginia.edu/collections/.
* Kansas was "Kansas Territory" at the 1860 federal census
** Colorado was "Colorado Territory" at the 1870 federal census
§ The terms "Colored Population" and "Negro Population" are the racial nomenclature used by the Census Bureau between 1860 and 1890.

that "Cherokee blood" needed protection now that slavery had been abolished. Traditional Cherokee culture viewed "blood" as a substance with either destructive or vital reproductive qualities. With the appropriation of Western forms of racial thinking, however, genealogical understandings of "blood" and human inheritance became racialized. The type of "blood" one possessed therefore defined one's social status and legal identification in the Cherokee Nation.[22]

But just how real was the threat of "African blood" and Cherokee-black miscegenation after the Civil War?[23] Census data indicates that the population of "colored people" in states adjoining the Cherokee Nation was sizeable, and grew steadily over the course of the 1870s and 1880s. These increases, which reflected both natural increase and migration, highlighted to Cherokee leaders just how vulnerable Cherokee "blood" was to potential dilution from growing migrant populations.[24]

Within Indian Territory, the census data reveals even more clearly why Cherokee leaders felt anxious about demographic changes. In 1890, the Bureau of the Census reported that 51,279 Native Americans resided in Indian Territory, as compared to 110,254 whites and 18,636 "Negroes."

By 1907, the year Oklahoma acquired statehood, the Native American population stood at 61,925, the white population 538,512, and the African American population 80,649. Whereas both the white and black populations had increased substantially, both absolutely and as a percentage of the total population, the percentage of Native Americans had declined, falling from 28.5 percent of the population in 1890 to 9.1 percent by 1907.[25]

Patterns also emerged in the geographical distribution of the black populations in the Cherokee Nation after the Civil War. By 1880, the "colored" population of the Cooweescoowee District was 546, or a little over 30 percent of the total population of 1,797. The·Cooweescoowee District was indeed ethnically diverse, with its inhabitants also including 220 whites, 290 Shawnees, and 690 Delaware Indians. A similar story of racial and ethnic diversity existed in the Illinois and Delaware Districts. For example, 274 whites, 101 blacks, 72 Delawares, and 290 Shawnees (out of a total population of 2,371) called the Delaware District home. In the Illinois District, a total population of 1,556 included 539 blacks and 155 Creeks.[26]

A similar story of demographic decline afflicted Cherokees living east of the Mississippi River. The federal census of 1890 estimated that 936 Cherokees lived in Georgia, 318 in Tennessee, and 11 in Alabama. There were also some Cherokees living in Kentucky and Virginia, but the census taker determined that they had been "sufficiently incorporated into the white population" and did not warrant enumeration as Cherokees. Both whites and blacks therefore far outnumbered those of Cherokee descent in these states.[27]

At the Qualla Boundary Reservation in North Carolina, Eastern Band Cherokees also encountered growing populations of both black and white Americans. In 1860, the slave population of North Carolina stood at approximately 331,059. By 1890, the state's African American population totaled 561,018. There were 518 black Americans in Jackson County and 225 in Swain County, where the Qualla Reservation cut through. While 742 African American residents in the immediate vicinity of the North Carolina Cherokee reservation was not a huge number of people, it was by no means insignificant. According to the 1890 census, the Eastern Band comprised a population of 1,520.[28]

When this demographic data is viewed in the broader social and political context of Reconstruction and the Gilded Age in American political and economic history, we see just how important the questions of marriage, migration, and race became to Cherokee identity during the late nineteenth century.[29] For example, political violence in the South prompted many black Americans to migrate westward, changing the demographic landscape of states like Kansas in the process. In 1870, Missouri-born African Americans constituted the largest share of the black population in Kansas, followed by blacks born in Kentucky and Tennessee. By 1880, the demographics had shifted. While most blacks in Kansas were now Kansas-born, those who migrated to the state came primarily from Mississippi, Texas, Louisiana, Virginia, West Virginia, and Arkansas.[30] The racial nature of the South's political violence partly explains black migration to states like Kansas. However, African Americans were also pulled toward Kansas by dreams of finding a "promised land" where they might farm and raise their families in peace and safety. Just as whites caught "Kansas fever" and headed toward the "geographical centre of the continent" during the 1870s, so too did blacks.[31]

In Indian Territory, directly south of Kansas, federal officials reported on the relations between Native Americans and blacks. Among the Seminole and Creek Indians, a majority of tribal members supported the incorporation of former slaves into their respective nations. In stark contrast, the Chickasaw and Choctaw reportedly displayed "a violent prejudice" against freedpeople, with racially motivated murders becoming commonplace in the decades after the Civil War. The Cherokee, true to their recent history, were divided in their attitudes toward the freedpeople in their Nation.[32]

If the Cherokee people were divided over the future status of freedpeople in the Cherokee's political homeland, their leaders were not.[33] Cherokee leaders remained determined to exclude former slaves, and blacks generally, from the Nation. For this reason, the members of the National Council took a keen interest in the migration of Southern blacks into Missouri and Kansas. While the majority of the black population in these states congregated around towns and cities like St. Louis—where employment opportunities were highest—several thousand African Americans settled near the Kansas-Cherokee Nation border.[34] Along the Cherokee Nation's northern borderland, Cherokee freedpeople encountered and intermarried with freedpeople from the American South. Applications for Cherokee citizenship from such couples confirmed the mixing of these two populations of freedpeople, adding further complexity to the already complex deliberations over the citizenship status of freedpeople.

The connection that the National Council had established between intermarriage and citizenship in the early nineteenth century was thus extended into late nineteenth-century lawmaking and legal practices.[35] Marriage was far from a private matter in the minds of Cherokee leaders. It was a very public issue, an institution upon which the balance and harmony of Cherokee communities rested. A citizen's choice of marital and/or sexual partner thus had the potential to reshape the demographic make-up of the Cherokee Nation.

The issue of intermarriage illuminates a very intimate dimension to the overlapping Cherokee and African American diasporas, especially in and around the Cherokee diaspora's political homeland. The case of freedman Samuel Barnes highlights the type of intermarriage that troubled Cherokee leaders. Barnes claimed that he had migrated to the Cherokee Nation from Arkansas in 1871. Once in the Nation, he met and married his wife, "whose father was part Cherokee." Despite presenting the CCC with documentation attesting to his father-in-law's Cherokee genealogy, Barnes, his wife, and their children were placed on the "doubtful roll" of Cherokee freedpeople. Barnes objected, insisting that he and his family had lived in the Sequoyah district for the best part of a decade, made improvements to their land, and sent their children to the local public schools. However, once the family's name was placed on the "doubtful roll," the Barnes family faced an uncertain future. To the Barnes family, the Sequoyah District was home. The Cherokee legal system now threatened the future stability of that home.[36]

Jane Hubbard found herself jumping through similar legal hoops in a bid to establish her right to Cherokee citizenship.[37] Hubbard was born in Tennessee but resided in Kansas at the time of her application, in May 1881. According to her sworn affidavit, Hubbard's mother "was what is termed a Quadroon and was owned and held as a slave by one Nathan Thomas of Williamson County in the state of Tennessee." Hubbard's father, also a slave and possessing no Cherokee "blood" according to census records, was a man named John Reese. Hubbard alleged that she was kidnapped sometime in the 1850s and subsequently enslaved in the Cherokee Nation in Indian Territory. John Reese tried desperately to raise the money to purchase his daughter's freedom, but his efforts failed. Undeterred, Reese hired a man to travel to the Cherokee Nation and "steal" his daughter from slavery. Evidently Reese's plot was discovered, and he and his wife were banished from Williamson County, Tennessee. Cherokee authorities, sensitive to slave plots following the slave rebellion in the Cherokee Nation in 1842, remained on guard against incursions from "intruders" like John Reese.

There is no question that Jane Hubbard had been a slave in the Cherokee Nation in the years before the Civil War. Kidnapped and enslaved at a young age, then eventually marrying and having four children, Hubbard did not possess Cherokee "blood" but could only ever recall life among the Cherokees. The same was true of her children. Thus her 1881 affidavit requested the rights of Cherokee citizenship on the grounds that she and her children "are Cherokee Indians entitled to all the rights[,] privileges and immunities in the Cherokee Nation." Hubbard claimed that her family had been "unjustly and unlawfully debarred of their rights in the Cherokee Nation," and demanded the reinstatement of their citizenship rights and protections on the basis of being enslaved in the Cherokee Nation prior to the American Civil War.

In her application Jane Hubbard made no explicit claims upon the Cherokee Nation's treasury or its territorial holdings. Instead, she requested that the Cherokee identity she coveted for herself and for her family be acknowledged by the Nation's leaders. Such acknowledgement would carry with it the legal protections afforded other freedpeople granted Cherokee citizenship in the Nation—a privileged set of rights that Cherokees living in diaspora likewise coveted—and would affirm Hubbard's abstract sense of belonging to an adopted nation.

Because cases like Jane Hubbard's raised the suspicions of Cherokee leaders, they reminded people of African descent of the importance of presenting reliable witnesses, keeping detailed files of past migrations, and producing documentation of marriages and/or the births of children to support their claims of Cherokee citizenship.[38] For instance, on April 4, 1883, Mrs. Flora Lane wrote an impassioned letter to the principal chief of the Cherokee Nation demanding that she and her husband receive recognition of their Cherokee citizenship.[39] Writing from Coffeeville, Kansas, a small town connected to the Cherokee Nation by rail lines, Lane began her letter by insisting, "I am a colored lady of the Cherokee Nation I.T." Having established her racial and national identity, Lane proceeded to outline the legal foundations upon which that identity rested. She wrote, "[I am] also a citizen of said territory by treaty of 1866 & have been recognized as such under the laws of said Nation. My husband took a claim in the Nation . . . [and] made lasting improvements on a good piece of land."[40]

Lane's letter suggests that she did not see her racial status as "colored" as an impediment to asserting a Cherokee identity. For Flora Lane, identity was tied to both her racial understanding of herself— "colored"—and her citizenship status—Cherokee. The legal recognition that she sought from the National Council would, Lane implied, protect the land that she and her husband claimed as their own and worked hard to improve.[41]

But who exactly was Flora Lane? This was certainly a question that the members of the CCC wanted answered. According to census data, Flora Lane was born about 1844 in Virginia. Her future husband, George Lane, was born around 1845. In 1870, census enumerators labeled Flora and George Lane as "mulatto" and noted that they resided in Athens, Alabama.[42] At the next decennial census, in 1880, George and Flora were still living together as man and wife in Alabama.[43] Thereafter, George and Flora Lane disappear, with no trace of them in government records. Where did they go?

Flora Lane's fate following her 1883 letter to the principal chief of the Cherokee Nation remains shrouded in mystery. Did she and her husband relocate to another part of the country? It's possible. In all of the census data that I have combed, the tax records, deeds to property, and death notices, Flora and George Lane are nowhere to be found. It is possible that they were Cherokee freedpeople, refugees from the western theater of the Civil War who just happened to make their way to Alabama during one of the most turbulent periods in United States history. But without more conclusive evidence, they could just as easily have been former Southern slaves who never had anything to do with the Cherokees, or any Native Americans for that matter. Their disappearance from Cherokee and federal government records, however, was not an uncommon conclusion to such stories. Citizenship requests like that of Flora and George Lane leave many unanswered questions, but they also reveal how migration and marriage were interconnected in the post-Civil War world, forcing Cherokee leaders to more firmly and clearly define what it meant to be Cherokee.[44]

Citizenship applications like Flora and George Lane's continued to emerge from the Cherokee borderlands and the vicinity of former refugee camps in and around Indian Territory during the late nineteenth century. These cases underscore the legal complexities created by migration and intermarriage, especially in the case of marriages between Cherokee freedpeople and freedpeople from the American South.[45] In 1888, for example, Elizabeth Henson began making inquiries about how she might establish her right to Cherokee citizenship. After hiring a Pennsylvania lawyer, Henson submitted documentation to the Secretary of the Interior that she believed established her Cherokee genealogy and migratory history.

According to a letter prepared by her lawyer, Henson spent most of the Civil War in Kentucky. It's not clear from the surviving documentation whether she had been enslaved in Kentucky or in the Cherokee Nation prior to 1861, but by war's end she came under the care of the Freedmen's Bureau in Kentucky. Described by her lawyer, J. A. R. Rogers, as a "colored girl, but with unmistakable Indian features," she received care from "one of the best families" in Philadelphia. She subsequently attended Oberlin College, and later married a Missouri man by the name of Samuel Bealer.

At the time of their marriage, Bealer possessed considerable land holdings and was financially comfortable. However, he lost his land at some point in the 1870s and the family subsequently fell on hard times. To Cherokee officials, such an application for citizenship was all too familiar. It had all the hallmarks of an opportunistic black couple trying to profit from the Cherokee Nation's meager treasury. Still, Henson's lawyer persisted. He claimed that his client had "full particulars of her Cherokee origin and gives persons and dates connected with her history and ancestry." To reinforce the validity of the couple's claim, Rogers insisted that Mr. Bealer "has some Cherokee blood" also.[46]

Such claims rarely met with success. They nonetheless continued to plague Cherokee officials, especially after the allotment policy became a full-blown crisis affecting Indian sovereignty and the land base of the Cherokee diaspora's political homeland. By the 1880s freedpeople recognized the changing political landscape of Indian Territory and increasingly turned to the Secretary of the Interior before going to the Cherokee Nation to demand their Cherokee citizenship rights. Surviving archival records reveal just how difficult the task confronting officials was in these cases. The migratory paths that Cherokee freedpeople took between the Cherokee Nation, Kansas, Missouri, Arkansas, and Texas, and the resulting intermarriages with blacks from the American South, compounded the difficulty of the bureaucratic task. As I noted earlier in this chapter, many of these freedpeople endeavored to settle in the Cooweescoowee District, a fact reflected in the Department of the Interior's case files. For example, Alice Alberty migrated from Kansas to Texas immediately after the Civil War, and eventually resettled in the Cooweescoowee District of the Cherokee Nation. Jesse Brown filed an application for Cherokee citizenship from nearby Coffeyville, Kansas, claiming that her Cherokee master had relocated her family to the Deep South during the Civil War.[47]

To Cherokee leaders, marriage was vital to the balance and harmony of their society. The National Council therefore moved to both amend and clarify its marriage laws so that applicants like those above would have no legal grounds upon which to claim Cherokee citizenship. While maintaining prohibitions on interracial marriages between blacks and Cherokees, by 1880 the National Council began explicit attempts to make "intermarriage law uniform and just to all citizens of Indian blood." Thus, if a white man wished to marry a "Delaware" Indian who had been adopted in the Cherokee Nation, so long as that man had "certificate of good character signed by Delaware citizens" he was entitled to all the rights and privileges of Cherokee citizenship.[48]

People of African descent were not included in these "uniform" laws. Different legal standards applied to them. Article 3, Section 5 of the Cherokee Nation's constitution (1881) made the position of people of African descent clear:

> The descendants of Cherokee men by all free women except the African race, whose parents may have been living together as man and wife, according to the customs and laws of the Nation, shall be entitled to all the rights and privileges of this Nation as well as the posterity of Cherokee women by all free men. No person who is of negro or mulatto parentage, either by the father' or mother's side, shall be eligible to hold any office of profit, honor or trust, under this government.[49]

This was an unapologetically racist document. Ratified in an era when anti-black racism was standard practice in American politics and law, the Cherokee constitution was part of a larger social and cultural milieu in which collective identities hinged on exclusionary ideologies.[50]

However, Cherokee leaders were in a bind. Treaty obligations required the Cherokee Nation to recognize Cherokee freedpeople as citizens so long as they conformed to the terms of the 1866 treaty. But national sentiment was against such incorporation, especially if a freedman brought along an African American spouse with no previous connection to the Cherokee Nation. Principal Chief Dennis Bushyhead recognized this when he addressed the "many-headed question of 'citizenship'" in his fourth annual message to the National Council in 1882. Bushyhead acknowledged public sentiment but maintained that under the terms of the treaty the Cherokee Nation was duty-bound to respect the citizenship rights of African Americans married to Cherokee citizens.[51]

Understanding the implications of Bushyhead's argument, the members of the National Council set about "perfecting" intermarriage laws.[52] To the members of the National Council, the question of intermarriage between Cherokee freedpeople and African Americans was not a matter of kinship or traditional notions of adoption—concepts that had not been applied to Cherokee slaves during the nineteenth century in any case—but of the racial composition of the Cherokee diaspora's political homeland. Prior to the Civil War, both the Cherokee Nation and the neighboring Creek Nation passed a series of laws prohibiting intermarriage between their citizens and people with African "blood."[53] In the post-Civil War context these laws were revisited to reinforce prohibitions on intermarriage between Cherokees and "persons of color."[54] In 1868, the Cherokees reprinted an intermarriage law dating from 1839, a law that prohibited intermarriage with slaves.

In the spirit of these laws, the CCC began its work with the goal preventing the Cherokee diaspora's political homeland from losing its distinctive Cherokee (and racial) character. Backed by the National Council's lawmaking powers, the CCC constructed major bureaucratic impediments to the acquisition of citizenship by Cherokee freedpeople and their African American spouses.[55] According to the National Council and their CCC allies, "refugee freedman" and people of "African blood" constituted one of the more visible and disconcerting aspects of the "intruder" problem.[56] As CCC rulings were handed down, the perception that all black people were "intruders" hardened in Cherokee political and popular consciousness.[57]

Still, Cherokee freedpeople and their African American spouses persisted in claiming citizenship. Some Cherokee freedpeople alleged that the Cherokee courts had stripped them of their citizenship despite the fact that they had never left the Nation during the war, or for any extended period thereafter. Such was the claim of Mayland Back, who in June 1879 testified, "I am a colored man born and raised in the Cherokee Nation have never left it for more than two or three months at a time and even then I was in government service."[58]

But as Cherokee officials saw things, the freedpeople were everywhere on the move. Was Mayland Beck really who (and what) he claimed to be? Or was he one of the "exodusters," Southern African Americans who migrated to Kansas dreaming of a better life for themselves in the 1870s?[59] Some of these "exodusters" married Cherokee freedpeople and subsequently applied for citizenship in the Cherokee Nation, citing their compliance with Cherokee intermarriage laws. In August 1877, for example, Rubin Still and his wife, "[a] maimed colored woman that claims Cherokee rights under Treaty," applied to the Commissioner of Indian Affairs for Cherokee citizenship—an application, it's worth noting, that bypassed the Cherokee National Council, thus revealing much about where freedpeople believed the real political power resided. The Stills applied from Cooweescoowee. Their application was denied because Still "is an intruder, and a bad man at that."[60]

Due to the overlapping diasporas of Cherokee and Southern freedpeople, the intermarriages that occurred as a result, and the different governing authorities receiving citizenship claims, there were many families with uncertain social and legal standing in the Cherokee Nation. These families lived primarily in the Cooweescoowee District of the Cherokee Nation, in towns like Coffeyville along the Cherokee-Kansas border, in Missouri, Arkansas, and Texas.[61]

The CCC received a number of applications for citizenship from freedpeople in Texas. Like other freedpeople, these applicants often discovered that they were ineligible for citizenship, either because they failed to meet the requirements for Cherokee citizenship established in the 1866 treaty, or they ran afoul of the Cherokee Nation's laws pertaining to freedpeople and "intruders." As the Cherokee Nation and its Citizenship Commissioners saw things, these freedpeople had made the decision to live a life in diaspora, and a sovereign nation had every right to include issues such as residency and race in the essential qualifications for citizenship.[62]

For freedpeople who followed migratory paths into and out of the Cherokee Nation during the Civil War and late nineteenth century, these laws and legal interpretations had devastating consequences. Cherokee freedpeople sometimes pooled their resources, drawing on relationships forged during slavery, to present united petitions for Cherokee citizenship rights. This was the case for Jeffrey Holt and his eleven co-claimants for citizenship in November 1875. All ex-slaves, Holt and his co-claimants filed affidavits testifying that they had returned to the Cherokee Nation within six months of the 1866 treaty. Holt added that he resided with his family in the Cherokee Nation, qualifying them for "equal [rights] with the Indians" under Cherokee law. For no clear reason other than that the Holt claimants possessed "African blood," their claim was denied.[63]

A number of CCC rulings cited issues of race and residency as justification for the denial of Cherokee citizenship claims from people possessing "African blood." In 1880, Cherokee freedman Alex Bean lodged an application for Cherokee citizenship. His application was rejected because he had relocated to Kansas in 1879. Defined by the Cherokee Nation as an "intruder," Bean was forced to move outside the Nation's territorial limits. US census takers recorded Bean living in Tyler, Texas, in 1880.[64] However, Cherokee immigration and citizenship laws were not applied evenly. For example, Alex Sloan, who according to Cherokee records possessed no "Negro" ancestry, moved to Texas with his family as a small boy. Despite spending less time in the Cherokee Nation than Alex Bean, Sloan was admitted to citizenship in 1881.[65] The different outcomes in the cases of Bean and Sloan highlight the importance of having Cherokee "blood" free of African "admixtures." Racial purity had the power to make Cherokee citizenship commissioners forget about their own residency requirements for citizenship. Conveniently, this amnesia was overcome when the applicant or applicants involved possessed black "blood."

Race—and the tangle of issues and human relationships bound up with it—proved to be *the* critical factor in deciding the fate of citizenship applications during the 1870s and 1880s. Louis Carter discovered this after turning to the Commissioner of Indian Affairs for assistance in his application for Cherokee citizenship. Carter explained, "I am a colored man and was once a slave in the United States that I married a colored woman and citizen of the Cherokee Nation." Enclosed with his letter was a copy of his marriage license, tangible evidence of both Carter's marriage and his conformity to Cherokee marriage laws. For good measure, Carter added, "I married her and complied with all the requirements of law regulating intermarriage with citizens of the U.S. and that of Cherokees." However, Carter's marriage was deemed to have breached intermarriage laws with "negroes" and was therefore null and void. The application was subsequently dismissed.[66]

While both the Cherokee National Council and the Department of the Interior often ruled in the negative on the citizenship claims of freedpeople, Cherokee freedmen and women sometimes tried to play off the two sovereign nations' legal systems and political institutions in an effort to acquire a favorable ruling.[67] Such was the case of one William Hudson.[68] Hudson's life reflected the overlapping nature of the

African American and Cherokee diasporas in the United States during the nineteenth century. Hudson claimed that he had been a slave in the American South prior to the Civil War. In those heady early years of freedom following the war and emancipation, Hudson set out for the West. By 1867, Hudson was living in the Cherokee Nation and married to "a colored woman." Conscious of the Cherokee Nation's intermarriage laws, he testified that "I procured license from the proper authorities and performed all the requirements of law regulating intermarriage with citizens of the U.S. and of the Cherokee Nation." As Hudson understood Cherokee intermarriage laws, they were not set up to police race, but to regulate marriages between people of different nations.

In 1870, the Cherokee Nation agreed that Hudson had complied with intermarriage laws and granted him citizenship. However, citizenship was a particularly malleable legal identity in the Cherokee Nation during the late nineteenth century; even once it was attained, there existed no guarantees that it would last for life. This proved to be Hudson's experience. He was subsequently placed "on the doubtful list together with all other colored people that had married in this country from the U.S."

Hudson responded to the Nation's suspicions by lodging his marriage certificate with the Supreme Court of the Cherokee Nation. And there his papers sat, or so he thought, while the Court deliberated on his case. Anxious for a decision, Hudson inquired into the Court's deliberations. The response proved disappointing. The clerk of the Supreme Court claimed that Hudson's papers "were lost." Despite the absence of material evidence, Hudson soon received a decision. On June 9, 1878, the CCC concluded that in 1865 Hudson was a citizen of the United States. He did indeed marry a Cherokee freedwoman, Phoebe Smith, who was owned by a citizen of the Cherokee Nation when the Civil War began. However, the Commission denied Hudson's application for Cherokee citizenship because the Supreme Court of the Cherokee Nation declared that his marriage license—the same license the Court's clerk claimed to have lost—had not been "procured from legal authority" within the Nation. As far as the Cherokee Nation was concerned, William Hudson was an "intruder," and a black one at that.[69]

William Hudson did not give up the fight for his Cherokee citizenship. In May 1880, Lewis Carter, Henry Clay, and Phillip Duncan—all freedmen who had married Cherokee citizens—joined Hudson in requesting the assistance of the United States Secretary of the Interior in overcoming the gross violations of their citizenship rights in the Cherokee Nation. Hudson, Carter, Clay, and Duncan all maintained that they were Cherokee citizens by virtue of their conformity to the intermarriage laws of the Nation. They explained,

> At the break out of the late war we were slaves, some of us owned by citizens of the United States, others by citizens of this Nation. That since coming to the Nation, since the war, we married colored women who under the Cherokee Treaty of 1866, Sec. 9, have all the rights and privileges of native Cherokees.

Hudson, Carter, Clay, and Duncan did not interpret Cherokee intermarriage laws to have any racial or color-conscious meaning; instead, they understood these laws to be part of a coordinated effort on the part of the Cherokee Nation to police marriages between individuals from different nation-states. Believing themselves in compliance with Cherokee intermarriage laws, the petitioners insisted that, based on Article 9 of the 1866 treaty between the Cherokee Nation and the United States, they were not "intruders," but "to all intents and purposes adopted citizens of the Cherokee Nation, by virtue of this marriage." Officials disagreed, deeming these men "intruders."[70]

White "intruders" far outnumbered black "intruders" in the Cherokee Nation in the two decades after the Civil War. But no group of intruders attracted such a visceral, emotional response from Cherokee lawmakers and judges as people of African descent. This was racism in its most transparent legal form. At issue was a stake in the Nation's treasure and its land, the demographic makeup of the political homeland of the Cherokee diaspora, and the ontological question of what constituted a Cherokee identity. The Commissioner of Indian Affairs recognized these interconnected concerns in relation to the Cherokee

Nation's freedpeople and their African American spouses from the United States, noting, "the Cherokees are determined to brush down the colored people who were their former slaves."[71]

The Cherokee Nation's institutional memory proved willfully short on the question of freedpeople, and African Americans in general. There were some Cherokee leaders, especially those in the Downing Party, who insisted that they recognized "no distinction between Cherokee citizens on account of colour & will do all we can to do away with any prejudices that may exist between 'Halfbloods' and 'Fullbloods.'" In general though, the lawyers, politicians, and bureaucrats who narrated the Cherokees' recent history, interpreted their laws, and prescribed the Nation's future aspirations attempted to eliminate people of African descent from the story of the "Cherokee family" during the late nineteenth century.[72]

The frequency with which Cherokee leaders used the language of "blood quantum" in legal and political discourse mirrored a similar exclusionary language used by federal and state officials throughout the United States. While Cherokee lawyers and politicians routinely applied the language of "blood quantum" in racially exclusionary terms, they endeavored to avoid charges of anti-black racism by emphasizing their sovereign right to determine the genealogy of citizenship applicants. It was a brilliant institutional strategy, which, when stripped of its artifice, had as its fundamental purpose the exclusion of as many Cherokee freedpeople and intermarried African Americans as the law would allow. By combining the language of genealogy with racialized interpretations of "blood," "tradition," and a "modern" Cherokee identity, Cherokee leaders did not simply deny the existence of African Cherokee identity, but engaged in a concerted institutional attempt to erase it from the collective life and memory of the Cherokee diaspora.

Despite the overarching institutional memory and narrative of the Cherokee Nation, such positions were not universally shared. Some Cherokees bucked the racist trajectory of the National Council and Cherokee courts and embraced ethnic and racial diversity as one of the hallmarks of Cherokee identity, the Downing Party platform being one example of these attitudes. Other Cherokee citizens celebrated the fact that refugee freedpeople had been allowed to re-enter the Cherokee Nation after the Civil War and acquire land and citizenship. This, they argued, was more than the United States was prepared to do for its black populations. Self-serving as this latter position may have been, it did allow the proponents of such ideas to emphasize that the central issue regarding Cherokee freedpeople was not race or intermarriage, but the sovereign right of the Cherokee Nation to determine on its terms whom to admit to the family of Cherokee citizens. As one writer put it:

> We have always had the right to govern ourselves. Our treaties guarantee to us this right. Our treaties have made the colored population of this country citizens and we have agreed that you should be equal in rights privileges and the same protection under our laws. We have done more, we have divided our birthright with you in the division of our lands and our money. Has the Govt. of the United States or any individual State done so much? Go and ask those shrinking philanthropists and bring back the answer. Listen to the advise [sic] of your friends, don't treat us as though you gained your homes by conquest or held your rights by force of arms, and if you would be respected always be respectful. If you wish to prove yourselves good citizens be obedient to, and, abide by the law of the country that has adopted you.[73]

According to this writer, the "afro-Cherokee" people had been "adopted" into the Cherokee Nation, but they must always comport themselves as "good citizens." The Cherokee people were keeping a very close eye on anyone claiming to be African Cherokee.

Diasporic Horizons

The future of the Cherokee people and the diaspora they established during the nineteenth century was anything but
assured as that tumultuous century neared its end. In the
trans-Mississippi West, the recent history of the "intruder
problem," the "refugee business," and disputes over the citizenship
status of Cherokee freedpeople all presented significant challenges to
Cherokee leaders hoping to clarify the legal dimensions of Cherokee
identity. Similarly, Cherokee leaders in western North Carolina fretted
over the impact of intermarriage and the opening of Cherokee lands to
the outside world following the Civil War. Cherokee leaders on both
sides of the Mississippi therefore recognized that the loss of land, migration, declining Indigenous populations, and biological and cultural
mixing posed serious challenges to the future of an identifiable Cherokee people, much less a Cherokee homeland (or homelands).[1] The federal government's Indian policy compounded the severity of these challenges. Between 1887 and 1934, the federal government moved to break
up communally held Indian lands and allot that land to Indigenous
people on an individual basis. This policy buttressed the broader objective of assimilating Native Americans into white society—a process
facilitated by the education of Indigenous children in federally funded
boarding schools.[2]

Allotment and assimilation also coincided with a period in United State history defined by corporate corruption, the greed of railroad monopolies, and the westward migration of homesteaders and Euroamerican squatters. Cherokee leaders did their best to resist these developments.[3] Like all Indigenous leaders in Indian Territory, they opposed land allotments, resisted the excesses of assimilation policy, and participated in anti-colonial movements into the twentieth century.[4]

Thus, in Indian Territory and the region surrounding the diaspora's political homeland, feelings of suspicion, uncertainty, and anxiety—be it of whites, blacks, other Indians, the intentions of the federal government, railroad corporations, or land speculators—hung over this era of Cherokee history. This remained the case for Cherokees on both sides of the Mississippi even after the allotment and assimilation era transitioned into the era of "termination" and "relocation," which began after Franklin Roosevelt entered the White House in 1932. The Indian Reorganization Act (1934), popularly referred to as the "Indian New Deal," was the centerpiece of the Roosevelt administration's Indian policy. It was designed to facilitate federal government efforts to return a limited form of self-government to Indigenous tribes and to reverse the privatization (or individual allotment) of communal landholdings under the Dawes Act (1877).[5]

It was against this complex historical backdrop that the twentieth-century Cherokee diaspora took shape. Like other diasporas, the Cherokee diaspora opened up new geographical vistas and socioeconomic opportunities. For Cherokees, life in diaspora and outside the homelands in Indian Territory and western North Carolina both challenged and revivified the significance of Cherokee identity. Between the late 1880s and the Second World War, a Cherokee's horizons were shaped and reshaped by experiences in the present, aspirations for the future, and understanding of the past. Thus, the intersection of the past and present, the significance of travel and migration, and shifting perceptions of "home," "blood," and the value placed on memory and historical narration all played significant (if uneven) roles in defining what it meant to be "Cherokee" in a diasporic context.

The Allotment of Cherokee Homelands

Due to changes in American demographics, the politics of tribal sovereignty, land rights, and identity were fraught with high emotion and uncertainty for Native Americans between 1887 and 1934.[6] This certainly proved to be the case for people of Cherokee descent living in the Cherokee Nation in Indian Territory, on the Qualla Boundary Reservation in North Carolina, or in the 25 or more states in the United States that Cherokees called home. According to federal census takers, Cherokees in diaspora in the United States were a racially mixed group. The 1910 federal census of Cherokees "by blood" (not "Cherokee citizens"—a legal category that included freedpeople), enumerated 6,900 Cherokee "full-bloods" and 24,329 mixed-race Cherokees living in the United States (but outside of Oklahoma); 5,919 "full-blood" and 23,440 "mixed-blood" Cherokees lived within Oklahoma; and 934 "full-blood" and 469 mixed-race Cherokees lived in North Carolina.[7]

As late nineteenth-century Cherokees sought to establish eligibility for land allotments, the program was complicated by the geographically diffuse and biologically mixed nature of the Cherokee diaspora within the United States.[8] The individual charged with determining who qualified for land allotments was not a Cherokee, but an American bureaucrat. Henry L. Dawes, whom the General Allotment Act (1887) was named after, headed a three-member commission that included Meredith Helm Kidd and Archibald S. McKinnon. Headquartered in Muskogee, Indian Territory, the commission set about convincing Native Americans of the virtues of receiving land in severalty.[9] With Cherokee leaders and their Creek allies holding out on allotment, the United States Congress passed the Curtis Act (1898). Signed by President William McKinley, the Curtis Act empowered the Dawes Commission to establish tribal "rolls" on the basis of blood quantum, dissolve tribal courts and extend United States law over citizens of Indigenous nations, and to allot almost 16,000,000 acres of land to individuals. Approximately 3,174,988 acres of communally owned Native American lands was now set aside and surveyed for railroad construction, new towns, churches and schools, and the mining of resources, such as coal.[10]

In the agreement that ultimately brought allotment to the Cherokee Nation, the Cherokee Agreement of 1902, Cherokees received more favorable terms than neighboring Indigenous nations.[11] Over opposition from members of Redbird Smith's NightHawk Keetoowahs, the Cherokee National Council agreed to divide seven million acres of communally owned land among 47,798 allottees (those of Cherokee "blood" and individuals with "prior claims"). The allotments averaged 110 acres. Still, the concessions that Cherokee leaders won on behalf of their people were minor in comparison to what was lost—the territorial basis of Cherokee nationhood, and with it, a legally defined place that Cherokees living in diaspora could confidently call "home."[12]

The federal government based its calculation of Indigenous identity and qualification for land allotments on blood quantum.[13] This legal and bureaucratic maneuvering resulted in Cherokees losing approximately ninety percent of their pre-allotment landholdings in Indian Territory.[14] If land was the material basis upon which Cherokee people identified their political homeland, then the federal government's use of blood quantum did much to undermine the social and cultural meanings of Cherokee identity.[15]

In North Carolina, where Cherokees were legally classified as citizens of that state, Cherokee leaders at the Qualla Reservation also struggled to preserve a distinctively Cherokee identity. In particular, Eastern Band leaders feared that interracial marriages would dilute the biological basis for Cherokee identity. They therefore pressed the federal government to include a clause in their allotment agreement that maintained a minimum "blood quantum" of one-sixteenth Cherokee "blood," a stipulation that equated identity with race.[16] In 1889, the North Carolina Cherokees came to an agreement with the federal government that gave them the status of a federally recognized tribe with corporate rights to their lands, but gave the United States government the authority to determine tribal membership. It was not until 1930 that the Eastern Band gained the legal power to remove people having less than one-sixteenth Cherokee blood from the reservation.[17]

In the trans-Mississippi West, anxieties about "blood quantum," land allotments, and the nature of Cherokee identity were exacerbated by political factionalism. In 1886, one year before the passage of the

Dawes Act, the campaign for principal chief of the Cherokee Nation was enlivened by accusations that one of the candidates was not qualified to run for office because he had been born outside of the Cherokee Nation. Resurrecting the intertwined issues of territoriality and citizenship, Joel B. Mayes, a "half-blood" and former major in the Confederate Army, claimed that his opponent, Rabbit Bunch, a "full-blood" Cherokee and member of the National Party, displayed questionable loyalty to the Cherokee Nation because Bunch had spent a significant amount of time outside of the Nation. Adding fuel to suspicions about Bunch's loyalty to the Cherokee Nation, his National Party colleagues used their private correspondence to express a racial preference for a "half-breed" to lead the party. For instance, Clint C. Lipe, a biracial Cherokee who married a white woman, expressed a desire to see "a half breed at the head of our government."[18] Lipe also expressed concern that diasporic political figures such as Richard M. Wolf, the Eastern Cherokees' president of the Permanent Council and the man who went on to lead legal efforts to have the Keetoowah Society incorporated, would be appointed to Bunch's Executive Committee should the National Party's candidate triumph.[19] Bunch, however, was not elected, prompting one National Party insider to observe that "we will never have another full blood Cherokee for Chief, for I am satisfied that their [sic] never will be another such effort to elect one."[20]

Political factionalism, enlivened by racial prejudices and questions of "national" loyalty, was nothing new in the Cherokee Nation; it did, however, complicate the tortured process of selecting leaders to see the Nation through the allotment process.[21]

Still, allotment and tribal dissolution were coming. As outlined in the Cherokee Agreement of 1902, the Cherokee Nation was scheduled for dissolution in 1906. Difficulties in allotting land postponed that date until 1914, during which time the Cherokee government continued to exist in limited form. The task of leading the Cherokee government to its inevitable death fell to William C. Rogers. Rogers was a Downing Party man, a Mason, and a successful farmer. His family lineage connected him "to the Black Coats, the Bushyheads, the Rattlingourds, the Little Terrapins and most of the principal families of Arkansas, including that of Oolootekea (also spelled Ooloodega) himself."[22] In 1903,

Rogers was elected principal chief of the Cherokee Nation, only to be impeached in 1905 when agitation from the Keetoowah Cherokees set the stage for Frank J. Boudinot to assume power. The federal government, however, stepped in to stifle this Cherokee political turmoil before it turned bloody. Rogers thus became the first in a long succession of Cherokee chiefs appointed by the president of the United States.[23]

William C. Rogers was under no illusions about the future of the Cherokee Nation. His was a melancholic task. Speaking before the Cherokee National Council in November 1904, Rogers outlined in simple yet provocative terms the Cherokee Nation's immediate future: "The [Cherokee] Government which our forefathers cherished and loved and labored so hard to perfect, has been sentenced to die."[24] The sovereignty of the Cherokee diaspora's political homeland was all but gone. Dutifully, Rogers remained in office until 1917, his primary task being the signing of deeds to allotted land.[25] The end, it seemed, had come.[26]

Not all Cherokees, however, were willing to accept this scenario and surrender to the federal government's allotment and assimilation policies. So-called traditionalist movements, such as the "ultra conservative" Cherokee Emigrant Indians under the leadership of Joe Fox and Coming Snell, refused to accept the end of Cherokee sovereignty. Similarly, the most famous early twentieth-century traditionalist movement, Redbird Smith's Nighthawk Keetoowahs, resisted both the federal government's policies and the Cherokee National Council's accession to federal dictates.[27]

Redbird Smith was a child of the Cherokee diaspora. His mother, a woman of mixed German and Cherokee ancestry, and his "full-blood" Cherokee father, Pig Smith, had just arrived in the Cherokee Nation from Arkansas when Redbird was born on July 19, 1850. Once settled in the Illinois District of the Cherokee Nation, Redbird's father became active in conservative politics and taught his son about Cherokee traditions and beliefs.[28] Redbird Smith ultimately applied this informal education to the movement he led, a movement that was both a political statement against allotment and assimilation, and a declaration of pride in the traditions that gave Cherokee identity its cultural meaning.

The cultural pride that Redbird Smith felt was linked to the Cherokee legend of their ancient origins. According to that legend the Keetoowah, (or Kituwah; Ani-gi-du-wa-gi, meaning "the covered or protected people") received their name from God, "the giver of all things." This God-given name was a critical part of their identity, or soul. The belief that the Cherokees were a providentially chosen people motivated the Keetoowah's ancient forebears—whom some scholars refer to as the Ani-Kutani— to leave an unnamed island in the Atlantic, traverse the ocean, and establish Kituwah, one of the seven Cherokee Mother Towns.[29]

Redbird Smith and his followers—among them the famous Cherokee outlaw Zeke Proctor—drew spiritual strength from these traditions. With the formation of the Nighthawk Keetoowahs at a ceremonial ground near Gore in 1902, Smith's "Nativistic revival" began, and opposition to allotment and assimilation received its organizational structure.[30] According to Redbird Smith and his followers, the trans-Mississippi Cherokees were connected to their ancient forebears by adherence to ancient traditions and narratives of creation, which included stories of migration. Their more recent descendants began migrating west in the 1760s in an attempt to preserve and protect Cherokee traditions from aggressive Euroamericans. A second wave of migrants moved west during the era of the Revolutionary War. Finally, a third wave, the Chickamauga warriors (or red chiefs) and their followers began migrating into the trans-Mississippi West during the early nineteenth century. Through these westward migrations, those Cherokees who believed themselves to be the descendants of the ancient Keetoowahs hoped to keep the flames of their sacred fires alight.[31]

Redbird Smith used this history to frame his opposition to allotment. He maintained that the Cherokees, being blessed with intelligence, industriousness, and a keen sense of loyalty, retained a mission to preserve "Our pride in our ancestral heritage" so that "our posterity" has a clear sense of Cherokee identity—of soul—to guide them through life.[32] Allotment and severalty did indeed come to the Cherokee Nation, but the pride Smith instilled in his followers continued to burn brightly long after his death.[33]

Figure 15: Keetoowah ceremony (no date). Courtesy of the Thomas Gilcrease Museum, Tulsa, Oklahoma.

Scattered over the Earth

During the late nineteenth and early twentieth centuries, Cherokees were scattered across the United States. Migrations involve calculations and choices, and many Cherokees living in diaspora chose not to return to the Cherokee Nation. Some who made that choice had their Cherokee citizenship recognized by the Cherokee Nation, while others, like Robert and Rebecca Carter of California, were denied legal recognition.[34] The fate of couples like the Carters reinforced the enduring importance of territoriality to the meaning of Cherokee citizenship during the era of allotment.

Cherokees living at the Qualla Reservation who decided to migrate to the Cherokee Nation were no more likely to meet with success during the allotment era.[35] Similarly, Cherokee freedpeople were rou-

Figure 16: Cherokee family on the porch of their home in western North Carolina (no date). Courtesy of the Thomas Gilcrease Museum, Tulsa, Oklahoma.

tinely barred from legal recognition as Cherokees because they had not "perfected their citizenship," or because they had breached Cherokee intermarriage laws when they married an African American.[36]

What such cases tell us is that the intertwined issues of "blood," travel, and migration muddied the legal waters of Cherokee citizenship and eligibility for land allotments at the same time that technology made travel and adventure more of a possibility than ever before. For example, Cherokee entertainer Will Rogers and his friends often took the train from the Cherokee Nation to Missouri, Texas, Arkansas, and as far as New York.[37] For other Cherokees, two world wars, the Dust Bowl, and the Great Depression of the 1930s all affected their decisions to travel to faraway places temporarily, or to migrate permanently. At the turn of the century, travel and migration prompted new questions about the nature of Cherokee identity and fresh assertions about what it meant to be Cherokee in the early twentieth century.

The First and Second World Wars had a profound economic and social impact on Cherokee people, with Cherokees serving in the armed forces in various capacities. Some Cherokees served in the navy; others experienced trench warfare, or served as "code talkers" for U.S. intelligence.[38] In other instances, Cherokees worked as auxiliary staff, cleaning latrines or preparing meals. In 1919 the *Seamen's Journal* published a celebratory essay on the history of Cherokee warriors engaged in military service on behalf of either the British or the United States. This activity spanned centuries, from fighting alongside George Washington's "Virginia Blues" during the French and Indian War, to service in Cuba during the Spanish American War and "in China at the time of the Boxer Uprising." But it was the recently ended First World War that occupied the foreground. Of Cherokee participation in the "Great War," the *Seamen's Journal* observed that "Cherokee citizens of eastern Oklahoma point with pride to the fact that the Cherokee in this war . . . have borne an honorable and valorous part."[39]

For some Cherokee men, active service in World War I provided an opportunity to assert their pride in being Cherokee. Carlyle T. Pinn enlisted as "A Cherokee Cadet" from his hometown of Jamaica Plain, Massachusetts. It is not clear whether Pinn ever lived with the Western or Eastern Cherokees, but his self-identification as a Cherokee Indian instilled pride in the significance of his service. "To my knowledge," Pinn recalled, "I am the first and only Indian ever enlisted in this old and excellent regiment, which has always performed wonderful and comfortable achievements."[40]

Cherokees' experiences during World War I were not all positive. When the United States military began administering psychologist Robert Yerkes' IQ tests, military officials used the results from these tests to confirm perceptions of both African American and Native American mental inferiority.[41] Officials also tended to equate poor English skills with a lack of intelligence. For example, Lieutenant F. B. Taylor complained of John Doublehead, who served in Taylor's Sixty-fourth Infantry Regiment, that Doublehead "does not speak very good English and perhaps this is one reason why he is poor in carrying verbal messages."[42] Oftentimes officers asserted that ignorance and mental deficiencies bred insubordination. For instance, Private John Ratt, a Cherokee from Wellington, Oklahoma, was charged with insubordination toward his superiors. Ratt attempted to excuse his actions by explaining that constant salutations were uncommon in the Cherokee community in which he lived.[43]

Cherokees who participated in World War I focused less on white racism and more on the opportunities that the war presented. This proved true for Private Ray C. Sanook. Sanook was born in North Carolina in 1894. As a youth, he attended the Carlisle Indian School in Pennsylvania, where he demonstrated excellent leadership qualities. When he was drafted for service during the First World War, Sanook was a resident of Allegheny County in western Pennsylvania.[44] During the War, Sanook was assigned to the First Battalion, 319th Infantry Regiment's Sniping, Observation, and Scouting Section.[45] Sanook's military career was not over, however, once the war ended. While he returned to civilian life in the inter-war years, with the outbreak of the Second World War, and the United States' entry into that war following the Japanese attack on Pearl Harbor in 1941, Sanook, now aged forty-eight, once again entered military service. At the time of his draft registration in 1942, Sanook lived in the small, largely white, rural township of St. Paul, in Champaign County, Ohio, and according to the federal census of 1930, was employed doing unspecified railroad work.[46] Census enumerators seem to have looked at Ray Sanook and assumed he and his wife Pearl were "White." Whether the Sanooks retained some personal connection to the Cherokee culture or language is open to speculation, but it appears that those around him in Ohio perceived Ray Sanook as a white man.[47]

Ray Sanook's ability to "pass" as white, however, did not extend to his military service. With a record of his prior service during World War I, Sanook's draft registration for the Second World War clearly labeled him as "Indian," a categorization that set him up for service involving menial labor. Sanook, however, was lucky in that he had previous wartime experience and relatively specialized skills, and therefore he served as a seaman during World War II. In 1943, for example, he returned to the port of New Orleans after serving on a vessel sent to the port of Cristobal, on the Atlantic Ocean side of the Panama Canal.

During the course of the war, Sanook moved between the Atlantic and the Pacific theaters.[48]

Like the other 25, 000 Native Americans who saw active service during World War II, Ray Sanook used his military service as an opportunity to travel to faraway and exotic parts of the world.[49] The events of World Wars I and II thus intersected with the lives of Cherokee people in unexpected ways. Other now-iconic events of the early twentieth century, such as the Dust Bowl and the so-called "Okie" and "Arkie" migrations that followed, the stock market crash of 1929, and the ensuing Great Depression, likewise altered the lives of Cherokees throughout the diaspora.[50]

Cherokees who did not see active service in either World War I or II generally confined their travels to the territorial borders of the United States in the early twentieth century. Such was the case for Stooeastah, or Dan McGhee. Stooeastah was the Cherokee grandfather of literary scholar Sean Kicummah Teuton. Teuton has written eloquently about his grandparents' journey to Oakland, California. They left the Cherokee Nation in Indian Territory in 1907 after the federal government systematically dismantled Cherokee sovereignty and Oklahoma became a state. Teuton details how his grandfather, who preferred his Cherokee name, Stooeastah, and his grandmother, Armada McGhee nee Jones (who was from Independence, Arkansas), traveled toward the setting sun—just as Stooeastah's own grandparents did when they were forced to migrate to Indian Territory in 1838. In northern California, where John Rollin Ridge penned his greatest literary works, a small but nonetheless visible population of Cherokees emerged after the Gold Rush years, and there Stooeastah lived his life and ultimately found his final resting place. Teuton notes that McGhee died the same year that the federal government began interning Japanese Americans during the Second World War.[51] The historical intersections of diasporic peoples' encounters with the United States' brand of colonial governance were as poetic as they were oppressive and tragic.[52]

While Cherokees saw service during both world wars, and also worked in war industries in the United States, Cherokee people were not unanimous in their support for the wars. At issue for some Indigenous leaders was both the nature of Native American involvement in the wars and the political remuneration that would follow from such service. On both sides of the Mississippi during the 1930s, Cherokees continued to press the federal government over land rights and tribal sovereignty. In North Carolina, Eastern Band leaders used global affairs as an opportunity to express their desire to opt out of the allotment process, a position that the United States Congress acceded to in 1931, effectively ending allotment among the North Carolina Cherokees.[53]

A growing number of Cherokees living throughout the United States made the difficult decision to leave behind the anxieties associated with land allotments, tribal sovereignty, and economic hardship and set out toward the "setting sun" in search of new opportunities.[54] This was especially true during the inter-war period, when Cherokee families attempted to settle in places as remote as Australia. In 1919, for example, the Commonwealth of Australia received an application from an American family outlining the "desire of Cherokee Indians to settle in Australia."[55] Very little of this application survives, but given that the Commonwealth's immigration policy revolved around the racially exclusive ideal of a "white Australia" it should come as little surprise that this particular application was summarily rejected.

In the early twentieth century, migrations of this distance were rare. For Cherokees who did strike out toward the setting sun, California proved to be the most popular destination. For the most part, we know precious little of how the early twentieth-century Cherokees who settled in California understood or narrated their sense of Cherokee identity. That era's ethnologists, anthropologists, and linguists, like Smithsonian Institution ethnologist James Mooney, focused on preserving "traditional" Indigenous cultures and languages. The personal histories and beliefs of Cherokees who migrated toward the Pacific Ocean therefore eluded early twentieth-century ethnographers, leaving posterity with only the odd black-and-white photograph, a few faint personal recollections, and the even more occasional archival insight on which to base speculation about how Cherokees in the Golden State saw themselves and the world around them.[56]

Reconstructing what it meant to be Cherokee in the Pacific world of the early twentieth century is therefore a difficult task. The Pacific is a massive space; the various inhabited lands, islands, and atolls can feel

Figure 17: Portrait of Pomo-Cherokee man from California during the early twentieth century. Courtesy of the Braun Research Library Collection, Autry National Center, Los Angeles, Photo # P.808 Braun Research Library, copyright photo by E. S. Curtis.

isolated and disconnected from other communities and cultures. Cherokee people likely felt these omissions with varying degrees of emotional intensity during the early twentieth century. The cultural construction of the Pacific as isolated pockets of settlement, however, runs against the grain of recent Indigenous historiography in the Pacific. According to Pacific Island scholar Epeli Hauʻofa, Pacific Islanders developed rich cultures, linguistic traditions, and economies of exchange that pre-date European colonization. Hauʻofa thus presented an empowering vision of the Pacific to its Indigenous people, a vision of a people with a history and a future not weighted down by dependency theory, or by the notion that economic life and culture radiate out from European metropoles to isolated and impoverished Pacific Island colonies.[57]

For Cherokees in the "Sea of Islands," a sense of connectedness to their faraway homeland and to Cherokee culture often seemed distant, even out of reach. In such a context, was any coherent and meaningful Cherokee identity possible? In California, people of Cherokee descent felt they could at least start a new life defined by stable family environments and better economic opportunities. Significantly, the Cherokee families who migrated to California were often racially mixed and culturally diverse. Some did find the material comforts they dreamed of, while many others remained mired in poverty. The children of these families also had a variety of experiences. Some thrived in California, excelling in their studies and extracurricular activities at the off-reservation schools they attended. Other children struggled. The records of the Sherman Institute, located from 1902 in Riverside, California, provide rare insights into the struggles of young men and women of Cherokee descent to understand their place in the settler colonial world of California.[58]

The Sherman Institute, one of twenty-four federally run off-reservation boarding schools, was founded in 1892 as the Perris Indian School in Perris, California. It relocated to Riverside, California, in 1902 and was renamed the Sherman Institute.[59] Modeled after Richard Henry Pratt's Carlisle Indian School, Sherman educated students from Indigenous communities and mixed-race native families from California, Arizona, New Mexico, Idaho, Oregon, Nevada, Oklahoma, Montana, Utah, South Dakota, Wisconsin, and Nebraska.[60] Prior to the Second World War, most Cherokee children were educated at the Cherokee Nation's public schools, male and female seminaries and orphan asylums, the "Negro high schools," or the Cherokee Boarding School in North Carolina.[61] By the late nineteenth and early twentieth centuries, however, the Cherokees were well and truly a diasporic people, and children of Cherokee descent regularly attended BIA boarding schools. Sherman enrolled forty-five children of Cherokee descent prior to World War II. These students came from towns and cities in California—Sacramento, Modesto, and Redding in northern California; Ontario, Los Angeles, and Anaheim in southern California—in addition to Oklahoma and Arizona. Official records indicate that these Cherokee students possessed "blood quantums," ranging from "full-blood" to 1/32 Cherokee blood. By far the most commonly recorded blood quantum was "one-quarter blood," with 19 students categorized in this group.[62] The recording of blood-quantum by BIA officials, however, was not simply a matter of assigning racial designations to determine eligibility for enrollment. Indeed, student records indicate the subtle racial and cultural battle that went on between federal officials' definition of a child's racial identity and the individual child's self-perception of his or her race and indigeneity.

Consider Charles Starr. In 1927, Charles Starr entered Sherman and quickly distinguished himself as a model student. He excelled in both his academic and vocational studies, and earned a reputation for being a brilliant public speaker. By 1932, Starr had endeared himself to students and staff and was elected "yell leader" of the Liberty Society, a student debate club.[63] In the minds of Sherman's white educators, Starr had become a model of Indian assimilation and an exemplar for other students. Starr, in other words, was living proof that Native American children had the potential "To learn the ways of the white people."[64]

To Sherman educators and BIA officials, a child like Starr was an ideal candidate for assimilation into American social and economic life. His father was purportedly three-quarters Cherokee, while BIA officials classified his mother as one-quarter Cherokee. While Starr appears to have classified himself as "half-blood Cherokee," officials enrolled him at Sherman as 3/8 Cherokee.[65] Perceived by Sherman enrollment officers as nearer to white than a "half-blood" Indian, Starr was therefore "taken care of, taught, and drilled" so that he could eventually assimilate into white society.[66]

In California, correspondence between the parents of Cherokee students and Sherman officials suggests that a number of these parents hoped to use federal Indian schools to equip their children with the necessary skills to eventually achieve economic independence. Such intentions are evident in the case files of students like Josephine Coleman, a "half-blood" Cherokee, who received her father's permission to participate in the "outing" program in 1929. Outing was a system in which students were placed with white employers during the summer recess.[67] Charles Coleman informed Superintendent Conser that "my daughter Josephine . . . has my permission to try a little outing." According to Mr. Coleman's letter, Josephine was eager to "try a little outing" because "She has been asking me for the past two years to go outing so I decided to let her try one year . . . I am sure she will gain a great deal outing."[68] While the vocational skills learned by Cherokee students reflected the gendered nature of early twentieth-century curriculums, some Cherokee children also expressed the hope that in acquiring practical skills they could become financially independent. For example, Frank Watson, a "quarter-blood" Cherokee from Grove, Oklahoma, insisted that "After learning my trade I wish to get a job and make a living hoping some day to own a shop of my own."[69]

Sherman was seen by some Cherokee diaspora parents as both a springboard to economic independence and a place of refuge for children.[70] Children like Elizabeth Hobbs, a "three-eighths" Cherokee from Sacramento, California, were reportedly growing up in an impoverished family environment. Hobbs's parents had apparently separated in a bitter divorce, her white father leaving California and relocating to the east coast. Although Elizabeth Hobbs "is a blond and . . . looks white," her mother was reported to be a "three-quarter blood" Cherokee who, officials insisted, "is not one of the Indians that present a problem."[71] Despite, or perhaps because of, the ongoing family feuding between Elizabeth Hobbs's parents, her mother enrolled her at Sherman, where she became a solid "B" grade student.[72] Little evidence survives to indicate the young woman's attitudes about her racial appearance and sense of Cherokee identity, if indeed she held on to one. Elizabeth's father did not even want her to visit her mother on weekends. But perhaps her mother's single-minded determination to maintain legal custody of her daughter was indicative of a close mother-daughter bond that Elizabeth ultimately translated into an adult acceptance of her Cherokee heritage.

Elizabeth Hobbs's home life may have been unstable, but in many ways she was fortunate in having a mother who loved her and was willing to fight the necessary legal battles to raise her to adulthood. Other children faced a much less certain future.[73] This was particularly the case in the 1930s, as the effects of the Great Depression gripped families across the nation.[74] Georgia Tanner, for example, was one of ten people living in her home in El Monte, California when her "half-breed" Cherokee father and white mother wrote to the Sherman Institute to request the admission of their daughter. The Tanners pled their case by stating the dire nature of their home life, claiming, "We can't provide properly for [Georgia's] education and properly cloth her due to the size of our family." They continued their plea on Georgia's behalf adding, "She is adapted to beauty culture and is desirous of studying the same."[75]

In the language of early twentieth-century social service workers, children like Georgia Tanner were considered "half orphans," or children whose parents—in some cases, a single parent—experienced difficulty providing a comfortable home for a child or children.[76] Such instances of the breakdown of traditional family and kin networks among the Cherokee led to the construction of the Cherokee Orphan Asylum in the Cherokee Nation.[77] However, these institutions could not accommodate every needy child, and many Cherokee families lived far from the Cherokee diaspora's political homeland. Some "half orphans" migrated west with their families and eventually entered off-reservation schooling in California, among them Ruth Whitley from Sells, Arizona. Whitley entered Sherman after her "half-blood" Cherokee mother died and her "one-quarter blood" father was unable to support her. As Whitley's aunt informed Sherman officials, "Her father has not been able to take care of her, taking her from place to place wherever he went and has not been able to take care of her."[78]

While many parents enrolled a child at Sherman in order to ease pressure on household finances or prevent a child from living the life of a tramp, many also expressed a desire to have their children receive the best education available. For mixed-race Cherokee children, the Sherman Institute seemed to offer a possible path to social mobility and economic independence. Richard Cooper's father enrolled his "half-blood" son at Sherman in 1938 because "it will be better for him." According to the elder Cooper, "There is too many bad boys here [in Paso Robles, California]. I want him away."[79] Students of Cherokee descent often echoed these sentiments, expressing a determination to acquire an education and become economically self-sufficient. Margaret Duncan and her sister Lucinda were completely overjoyed at gaining admission to Sherman, certain that they would be "happy there and obtain a good and useful education." The Duncan girls, from Clovis, New Mexico, migrated to California with their "7/8 blood" Cherokee father and "5/8 blood" Cherokee mother. Just how the Duncan girls ought to be classified confused and at times confounded Sherman officials. Some official documents categorize them as "3/4 blood" Cherokee, while others note that they were "half-blood Cherokee."[80] To officials, blood quantum was no small matter; it determined a student's curriculum, and as such, future employment opportunities. Even more revealing, however, was the language that Margaret and Lucinda Duncan used to describe their aspirations, aspirations that underscore how off-reservation schooling prescribed the economic and social horizons of Indigenous children. For most students at Sherman, the loftiest of dreams meant becoming a skilled member of the American working class, while the vast majority took up menial jobs and became part of the United States' unskilled proletariat.[81]

A number of Sherman's Cherokee students echoed the Institute's promotional literature and expressed a determination to "obtain a good and useful education."[82] However, an equal number of students had negative experiences during their time at the Institute, among them brothers Robert and Kay Beldon, who entered Sherman from Sacramento, in northern California, in 1926. Officials described the boys as "quarter-blood" Cherokee, although they appear to have seen themselves as "full white."[83] On September 2, 1926, Kay Beldon, the younger of the two, wrote an impassioned letter to his mother that outlined the horrors of the Sherman Institute. Kay informed his mother:

> This is the worst school I ever been to. The first day I came here, I had to take a shower, and there was shit all over the shower house, all boys pick on me and hit me, and that's why I don't like it here. There is one boy here, that is going home and his brother is coming after him in his auto, and we are going with him, he passes us right through Sac. If his brother

don't come I will write to you and tell you, so you can send us some money . . . Bob don't like it here at all. [The school] is the dirtiest I ever was in.[84]

Few surviving statements from former students more clearly and directly contradict the vision of educational utopia that Sherman Institute literature promoted. According to Kay Beldon, he and his brother never felt at ease at Sherman. Perhaps this had something to do with the unsanitary facilities that he described for his mother; or maybe it had more to do with the brothers' self-identification as "full white," which may have inspired hostility from other students and precipitated the bullying that Kay Beldon complained about. Whatever the reasons for the brothers' discomfort at Sherman, shortly after Kay sent that letter on September 2, 1926, they made good on their promise and absconded.

This, however, was not the first time that the Beldon brothers had fled the school grounds. They had previously taken flight in August 1926. After that instance Superintendent Conser expressed his willingness to "give the boys another chance."[85] However, by mid-September, with the brothers once again absconding, the stakes appear to have risen. Indeed, the boys' parents, Robert Beldon, Sr., a "half-blood" Cherokee, and Hazel Wright, who was white, expressed great concern. Beldon, Sr., was clearly angered by his sons, writing to Superintendent Conser on September 21, 1926, "I want you to get the Boys Back [sic] and punish them so they won't repeat it again."[86] Wright's anxiety was more nurturing in character; she complained in a letter to her husband that "They dont [sic] take them back or make any effort to find them. When the girls run away they do try to get them."[87] Hazel Wright clearly felt that the authorities at Sherman showed a greater duty of care towards female students who absconded from the Institute's grounds. Whatever the actual reason, the Beldon boys were refused re-admission in 1929. Writing of Robert Beldon, the school's disciplinarian Ralph E. Johnson informed Superintendent Conser that "Robert Beldon's promises to us mean very little, as he was constantly promising to do better. Robert has to be called into this office and reprimanded daily and at each of these occasions he faithfully promised to make his bed and clean his locker or to go to his vocational dept. and school even to his bathing."

Johnson's harsh assessment of Robert Beldon prompted him to conclude, "I do not believe it good judgment to bring the boys back to this Institution."[88] The Beldon case thus epitomized the fate of mixed-race children of the Cherokee diaspora who felt disconnected from family and community, and who felt even more out of place in a rigid institutional setting like Sherman.[89]

Memory and Identity

By the late 1930s, Cherokee people young and old had a long history of dealing with both the institutions and the individual agents of settler colonialism.[90] The recent history of allotment and assimilation, the beginnings of "termination" and "relocation" programs, and Cherokees' childhood experiences in institutions like Sherman contributed to the texture of life in the Cherokee diaspora. It was also in this general context that Cherokees structured their collective historical consciousness. One event stood above all others in anchoring a modern Cherokee historical consciousness: the Trail of Tears.

The origin of the term "Trail of Tears" remains shrouded in conjecture. In the nineteenth century, references to "trails" and "tears" appeared in various literary formats in reference to the violence of Spanish colonialism.[91] At some point during the late nineteenth and early twentieth centuries, the Trail of Tears entered the American vernacular as shorthand for the territorial dispossession of Native Americans and their forced migration into the West in the 1830s. In *A History of Oklahoma* (1908), government bureaucrats Joseph B. Thoburn and Isaac M. Holcomb, traced "the roads over which the Southern tribes came into their new inheritance."[92] Their sentimental narrative focused not on the hardships of the journey and the loss of friends and relatives, but on a positive story of the tribes' "new inheritance" in the West. In light of the processes of allotment, detribalization, and the admission of Oklahoma to statehood in 1907, one might be forgiven for thinking that Thoburn and Holcomb were telling a crude joke at the Indian's expense.

Thoburn and Holcomb were not joking, and as a result it was left to early twentieth-century Native American writers to explore the depth of emotions that Indigenous people associated with the phrase "Trail of

Tears." The durability of the imagery of the Trail of Tears and the belea-guered Cherokee Nation owes much to the histories and biographies of prominent Cherokees written during the early twentieth century. Rachel Caroline Eaton penned one of the most important works of Cherokee history during the decades between the First and Second World Wars,[93] *John Ross and the Cherokee Indians* (1914), a book that followed in the biographical tradition of Cherokee educators Mary Jane Ross and Ma-bel Washbourne Anderson.[94] Eaton's book, however, focused less on the celebration of prominent individuals and more on dispersal, sickness, death, "homesickness and mental depression,"[95] noting, "For many years the road the exiles travelled on this fateful journey was known to the Indians by a word in their language meaning the 'Trail of Tears.'"[96]

Anne Ross, an actress and John Ross's granddaughter, also helped to raise awareness about the phrase "Trail of Tears" during a speaking tour of the United States in 1916. Styling herself Princess Galilolle, and attired in the outfit of a Plains Indian woman—a culturally contrived identity—Ross labeled Cherokee removal a "Trail of Tears."[97] The Cherokee poet Ruth Margaret Muskrat's 1922 poem "The Trail of Tears" gave voice to the emotional pain that she imagined many Cherokees must have felt being forced into a life of exile far from the mountains and rivers of their Southeastern homeland.[98]

The phrase "Trail of Tears" evoked images of Cherokees march-ing overland through sleet and snow, and over windswept prairies and endless plains. During the early twentieth century, this imagery served a purpose, underscoring the hardship, suffering, and loss that those forced to march into the trans-Mississippi West experienced. While such imagery served to give meaning to this most significant event in modern Cherokee history, it did not always reflect the reality of the re-moval process. Cherokees did not always complete the journey into the trans-Mississippi West by foot. According to Cherokee scholar Daniel Littlefield, water was the most common means of westward travel, with steamboats, keelboats, flatboats, canal boats, and sailing ships all be-ing used. Transportation was also provided by horses, carts, wagons, and even the railroad.[99] Despite Littlefield's perspective, the imagery of Cherokees marching overland, especially through snow and sleet, per-sists today, just as vivid as it was during the early twentieth century.

Cherokees, like other Native American exiles, did not forget the significance of the Trail of Tears. Indeed, the phrase "Trail of Tears" appears to have become embedded in Cherokee historical consciousness by the time federal employees began work on the Works Project Administration's Indian Pioneer Papers (IPP) in the late 1930s. Like the Works Project Administration interviews conducted with former slaves at that same time, the IPP interviews come with methodological and interpretive challenges. In an era when race was omnipresent in American society and culture, the answers of respondents must be weighed in the context of the racial or ethnic identity of the interviewer. Similarly, the reader needs to scrutinize the types of questions asked, to account for cases when an interviewer asks a leading question.[100]

Despite these interpretive challenges, the IPP documents nonetheless offer invaluable insights into the place of the Trail of Tears in the oral histories of Native Americans in Oklahoma. Interviewees typically spoke about the date and location of their birth, their education, work and family life, and occasionally digressed into narrations of particularly memorable people or events. More often than not, the Trail of Tears was the narrative pivot, the focal point for a description of the hardships and cruelty of settler colonial oppression. For example, Washington Lee recalled the base injustice that the United States government imposed on the Cherokees, insisting that her grandfather "was driven from his home in Georgia over the Trail of Tears with all the other Cherokee Indians and while on the trail somewhere he lost his father and mother and sister, and never saw them any more."[101] The Cherokee woman Estella Stickle had a similarly grim story to tell, remembering the Trail of Tears as "A Real American Tragedy." In Stickle's memory, the Trail of Tears involved "Walking, walking, walking. Unrelieved walking. Days of walking. Weeks of walking. Months of walking. Continuous walking. Monotonous walking. Maddening walking."[102]

Stickle's characterization of removal was punctuated with evocative images of the hardships she imagined the removal generation experiencing. She was not, however, simply being descriptive; she had a moral to convey. After emphasizing the endurance needed to survive the long walk into the trans-Mississippi West, she emphasized how "Pain, hunger, illness, death," were all too common along the "Trail of

Tears." She explained that through "Nights of exposure," through the rain, the cold, and the winds, the Cherokee and other Southeastern Native Americans kept walking until they reached Indian Territory.[103] Why did such suffering occur? Stickle had a blunt answer, stating that it "was the white man's insatiable hunger for land, for wealth, that caused him to forget his [treaty] promise and drive the red man farther west."[104]

These memories of removal were filtered through at least four or five generations of family histories.[105] This was the case for Ella Robinson's memories of the Trail of Tears. Robinson's parents were born in Georgia in 1836 and 1837 respectively. Her father, David Israel, was "a full blood Cherokee," and her mother, Martha Jane Miller Israel, "a quarter Cherokee." Given that David and Martha were infant children during removal, they were unlikely to have recalled many details about the Trail of Tears. Evidently David and Martha Israel's parents passed down their recollections of removal, thus generating the family's connection to this most traumatic event in modern Cherokee history. From the stories David and Martha Israel heard as they grew to adulthood, they formed a mental picture of life in "the old nation" back east, of the hardships of removal, and the uncertainty of starting life anew in Indian Territory. It was from these family recollections that Ella's understanding of the Trail of Tears slowly took shape.[106]

If firsthand recollections of the Trail of Tears were hard to come by during the late 1930s, tales of hardship were not. This word—"hardship"—was repeated many times in the oral histories collected for the IPP. It is a word that evokes images of the struggle to survive, to endure against great odds. Cherokee Jim McCurtin narrated a history replete with hardships. He informed his interviewer that his wife's parents "told her of the many hardships they endured on the way to the west during the removal. On this side of the Mississippi, they had trenches laid off and the Indians were not allowed to cross the trenches. There was much rain and snow. Many of their horses died, and finally smallpox broke out and the Chickasaw began to die."[107]

"Hardship" seemed to follow Cherokees during the nineteenth and early twentieth centuries. According to the interviewees in the IPP, these hardships began during removal in the late 1830s. Hardship was, quite simply, a product of American settler colonialism. Detailing the "hardships" experienced by Cherokees in Indian Territory in the wake of removal, Amos Green explained that "Many of those early day Indians had been through sickness, loss of all the few possessions they had and the starvations as well as the deaths that occurred without number."[108] Rachel Dodge also told a tale of the "many hardships of the trip" to Indian Territory, learned from her Cherokee grandmother.[109] Dodge, who was born in the Cherokee Nation in Indian Territory in 1886, informed her interviewer that her ancestors experienced "chills and fever from the exposure" and that efforts to remedy the ills of the sick and provide comfort to the dying were complicated by the foreignness of the landscape. Dodge explained, "Indian Doctors couldn't find the herbs they were used to and didn't know the ones they did find, so they couldn't doctor them as they would have at home."[110] In addition to the physical hardships of forced relocation, then, the exile experienced by the removal generation heightened their feelings of vulnerability and uncertainty.

If the forces of American settler colonialism had fractured the Cherokee past, made the present uncertain, and the future—in the allotment and assimilation era—only a tenuous possibility, then memories of the "Trail of Tears" brought this history into focus. As one interviewee explained:

> "The Indians will vanish" has been the talk of the older Indians ever since the white people first came to mingle among them. They seemed to prophesy that the coming of the white man would not be for their good and when the step towards their removal to a country to the West was just beginning, it was the older Indians that remarked and talked about themselves by saying, "Now, the Indian is now on the road to disappearance." The elders feared that removal from ancestral homelands would result in "their leaving of their ways."[111]

Forced to leave their "ancient" homeland, Cherokee elders felt that their place in the world was no longer certain. Their sense of direction, place, and connection to the lands where the customs of their ancestors were kept alive, medicine practiced, and game hunted was abruptly ended with removal. The Trail of Tears promised an uncertain future, or no future at all.[112] The elders, after all, viewed the West as a dark land where death was the only guarantee.

But change had come to the Cherokee. For some the Trail of Tears brought physical death, for others fears about spiritual death, and it portended an uncertain future for all. Cherokee people had been trying to make sense of these emotions and historical experiences since the early nineteenth century—in both written and oral form.[113] In the late 1930s, the descendants of the Cherokees forced into exile continued the work of ordering their intergenerational memories in ways that both they and white Americans might understand. Margaret Drew's father, John Thompson Drew, was a leader of one of the Cherokee companies forced to march west from Georgia in 1838. The Drews left their homeland with heavy hearts, but they survived the journey and eventually prospered in the West. Availing themselves of the best educational facilities in the Cherokee Nation, Arkansas, and Texas, the Drews remained a respected Cherokee family, and Margaret went on to become a teacher of considerable esteem.[114]

For the descendants of the Trail of Tears exiles, appropriating the narrative structures embedded in linear histories provided a way to imagine a connection to the ancestral homeland of their parents and grandparents in the cis-Mississippi. Elizabeth Watts, a "full-blood Cherokee Indian," born in the Canadian District of the Cherokee Nation in 1859, offers an example. Watts's identity was structured not simply by anxieties over land allotments or the early-twentieth-century obsession with "blood quantum," but also through her family connection to what she saw as the ancestral homeland in the Southeast, and the trauma of removal. Watts recalled with pride how her mother, Nancy Tony-Miller, was born "on the East bank of the Mississippi River near Memphis, Tennessee, in 1837, as her "grandparents were en route from Georgia on the 'Trail of Tears.'" Given the chronology of Elizabeth Watt's narrative, it is actually possible that her grandparents were among those Cherokee migrants who set out for the trans-Mississippi West prior to the forced removals of the Cherokees in 1838 and 1839. This, however, was not really the point of Watts' family history; the point she was trying to make was that despite the brutalities of American settler colonialism—the "hardships" of the Trail of Tears, the disease, and the death suffered by the very young and very old on that melancholic journey into exile— Watts' mother, Nancy, was born.[115] In the circumstances of her birth, Nancy was a child of the Cherokee diaspora—conceived in the Cherokee people's "ancient" homeland and born on a barge on the Mississippi River, a riverine borderland between the cis-and trans-Mississippi. Elizabeth Watts's mother survived her traumatic entry into the world and was raised in what became the new political homeland of the Cherokee diaspora. The imagery evoked, ordered, and narrated by Elizabeth Watts tells a powerful tale. While the specter of death and the uncertainty of exile underpin her narrative, her personal history is a story of birth and rebirth, a narrative arc that connects the past to the present, the east to the west.

No group's culture, social relations, or political institutions remain unchanged. This certainly proved to be true for the Cherokee in the century after removal. Historian Rose Stremlau has demonstrated, for example, how late nineteenth-century Cherokee families struggled to keep bonds of kinship alive. In the wake of the impact of settler colonialism on Cherokee life during the nineteenth century, Cherokee kinship practices on both sides of the Mississippi River evolved to help family members feel a sense of connectedness to "tradition," while simultaneously reimagining family relations in ways that made kin identities meaningful in the context of the late nineteenth and early twentieth centuries.[116]

The reimagining of kin relations can be seen in the interviews collected in the IPP, such as the account of Magnolia Adair Jones, born in the Flint District of the Cherokee Nation. Her father, Edward Adair, was reportedly a "one eighth Cherokee," while her mother, Melissa Harrison Adair, met and married Edward in Georgia. Magnolia's parents remained in the cis-Mississippi in the decades after removal, but a longing to reconnect with family prompted them to move to the West. The Adair family migrated to the Cherokee Nation in Indian Territory in 1870. Two years later they had a daughter, whom they named Magnolia. Through the processes of migration, marriage, and the birth of children in diaspora, kin relations long dormant and separated by vast distances received new life from Cherokee people who chose to relocate among family and friends, start families, and thereby breathe new life into what it meant to be Cherokee in the early twentieth century.[117]

The Cherokee kinship system was certainly tested, and indeed frayed, by the pressures imposed on it by nineteenth-century settler colonialism, and especially by the hardships of the Trail of Tears. This did not mean, however, that Cherokee kinship was simply forgotten and left to die a slow cultural death. Myrtle Emery explains how the people who gave Cherokee kinship ties their meaning also adapted kinship systems to meet their contemporary social and economic needs. Emery was living on a farm in the Dutches Creek bottom when a federal employee interviewed her in 1937. She had no recollection of her parents as they had died when she was still an infant. Emery underscored the durability of Cherokee kinship systems, however, when she explained how she was adopted and raised by Hiram and Susan Early, who lived eight miles east of Texanna, as though she were their biological child. Emery's adoption reflected how extended family networks emerged as an important source of kinship in diaspora.[118]

Narratives in the IPP were also punctuated with remembrances of the Western Cherokees, or "Old Settlers," and the Texas Cherokees, who left the "ancient homeland" behind them and set off "in canoes seeking a new land in which to live" under the leadership of "Chief Bowl."[119] Such stories became part of the rich fabric of diasporic Cherokee identities, just as Cherokees recalled the disruptive impact of the Civil War, migrations to work in the cattle business in Kansas and Missouri, or the importance of maintaining a biological connection to one's Cherokee ancestry by selecting a marital partner of "Cherokee extraction."[120]

The language of race and "blood quantum" was foremost in the minds of many respondents during the 1930s. It was on Richard L. Cox's mind when he recounted his personal history to an IPP interviewer in April 1938. Cox reported that he had settled in Oklahoma in 1900. To underscore the legitimacy of his decision of relocate and settle among the Cherokee in Indian Territory, Cox claimed to be of Cherokee blood through his mother's side of the family: "I trace my Indian blood from my mother's side. Her grandfather was presumed to be over one-half blood Cherokee. Her grandfather's folks lived in Kentucky but in 1832 all were not in harmony because of differences of opinion on the removal question." Cox insisted that although his mother's family "were very comfortably fixed in land," they decided it was in their best interest to move to Indian Territory."[121]

The issue of racial mixture and migration is a significant part of the story of the Cherokee diaspora, as it is for the story of settler colonialism in North America more generally. The IPP oral histories underscore the complex web of genealogical connections made by people of Cherokee descent in the late 1930s. These connections crossed lines of "race," culture, geography, and vast historical epochs. In her work for the IPP, Elizabeth Ross uncovered the story of Archibald Campbell, a Cherokee who was something of a folklore legend among early twentieth-century Cherokees. Archibald Campbell—"Arch" to his family and friends— provided a clear example of these labyrinthine connections. Witnesses testified that Campbell was born in the "old nation east of the Mississippi river." His father was Scottish, though Arch reportedly possessed "Indian characteristics." Arch spoke Cherokee, with a smattering of English. American colonialism, however, had a major impact on his life. In 1812 he was reputedly a member of the Cherokee warrior party who fought alongside Andrew Jackson at the famous Battle of Horseshoe Bend. In 1818 Campbell was part of a Cherokee war party sent west to fight Osage warriors, who, according to western Cherokee settlers, were invading their homesteads, killing and stealing livestock, and harassing women and children. The following year, Arch Campbell made a brief visit to Indian Territory, a faraway land he thought he would never see again. However, in 1838 he became part of the Trail of Tears. Arch survived the journey and made his home—a two-story log structure with "a stack or double chimney"—a short distance from the new Cherokee capital at Park Hill.[122]

Arch Campbell was the embodiment of the Cherokee people's adaptiveness and innovative spirit. Wherever they traveled, Cherokees took old stories about who they were and added new details, new layers of meaning that helped them to understand changes in their social and interpersonal environments. But this spirit of accommodation and innovation had its limits. And in the nineteenth and early twentieth century no group ran up against those limits more than Cherokees of African descent. That said, African American and mixed race African

Cherokee people were as much a part of the Cherokee diaspora as were people of myriad other racial and ethnic backgrounds. Mary Ann Mc-Coy, an ex-slave once owned by the Cherokee Bill McCoy, was one such person. She was among the Cherokees who settled "in Northeast Texas under the terms of a treaty made with the Republic of Texas during its brief existence. This band later returned to the Indian Territory." Mc-Coy's take on the hardships and iniquities of removal was influenced by the experiences of racial slavery. Three generations of women in Mc-Coy's family had been enslaved in Mississippi and traded back and forth between the Choctaws and the Cherokee. Her father, a Cherokee man by the name of Bob Parrot, died before he had the opportunity to enroll his progeny as citizens in the Cherokee Nation, and Mary Ann Mc-Coy, like so many Cherokee freedpeople, was denied citizenship in the Cherokee Nation after the Civil War. McCoy recalled that having her Cherokee ancestry legally recognized proved impossible, and she was "granted the privileges of a Freedman only."[123]

If late nineteenth- and early twentieth-century Cherokee officials were inclined to deny that a significant number of people of African ancestry also possessed Cherokee "blood," African Cherokee people were inclined to both remember and celebrate their mixed racial ancestry. For example, Jeff D. Randolph situated his identity in his "Cherokee, Creek, and Negro" ancestry. Randolph, who was born in 1862, stated that "In 1832, when the Indians moved with blood relatives of negro extraction, many Indians brought their own slaves with them to Oklahoma."[124] The Cherokee freedman Joe Bean had a similar story to tell about slavery and the Trail of Tears. Bean claimed that "Our old slave family was a big one," and that a Georgia Cherokee had once owned his mother and had forced her to migrate west at the end of the 1830s.[125] Nannie Gordon's father and grandfather not only accompanied the Cherokees along the Trail of Tears but were instrumental in helping Cherokees to cross the Ohio River on the journey toward Indian Territory.[126]

Memories of migration from East to West ran through many of the oral histories of former Cherokee slaves and their descendants at the end of the 1930s. Sam Jordan, for example, claimed that he was born in Alabama, his father a "half-breed" Cherokee, his mother a slave. According to Jordan, slavery in Cherokee society could be brutal because overseers were both poor and mean. Jordan claimed that the overseers he knew as a slave "would punish by whipping with bullwhip if the slaves failed to work to suit them." Jordan recalled that things improved little for Cherokee freedpeople after the Civil War—he could not forget the determination with which Cherokees worked to prevent African Cherokees and freedpeople from gaining access to land and citizenship in the Cherokee Nation.[127]

Other former Cherokee slaves and their descendants had similar stories to tell during the late 1930s. Mattie Logan claimed that her grandmother was a "half-blood" Cherokee from Virginia. Like Joe Bean, Logan was part of a big family. She spent part of her life as a slave in Mississippi before being sent to a Cherokee plantation prior to the Civil War. Mattie Logan's memories of life in the United States and among the Cherokee paralleled those of other African Cherokees, defined by slave sales and forced migrations, membership in large extended families, and, significantly, a mythical connection to a Cherokee forebear who hailed from some faraway place. For Mattie Logan, that ancestor was a "mixed-blood" Cherokee grandmother from Virginia. Other freedpeople and their descendants claimed historical connections to the Cherokee either through a mixed racial ancestry, being a slave on a Cherokee plantation in the Southeast, or both.[128] R. C. Smith typified such claims, insisting that while his forebears hated being slaves, they possessed connections to prominent figures in Cherokee history. "My father was half Cherokee Indian," Smith insisted. "His father was bought by an Indian woman and she took him for her husband. She died and my grandfather, father and auntie were bought by John Ross."[129] Some Cherokee freedpeople evidently believed that by establishing genealogical connections to prominent Cherokees, they would legitimate their legal and cultural claims to Cherokee identity.

These imagined bonds of kinship were important to the descendants of Cherokee freedpeople and mixed race African Cherokees also because they helped to establish a collective sense of belonging, through stories of historical struggle and hardship. Whether learned through the hushed whispers of family history, or through encounters with the bureaucratic apparatus of the Cherokee Nation, African Cherokees assertions of "blood" connections to prominent Cherokees, and freedpeople's recollections of toiling on plantations in either the cis-Mississippi or Indian territory, enabled people of African descent to insist that they were a part of Cherokee history, measureable, tangible, and provable in a material sense.[130]

However, one particularly important aspect of identity that African Cherokees and the descendants of freedpeople laid claim to in the late 1930s was a deeply rooted racial and cultural affiliation with Cherokee society. This connection was expressed in a number of ways. For example, Aunt Chaney McNair, who "got free in Kansas," reveled in details of her parent's connection to the Georgia Cherokee but wondered out loud why "God had made me black and ugly."[131] More commonly, Cherokee freedpeople deemphasized their racial appearance and highlighted their linguistic and cultural identification with the Cherokee. Patsy Perryman insisted that she was born in the Cherokee Nation and that her mother spoke fluent Cherokee. She added that her brother was also well versed in the Cherokee language, married a "full-blood Indian woman," and was assimilated into Cherokee culture. Perryman claimed that her brother's assimilation into Cherokee society was so complete that he preferred to distance himself from his black ancestry and was fond of declaring: "I darn tired looking at Negroes!"[132]

Expressions of linguistic, cultural, or even biological affinity with Cherokees were important to mixed-race African Cherokees and freedpeople and their descendants, especially those born outside of the Cherokee ancestral or political homelands. Phyllis Petite, for instance, was born in Rusk, Texas, the same location where the Texas Cherokees settled and were expelled by the Republic of Texas in the early nineteenth century. Petite insisted that her relatives retained a trove of memories that centered around the buying and selling of members of the family by white Texans and prominent Cherokee families, such as the Vanns. For other freedpeople, fluency in the Cherokee language and memories of kind Cherokee masters underlay their loyalty to the Cherokee Nation.[133] This was the case for Chaney Richardson. Despite the Civil War's destructive effects on families, through death, separation, or both, Richardson's sense of Cherokee identity was sustained by his knowledge of the Cherokee language and fond memories of kind Cherokee slave owners.[134] Morris Shephard held similarly fond feelings for the Cherokee people. Despite the sale of family members during slavery times, and the splintering of his family during the Civil War, Shephard remained proud of his Cherokee identity. He received an allotment near Coffeeville, Kansas, a popular location among Cherokee freedpeople, and married a former Cherokee slave, Nancy Hildebrand, whom he claimed had once been owned by the prominent Cherokee slave owner Joe Hildeband.[135]

While Cherokee leaders found it politically expedient to affirm the importance of Cherokee "blood" by finding legal and bureaucratic ways to exclude qualified freedpeople from receiving land within the Cherokee Nation, nonetheless a number of freedpeople did receive land allotments in the early twentieth century.[136] But land was not the only motivating factor behind African Cherokees' and freedpeople's sense of loyalty to the Cherokee diaspora's political homeland and attachment to their Cherokee identity. Shared historical experiences, such as enslaved ancestors being part of the Trail of Tears or family memories of kind Cherokee masters, and fluency in the Cherokee language and assimilation into Cherokee culture, all contributed to a sense of Cherokee identity for freedpeople, African Americans married to Cherokee freedpeople, and mixed-race African Cherokees.[137]

The Cherokee people proved to be particularly well equipped for life in diaspora. Well before the forced removals of the 1830s came to form a major part of Cherokee historical consciousness in the early twentieth century, Cherokee people nurtured origin narratives and folktales that both emphasized the importance of travel and migration, and reminded Cherokee people of who they were, irrespective of where their journeys took them. It was not that land was not important to Cherokees; it was. From the eighteenth-century towns that structured Cherokee social and political life to the hard-fought but ultimately failed resistance to the allotment process at the end of the nineteenth century, Cherokee people recognized the significance of the land and the water. However, in the evolving colonial contexts that shaped the narrative arc of Cherokee history from the 1760s to the 1940s, being Cherokee required more than an unbroken connection to the "ancient" homeland in the cis-Mississippi.

In the two centuries before the outbreak of World War II, Cherokees traveled across the Atlantic Ocean to England, braved the vast Pacific Ocean en route to Hawaii and tried, albeit unsuccessfully, to navigate the "white Australia" policy and settle in the island continent. In the Americas, Cherokee people clung loyally to a small piece of their "ancient" homeland in western North Carolina, built a new political homeland in Indian Territory, and migrated and settled in places as diverse as Tennessee, Georgia, Alabama, New York, Pennsylvania, Connecticut, Ohio, and Washington, DC. Emigrant Cherokees like Andrew Vann found their final resting place in locales as exotic as Havana, Cuba.[138] Despite continued colonial challenges to the culture, language, land base, and political sovereignty of the eighteenth- and nineteenth-century Cherokees, by the twentieth century the Cherokee people had established on the ruins of Anglo-American settler colonialism a diaspora that was as geographically vast as its population was racially and culturally diverse.

Epilogue

I began this book with an unlikely discovery and lots of unanswered questions: how did an application from a mixed-race Cherokee family for permanent residency status in the Commonwealth of Australia come to be? Tucked away in the National Archives of Australia, this document is, to my knowledge, exceptional; I have not found too many more like it in Australia, or anywhere else outside the United States. That is not to say that such documents do not exist, but it does reflect the fact that during the latter half of the twentieth century the vast majority of people claiming Cherokee descent generally confined their migration and resettlement patterns to the continental United States.[1]

The reasons for this movement, migration, and relocation after World War II were manifold: a quest for better economic opportunities, a desire to accompany a spouse on an exciting new adventure, a determination to reunite with long-lost relatives, and the impact of the federal government's termination and relocation program. Through the Bureau of Indian Affairs, the federal government strove to complete the work of assimilation by relocating Native Americans to urban centers and integrating them into the labor force. In addition, officials hoped to liquidate tribal assets.[2] Wilma Mankiller was a child when she became part of the federal government's relocation scheme. Writing of her family's migration to California, Mankiller recalled:

I experienced my own Trail of Tears when I was a young girl. No one pointed a gun at me or members of my family. No show of force was used. It was not necessary. Nevertheless, the United States government, through the Bureau of Indian Affairs, was again trying to settle the "Indian problem" by removal. I learned through this ordeal about the fear and anguish that occur when you give up your home, your community, and everything you have ever known to move far away to a strange place. I cried for days, not unlike the children who stumbled down the Trail of Tears so many years ago.[3]

The termination policy that saw Mankiller and her family relocated to California remained in effect until President Richard Nixon overturned it in 1970. The connection Mankiller draws to the forced removals of 1838 and 1839 reveals how that traumatic nineteenth-century event still resonated with Cherokees through the late twentieth century. It structured their historical consciousness and their sense of American injustice, and contextualized the enduring nature of settler colonial prejudice against Indigenous people. Moreover, Mankiller's historical consciousness framed her lived memory of being a diaspora Cherokee in late twentieth-century America. Just as black Americans contextualized racial prejudice through the historical prisms of slavery and Jim Crow segregation and violence, so Cherokees continued to nurture their own historical sense of what it meant to be Cherokee.

But America had changed by 1970. President Richard Nixon's abolishment of the termination program, along with the civil rights movement, the Black Power and Latino/a movements, the women's rights movement, and the American Indian Movement (AIM) all changed America politically, socially, and culturally. As some marched, others donned black leather jackets and bore arms, and still others nurtured cultural pride and language revitalization programs, some Cherokees worked within the American political system to change the relationship between the Cherokee people and the United States government. W. W. Keeler, a one-sixteenth Cherokee who was born in Texas in 1908, was a leader in this effort. A biography that does justice to Keeler's life and accomplishments remains to be written. What we do know about Keeler is that he was a graduate of the University of Kansas, and spent much of World War II in Mexico. In 1949, President Harry Truman appointed Keeler, a son of the Cherokee diaspora, to the position of chief of the Cherokee Nation. From this position, Keeler played a leading role in reinvigorating Cherokee culture and language, and, in 1971, achieved his ultimate goal: the reestablishment of Cherokee sovereignty and self-government. Keeler subsequently became the first elected chief of the Cherokee Nation since 1903.[4]

Suddenly, everyone was Cherokee, or at least some generic version of an American Indian. Cherokees did indeed live, work, and thrive in cities as diverse as Chicago, Toronto, and San Francisco by the late twentieth century.[5] In the Bay Area of San Francisco, however, hippies walked down Haight-Ashbury during the late 1960s and 1970s dressed like Indians; some channeled the myth of the "ecological Indian" in helping to start an environmental movement, replete with "earth day" celebrations, tie-dye t-shirts, peace pipes, organic corndogs, and ceremonial dances. It was easy to be cynical about all this, and some Cherokees were.[6] But the price of political success, cultural revitalization, and language immersion programs was increased visibility for Cherokees and Cherokee culture. Virtually every American wanted to be a Cherokee, and even those who didn't suspected they had a drop or two of Cherokee "blood."[7]

Such vagueness about the nature of Cherokee identity has proven a boon for the Cherokee population as recorded by the United States Bureau of the Census. In an age when self-reporting of racial and ethnic status has become commonplace, the Cherokee diaspora's population has increased steadily. In the 2000 United States census, "Cherokee" was the largest segment of the Native American population, with approximately 729, 533 people self-identifying as Cherokees. The second largest tribal group, Navajo, comprised just under 269, 202 people. Of those self-reporting as Cherokee, 281, 069 claimed no racial mixture and declared themselves "Cherokee alone." The vast majority of people who self-identified as Cherokee—68 percent—reported that they were "mixed" with at least one other race.[8] A decade later, the 2010 census of the 566 federally recognized Native American tribes—of which there are three federally recognized Cherokee tribes—found the population of the Cherokee diaspora continuing to grow. Cherokees remain the largest segment of the Native American population, with 819, 105 people self-reporting as Cherokee. Of this number, 314, 000 claimed citizenship in the Cherokee Nation of Oklahoma.[9]

There are problems with self-identification and the self-reporting methodologies used by the Census Bureau in ascertaining the diasporic Cherokee population. Anthropologist Circe Sturm points out that "racial shifters" have proven a particular challenge for the three federally recognized Cherokee tribes—the Cherokee Nation of Oklahoma, the Eastern Band of Cherokee Indians, and the United Keetoowah Band of Cherokees.[10] Late twentieth- and early twenty-first-century Americans have shown a particular propensity for regularly shifting their racial and ethnic identities, adding new and often highly contrived layers of meaning, submitting blood samples for DNA testing to "scientifically" prove their Cherokee ancestry, and elaborating on family legends to flesh out the meaning of their Cherokee selfhood.[11] This quest might be rooted in the romantic historical images that portray native peoples as being more spiritually attuned to the rhythms of the earth and cycles of life, but it has also gained cultural traction by virtue of the post-civil rights movement ethnic revivals—and outward displays of pride in ethnic identities such as Irish-American and Italian-American—that have come to dominate the American cultural landscape.[12]

In response to these developments, the Cherokee Nation of Oklahoma has faced pressure from some of its tribal members to narrow the legal definition of Cherokee citizenship. This ongoing legal and political drama has hit the descendants of Cherokee freedpeople particularly hard. In March 2006 the Cherokee Supreme Court ruled that the descendants of Cherokee freedmen had been unconstitutionally prevented from enrolling as citizens of the Cherokee Nation. Shortly after that ruling a petition began circulating for a referendum that would restrict membership in the nation to people with Cherokee "blood" only. Some Cherokees lobbied for an amendment to the Cherokee Nation's constitution designed to strip the descendants of Cherokee freedpeople of their citizenship. A special election in March 2007 led to the passage of that amendment, and as a result, the Cherokee citizenship of approximately 2,800 descendants of Cherokee freedpeople was revoked.[13]

The North Carolina Cherokees have also experienced political controversies over questions of identity and tribal membership. Some Cherokee officials in North Carolina have endeavored to narrow the definition of Cherokee identity by instituting a "fraud list," and in 2011 the Eastern Band of Cherokee Indians established the Cherokee Identity Protection Committee. With historical echoes of the late nineteenth-century Cherokee Citizenship Commission in the Cherokee Nation, the Eastern Band resolved to create the Committee because, as Big Cove representative Perry Shell observed, "Many times people are taking our identity."[14] Americans are "taking our identity," as Shell puts it, because over two hundred years of migration, racial mixing and intermarriage, and cultural change has made the cultural terrain of memory and identity as malleable as it is contested. However well-intentioned their efforts, Cherokee officials might learn from the experiences of their forebears that adopting concepts like "nation," "citizenship," and "blood quantum" creates as many new challenges in the identity labyrinth as it solves.

This was brought home to me when I sat one brisk August evening in 2011 at the Morningside Theater in Cherokee, North Carolina. I was there to watch Kermit Hunter's rewritten outdoor drama *Unto These Hills*. The racially mixed cast included local Cherokee, non-Cherokee, and white performers, an unwitting nod to the racially and ethnically diverse nature of the twenty-first-century Cherokee diaspora. Hunter's script, rewritten by Cherokee playwright Linda Squirrel, tells the story of Cherokee history from the beginning of time (as Cherokees understand that concept) to the era of removal and Tsali's self-sacrificing acts of resistance. Despite the rewrites to this epic drama, *Unto These Hills* remains a simplified version of the Cherokee past, packaged and presented for tourists. But the production's concluding line, *Ni-go-hi-Tsala-ga*, "Cherokee forever," is as much a statement about survival and defiance in the face of settler colonial oppression as it is an affirmation of Cherokeeness.

Perhaps Cherokee Meeks had this phrase in mind when she and her family tried to migrate to Australia in the 1960s. Indeed, it may be that this single phrase was (and is) enough to remind diaspora Cherokees of where they came from, who their ancestors were, and how they continue to both be and become Cherokee. There's a simple beauty to

Ni-go-hi-Tsa-la-ga, a poetry that conceals within it an assertiveness of identity that remains tied to an historical consciousness and the myriad experiences and beliefs that define Cherokee identity.

With one hundred or so other patrons, I left the Morningside Theater that evening in August 2011 cold but satisfied with the evening's entertainment. At the same time, I couldn't help wondering: What will that phrase—Ni-go-hi-Tsa-la-ga—mean a hundred years from now?

Glossary

Glossary of Names

Note: Given the nature of the colonial records used in this book and the phonetic makeup of the Cherokee syllabary, the spelling of names, places, and events sometimes varies. Every effort has been made to spell Cherokee names consistently in this book; however, on occasion hyphens and spaces between syllables have been left in place to convey to the reader a sense of the historical context in which they were used. This glossary of names is included to clarify any confusion that may arise from the various records in colonial archives and the multiple spellings of Cherokee names.

Cherokee name(s)	English name(s)
Agili	George Lowrey
Amo-adawehi (or Ama-edohi)	Moytoy
Attakullakulla (or Ada-gal'kala, Attacullaculla)	Little Carpenter
Chees-quat-a-law-ny	John Rollin Ridge, Yellow Bird
Connetoo	John Hill
Cooweeskoowee	John Ross
Cunne Shote	Stalking Turkey (also known as Standing Turkey)
Degadoga	Stand Watie
Duwali (or Di'wali)	Chief John Bowles (also known as The Bowl, Bowl, and Colonel Bowles

Gatun-wali	Big Mush or Hard Mush
Junaluska (also known as Tsuhnuhlahuhski)	
Kahmungdaclageh	Major Ridge
Kanagatoga	Old Hop
Kana'ti	Lucky Hunter
Lewi-za-wau-na-skie	Lewis Downing
Nanyehi	Nancy Ward
Nunna-tihi	Pathkiller
Nunna-tsune-ga	White Path
Onitossitah	Old Tassel (also known as Corntassel, Old Corn Tassel)
Oochilla	
Oothcalooga	Calhoun
Opothleyohola	Old Gouge
Ostenaco (or Austenaco, Ustenach)	Judd's Friend, Mankiller
Scholanuetta	Hanging Maw
Sehoya	Susanna Wickett Ridge
Selu	Corn Mother
Sequoyah	George Guess, George Gist
Skahtlelohskee	John Ridge
Stooeastah	Dan McGhee
Tah-chee	Dutch
Tallantusky (or Toluntuskee, Tahlonteeske)	
Tal-tsu'tsa	Doublehead (or Incalatanga)
Tekuh nah ste sky (also known as Buck OoWatie)	Elias Boudinot
Tsali	Charley
Unacata	White Man Killer
Wohsi	Moses Price
Wrosetasetow (also known as Outacite)	Mankiller
Yonagaska	Drowning Bear (or Bear Drowning Him)

Abbreviations

AGI	Archivo General de Indias, Serville, Spain
AHR	*Arkansas Historical Quarterly*
AICRJ	*American Indian Culture and Research Journal*
AIQ	*American Indian Quarterly*
APS	American Philosophical Society, Philadelphia, Pennsylvania
ASR	*American Sociological Review*
AQ	*American Quarterly*
BIA	Bureau of Indian Affairs
CHS	Cornwell Historical Society, Cornwell, Connecticut
CFL	Cornwall Free Library, Cornwall, Connecticut
CL	Manuscripts Division, William L. Clements Library, University of Michigan, Ann Arbor
CO	*Chronicles of Oklahoma*
CP	*Cherokee Phoenix, and Indian Advocate*
DRML	David M. Rubenstein Rare Book & Manuscript Library, Duke University, Durham, North Carolina
EAS	*Early American Studies*
FHQ	*Florida Historical Quarterly*
GHQ	*Georgia Historical Quarterly*
HHL	Henry E. Huntington Library, San Marino, California
HL	Houghton Library, Harvard University, Cambridge, Massachusetts
IPP	Indian Pioneer Papers, University of Oklahoma, Norman, Oklahoma
JAH	*Journal of American History*
JAS	*Journal of American Studies*
JCS	*Journal of Cherokee Studies*

JES	*Journal of Ethnic Studies*
JNH	*Journal of Negro History*
JSH	*Journal of Southern History*
JWH	*Journal of World History*
KH	*Kansas History*
KHS	Kansas Historical Society, Topeka, KS
KHQ	*Kansas Historical Quarterly*
LC	Library of Congress, Washington, DC
MVHR	*The Mississippi Valley Historical Review*
NAA	National Anthropological Archives, Smithsonian Institution, Suitland, Maryland
NAAA	National Archives of Australia, Canberra, Australia
NARA	National Archives Record Administration
NCHR	*North Carolina Historical Review*
NL	Newberry Library, Chicago
NS	*Native South*
NWR	*Niles' Weekly Register*
OHS	Oklahoma Historical Society, Oklahoma City, Oklahoma
PBP	William L. Anderson, Jane L. Brown, and Anne F. Rogers, eds., *The Payne-Butrick Papers: Volumes I-VI* (Lincoln: University of Nebraska Press, 2010)
RHR	*Radical History Review*
SLR	*Stanford Law Review*
SML	Sterling Memorial Library, Yale University, New Haven, Connecticut
STSW	State Historical Society of Wisconsin, Madison, WI
SWQ	*Southwestern Historical Quarterly*
TGM	Thomas Gilcrease Museum, Tulsa, Oklahoma
TNS	The National Archives of the United Kingdom
VHS	Virginia Historical Society, Richmond, Virginia
WHC	Western Historical Collections, University of Oklahoma, Norman, Oklahoma
WHQ	*Western Historical Quarterly*
WMQ	*William & Mary Quarterly*, 3rd Series
WSR	*Wicazo Sa Review*

Notes

PROLOGUE

1. "Application for Entry for Residence completed December 17, 1965," A12513, NAAA.

2. In Australia, the term "half-caste" also proved a popular racial epithet, directed particularly at people of Euro-Australian and Aboriginal heritage.

3. Ariela J. Gross, *What Blood Won't Tell: A History of Race on Trial in America* (Cambridge, MA: Harvard University Press, 2008), Chapter 5; Peggy Pascoe, *What Comes Naturally: Miscegenation Law and the Making of Race in America* (New York: Oxford University Press, 2009), 94–96.

4. Rose Stremlau, *Sustaining the Cherokee Family: Kinship and the Allotment of an Indigenous Nation* (Chapel Hill: University of North Carolina Press, 2011), 119; Paula Gunn Allen (Laguna Pueblo), *The Sacred Hoop: Recovering the Feminine in American Indian Traditions* (Boston: Beacon Press, 1986), 78.

5. Emma Willard, *A Series of Maps to Willard's History of the United States, or, Republic of America. Designed for Schools and Private Libraries* (New York: White, Gallaher, and White, 1828); William D. Walters, Jr., "Emma Willard's Geographies," *Pennsylvania Geographer* 37, no. 1 (Spring/Summer 1999): 118–38.

6. Albert S. Gatschet, *A Migration Legend of the Creek Indians* (Philadelphia: D.G. Brinton, 1884); James H. Merrell, *The Indians' New World: Catawbas and Their Neighbors from European Contact through the Era of Removal* (Chapel Hill: University of North Carolina Press, 1989), 5, 23, 95; Alan Gallay, *The Indian Slave Trade: The Rise of the English Empire in the American South, 1670–1717* (New Haven, CT: Yale University Press, 2002), 7, 41, 74, 261; William Engelbrecht, *Iroquoia: The Development of a Native World* (Syracuse, NY: Syracuse University Press, 2003), 111–14; Gary Warrick, *A Popula-*

tion History of the Huron-Petun, A.D. 500–1650 (New York: Cambridge University Press, 2008), 6, 38, 40, 83; Stephen Warren, *The Worlds the Shawnees Made: Migration and Violence in Early America* (Chapel Hill: University of North Carolina Press, 2014).

7. *PBP, I-III*, 7. On Willard's career as an educator see Mary J. Fairbanks, ed., *Emma Willard and Her Pupils, or Fifty Years of Troy Female Seminary, 1822–1872* (New York: Mrs. R. Sage, 1898), 6.

8. James Mooney, *History, Myths, and Sacred Formulas of the Cherokees* (1900; repr. Fairview, NC: Bright Mountain Books, 1992).

9. Horatio Hale, *Indian Migrations, as Evidenced by the Language* (Chicago: Jameson and Morse, 1883), 11; Grace Steele Woodward, *The Cherokees* (Norman: University of Oklahoma Press, 1963), 13; Thomas E. Mails, *The Cherokee People: The Story of the Cherokees from Earliest Origins to Contemporary Times* (Tulsa, OK: Council Oak Books, 1992), 25; Stanley Hoig, *The Cherokees and Their Chiefs: In the Wake of Empire* (Fayetteville: University of Arkansas Press, 1998), 8.

10. Duane H. King, "Introduction" in *The Cherokee Nation: A Troubled History*, ed. Duane King (Knoxville: University of Tennessee Press, 1979), ix; V. Richard Persico, Jr., "Early Nineteenth-Century Cherokee Political Organization" in *The Cherokee Nation*, ed. Duane, 106–7; William G. McLoughlin, *Cherokee Renascence in the New Republic* (Princeton, NJ: Princeton University Press, 1986), 7; Robert J. Conley, *The Cherokee Nation: A History* (Albuquerque: University of New Mexico Press, 2005), 31; Brice Obermeyer, *Delaware Tribe in the Cherokee Nation* (Lincoln: University of Nebraska Press, 2009), 48.

11. Henry T. Malone, *Cherokees of the Old South: A People in Transition* (1956; repr. Athens, GA: University of Georgia Press, 2010), 24–25; McLoughlin, *Cherokee Renascence*, 11; Mails, *The Cherokee People*, 79–82; Tom Hatley, *The Dividing Path: Cherokees and South Carolinians through the Revolutionary Era* (New York: Oxford University Press, 1995), 119–26; Tyler Boulware, *Deconstructing the Cherokee Nation: Town, Region, and Nation among Eighteenth-Century Cherokees* (Gainesville: University Press of Florida, 2011); Ian Chambers, "The Movement of Great Tellico: The Role of Town and Clan in Cherokee Spatial Understanding," *Native South* 3 (2010): 90; Theda Perdue, *Cherokee Women: Gender and Culture Change, 1700–1835* (Lincoln: University of Nebraska Press, 1998), 46; Circe Sturm, *Blood Politics: Race, Culture, and Identity in the Cherokee Nation of Oklahoma* (Berkeley: University of California Press, 2002), 31–32; Virginia M. Carney, *Eastern Band Cherokee Women: Cultural Persistence in Their Letters and Speeches* (Knoxville: University of Tennessee Press, 2005), 29.

12. Charles Hudson, *The Southeastern Indians* (Knoxville: University of Tennessee Press, 1978), 19; Charles Hudson, "Some Thoughts on the Early Social History of the Cherokees" in *The Conference on Cherokee Prehistory*, ed. David G. Moore (Swannanoa, N.C.: Warren Wilson College, 1986), 139–53; Theda Perdue, *Slavery and the Evolution of Cherokee Society, 1540–1866* (Knoxville: University of Tennessee Press, 1979), 12–18; Katja May, *African Americans and Native Americans in the Creek and Cherokee Nations, 1830s to 1920s* (New York and London: Routledge, 1996), 39; Chambers, "The Movement of Great Tellico," 95; Barbara Krauthamer, *Black Slaves, Indian Masters: Slavery, Eman-*

cipation, and Citizenship in the Native American South (Chapel Hill: University of North Carolina Press, 2013), 18–19.

13. John P. Brown, *Old Frontiers: The Story of the Cherokee Indians from Earliest Times to the Date of Their Removal to the West, 1838* (Kingsport, TN: Southern Publishers, Inc., 1938); William L. Anderson, ed., *Cherokee Removal: Before and After* (Athens: University of Georgia Press, 1991); John Ehle, *Trail of Tears: The Rise and Fall of the Cherokee Nation* (New York: Anchor Books); Theda Perdue and Michael D. Green, *The Cherokee Removal: A Brief History with Documents* (New York: Bedford/St. Martin's, 2004); Amy H. Sturgis, *The Trail of Tears and Indian Removal* (Westport, CT: Greenwood Publishing, 2007); Brian Hicks, *Toward the Setting Sun: John Ross, the Cherokees, and the Trail of Tears* (New York: Atlantic Monthly Press, 2011); Daniel Blake Smith, *An American Betrayal: Cherokee Patriots and the Trail of Tears* (New York: Henry Holt, 2011).

14. An argument can be made that Cherokee governance, as with the government of other Indigenous peoples in the South, had not been as centrally concentrated in the hands of a few chiefs since the era of the Mississippi Chiefdoms. See Hoig, *The Cherokees and Their Chiefs*, 8–9; James Taylor Carson, *Searching for the Bright Path: The Mississippi Choctaws from Prehistory to Removal* (Lincoln: University of Nebraska Press, 1999), 11–13; Claudio Saunt, *A New Order of Things: Property, Power, and the Transformation of the Creek Indians* (New York: Cambridge University Press, 1999), 2–3; Robbie Ethridge, *From Choctaw to Chickasaw: The European Invasion and the Transformation of the Mississippian World, 1540–1715* (Chapel Hill: University of North Carolina Press, 2010), 1–3.

15. John R. Finger, *The Eastern Band of Cherokees, 1819–1900* (Knoxville: University of Tennessee Press, 1984); Finger, *Cherokee Americans: The Eastern Band of Cherokees in the Twentieth Century* (Lincoln: University of Nebraska Press, 1993); Stremlau, *Sustaining the Cherokee Family*.

16. Some of Theda Perdue's most influential and oft-cited works include, *Slavery and the Evolution of Cherokee Society; Cherokee Women;* and *Mixed Blood Indians: Racial Construction in the Early South* (Athens: University of Georgia Press, 2003). See also Perdue's edited volumes *Nations Remembered: An Oral History of the Cherokees, Chickasaws, Choctaws, Creeks, and Seminoles in Oklahoma, 1865–1907* (Norman: University of Oklahoma Press, 1993); *Cherokee Editor: The Writings of Elias Boudinot* (Athens: University of Georgia Press, 1983); *Sifters: Native American Women's Lives* (New York: Oxford University Press, 2001).

17. Alexandra Harmon, "Wanted: More Histories of Indian Identity" in *A Companion to American Indian History*, ed. Philip J. Deloria and Neal Salisbury (Malden, MA: Blackwell Publishing, 2004), 254.

18. Carolyn Ross Johnston, *Cherokee Women in Crisis: Trail of Tears, Civil War, and Allotment, 1838–1907* (Tuscaloosa: University of Alabama Press, 2003), 19.

19. Michel Foucault, *The Order of Things: An Archeology of the Human Sciences* (1970; repr. New York: Vintage Books, 1994), 50; Pierre Bourdieu, *The Logic of Practice* (Stanford, CA: Stanford University Press, 1990), 54; Charles Lemert, *Social Things* (Lanham, MD: Rowman and Littlefield, 1992), 10, 28, 92. For analysis of Cherokee responses

to disease transfer see Paul Kelton, *Cherokee Medicine, Colonial Germs: An Indigenous Nation's Fight Against Smallpox, 1518–1824* (Norman: University of Oklahoma Press, 2015).

20. The exception is Julia Coates, "'None of Us Are Supposed to Be Here': Ethnicity, Nationality, and the Production of Cherokee Histories" (Ph.D. diss., University of New Mexico, 2002).

21. Russell Thornton, *The Cherokees: A Population History* (Lincoln: University of Nebraska Press, 1990), 147–48.

22. This aspect of my analysis expands on the work of Theda Perdue, *Mixed Blood Indians: Racial Construction in the Early South* (Athens: University of Georgia Press, 2005), ch. 3.

23. David S. Brose, C. Wesley Cowan, and Robert C. Mainfort, *Societies in Eclipse: Archeology of the Eastern Woodlands Indians, A.D. 1400–1700* (Washington, DC: Smithsonian Institution Press, 2001); Thomas M. N. Lewis and Madeline Kneberg, *Tribes That Slumber: Indians of the Tennessee Region* (Knoxville: University of Tennessee Press, 1958), 113–15.

24. David G. Anderson, "Political Change in Chiefdom Societies: Cycling in the Late Prehistoric Southeastern United States" (Ph.D. diss., University of Michigan, 1990); Ned J. Jenkins, "Tracing the Origins of the Early Creeks, 1050–1700 CE" in *Mapping the Mississippian Shatter Zone: The Colonial Indian Slave Trade and Regional Instability in the American South*, ed. Robbie Ethridge and Shri M. Shuck-Hall (Lincoln: University of Nebraska Press, 2009), 191. Historians Theda Perdue and Michael D. Green note that archeologists sometimes date the chiefdom period as 900 CE–1650 CE. See *The Columbia Guide to American Indians in the South* (New York: Columbia University Press, 2001), 31.

25. Richard B. Drake, *A History of Appalachia* (Lexington: University of Kentucky Press, 2001).

26. Kathleen Duval, "Interconnectedness and Diversity in 'French Louisiana'" in *Powhatan's Mantle: Indians and the Colonial Southeast*, ed. Gregory Waselkov, Peter Wood, and M. Thomas Hatley (Lincoln: University of Nebraska Press, 2006), 135; Stephen Kowalewski, "Coalescent Societies" in *Light on the Path: The Anthropology and History of the Southeastern Indians*, ed. Thomas J. Pluckhahn and Robbie Ethridge (Tuscaloosa: University of Alabama Press, 2006), 118–19

27. Christopher B. Rodning, "Reconstructing the Coalescence of Cherokee Communities in Southern Appalachia" in *The Transformation of the Southeastern Indians, 1540–1760*, ed. Robbie Ethridge and Charles Hudson (Jackson: University Press of Mississippi, 2002), 157; Christopher B. Rodning, *Center Places and Cherokee Towns: Archaeological Perspectives on Native American Architecture and Landscape in the Southern Appalachians.* (Tuscaloosa: University of Alabama Press, 2015).

28. Raymond Fogelson, "The Cherokee Ballgame Cycle: An Ethnographer's View," *Ethnomusicology* 15, no. 3 (September 1971): 327–28; Christopher B. Rodning, "William Bartram and the Archaeology of the Appalachian Summit" in *Between Contacts and Colonies: Archeological Perspectives on Protohistoric Southeast*, ed. Cameron B. Wesson and Mark A. Rees (Tuscaloosa: University of Alabama Press, 2002), 67–76; Ian Chambers, "The Movement of Great Tellico: The Role of Town and Clan in Cherokee Spatial Understanding," *NS* 2 (2010): 89–90.

29. Gregory E. Dowd, *A Spirited Resistance: The North American Indian Struggle for Unity, 1745–1815* (Baltimore: Johns Hopkins University Press, 1992), xv.

30. Fay A. Yarbrough, *Race and the Cherokee Nation: Sovereignty in the Nineteenth Century* (Philadelphia: University of Pennsylvania Press, 2008), 8.

31. James Chambers to Capt. George Campbell, September 19, 1776, Fol 203, CO 5/7, Original Correspondence Secretary of State, 1755–1779, TNS. Dowd, *A Spirited Resistance*, 145; Alden T. Vaughan, *Transatlantic Encounters: American Indians in Britain, 1500–1776* (New York: Cambridge University Press, 2006); Carolyn T. Foreman, *Indians Abroad, 1493–1938* (Norman: University of Oklahoma Press, 1943); William E. Mays, *Indian Trails of the Southeast* (Nashville: Blue and Grey Press, 1971), 1–2, 15–16, 24, 39, 43, 100.

32. Raymond D. Fogelson, "Perspectives on Native American Identity," in *Studying Native America: Problems and Prospects*, ed. Russell Thornton (Madison: University of Wisconsin Press, 1998): 40–59; Tyler Boulware, "Native Americans and National Identity in Early North America," *History Compass* 4, no. 5 (September 2006): 927–32.

33. William Eubanks, "The Red Race: Originators of the Ancient Apollo Worship," *Cherokee Advocate*, January 12, 1901, accessed January 14, 2013, http://www.ualr.edu/sequoyah/uploads/2011/11/WehEuba.html#RedRace.

34. Hoig, *The Cherokees and Their Chiefs*, 9.

35. Mooney, *Myths*, 242–45.

36. Nathaniel Shiedley, "Hunting and the Politics of Masculinity in Cherokee Treaty-Making, 1763–74," in *Empire and Others: British Encounters with Indigenous Peoples, 1600–1850*, ed. Martin Daunton and Rick Halpern (Philadelphia: University of Pennsylvania Press, 1999), 172–73; Perdue, *Cherokee Women*, 13–15; Daniel Heath Justice, *Our Fire Survives the Storm: A Cherokee Literary History* (Minneapolis: University of Minnesota Press, 2006), 28; Sturm, *Blood Politics*, 35.

37. Mooney, *Myths*, 246.

38. Mooney, *Myths*, 246–48.

39. Mooney, *Myths*, 431.

40. Edward Everett Dale and Gaston Litton, eds., *Cherokee Cavaliers: Forty Years of Cherokee History as Told in the Correspondence of the Ridge-Watie-Boudinot Family* (Norman: University of Oklahoma Press, 1939), 71; McLoughlin, *Cherokee Renascence*, 451.

41. *CP* 5 (September 1, 1832): 2.

42. Raymond D. Fogelson, "Perspectives on Native American Identity," 40–45.

43. Mooney, *Myths*, 100, 391–93; Herman J. Viola, *Diplomats in Buckskins: A History of Indian Delegations in Washington City* (Norman: University of Oklahoma Press, 1995), 18–20.

44. Mary Young, "The Cherokee Nation: Mirror of the Republic," *AQ* 33, no. 5 (Winter 1981): 502–24.

45. William G. McLoughlin, *After the Trail of Tears: The Cherokees' Struggle for Sovereignty, 1839–1880* (Chapel Hill: University of North Carolina Press, 1993); Andrew Denson, *Demanding the Cherokee Nation: Indian Autonomy and American Culture, 1830–1900* (Lincoln: University of Nebraska Press, 2004).

46. Peter Wagner, *A Sociology of Modernity: Liberty and Discipline* (New York and London: Routledge, 1994), 9, 27, 48–49, 126.

47. McLoughlin, *Cherokee Renascence,* 109–67; 206–46; 397–98.

48 . Michel Foucault, *Security, Territory, Population: Lectures at the College de France, 1977–1978* (New York: Palgrave, 2007), 29.

49. Mark Rifkin, "Representing the Cherokee Nation: Subaltern Studies and Native American Sovereignty," *Boundary 2* 32, no. 3 (2005): 48–55.

50. Erik Erikson, *Childhood and Society* (New York: W.W. Norton, 1950); *Young Man Luther* (New York: W.W. Norton, 1958); "Identity, Psychosocial," in *International Encyclopedia of Social Sciences* (New York: Macmillan, 1968), 61–65.

51. Theorists of identity contend that identities can be studied at the micro level of the individual and/or local community, and at a macro-level of analysis, that is, on a regional, national, or transnational level. See Raymond D. Fogelson, "Person, Self, and Identity: Some Anthropological Retrospectives, Circumspects, and Prospects" in *Psychosocial Theories of the Self,* ed. Benjamin Lee (New York and London: Plenum Press, 1982), 67–109.

52. Johannes Fabian, *Anthropology with an Attitude: Critical Essays* (Stanford, CA: Stanford University Press, 2001), 176–77; Melissa L. Meyer, "Race and Identity in Indian Country," *Ethnohistory* 51, no. 4 (2004): 800; William E. Unrau, *Mixed-Bloods and Tribal Dissolution: Charles Curtis and the Quest for Indian Identity* (Lawrence: University Press of Kansas, 1989); James F. Brooks, ed., *Confounding the Color Line: The Indian Black Experience in North America* (Lincoln: University of Nebraska Press, 2002); Sturm, *Blood Politics*; Tiya Miles, *Ties that Bind: The Story of an Afro-Cherokee Family In slavery and Freedom* (Berkeley: University of California Press, 2005), 111; Celia E. Naylor, *African Cherokees in Indian Territory: From Chattel to Citizens* (Chapel Hill: University of North Carolina Press, 2008), 10–13; Claudio Saunt, "The Native South: An Account of Recent Historiography," *NS* 1, no. 1 (2008): 50; Yarbrough, *Race and the Cherokee Nation.* Theda Perdue, "Race and Culture: Writing the Ethnohistory of the South," *Ethnohistory* 51, no. 4 (2004): 701–23.

53. *PBP, I–III,* 13–15, 211–12; Anderson, Brown, and Rogers, eds., *PBP, IV–VI,* 29–30.

54. *PBP, I–III,* 45; Giocchino Campese, "Beyond Ethnic and National Imagination: Toward a Catholic Theology of U.S. Immigration" in *Religion and Social Justice for Immigrants,* ed. Pierrette Hondagneu-Sotelo (New Brunswick: Rutgers University Press, 2007), 177–78.

55. Akhil Gupta and James Ferguson, "Beyond 'Culture': Space, Identity, and the Politics of Difference," *Cultural Anthropology* 7, no. 1 (February 1992): 6–23; Liisa H. Malkki, *Purity and Exile: Violence, Memory, and National Cosmology among the Hutu Refugees in Tanzania* (Chicago: University of Chicago Press, 1995), 197.

56. Gupta and Ferguson, "Beyond 'Culture,'" 6–23; Tony Judt, "The Past Is Another Country: Myth and Memory in Postwar Europe," *Daedalus* 121, no. 4 (Fall 1992): 83–118.

57. Yasmin Saikia, "Landscape of Identity: Transacting the Labels 'Indian,' 'As-

samese' and 'Tai-Ahom' in Contemporary Assam," *Contemporary South Asia* 10, no. 1 (March 2011): 73–93; Allaine Cerwonka, *Native to the Nation: Disciplining Landscapes and Bodies in Australia* (Minneapolis: University of Minnesota Press, 2004), 236.

58. Yael Zerubavel, *Recovered Roots: Collective Memory and the Making of Israeli National Tradition* (Chicago: University of Chicago Press, 1995), xvii.

59. Shari M. Huhndorf, *Going Native: Indians in the American Cultural Imagination* (Ithaca: Cornell University Press, 2001), 165.

60. Zerubavel, *Recovered Roots*, 7, 22.

61. Cathryn McConaghy, "On Pedagogy, Trauma and Difficult Memory: Remembering Namatjira, Our Beloved," *The Australian Journal of Indigenous Education* 32 (2003): 11–20; Christopher Schmidt-Nowara, "After 'Spain': A Dialogue with Josep M. Fradera on Spanish Colonial Historiography" in *After the Imperial Turn: Thinking with and through the Nation*, ed. Antoinette Burton (Durham, NC: Duke University Press, 2003), 168; Gayatri Chakravorty Spivak, "Nationalism and the Imagination," *Lectora* 15 (2009): 75–98.

62. Nancy Marie Mithlo, "Blood Memory and the Arts: Indigenous Genealogies and Imagined Truths," *AICRJ* 35, no. 4 (2011): 103–18. See also Dave Palmer, "Indigenous Young People and Victimhood," *Social Alternatives* 18, no. 2 (April 1999): 52–56; Jeannie Wright, K.W. Steve Land, Sue Comforth, "Fractured Connections: Migration and Holistic Models of Counselling," *British Journal of Guidance and Counselling* 39, no. 5 (November 2011): 471–96; Yolande Cohen, "The Migration of Moroccan Jews to Montreal: Memory, (Oral) History and Historical Narrative," *Journal of Modern Jewish Studies* 10, no. 2 (July 2011): 245–62.

63. W. R. L. Smith, *The Story of the Cherokees* (Cleveland: The Church of God Pub. House, 1928), 13; Richard S. Kim, "Diasporic Politics and the Globalizing of America: Korean Immigrant Nationalism and the 1919 Philadelphia Korean Congress" in *Asian Diasporas: New Formations, New Conceptions*, ed. Rhacel Parrenas and Lok Siu (Stanford: Stanford University Press, 2007), 221.

64. Daniel Heath Justice, "Beloved Woman Returns: The Doubleweaving of Homeland and Identity in the Poetry of Marilou Awaikta" in *Speak to Me Words: Essays on Contemporary American Indian Poetry*, ed. Dean Rader and Janice Gould (Tempe: University of Arizona Press, 2003), 76.

65. Gregory D. Smithers, *Science, Sexuality, and Race in the United States and Australia, 1780s–1890s* (New York and London: Routledge, 2009), 9; Teresia K. Teaiwa, "Native Thoughts: A Pacific Studies Take on Cultural Studies and Diaspora," in *Indigenous Diasporas and Dislocations*, ed. Graham Harvey and Charles D. Thompson, Jr. (Aldershot, UK: Ashgate Publishing Limited, 2005), 26.

66. An important study of homelands in Native American history is Douglas A. Hurt, "Defining American Homelands: A Creek Nation Example, 1828–1907," *Journal of Cultural Geography* 21, no. 1 (2003): 19–43. On the concept of diasporic peoples being "traveling cultures" and re-planting their beliefs and institutions in diaspora see James Clifford, "Diasporas," *Cultural Anthropology* 9, no. 3 (August 1994): 311, 318–19; Kevin Kenny, "Diaspora and Comparison: The Global Irish as a Case Study," *JAH* 90, no 1

278 NOTES TO PAGES 23–29

(June 2003): 134–62, esp. 159; Rogers Brubaker, "The 'Diaspora' Diaspora," *Ethnic and Racial Studies* 28, no. 1 (2005): 1–19.

67. Jana Evans Braziel and Anita Mannur, "Nation, Migration, Globalization: Points of Contention in Diaspora Studies" in *Theorizing Diaspora*, ed. Jana Evans Braziel and Anita Mannur (Malden, MA: Blackwell Publishing, 2003), 1.

68. Jasmin Habib, *Israel, Diaspora, and the Routes of National Belonging* (Toronto: University of Toronto Press, 2004) 4.

69. C.L. Webster, "Prof. D.W.C Duncan's Analysis of the Cherokee Language," *The American Naturalist* 23, no. 273 (September 1889): 779; Justice, *Our Fire Survives the Storm*, 171; Stremlau, *Sustaining the Cherokee Family*, 118–19; Christopher Teuton, *Cherokee Stories of the Turtle Island Liars' Club* (Chapel Hill: University of North Carolina Press, 2012), 8; Thomas A. Tweed, *Our Lady of the Exile: Diasporic Religion at a Cuban Catholic Shrine in Miami* (New York: Oxford University Press, 1997), 86; Devesh Kapur, *Diaspora Development and Democracy: The Domestic Impact of International Migration from Indian* (Princeton, NJ: Princeton University Press, 2010), 37; Ellen Cushman, *The Cherokee Syllabary: Writing the People's Perseverance* (Norman: University of Oklahoma Press, 2011), 88.

70. Leonard Thompson and Howard Lamar, "Comparative Frontier History" in *The Frontier in History: North America and Southern Africa Compared*, ed. Leonard Thompson and Howard Lamar (New Haven, CT: Yale University Press, 1981), 7; Pekka Hämäläinen, *The Comanche Empire* (New Haven, CT: Yale University Press, 2008), 8; Pekka Hämäläinen and Samuel Truett, "On Borderlands," *JAH* 98, no. 2 (September 2011): 338.

ONE   The Origins of the Cherokee Diaspora

1. Duane Champagne, "Symbolic Structures and Political Change in Cherokee Society," *JCS* 8, no. 2 (Fall 1983): 87–96; Michael Morris, "The High Price of Trade: Anglo-Indian Trade Mistakes and the Fort Loudoun Disaster," *JCS* 17 (1996): 3.

2. Duane King, "Introduction" in *The Cherokee Indian Nation: A Troubled History*, ed. Duane King (Knoxville: University of Tennessee Press, 1986), xiii; Tom Hatley, "Cherokee Women Farmers Hold Their Ground" in *Powhatan's Mantle: Indians in the Colonial Southeast*, rev. ed., eds. Gregory A. Waselkov, Peter H. Wood, and Tom Hatley (Lincoln: University of Nebraska Press, 2006), 325.

3. July 2, 1737, William Byrd Letterbook, 1736/7, March 20 –July 20, Mss5:2 B9966:4, VHS; Russell Thornton, *The Cherokees: A Population History* (Lincoln: University of Nebraska Press, 1990), 63–65; Theda Perdue and Michael Green, *The Cherokee Nation and the Trail of Tears* (New York: Penguin, 2007), xiv; Tyler Boulware, "The Effect of the Seven Years' War on the Cherokee Nation," *EAS* 5, no. 2 (Fall 2007), 395–426.

4. See the introduction of this book for a summation of the Cherokee clan system.

5. James Adair, *History of the American Indian* (1775) in *Voices of the Old South: Eyewitness Accounts, 1528–1681*, ed. Alan Gallay (Athens: University of Georgia Press, 1994), 55–56; Henry Thompson Malone, *Cherokees of the Old South: A People in Transi-*

tion (1956; repr. Athens: University of Georgia Press, 2010), 24–25; *PBP, I-III*, 215; *PBP, IV-VI*, 432; 446; John R. Finger, *The Eastern Band of the Cherokees, 1819–1900* (Knoxville: University of Tennessee Press, 1984), 3–4; William G. McLoughlin, *Cherokee Renascence in the New Republic* (Princeton, NJ: Princeton University Press, 1986), 11–12; Robert J. Conley, *The Cherokee Nation: A History* (Albuquerque: University of New Mexico Press, 2005), 25; Thornton, *The Cherokees*, 23–25.

6. Neal Salisbury, "The Indians' Old World: Native Americans and the Coming of Europeans," *WMQ*, 3rd Series, 53, no. 3 (July 1996): 445–47; McLoughlin, *Cherokee Renascence*, 7; Malone, *Cherokees of the Old South*, ch. 1; Theda Perdue, *Cherokee Women: Gender and Cultural Change, 1700–1835* (Lincoln: University of Nebraska Press, 1998), 8–9; Amy H. Sturgis, *The Trail of Tears and Indian Removal* (Westport, CT: Greenwood Press, 2007), 68.

7. Christopher B. Rodning, "Reconstructing the Coalescence of Cherokee Communities in Southern Appalachia" in *Transformation of the Southeastern Indians, 1540–1760*, ed. Robbie Ethridge and Charles Hudson (Jackson: University of Mississippi Press, 2002), 160–66.

8. Marvin T. Smith, "Aboriginal Population Movements in the Postcontact Southeast" in *Transformation of the Southeastern Indians*, ed. Ethridge and Hudson, 7–8.

9. Israel Shreve Diary, CL 1: 51–53. Quotation is from p. 53. See also William E. McGoun, "Adoption of Whites by 18th Century Cherokees," *JCS* 9, no. 1 (Spring 1984): 37–42.

10. "Father and Mother" to Agnes and James Lock, October 22, 1774, Robert McCallen Papers, CL, Box 47, Folder 33. See similarly Andrew Burnaby, *Travels through the Middle Settlements in North America* (London: T. Payne, 1775), 58; John Filson, *The Discovery, Purchase and Settlement, of Kentucke* (Wilmington: Printed by James Adams, 1784), 57, 63.

11. *PBP, I-III*, 14–15; Clara Sue Kidwell, "Indian Women as Cultural Mediators," *Ethnohistory* 39, no. 2 (Spring 1992): 97–107, esp. 102; Norma Tucker, "Nancy Ward, Ghighau of the Cherokees," *GHQ* 53, no. 2 (June 1969): 192–200; Tiya Miles, "'Circular Reasoning': Recentering Cherokee Women in the Antiremoval Campaigns," *AQ* 61, no. 2 (June 2009): 221–43.

12. Champagne, "Symbolic Structures and Political Change in Cherokee Society," 87.

13. Lynne P. Sullivan and Christopher B. Rodning, "Gender, Tradition, and the Negotiation of Power Relationships in Southern Appalachian Chiefdoms" in *The Archeology of Traditions: Agency and History Before and After Columbus*, ed. Timothy R. Pauketat (Gainesville: University Press of Florida, 2001), 108–10; David Hally, *King: The Social Archeology of a Late Mississippian Town in Northwestern Georgia* (Tuscaloosa: University of Alabama Press, 2008), 18; Robbie Ethridge, *From Chicaza to Chickasaw: The European Invasion and the Transformation of the Mississippian World, 1540–1715* (Chapel Hill: University of North Carolina Press, 2010), 3–4 .

14. Hally, *King*, 10.

15. Dixie Ray Haggard, "Internalizing Native American History: Comprehending Cherokee and Muscogulge Identities," *Indigenous Nations Studies Journal* 1, no. 2 (Fall

2000): 14. See also Christopher B. Rodning and Amber M. VanDerwarker, "Revisiting Coweeta Creek: Reconstructing Ancient Cherokee Lifeways in Southwestern North Carolina," *Southeastern Archeology* 21, no. 1 (Summer 2002): 6; Hally, *King*, 22.

16. Tyler Boulware, *Deconstructing the Cherokee Nation: Town, Region, and Nation among Eighteenth-Century Cherokees* (Gainesville: University Press of Florida, 2011), 2–3, 10; Rodning, "Reconstructing the Coalescence of Cherokee Communities in Southern Appalachia," 172.

17. Earl of Egremont to Gov. Boone, August 7, 1762, Fol. 288, CO 5/214, Entry Book of Letters and Dispatches, 1759–1763, TNS; Letter from Upper Creeks to Gov. Johnson, May 16, 1766, Fol. 15, CO 5/67, Original Correspondence Secretary of State, Indian Affairs, 1766–1767. Carolyn T. Foreman, *Indians Abroad, 1493–1938* (Norman: University of Oklahoma Press, 1943); Alden T. Vaughan, *Transatlantic Encounters: American Indians in Britain, 1500–1776* (New York: Cambridge University Press, 2006), Chs. 7–8.

18. John E. Worth, "Spanish Missions and the Persistence of Chiefly Power" in *The Transformation of the Southeastern Indians*, ed. Ethridge and Hudson, 61–62; R. David Edmunds, "Native Americans, New Voices: American Indian History, 1895–1995," *AHR* 100, no. 3 (June 1995): 733; Wilma Dunaway, "Incorporation as an Interactive Process: Cherokee Resistance to Expansion of the Capitalist World-System, 1560–1763," *Sociological Inquiry* 66, no. 4 (November 1996): 457 ("ethnic reorganizations"); Boulware, "The Effects of the Seven Years' War on the Cherokee Nation," 397; Hatley, *The Dividing Paths*, 13, 82.

19. Hatley, *Dividing Paths*, 161; Alan Taylor, *American Colonies: The Settling of North America* (New York: Penguin, 2001), 228–29.

20. Dunaway, "Incorporation as an Interactive Process," 461–63; Boulware, "The Effect of the Seven Years' War on the Cherokee Nation," 398; Finger, *The Eastern Band of Cherokees*, 6; McLoughlin, *Cherokee Renascence*, 17–18, 27, 29; Hatley, *Dividing Paths*, 155–60.

21. Cherokees. Headman Copy of a Talk to Capt. Raymond Demere, Fort Prince George September 18, 1756, Box 2, William Henry Lyttelton Papers, 1730–1806, CL; Walter Alves Cy to Cherokees, Copy of portions of land deeds giving extent of Kentucky, lands granted to Richard Henderson and Company (Transylvania Company) by the Cherokees by the Treaty of Sycamore Shoals, March 1775, Native American History Collection, 1689–1921, Box 1, CL.

22. *The Annual Biography and Obituary, for the Year 1819*, vol. 3 (London: Longman, Hurst, Rees, Orme, and Brown, 1819), 163.

23. *The Annual Biography and Obituary*, 3: 164.

24. McLoughlin, *Cherokee Renascence*, 9.

25. James Mooney, *James Mooney's History, Myths, and Sacred Formulas of the Cherokees* (1891, 1900; repr., Fairview, NC: Bright Mountain Books, 1992), 229; Horatio Hale, *Indian Migrations: As Evidenced by Language* (Chicago: Jameson and Morse, Printers, 1883), 3–11; Haggard, "Internalizing Native American History," 18; Dawn E. Bastian and Judy K. Mitchell, *Handbook of Native American Mythology* (New York: Oxford University Press, 2004), 114–15; James T. Carson, "Ethnogeography and the Native American Past," *Ethnohistory* 49, no. 4 (Fall 2002): 773, 777, 782.

26. This was, and remains, the view of Keetoowah Cherokees. See Georgia Rae Leeds, *The United Keetoowah Band of Cherokee Indians in Oklahoma* (New York: Peter Lang, 1996), 4–5; Haggard, "Internalizing Native American History," 18.

27. Heidi M. Altman and Thomas N. Belt, "Reading History: Cherokee History through a Cherokee Lens," *NS* I (2008): 91; Conley, *The Cherokee Nation*, 7.

28. Thornton, *The Cherokees*, 8–9.

29. Thornton, *The Cherokees*, 6–7.

30. William Bartram, *Travels through North and South Carolina, Georgia, East and West Florida, the Cherokee Country, the Extensive Territories of the Muscogulges, or Creek Confederacy, and the Country of the Chactaws* (Philadelphia: Printed by James and Johnson, 1791) in *William Bartram on the Southeastern Indians*, ed. Gregory A. Waselkov, Kathryn E. Holland Bruand (Lincoln: University of Nebraska Press, 1995), 140.

31. Bartram, *Travels*, 141.

32. Vicki Rozema, ed., *Cherokee Voices: Early Accounts of Cherokee Life in the East* (Winston-Salem, NC: John F. Blair, Publishing, 2006), 95.

33. Traditions of the Cherokees, John Howard Payne Papers, 1794–1841, vol. 1, Ayer Ms. 689, NL, 14.

34. Henry Rowe Schoolcraft, *Notes on the Iroquois: Or, Contributions to American History, Antiquities, and General Ethnology* (New York: Bartlett and Welford, 1846), 359.

35. Altman and Belt, "Reading History," 93. See also Schoolcraft, *Notes on the Iroquois*, 360; Fogleson, "Who Were the Ani-Kutani?" 255–63.

36. See for example the 1755 report detailing the arrival of twelve Cherokee warriors at the home of Pennsylvania's governor as they returned to Cherokee Country after fighting the "French Indians." Samuel Hazard, ed., *Minutes of the Provincial Council of Pennsylvania, From the Organization to the Termination of the Proprietary Government*, vol. 6 (Harrisburg: Theo. Fenn, 1851), 276. See also Paul Demere to William H. Lyttelton, October 11, 1757, Box 6, Lyttelton Papers, CL.

37. David H. Corkran, *The Cherokee Frontier: Conflict and Survival, 1740–62* (Norman: University of Oklahoma Press, 1962), 28–29; W. Stitt Robinson, *James Glen: From Scottish Provost to Royal Governor of South Carolina* (Westport, CT: Greenwood Publishing Group, 1996), 90; Colin G. Calloway, *The American Revolution in Indian Country: Crisis and Diversity in Native American* Communities (New York: Cambridge University Press, 1995), 186.

38. Willinawa's Talk, October 9, 1757, Box 6, Lyttelton Papers, CL. See also Malone, *Cherokees of the Old South*, 13–14; Michael P. Morris, *The Bringing of Wonder: Trade and the Indians of the Southeast, 1700–1783* (Westport, CT: Greenwood Publishing Group, 1999), 120; Hatley, *Dividing Path*, 160.

39. Willinawa's Talk, October 9, 1757.

40. General Amherst Report, October 22, 1759, T1/389/76–77, Treasury Board Papers and In-Letters, NTS. *The Annual Register, or the View of the History, Politicks, and Literature, of the Year 1760* (London: R. and J. Dodsley in Pall-Mall, 1761), 234; Corkran, *The Cherokee Frontier*, 147.

41. Clement Reade to Robert Dinwiddie, April 9, 1757, in *Amherst Papers, 1756–1763: The Southern Sector: Dispatches from South Carolina, Virginia and His Majesty's*

Superintendent of Indian Affairs, ed. Edith Mays (Bowie, MD: Heritage Books, 1999), 7; *Maryland Gazette*, December 18, 1760, Lyman Copeland Draper Papers, 1 JJ 642–651, SHSW; Alexander Hewatt, *An Historical Account of the Rise and Progress of the Colonies of South Carolina and Georgia*, vol. 2 (London: Printed for Alexander Donaldson, 1779), 227; James C. Kelly, "Oconostota," *JCS* 3, no. 4 (Fall 1978): 221–38; John Oliphant, *Peace and War on the Anglo-Cherokee Frontier, 1756–63* (Baton Rouge: Louisiana State University Press, 2001), 86; Corkran, *The Cherokee Frontier*, 180–212; Douglas M. Wood, "'I Have Now Made a Path to Virginia': Outacite Ostenaco and the Cherokee-Virginia Alliance in the French and Indian War," *West Virginia History* 2, no. 2 (Fall 2008): 31–60.

42. Archibald Montgomery to Amherst, May 24, 1760; James Grant to Jeffrey Amherst, January 17, 1761; Amherst to Col. Grant, August 1, 1761, Mays, *Amherst Papers*, 104, 176, 286.

43. Hewatt, *An Historical Account*, 2: 214; Malone, *Cherokees of the Old South*, 24; Fred Anderson, *Crucible of War: The Seven Years' War and the Fate of Empire in British North America, 1754–1766* (New York: Vintage, 2000), 72, 459; Oliphant, *Peace and War*, 24, 70–71, 119. The quote "pick up the hatchet" is at 88; Jill Norgen, *The Cherokee Cases: Two Landmark Federal Decisions in the Fight for Sovereignty* (Norman: University of Oklahoma Press, 2003), 32–33; Susan C. Powers, *Art of the Cherokee: Prehistory to the Present* (Athens: University of Georgia Press, 2007), 74; Fay A. Yarbrough, *Race and the Cherokee Nation: Sovereignty in the Nineteenth Century* (Philadelphia: University of Pennsylvania Press, 2008), 15.

44. In a very small number of cases, some Cherokee people reportedly migrated in a southeasterly direction toward Spanish Florida. See John T. Juricek, "The Westo Indians," *Ethnohistory* 11, no. 2 (Spring 1964): 146, 152; Patrick Riordan, "Finding Freedom in Florida: Native Peoples, African Americans, and Colonists, 1670–1816," *FHQ* 75, no. 1 (Summer 1996): 24–43.

45. McLoughlin, *Cherokee Renascence*, 20, 37; Hatley, *Dividing Path*, 54; Jennifer M. Spear, *Race, Sex, and Social Order in Early New Orleans* (Baltimore: Johns Hopkins University Press, 2009), 26; Gregory D. Smithers, *Science, Sexuality, and Race in the United States and Australia, 1780s–1890s* (New York and London: Routledge, 2009), 26.

46. "Friends and Brothers" from William Preston, June 11, 1774, Preston Davie Papers, 1750–1967, Section 6, Reel C15, Mss1 D2856 d, VHS. For analysis of the Revolutionary War and its impact on the frontier history of the United States see Claudio Saunt, *West of Revolution: An Uncommon History of 1776* (New York: W. W. Norton and Company, 2014).

47. Onitossitah's address was delivered on October 10, 1784. Walter Clark, ed., *The State Records of North Carolina, 1781-'85* (vol. 17, Goldsboro, NC: Nash Brothers, 1899), 175.

48. William Preston to Captain William Ferguson to Occanastota, Atacullaculla and the Other Chiefs and Warriors of the Cherokee Nation, August 23, 1776, Preston Papers; Mr. Thomas Hutchins, September 13, 1786, Josiah Harmar Papers, 1681–1937, CL; E. Lane to Lt. Smith, September 25, 1786, Harmer Papers, CL; El Baron de Carondelet to el Conde de Floridablanca, February 25, 1792, Letters to the Ministers, 1780–1792,

Cuba 177B, AGI; Edward Countryman, "Indians, the Colonial Order, and the Social Significance of the American Revolution," *WMQ*, 3rd Series, 53, no. 2 (April 1996): 354; McLoughlin, *Cherokee Renascence*, 19–20.

49. Doublehead did not move west with the Arkansas Cherokee. He remained in the East, where most Cherokee considered him a "betrayer" of the people. John Howard Payne Papers, 1794–1841, Ayer Ms. 689, NL, 2: 42, 46.

50. Edmund Randolph, Gov of VA, 9 DD 74, 1780s, Lyman Copeland Draper Papers, STSW; Countryman, "Indians, the Colonial Order, and the Social Significance of the American Revolution," 355.

51. McLoughlin, *Cherokee Renascence*, 62–63; Perdue, *Cherokee Women*, 80.

52. Colonial officials were eager to see Cherokee warriors put down the "war hatchet," especially with their long-time rivals the Creeks. Peace between tribal nations, colonial officials believed, would aid in solidifying imperial governance, help extend trade networks, and ensure the safety of frontier settlers. See James Staats Morris ALS to Lewis Morris, December 16, 1793, Native American History Collection, 1689–1921; "Answer to the Question: Is the Prosecution of the Present Indian War an Advantage to the United States," October 29, 1794, Box 1, CL; Cletus F. Fortwendel, Jr., "Silas Dinsmoor and the Cherokees: An Examination of One Agent of Change," *JCS* 27 (1996): 33.

53. John P. Brown, "Eastern Cherokee Chiefs," *CO* 16, no. 1 (March 1938): 20; McLoughlin, *Cherokee Renascence*, 60; Hoig, *Cherokees and Their Chiefs*, 77, 82; Cumfer, *Separate Peoples, One Land*, 55–56; Theda Perdue, "Women, Men, and American Indian Policy: The Cherokee Response to Civilization" in *Negotiators of Change: Historical Perspectives on Native American Women*, ed. Nancy Shoemaker (New York and London: Routledge, 1995), 97.

54. For more on this point, see Chapter 2 of this book.

55. Gary C. Stein, "'And the Strife Never Ends': Indian-White Hostility as seen by European Travelers in America, 1800–1860," *Ethnohistory* 20, no. 2 (spring 1973): 175.

56. Gov. Martin to Brig. Gen. McDowell, July 23, 1782, vol. 16, CSR Documents by Martin, Alexander, 1740–1807, 697–98, accessed August 23, 2011, http://docsouth.unc .edu/csr/index.html/creators/csr10076; Thornton, *The Cherokees*, 39; Kristofer Ray, *Middle Tennessee, 1775–1825: Progress and Popular Democracy on the Southern Frontier* (Knoxville: University of Tennessee Press, 2007), 23; 25–26, 28.

57. Thomas D. Clark, *A History of Kentucky* (New York: Prentice-Hall, 1937), 112; Mark T. Banker, *Appalachians All: East Tennesseans and the Elusive History of an American Region* (Knoxville: University of Tennessee Press, 2010), 25.

58. Banker, *Appalachians All*, 26–7, 30–1.

59. Gaston L. Litton, "The Principal Chiefs of the Cherokee Nation," *CO* 15, no 3 (September 1937): 258.

60. McLoughlin, *Cherokee Renascence*, 59–60.

61. Gary Moulton, *John Ross, Cherokee Chief* (Athens: University of Georgia Press, 1978), 5.

62. Gary E. Moulton, ed., *The Papers of Chief John Ross, 1807–1839*, 2 vols. (Norman: University of Oklahoma Press, 1985), 1: 17. Hereafter *Ross Papers*.

63. Oolootekea also appears as "Oo-Loo-te-ka" in some contemporary documents. Thomas Nuttall, *A Journal of Travels into the Arkansa Territory, During the Year 1819, with Occasional Observations on the Manners of the Aborigines, Illustrated by a Map and Other Engravings* (Philadelphia: Thos. M. Palmer, 1821), 129.

64. Notes on Cherokee History, vol. 6, John Howard Payne Papers, 1794–1841, Ayer Ms. 689, NL, 206–7. See also Colin G. Calloway, *White People, Indians, and Highlanders: Tribal People and Colonial Encounters in Scotland and America* (New York: Oxford University Press, 2010).

65. Douglas W. Owsley and Helen L. O'Brien, "Stature of Adult Cherokee Indians during the Eighteenth Century," *JCS* 7, no. 2 (Fall 1982): 75.

66. Nuttall, *A Journal of Travels into the Arkansa Territory*, 182

67. Emmet Starr, *History of the Cherokee Indians and Their Legends and Folk Lore* (Oklahoma City: The Warden Company, 1921), 40–41; S. Charles Bolton, "Jeffersonian Indian Policy and the Emergence of Arkansas Territory," *AHQ* 62, no. 3 (Autumn 2003): 266; McLoughlin, *Cherokee Renascence*, 95–96; Kathleen DuVal, *The Native Ground: Indians and Colonists in the Heart of the Continent* (Philadelphia: University of Pennsylvania Press, 2006), 10, 198, 246; Alan Gallay, *The Indian Slave Trade: The Rise of the English Empire in the American South, 1670–1717* (New Haven, CT: Yale University Press, 2002), 30.

68. Perdue, "Race and Culture," 712–13.

69. *Ross Papers*, I, 28.

70. John P. Reid, *A Law of Blood: The Primitive Law of the Cherokee Nation* (New York: New York University Press, 1970); Rennard Strickland, *Fire and the Spirits: Cherokee Law from Clan to Court* (Norman: University of Oklahoma Press, 1975), 23–24; McLoughlin, *Cherokee Renascence*, 120–21; Perdue and Green, *The Cherokee Nation and the Trail of Tears*, 37–38; Thurman Wilkins, *Cherokee Tragedy: The Ridge Family and the Decimation of a People* (Norman: University of Oklahoma Press, 1986), 39–40.

71. *Register of Debates in Congress, Comprising the Leading Debates and Incidents of the First Session of the Twenty-First Congress: Together with an Appendix* (Washington, DC: Gales and Seaton, 1830), 1066.

72. Theda Perdue, "The Conflict Within: Cherokees and Removal" in *Cherokee Removal: Before and After*, ed. William L. Anderson (Athens: University of Georgia Press, 1991), 58–59.

73. William McLoughlin, "Thomas Jefferson and the Beginnings of Cherokee Nationalism," *WMQ*, 3rd Edition, 32, no. 4 (October 1975): 547–80.

74. Jefferson's letter to the Cherokee chiefs was dated May 4, 1808. *The Writings of Thomas Jefferson* vol. 8 (Washington, DC: Taylor and Maury, 1854), 213.

75. Edward E. Dale, "Arkansas and the Cherokees," *AHQ* 8, no. 2 (summer, 1949): 96; Lonnie J. White, "Arkansas Territorial Indian Affairs," *AHQ* 21, no. 3 (Autumn 1962): 203; Morris S. Arnold, *Colonial Arkansas, 1686–1804: A Social and Cultural History* (Fayetteville: University of Arkansas Press, 1991), 64–65.

76. DuVal, *Native Ground*, 198.

77. Dan L. Thrapp, *Encyclopedia of Frontier Biography* (vol. 3, Lincoln: University of Nebraska Press, 1998), 1398.

78. Payne Papers, 1794–1841, Ayer Ms. 689, 2: 15.

79. Nuttall, *A Journal of Travels into the Arkansa Territory*, 124–25; J. J. Abbert, Colonial Topographical Engineer, June 1846 in *The New American State Papers: Explorations and Surveys, Continental North America*, vol. 3, ed. Thomas C. Cochran (Wilmington, DE: Scholarly Resources, Inc., 1972), 96.

80. Grant Foreman, *Pioneer Days in the Early Southwest* (1926; repr. Lincoln: University of Nebraska Press, 1994), 28–30.

81. Foreman, *Pioneer Days in the Early Southwest*, 29; Bolton, "Jeffersonian Indian Removal," 264–66.

82. Joseph Patrick Key, "Indians and Ecological Conflict in Arkansas," *AHQ* 59, no. 2 (Summer 2000): 143.

83. The Arkansas Cherokees also encountered Euroamerican settlers and their slaves fleeing the infertile swamplands of the Ohio Valley and Missouri for a new life in Arkansas. Historians also point out that during the early eighteenth century, Delaware and Shawnee refugees also established settlements in the upper Ohio Valley. Penelope B. Drooker, "The Ohio Valley, 1550–1750: Patterns of Sociopolitical Coalescence and Dispersal" in *The Transformation of the Southeastern Indians*, ed. Ethridge and Hudson, 128; Scott Weidensaul, *The First Frontier: The Forgotten History of Struggle, Savagery, and Endurance in Early America* (New York: Houghton Mifflin Harcourt Publishing Company, 2011), xiii, 261; Stephen Warren, *The Worlds the Shawnees Made: Migration and Violence in Early America* (Chapel Hill: University of North Carolina Press, 2014); Sami Lakomäki, *Gathering Together: The Shawnee People through Diaspora and Nationhood, 1600–1870* (New Haven: Yale University Press, 2014) 50, 68, 100.

84. Dale, "Arkansas and the Cherokees," 96–97; Arnold, *Colonial Arkansas*, 124; Key, "Indians and Ecological Conflict in Arkansas," 128; Theda Perdue, *"Mixed Blood" Indians: Racial Construction in the Early South* (Athens: University of Georgia Press, 2003), 2–4; Bolton, "Jeffersonian Removal," 257–58, 264; Perdue, "Race and Culture," 712.

85. Perdue, *Cherokee Women*, 118–20.

86. Key, "Indians and Ecological Conflict in Arkansas," 127.

87. Arch C. Johnson and Eugene S. Schweig, "The Enigma of the New Madrid Earthquakes of 1811–1812," *Annual Review of Earth and Planetary Sciences* 24, no. 1 (May 1996): 339–84; Mary E. Young, "Indian Removal and Land allotment: The Civilized Tribes and Jacksonian Justice," *AHR* 64, no. 1 (October 1958): 32.

88. Duane H. King, "Cherokee in the West: History since 1776" in *Handbook of North American Indians: Southeast*, ed. Raymond Fogleson (Washington, DC: Smithsonian Institute, 2004), 356.

89. The Cherokee prophet Skawuaw (or The Swan) argued in June 1812 that the Cherokee people's adoption of Anglo-American sociopolitical and cultural practices must be given up, lest they encounter future shocks of the magnitude visited upon them by the New Madrid Earthquakes.

90. Taloteske and Cunnetue to Return Meigs, June 23, 1810, Records of the BIA Affairs, Records of the Cherokee Indian Agency, East, Record Group 75, 19, 8, NARA, Washington, DC.

91. Nuttall, *A Journal of Travels into the Arkansa Territory*, 181.

92. Duval, *Native Ground*, 219.

93. Cephas Washburn, *Reminiscences of the Indians, with a Biography of the Author by Rev. J.W. Moore* (Richmond, VA: Presbyterian Committee of Publication, 1869), 79; William Kennedy, *Texas: The Rise, Progress, and Prospects of the Republic of Texas*, vol. 2 (London: R. Hastings, 1841), 312; Dianna Everett, *The Texas Cherokees: A People Between Two Fires, 1819–1840* (Norman: University of Oklahoma Press, 1990), 10–11, 23, 26.

94. Larry S. Watson, "What Cherokee Records Should You Search?" *Journal of American Indian Family Research* 9, no. 4 (1988): 4. See chapter 3 for further analysis of the Texas Cherokee.

95. Stephen F. Austin, Benjamin R. Milam, and David G. Burnet, "Memorial to His Excellency, Gen. Bustamente, Commander-in-Chief, &c., &c.," July 2, 1827, San Felipe de Austin, in William Bollaert, *Cherokee Memos*, VAULT Ayer Ms. 89, NL; *Literary Gazette*, May 15, 1841, 309; Everett, *Texas Cherokees*, 40.

96. Tiya Miles, "'Circular Reasoning,'" 226, 228.

97. Patrick Wolfe, *Settler Colonialism and the Transformation of Anthropology: The Politics and Poetics of an Ethnographic Event* (New York: Continuum, 1999), 1–3, 29.

98. Everett, *Texas Cherokees*, 104, 110, 115.

TWO   Colonialism, Christianity, and Cherokee Identity

1. William G. McLoughlin, "Cherokee Anomie, 1794–1890: New Roles for Red Men, Red Women, and Black Slaves" in *Uprooted Americans: Essays to Honor Oscar Handlin*, ed. Richard L. Bushman, Neil Harris, David Rothman, Barbara Miller Solomon, and Stephan Thernstrom (Boston: Little, Brown, and Company, 1979), 453; Willam G. McLoughlin, *Cherokee Renascence in the New Republic* (Princeton, NJ: Princeton University Press, 1986), 167, 205, 428; Robert J. Conley, *The Cherokee Nation: A History* (Albuquerque: University of New Mexico Press, 2005), 250. Various historians employ slightly different periodization to denote the era of the early republic. Gordon Wood defines the early republic as the period between 1789 and 1815, while J. C. A. Stagg sets the early republic's chronology at 1783–1830. See Gordon S. Wood, *Empire of Liberty: A History of the Early Republic, 1789–1815* (New York: Oxford University Press, 2011); J. C. A. Stagg, *Mr. Madison's War: Politics, Diplomacy and Warfare in the Early American Republic, 1783–1830* (Princeton, NJ: Princeton University Press, 1983).

2. John R. Finger, *The Eastern Band of the Cherokees, 1819–1900* (Knoxville: University of Tennessee Press, 1984), 6; McLoughlin, *Cherokee Renascence*, 29–30; John P. Bowes, *The Trail of Tears: Removal in the South* (New York: Chelsea House, 2007), 102; Theda Perdue and Michael D. Green, *The Cherokee Nation and the Trail of Tears* (New York: Penguin, 2007), 146–50; Henry Thompson Malone, *Cherokees of the Old South: A People in Transition* (1956; repr., Athens: University of Georgia Press, 2010), 7.

3. McLoughlin, *Cherokee Renascence*, xv, passim; Priscilla Wald, "Terms of Assimilation: Legislating Subjectivity in the Emerging Nation" in *American Indian Persistence and Resurgence*, ed. Karl Kroeber (Durham, NC: Duke University Press, 1994), 89–90; Andrew Denson, *Demanding the Cherokee Nation: Indian Autonomy and Ameri-*

can Culture, 1830–1900 (Lincoln: University of Nebraska Press, 2004), 16; Perdue and Green, *Cherokee Nation and the Trail of Tears*, 53.

4. Duane Champagne, *Social Order and Political Change: Constitutional Governments among the Cherokee, the Choctaw, the Chickasaw, and the Creek* (Palo Alto, CA: Stanford University Press, 1992), 246.

5. Joan Greene, "Civilize the Indian: Government Policies, Quakers, and Cherokee Education," *JCS* 10, no. 2 (Fall 1985): 192–93; Laura L. Mielke, *Moving Encounters: Sympathy and the Indian Question in Antebellum Literature* (Amherst: University of Massachusetts Press, 2008), 20.

6. Carmeleta L. Monteith, "Literacy among the Cherokee in the Early Nineteenth Century," *JCS* 9, no. 2 (Fall 1984): 62–63.

7. E. C. Routh, "Early Missionaries to the Cherokees," *CO* 15, no. 4 (December 1937): 449; Malone, *Cherokees of the Old South*, 92; William G. McLoughlin, *The Cherokees and Christianity, 1794–1870: Essays on Acculturation and Cultural Persistence*, ed. Walter H. Conser, Jr. (Athens: University of Georgia Press, 1994), 198; Rowena McClinton, ed., *The Moravian Springplace Mission to the Cherokees*, abr. ed. (Lincoln: University of Nebraska Press, 2010), 2, 16–17.

8. McLoughlin, *Cherokee Renascence*, 281.

9. Cynthia L. Lyerly, *Methodism and the Southern Mind, 1770–1810* (New York: Oxford University Press, 1998), 47–48; Charity R. Carney, *Ministers and Masters: Methodism, Manhood, and Honor in the Old South* (Baton Rouge: Louisiana State University Press, 2011), 8, 36, 123.

10. "Black River Conference, M.E. Church," *St. Louis Christian Advocate*, June 24, 1858, 2.

11. Jeffrey Williams, *Religion and Violence in Early American Methodism: Taking the Kingdom by Force* (Bloomington: Indiana University Press, 2010), 125.

12. McLoughlin, *Cherokees and Christianity*, 47, 69, 78; Patrick Minges, *Slavery and the Cherokee Nation: The Keetoowah Society and the Defining of a People* (New York and London: Routledge, 2003), 66–67.

13. Stephen S. Smith to Jane Morse, July 25, 1821, Native American Collection, CL; McLoughlin, *Cherokees and Christianity*, 66.

14. *Christian Observer* 35 (November 1840), 683. See also *CP*, May 19, 1832, 2–3; Clara Sue Kidwell, *Choctaws and Missionaries in Mississippi, 1818–1918* (Norman: University of Oklahoma Press, 1995), 84.

15. Not until the secession crisis, and the Presbyterian Church's formation of its own missionary society in 1870, did the American Board lose many of its Calvinistic members and assume an identity as an almost wholly Congregationalist institution.

16. Jack Frederick Kilpatrick and Anna Gritts Kilpatrick, eds., *New Echota Letters: Contributions of Samuel A. Worcester to the Cherokee Phoenix* (Dallas: Southern Methodist University Press, 1968), 3.

17. McLoughlin, *Cherokees and Christianity*, 124.

18. Cephas Washburn, *Reminiscences of the Indians, with a Biography of the Author by Rev. J.W. Moore* (Richmond, VA: Presbyterian Committee of Publication, 1869), 33.

19. Dawn Elaine Bastian and Judy K. Mitchell, *Handbook of Native American Mythology* (Santa Barbara, CA: ABC-CLIO, 2004), 49.

20. John Smolenski, *Friends and Strangers: The Making of a Creole Culture in Colonial Pennsylvania* (Philadelphia: University of Pennsylvania Press, 2010), 173–74.

21. Elizur Butler to Evarts, September 13, 1826, ABCFM 18.3.1, v. 4, 67–74. D. S. Butrick, Journal, December 1823, ABCFM 18.3.1, v. 3, 156–62.

22. Cyrus Kingsbury to Samuel Worcester, June 30, 1817, ABCFM 18.3.1, v. 3, 7–12.

23. A. Hoyt to Jeremiah Evarts, January 8, 1819, ABCFM 18.3.1, v. 3, 34–41.

24. Kingsbury to Worcester, October 15, 1816, ABCFM 18.3.1, v. 3, 1–6.

25. Kingsbury to Worcester, May 8, 1816; Kingsbury to Worcester, November 28, 1816, ABCFM 18.3.1, v. 3, 1–6; Laura Potter to David Greene, August 30, 1833, ABCFM 18.3.1, v. 8, 17–18.

26. Butler claimed that his proposal for a Cherokee colony in Texas had the support of John Ross. Butler to D. Greene, February 27, 1830, ABCFM 18.3.1, v. 4, 80–85; Hoyt to Evarts, December 22, 1819, ABCFM 18.3.1, v. 3, 47–50.

27. Thurman Wilkins, *Cherokee Tragedy: The Ridge Family and the Decimation of a People* (Norman: University of Oklahoma Press, 1986).

28. Mabel W. Anderson, *The Life of General Stand Watie: The Only Indian Brigadier General of the Confederate Army and the Last General to Surrender* (Pryor, OK: n.p., 1931), 11; Kenny A. Franks, *Stand Watie and the Agony of the Cherokee Nation* (Memphis, TN: Memphis State University Press, 1979), 3–5; Anne J. Bailey, *Invisible Southerners: Ethnicity in the Civil War* (Athens: University of Georgia Press, 2006), 31

29. Wilkins, *Cherokee Tragedy*, 31.

30. In May 1819, President James Monroe visited Brainerd and expressed how he was "much pleased" with the educational progress of the Cherokee pupils in attendance. See Robert P. Forbes, *The Missouri Compromise and Its Aftermath: Slavery and the Meaning of America* (Chapel Hill: University of North Carolina Press, 2007), 55.

31. Malone, *Cherokees of the Old South*, 95–96; Bernd Peyer, *American Indian Nonfiction: an Anthology of Writings, 1760s–1930s* (Norman: University of Oklahoma Press, 2007), 124; Wilkins, *Cherokee Tragedy*, 4, 6; A. J. Langguth, *Driven West: Andrew Jackson and the Trail of Tears to the Civil War* (New York: Simon and Schuster, 2010), 30.

32. William Potter to Evarts, April 18, 1831, ABCFM 18.3.1, v 8, 1–2.

33. Deborah L. Duvall, *An Oral History of Tahlequah and the Cherokee Nation* (Chicago: Arcadia Publishing, 2000), 37.

34. See for example, Hoyt to Evarts, May 22, 1823, ABCFM 18.3.1 v. 3, 98–102; Butrick to Worcester, July 2, 1818, ABCFM 18.3.1 v. 3, 98–102. See also Carolyn T. Foreman, "A Cherokee Pioneer," *CO* 7, no. 4 (December 1929): 364.

35. *CP*, March 27, 1828, 2; Fay A. Yarbrough, *Race and the Cherokee Nation: Sovereignty in the Nineteenth Century* (Philadelphia: University of Pennsylvania Press, 2008), 36–37. See also the forthcoming work by Ann McGrath, *Illicit Love: Interracial Sex and Marriage in the United States and Australia* (Lincoln: University of Nebraska Press, 2015).

36. *CP*, March 13, 1828, 2.

37. As Fay Yarbrough correctly observes, the question of Cherokee men marrying white women was demographically not perceived as serious an issue as white men marrying Cherokee women. See Yarbrough, *Race and the Cherokee Nation*, 36.

38. *The Life and Times of Hon. William P. Ross* (Fort Smith, AK: Weldon and Williams, Printers, 1893), 1–3. In his choice of marriage partner, "blood" proved a critical determinant for Ross. He married his first-cousin, Mary Jane Ross. See Emmet Starr, *History of the Cherokee Indians and Their Legends and Folk Lore* (Oklahoma City: The Warden Company, 1921), 411.

39. *Ross Papers*, I, 554–55.

40. Jack F. Kilpatrick, "An Adventure Story of the Arkansas Cherokees, 1829," *AHQ* 26, no. 1 (Spring 1967): 41.

41. Butrick to Evarts, February 22, 1825, ABCFM 18.3.1, v. 4, 8–11. George R. Gilmer, *Sketches of Some of the First Settlers of Upper Georgia, of the Cherokees, and the Author* (1855; repr. Baltimore, MD: Genealogical Publishing Company, 1970), 313; Butrick to Evarts, April 3, 1824, ABCFM 18.3.1, v. 4, 8–11.

42. Laura Potter to David Greene, May 7, 1832, ABCFM 18.3.1, v. 8, 10–16. See also John Demos, *The Heathen School: A Story of Hope and Betrayal in the Age of the Early Republic* (New York: Vintage, 2014).

43. Gregory D. Smithers, *Science, Sexuality, and Race in the United States and Australia, 1780s–1890s* (New York: Routledge, 2009), ch. 2.

44. Reverend Mr. Herman Daggett to Jeremiah Evarts, April 12, 1823, ABCFM 8.2.13.

45. Ridge Wedding Record, January 27, 1824, 2009.57.05, CHS.

46. Emily Fox quoted in Theodore S. Gold, *Historical Records of the Town of Cornwall, Litchfield County Connecticut*, 2nd ed. (Hartford, Conn.: Case, Lockwood, and Brainard Co., 1904), 33–34.

47. Lillian Delly, "Episode at Cornwall," *CO* 51, no. 4 (Winter 1973–74): 446.

48. William C. Sturtevant, ed., "John Ridge on Cherokee Civilization in 1826," *JCS* 6, no. 2 (Fall 1981): 88.

49. "Mission to the Cherokees," *Baptist Missionary Magazine*, June 1841, 175.

50. Laura Potter to Greene, August 30, 1833; William Potter to David Greene, July 7, 1835, ABCFM 18.3.1, v. 8, 19–23.

51. Laura Potter to Greene, August 30, 1833; William Potter to David Greene, July 7, 1835, ABCFM 18.3.1, v. 8, 19–23.

52. *Ross Papers*, I, 598; Theda Perdue, "Letters from Brainerd," *JCS* 4, no. 1 (Winter 1979): 6.

53. John Ridge to Elizur Butler, July 7, 1826, ABCFM 18.3.1, v. 4, 67–74.

54. I. Proctor to J. Evarts, July 10, 1828, ABCFM 18.3.1, v. 4, 92–96.

55. On Methodism, Cherokee syncretism, and nationalism see McLoughlin, *Cherokees and Christianity*, 204. On Cherokee Baptists and syncretism see Minges, *Slavery and the Cherokee Nation*, 71.

56. McLoughlin, *Cherokee Renascence*, 277; William G. McLoughlin, *The Cherokee Ghost Dance: Essays on the Southeastern Indians, 1789–1861* (Macon, GA: Mercer University Press, 1984), 422.

57. McLoughlin emphasizes the generational and educational divisions that emerged among the Cherokee by the 1820s. These divisions often found expression in the language of race and class difference. See *Cherokee Renascence*, 326. To the emergence of these sociocultural and economic divisions should be added changes in Cherokee gender relations and significant alterations in the way Cherokee men and women negotiated space and distance.

58. Duvall, *Oral History of Tahlequah*, 14.

59. *Laws of the Cherokee Nation: Adopted by the Council at Various Periods. Printed for the Benefit of the Nation* (Tahlequah, CN: Cherokee Advocate Office, 1852; repr. Wilmington, DE: Scholarly Resources Inc., 1973), 10, 38, 58.

60. McLoughlin, *Cherokee Renascence*, 366, 384, 388; David LaVere, *Contrary Neighbors: Southern Plains and Removed Indians in Indian Territory* (Norman: University of Oklahoma Press, 2000) 13; Tiya Miles, *Ties that Bind: The Story of an Afro-Cherokee Family In Slavery and Freedom* (Berkeley: University of California Press, 2005), 123–24.

61. J. W. Powell, *Annual Report of the Bureau of American Ethnology to the Smithsonian Institute, 1897–98* (Washington, DC: Government Printing Office, 1900), 132; Perdue and Green, *Cherokee Nation and the Trail of Tears*, 53; Mark Rifkin, "Representing the Cherokee Nation: Subaltern Studies and Native American Sovereignty," *Boundary 2* 32, no. 3 (2005): 58–59.

62. Tom Hatley, *The Dividing Paths: Cherokees and South Carolinians through the Revolutionary Era* (New York: Oxford University Press, 1995), 235.

63. *PBP, I-III*, 132–43; Gabriel Harrison, *John Howard Payne: Dramatist, Poet, Actor, and Author of Home, Sweet Home* (1884; revised ed. Philadelphia: J.B. Lippincott and Co., 1885), 291.

64. Payne Papers, 2: 116.

65. Payne Papers, 2: 116; Charles Henry Brainard, *John Howard Payne: A Biographical Sketch of the author of "Home, Sweet Home* (Washington, DC: George A. Coolidge, 1885), 42; 163; Rosa P. Chiles, *John Howard Payne: American Poet, Actor, Playwright, Consul and the Author of "Home, Sweet Home"* (Washington, DC: Columbia Historical Society, 1930), 61.

66. Willard Walker, "Notes on Native Writing Systems and the Design of Native Literacy Programs," *Anthropological Linguistics* 11, no. 5 (May 1969): 153; Monteith, "Literacy among the Cherokee in the Early Nineteenth Century," 65–66.

67. Payne Papers, 2: 137.

68. Samuel C. Williams, "The Father of Sequoyah: Nathaniel Gist," *CO* 15, no. 1 (March 1937): 4; Walter A. Russell, *Descendants of Matthew Russell and Related Families of Jackson County, Alabama: A Collection of Genealogies* (Bloomington, IN: Author House, 2009), 207.

69. Payne Papers, 2: 117.

70. Payne Papers, 2: 119–20.

71. Payne Papers, 2: 120.

72. Payne Papers, 2: 125.

73. Payne Papers, 2: 127.

74. Payne Papers, 2: 131; *Maryland Gazette*, December 18, 1760; Vicki Rozema, ed., *Cherokee Voices: Early Accounts of Cherokee Life in the East* (Winston-Salem, NC: John F. Blair, Publishing, 2006), 73.

75. "The West," *The People's Magazine* 2, no. 25 (February 21, 1835): 37–38; Ellen Cushman, "'We're Taking the Genius of Sequoyah into This Century': The Cherokee Syllabary, Peoplehood, and Perseverance," *WSR* 26, no. 1 (Spring 2011): 68, 72.

76. William Pulte and Kathy Altom, "The Mexican Cherokees and the Kickapoo of Nacimiento, Mexico: A Previously Underreported Relationship," *JCS* 9, no. 1 (Spring 1984): 35.

77. See Theda Perdue's introduction in her *Cherokee Editor: The Writings of Elias Boudinot* (Athens: University of Georgia Press, 1996), 3–4.

78. Perdue, *Cherokee Editor*, 41.

79. The Cherokee students at Cornwall during Boudinot's time there were James Hicks; Thomas Basset; Daniels S. Tau-chia-chy; John Ridge, John Vann. See 2009.63.04: Members of the Foreign Mission School, Nov 1st 1819, CHS; Andrew Wiget, "Elias Boudinot, Elisha Bates and *Poor Sarah*: Frontier Protestantism and the Emergence of the First Native American Fiction," *JCS* 8, no. 1 (Spring 1983): 7.

80. Perdue, *Cherokee Editor*, 43.

81. Perdue, *Cherokee Editor*, 46.

82. Elias Boudinot, *An Address to the Whites: Delivered in the First Presbyterian Church, on the 26th May, 1826* (Philadelphia: William F. Geddes, 1826).

83. McLoughlin and Conser, Jr., take a different view, arguing that no Cherokee offered a systematic statement on race prior to the Civil War. See William G. McLoughlin and Walter H. Conser, Jr., "'The First Man was Red:' Cherokee Responses to the Debate Over Indian Origins, 1760–1860," *AQ* 41, 2 (June, 1989), 244.

84. Sturm, *Blood Politics*, 2; Miles, *Ties that Bind*, 111; Celia E. Naylor, *African Cherokees in Indian Territory: From Chattel to Citizens* (Chapel Hill: University of North Carolina Press, 2008), 10–13; Claudio Saunt, "The Native South: An Account of Recent Historiography," *NS* 1, no. 1 (2008): 50; Yarbrough, *Race and the Cherokee Nation*. See also the following important essay and response in *Ethnohistory*: Theda Perdue, "Race and Culture: Writing the Ethnohistory of the South," *Ethnohistory* 51, no. 4 (Fall 2004), 701–23; Claudia Saunt, Barbara Krauthamer, Tiya Miles, Celia Naylor, and Circe Sturm, "Rethinking Race and Culture in the Early South," *Ethnohistory* 53, no. 2 (Spring 2006), 399–405.

85. Lonnie J. White, "James Miller: Arkansas' First Territorial Governor," *AHQ* 19, no. 1 (Spring 1960): 12–30; Lonnie J. White, "Arkansas Territorial Indian Affairs," *AHQ* 21, no. 3 (Autumn 1962): 204–7.

86. Cyrus Kingsbury to Samuel Worcester, October 15, 1816, Washington, Shea County, East Tennessee, ABCFM 18.3.1 Cherokee Mission 1824–1871, vol. 3. On the theory and application of evolutionary stage theory in the early nineteenth century see Smithers, *Science, Sexuality, and Race*, 51.

87. Boudinot, *An Address to the Whites*, 3–4.

88. Claudio Saunt, "Telling Stories: The Political Uses of Myth and History in the Cherokee and Creek Nations," *JAH* 93, no. 3 (2006): 673–97;

89. Richard J. Perry, *From Time Immemorial: Indigenous Peoples and State Systems* (Austin: University of Texas Press, 1996), 32.

90. Cherokee Nation, *Address of the "Committee and Council of the Cherokee Nation, in General Council Convened," to the People of the United States* (n.d. Pamphlet is housed in the Library Company of Philadelphia), 7.

91. William G. McLoughlin and Walter H. Conser, "The Cherokees in Transition: A Statistical Analysis of the Federal Cherokee Census of 1835," *JAH* 64, no. 3 (December 1977), 678–703; Thornton, *The Cherokees*, 53; Thornton, "The Demography of the Trail of Tears Period: A New Estimate of Cherokee Population Losses" in *Cherokee Removal*, ed. Anderson, 87. In an address to the Cherokee of the Coosewatee District, Elijah Hicks echoed Boudinot's sentiments, arguing in 1828 that a racially mixed Cherokee population had "converted our tomahawks to the woodman's axe and opened the sublime Elysian vales, for the still sublimely ample fields." See *CP*, July 21, 1828, 2. See also Boudinot, *Address*, 6–7

92. Perdue, *Cherokee Editor*, 43–8, 102–3.

93. Boudinot, *Address*, 8–9. See also Perdue, *Cherokee Editor*, 46.

94. Boudinot, *Address*, 3–4, 9; Perdue, *Cherokee Editor*, 43–44.

95. *CP*, July 15, 1829, 1; Perdue, *Cherokee Editor*, 48, 95, 102–3, 105; Theresa Strouth Gaul, ed., *To Marry an Indian: The Marriage of Harriet Gold and Elias Boudinot in Letters, 1823–1839* (Chapel Hill: University of North Carolina Press, 2005), 4–5.

96. *Laws of the Cherokee Nation*, 3, 120, 150; Rennard Strickland, *Fire and Spirit: Cherokee Law from Clan to Court* (Norman: University of Oklahoma Press, 1982); Miles, *Ties that Bind*, 104.

97. *Laws of the Cherokee Nation*, 24, 34, 37.

98. Boudinot, *Address*, 10.

99. *Ross Papers*, I, 283.

100. See for example Perdue's remarks in Perdue, *Cherokee Editor*, 33.

101. Boudinot, *An Address to the Whites*, 10–11.

102. Thornton, *The Cherokees*, 52–53.

103. Quoted in Smithers, *Science, Sexuality, and Race*, 104.

104. This literature is large and growing by the year. See for example Katja May, *African Americans and Native Americans in the Cherokee and Creek Nations* (New York: Garland, 1996); Theda Perdue, *Mixed-Blood Indians: Racial Construction in the Early South* (Athens: University of Georgia Press, 2003); Miles, *Ties that Bind*; Yarbrough, *Race and the Cherokee Nation*; Cynthia Cumfer, *Separate Peoples, One Land*; Smithers, *Science, Sexuality, and Race*, ch. 4.

105. Yarbrough, *Race and the Cherokee Nation*, 32.

106. Boudinot, *Address*, 11.

107. Smithers, "The 'Pursuits of the Civilized Man,'" 260–61.

108. Boudinot Wedding Record, March 28, 1826, 2009.57.06, Cornwell Historical Society. See also Gaul, *To Marry an Indian*, 222. See also Miles, *Ties that Bind*, 22, 86; Smithers, *Science, Sexuality, and Race*, 104.

109. Gaul, *To Marry an Indian*, 89–90, 92, 94, 97, 108. See also Herman Vaill to Harriet Gold, July 1, 1825; Brinsmaid to Vaill, July 14, 1825, Herman Landon Vaill Collection, MS. 519, SML; "The Romance of Elias Boudinot and Harriet Gold," Box 5, Folder 16, Item 1, Grant Foreman Collection, OHS, 2.

110. Gaul, *To Marry an Indian*, 130.

111. "The Romance of Elias Boudinot and Harriet Gold," 3.

112. Gaul, *To Marry an Indian*, 162, 174–75. See also Vaill to Gold, March 5, 1826, Vaill Collection; *CP* (March 13, 1828), 2; Barbara Austen, "Marrying Red: Indian / White Relations and the Case of Elias Boudinot and Harriet Gold," *Connecticut History* 45 (Fall 2006): 256–60.

113. Hiram Carleton, *Genealogical and Family History of the State of Vermont* (New York: The Lewis Publishing Company, 1909), 153; Zella Armstrong, *The History of Hamilton County and Chattanooga, Tennessee* (1931; repr. Johnson City, TN: The Overmountain Press, 1993), 39; James W. Parins, *Elias Cornelius Boudinot: A Life on the Cherokee Border* (Lincoln: University of Nebraska Press, 2006), 12.

114. McGrath, *Illicit Love*.

115. Perdue, *Cherokee Editor*, 163; "Notes on Cherokee History," Payne Papers, Ayer Ms. 689, 26.

116. Boudinot, *An Address to the Whites*, 3; Smithers, *Science, Sexuality, and Race*, 104.

THREE   Removal, Reunion, and Diaspora

1. Alfred A. Cave, "Abuse of Power: Andrew Jackson and the Indian Removal Act of 1830," *The Historian* 65, no. 6 (December 2003): 1330–53. Cave argues that the Indian Removal Act (1830) did not give Jackson the authority to forcibly remove the Cherokees from their homes and breached the Indian Trade and Intercourse Act (1802).

2. Brad Agnew, *Fort Gibson: Terminal on the Trail of Tears* (Norman: University of Oklahoma Press, 1989); Vicki Rozema, ed., *Voices from the Trail of Tears* (Winston-Salem, NC: John F. Blair, Publisher, 2002), 21; Sarah H. Hill, *Cherokee Removal: Forts Along the Georgia Trail of Tears* (n.p.: National Parks Service and the Georgia Department of Natural Resources/Historic Preservation Division, 2005).

3. William McLoughlin, *Cherokee Renascence in the New Republic* (Princeton, NJ: Princeton University Press, 1986), xvii; Ronald N. Satz, "Rhetoric Versus Reality: The Indian Policy of Andrew Jackson" in *Cherokee Removal: Before and After*, ed. William L. Anderson (Athens: University of Georgia Press, 1992), 29–54; Andrew Denson, *Demanding the Cherokee Nation: Indian Autonomy and American Culture, 1830–1900* (Lincoln: University of Nebraska Press, 2004), 4, 16; Theda Perdue and Michael D. Green, *The Cherokee Nation and the Trail of Tears* (New York: Viking, 2007), 38–39.

4. Denson, *Demanding the Cherokee Nation*, 38–40; Daniel Heath Justice, *Our Fire Survives the Storm: A Cherokee Literary History* (Minneapolis: University of Minnesota Press, 2006), 78–80.

5. Ronald N. Satz, *American Indian Policy in the Jacksonian Era* (Lincoln: University of Nebraska Press, 1975), 64; James R. Christianson, "Removal: A Foundation for the Formation of Federalized Indian Policy," *JCS* 10, no. 2 (Fall 1985): 221–22; Duane Champagne, *Social Order and Political Change: Constitutional Governments among the Cherokee, the Choctaw, the Chickasaw, and the Creek* (Stanford, CA: Stanford University Press, 1992), 132–33; Anthony F. C. Wallace, *The Long Bitter Trail: Andrew Jackson and the Indians* (New York: Hill and Wang, 1993), 70.

6. Francis J. Scully, "Across Arkansas in 1844," *AHR* 13, no. 1 (Spring 1954): 32; Mary W. Clarke, *Chief Bowles and the Texas Cherokees* (1971; repr. Norman: University of Oklahoma Press, 1971), 112; A. M. Gibson, *The Kickapoos: Lords of the Middle Border* (Norman: University of Oklahoma Press, 1963), 145, 155, 158.

7. Rennard Strickland, *Fire and the Spirits: Cherokee Law from Clan to Court* (Norman: University of Oklahoma Press, 1975), 68.

8. Joyce B. Phillips and Paul Gary Phillips, eds., *The Brainerd Journal: A Mission to the Cherokees, 1817–1823* (Lincoln: University of Nebraska Press, 1998), 53; Strickland, *Fire and the Spirits*, 69.

9. Strickland, *Fire and the Spirits*, 68

10. Gary E. Moulton, ed., *The Papers of Chief John Ross, 1807–1839*, 2 vols. (Norman: University of Oklahoma Press, 1985), 1: 89, 98. (hereafter cited as *Ross Papers*)

11. *Ross Papers*, 1: 92, 103, 144, 151.

12. Emmet Starr, *History of the Cherokee Indians and Their Legends and Folk Lore* (Oklahoma City, OK: The Warden Company, 1921), 55.

13. *CP*, November 25, 1829, 3; December 10, 1829, 1; April 20, 1833, 1.

14. *Ross Papers*, 1: 195, 198, 210, 218.

15. *Speech of Mr. Everett, of Massachusetts, on the Bill for Removing the Indians from the East to the West Side of the Mississippi, May 19, 1830* (Washington, DC: Gales and Seaton, 1830), 5; David S. Heidler and Jeanne T. Heidler, eds., *Indian Removal: A Norton Casebook* (New York: W.W. Norton and Company, 2007), 138.

16. Heidler and Heidler, *Indian Removal*, 123.

17. Christopher Herbert, *Culture and Anomie: Ethnographic Imagination in the Nineteenth Century* (Chicago: University of Chicago Press, 1991), 161; Colin G. Calloway, *White People, Indians, and Highlanders: Tribal People and Colonial Encounters in Scotland and America* (New York: Oxford University Press, 2008), 66.

18. Heidler and Heidler, *Indian Removal*, 128.

19. Mary Hershberger, "Anticipating Abolition: The Struggle against Indian Removal in the 1830s," *JAH* 86, no. 1 (June 1999): 15–40.

20. *Speech of Mr. Foster, of Georgia, on the Bill to Provide the Removal of the Indians West of the Mississippi, May 17, 1830* (Washington, DC: Duff Green, 1830), 3.

21. Heidler and Heidler, *Indian Removal*, 140–41.

22. *Ross Papers*, 1: 231.

23. George W. Bonnell, *Topographical Description of Texas. To Which is Added, an Account of the Indian Tribes*, 3 vols. (Austin, TX: Clark, Wing, and Brown, 1840), 1: 140.

24. *History of the Claim of the Texas Cherokee* (New York: Morgan, Combs and Lawrence, 1873), 3; Dianna Everett, *The Texas Cherokees: A People Between Two Fires, 1819–1840* (Norman: University of Oklahoma Press, 1995), 22–25, 27; Ben Kiernan, *Blood and Soil: A World History of Genocide and Extermination from Sparta to Darfur* (New Haven, CT: Yale University Press, 2009), 338–39.

25. *History of the Claim of the Texas Cherokee*, 3; Everett, *The Texas Cherokees*, 22–25.

26. *History of the Claim of the Texas Cherokee*, 4–5. See also John Ridge, *The Cherokee Warpath, 1836–1840*, mssHM1730, HHL, 9–12.

27. *History of the Claim of the Texas Cherokee*, 4–5; Everett, *Texas Cherokees*, 99; Mary W. Clarke, *Chief Bowles and the Texas Cherokee* (Norman: University of Oklahoma Press, 2001), 50; Amy S. Greenberg, *Manifest Manhood and the Antebellum American Empire* (New York: Cambridge University Press, 2005), 30.

28. Sam Houston to Duwali, November 22, 1835, Amelia W. Williams and Eugene C. Barker, eds. *The Writings of Sam Houston, 1813–1863*, December 20, 1822 to January 31, 1844, 8 vols. (Austin: The University of Texas Press, 1940), 3: 7.

29. Alfred M. Williams, ed., *Sam Houston and the War of Independence in Texas* (Boston: Houghton, Mifflin and Company, 1895), 135.

30. *NWR*, October 1, 1836, 67.

31. *NWR*, May 26, 1838, 1; *Proceedings of the General Convention of Delegates Representing the Citizens and Inhabitants of Texas* (Brazoria, Texas, 1832), 546; William Kennedy, *Texas: The Rise, Progress, and Prospects of the Republic of Texas*, vol. 2 (London: R. Hastings, 1841), 311–14; N. Doran Maillard, *The History of the Republic of Texas, from the Discovery of the Country to the Present Time; and the Cause of Her Separation from the Republic of Mexico* (London: Smith, Elder, and Co., 1842), 200.

32. Frederick Marryat, *Narrative of Travels and Adventures of Monsieur Violet, in California, Sonora, and Western Texas* (Leipzig: Tauchnitz, 1843), 259–60; Everett, *The Texas Cherokees*, 87–90.

33. "On the Removal of the Capital from Austin," December 2, 1839 in Williams and Barker, *The Writings of Sam Houston*, 2: 317.

34. "In Behalf of the Cherokee Land Bill, 1839" in Williams and Barker, *The Writings of Sam Houston*, 2: 323.

35. *History of the Claim of the Texas Cherokee*, 4; Everett, *The Texas Cherokees*, 96; Kiernan, *Blood and Soil*, 341–44.

36. President Lamar to Bowl and Other Headmen, May 26, 1839 in *The Papers of Mirabeau Buonaparte Lamar*, 6 vols., ed. Charles Adams Gulick, Jr. (Austin, TX: A.C. Baldwin and Son, 1922), 2: 590, 592–93.

37. *Annual Report of the Commissioner of Indian Affairs, Transmitted with the Message of the President at the Opening of the Second Sessions of the Twenty-Sixth Congress, 1839–1840* (Washington, DC: J. Gideon, Jr., Printer, 1840), 31.

38. *Memorial of the Delegates and Representatives of the Cherokee Nation, West, April 1, 1840*, 26th Congress, 1st Session, Doc. No. 162, House of Representatives (Washington, DC: Government Printing Office, 1840), 4–5.

39. Treaty with the Cherokee, 7 Stat., 156, Proclaimed December 26, 1817, in *Indian Affairs: Laws and Treaties*, 7 vols., ed. Charles J. Kappler (Washington, DC: Government Printing Office, 1904), 2: 141–43; Treaty with the Cherokees, 1819, 7 Stat., 195, Proclaimed March 10, 1819, in *Indian Affairs* 2: 177–81.

40. *Register of Debates in Congress Comprising the Leading Debates and the Incidents of the First Session of the Twenty-First Congress Together With an Appendix Containing Important State Papers and Public Documents, and the Laws Enacted During the Session with a Copious Index of the Whole* (vol. 4, Washington, DC: Gale and Seaton, 1830), 1096.

41. Ibid, 1096; Harvey Dan Abrams, *Cherokee Indians Relocation Papers, 1815–1838*, MS 927, Georgia Historical Society Manuscript Collection; Isaac McLellan, *The Fall of the Indian: With other Poems* (Boston: Carter and Hendee, 1830), 9.

42. Cave, "Abuse of Power," 1336.

43. Isaac M'Coy, *Remarks on the Practicability of Indian Reform, Embracing Their Colonization*, 2nd ed. (New York: Gray and Bunce, 1829), 49; Jeremiah Evarts, *Essays on the Present Crisis in the Condition of the American Indians* (Boston: Perkins and Marvin, 1829), 91; Robert Hare, *A Vindication of the Cherokee Claims, Addressed to the Town Meeting in Philadelphia, on the 11th of January, 1830* (Philadelphia: n.p., 1830), 3; "William Penn," *A Brief View of the Present Relations between the Government and People of the United States and the Indians within our National Limits* (1828), 1, CL; Jeremiah Evarts, George B. Cheever, and Convers Francis, *The Removal of the Indians, an Article from the American Monthly Magazine: An Examination of an Article in the North American Review; and an Exhibition of the Advancement of the Southern Tribes, in Civilization and Christianity* (Boston: Peirce and Williams, 1830), 1; William Frelinghuysen, *Speech of Mr. Frelinghuysen, of New Jersey, Delivered in the Senate of the United States, April 6, 1830* (Washington, DC: The Office of the National Journal, 1830).

44. John R. Finger, "The Impact of Removal on the North Carolina Cherokees" in *Cherokee Removal: Before and After*, ed. William L. Anderson (Athens: University of Georgia Press, 1991), 101.

45. Susan M. Ryan, *The Grammar of Good Intentions: Race and the Antebellum Culture of Benevolence* (Ithaca, NY: Cornell University Press, 2003), 26, 31.

46. Ronald Wright, *Stolen Continents: Five Hundred Years of Conquest and Resistance in the Americas* (New York: Mariner Books, 2005), 214; Reginald Horsman, *Race and Manifest Destiny: The Origins of American Racial Anglo-Saxonism* (Madison: University of Wisconsin Press, 1981), 100; Anderson, *Cherokee Removal*, 3; Paul Andrew Hutton, *Phil Sheridan and His Army* (Norman: University of Oklahoma Press, 2003), 180

47. *NWR*, April 4, 1835, 83; Kenneth Penn Davis, "Chaos in the Indian Country: The Cherokee Nation, 1828–35" in *The Cherokee Indian Nation: A Troubled History*, ed. Duane King (Knoxville: University of Tennessee Press, 1986), 129; Jill Norgren, *The*

Cherokee Cases: Two Landmark Federal Decisions in the Fight for Sovereignty (Norman: University of Oklahoma Press, 2004), 42–43.

48. *CP*, July 10, 1830, 4.

49. "Short Reviews and Notices—The Case of the Cherokee Nation against the State of Georgia," *American Jurist and Law Magazine* 6 (July-October 1831): 211; Lewis Cass, *Review of an Article in the North American for January 1830, on the Present Relations of the Indians* (Boston: Peirce and Parker, 1830), 1, 13. Cass argued that to "contend that the Cherokees have a title to the soil, but not to jurisdiction," as Jackson's supporters did, "is an outrage upon common sense." See also Charles C. Royce, *The Cherokee Nation of Indians* (1887; repr. New Brunswick, NJ: Transaction Publishers, 2007), 134; Joseph C. Burke, "The Cherokee Cases: A Study in Law, Politics, and Morality," *SLR* 21 (1968–69): 500–531; Champagne, *Social Order and Political Change*, 144; Perdue and Greene, *The Cherokee Nation*, 77–83.

50. *Cherokee Nation v. Georgia*, 30 U.S. 5 Pet. 1 (1831)

51. *Worcester v. Georgia*, 31 U.S. 6 Pet. 515 (1832)

52. Matthew T. Gregg and David M. Wishart, "The Price of Removal," *Explorations in Economic History* 49 (2012): 423–42.

53. Jackson quoted in Ronald N. Satz, *American Indian Policy in the Jacksonian Era* (Norman: University of Oklahoma Press, 1975), 49.

54. *CP*, July 24, 1830, 1; January 26, 1833, 3. See similarly *CP*, March 29, 1834, 1.

55. John Ridge to Hon. George Gilmer, n.d., John Ridge, ca. 1821–1835, Box Ayer, MS. 761, NL.

56. Russell Thornton, *The Cherokees: A Population History* (Lincoln: University of Nebraska Press, 1990), 51–53; William G. McLoughlin and Walter H. Conser, "The Cherokees in Transition: A Statistical Analysis of the Federal Cherokee Census of 1835," *JAH* 64, no. 3 (December 1977): 681; Dianna Everett, *The Texas Cherokees: A People Between Two Fires, 1819–1840* (Norman: University of Oklahoma Press, 1990), 50–51.

57. R. Douglas Hurt, *The Indian Frontier, 1763–1846* (Albuquerque: University of New Mexico Press, 2003), 159–60. Scholars have debated whether the Keetoowah Society was a functional organization prior to 1838 with the structural capacity to coordinate opposition to removal. See Russell Thornton, "Nineteenth-Century Cherokee History," *ASR* 50, no. 1 (February 1985): 126; Duane Champagne, "Cherokee Social Movements: A Response to Thornton," *ASR* 50, no. 1 (February 1985): 128–29; Champagne, *Social Order and Political Change*, 145. In general, historians of Cherokee history date the origins of the modern Keetoowah to the 1850s. See McLoughlin, *Cherokees and Christianity*, 246; Patrick Minges, *Slavery and the Cherokee Nation: The Keetoowah Society and the Defining of a People* (New York and London: Routledge, 2003), 1–2; Claudio Saunt, "Telling Stories: The Political Uses of Myth and History in the Cherokee and Creek Nations," *JAH* 93, no. 3 (December 2006): 692.

58. *CP* 1, no. 21 (July 21, 1828); *CP* 1, no. 1 (February 21, 1828): 2; *CP* 2, no. 40 (January 20, 1830): 2; Champagne, *Social Order and Political Change*, 143, 145.

59. *Correspondence on the Subject of the Emigration of Indians, Between the 30th November, 1831, and 27th December, 1833, with Abstracts of Expenditures by disbursing*

Agents, in the Removal and Subsistence of Indians, &c., &c. vol. 2 (Washington, DC: Duff and Green, 1835), 910. The full text of the Treaty of New Echota is available from Kappler, *Indian Affairs: Laws and Treaties* 2: 439–49. See also Moulton, *John Ross*, 72; Hurt, *The Indian Frontier*, 159.

60. Theda Perdue, ed., *Cherokee Editor: The Writings of Elias Boudinot* (Athens: University of Georgia Press, 1996), 160; Strickland, *Fire and the Spirits*, n. 38, p. 78.

61. John G. Wool Address to the Cherokee People, New Echota, Georgia, March 22, 1837, Indian File, HM13240 A&B, HHL.

62. In a letter from John Ridge to Eliza Northrup, dated November 1, 1836, plans for Cherokee migrations to Arkansas are discussed in some detail. See Manuscripts Pertaining to the Foreign Mission School, CFL, 4704.

63. "Memorial of a Delegation of the Cherokee Nation, Remonstrating against the Instrument of Writing (Treaty) of December 1835," January 15, 1838, 25th Congress, 2^d Session, House of Representatives, Doc. No. 99, 2. CL.

64. *Ross Papers*, 1: 308.

65. *Ross Papers*, 1: 261.

66. *Ross Papers*, 1: 316–17.

67. *Ross Papers*, 1: 283.

68. See the statement of the Eastern and Western Delegates to the President of the United States, March 16, 1837, in "Memorial of a Delegation of the Cherokee Nation, Remonstrating against the Instrument of Writing (Treaty) of December 1835," January 15, 1838, 25th Congress, 2^d Session, House of Representatives, Doc. No. 99, 19–20. CL.

69. *Memorial of a Delegation from the Cherokee Indians, Presented to Congress January 18, 1831* (Washington, DC: Government Printing Office, 1831), 7.

70. Census Office, *The Five Civilized Tribes in Indian Territory* (Washington, DC: United States Printing Office, 1894), 25.

71. Cave, "Abuse of Power," 1330. See also *CP*, February 18, 1832, 1.

72. Thornton, *The Cherokees*, 68.

73. Paul Kutsche, "The Tsali Legend: Culture, Heroes, and Historiography," *Ethnohistory* 10, no. 4 (Autumn 1963): 329, 332–35; 345.

74. Charles Lanman, "Euchella and Tsali from Letters from the Allegany Mountains," *JCS* 4, no. 4 (1979): 235–36; Nicol N. Auguste, "The Rhetoric of Nuna Dual Tsuny: Retelling the Cherokee Trail of Tears" (Ph.D. diss., University of North Carolina at Greensboro, 2006), 2, 114.

75. Catherine L. Albanese, "Exploring Regional Religion: A Case Study of the Eastern Cherokee," *History of Religions* 23, no. 4 (May 1984): 347; Althea Bass, "Tsali of the Cherokees," *Sewanee Review* 50 (1942): 6–8; John R. Finger, "The Saga of Tsali: Legend Versus Reality," *NCHR* 56 (1979): 1–18; "Primary Accounts of the Tsali Incident," *JCS* 4 (1979): 213–33.

76. Duane H. King, "The Origins of the Eastern Cherokees as a Social and Political Entity" in *The Cherokee Indian Nation*, ed. King, 166. See chapter 4 for more on the North Carolina Cherokee in the decades after removal.

77. Perdue, *Cherokee Editor*, n. 2, 226.

78. See chapter 8, for more on the significance of memory and what became known as the "Trail of Tears" during the late nineteenth and early twentieth centuries.

79. Grace S. Woodward, *The Cherokees* (Norman: University of Oklahoma Press, 1963), 215; Christopher C. Meyers, *The Empire State of the South: Georgia History in Documents and Essays* (Macon, GA: Mercer University Press, 2008), 90.

80. The recollections of Cherokees differ sharply from official accounts about removal. "Throughout their collection and emigration," the Commissioner of Indian Affairs reported in 1838, "the Cherokees have manifested proper temper, and an inclination to do whatever is required, with fewer exceptions than might have been expected, and these not of an important nature." See *Annual Report of the Commissioner of Indian Affairs, transmitted with the Message of the President at the Opening of the Third Session of the Twenty-Fifth Congress, 1837–1838* (Washington, DC: Blair and Rivers, Printers, 1838), 5.

81. Ethan A. Hitchock, "Trail of Tears" in *The Cherokee Removal*, ed. Anderson, 171.

82. *Cherokee Legends and the Trail of Tears: From the Nineteenth Annual Report of the Bureau of American Ethnology* (Knoxville, TN: S.B. Newman Printing Co., 1956), 22.

83. Rozema, *Voices from the Trail of Tears*, 31.

84. John R. Butterly and Jack Shepherd, *Hunger: The Biology and Politics of Starvation* (Lebanon, NH: University Press of New England, 2010), 185.

85. Amy H. Sturgis, *The Trail of Tears and Indian Removal* (Westport, CT: Greenwood Press, 2006), 60.

86. On the concept of exile in Native American history see John P. Bowes, *Exiles and Pioneers: Eastern Indians in the Trans-Mississippi West* (New York: Cambridge University Press, 2007).

887. Howard Wettstein, "Coming to Terms with Exile" in *Diasporas and Exiles: Varieties of Jewish Identity*, ed. Howard Wettstein (Berkeley: University of California Press, 2002), 47–48.

88. *Memorial of the Delegates and Representatives of the Cherokee Nation, West*, 5, 8.

FOUR Uncertain Futures

1. Nicole Etcheson, *The Emerging Midwest: Upland Southerners and the Political Culture of the Old Northwest, 1787–1861* (Bloomington: Indiana University Press, 1995), 16; James D. Miller, *South by Southwest: Planter Emigration and Identity in the Slave South* (Charlottesville: University of Virginia Press, 2002), 87–89.

2. John Love to "My dear father," May 6, 1840, John Love Papers, Box 1, CL. See also *The Boston Quarterly* 2 (April 1839), 255.

3. Samuel G. Drake, *Indian Captivities* (Boston: Antiquarian Bookstore and Institute, 1839), v; Benjamin Slight, *Indian Researches; Or, Facts Concerning the North American Indians* (Montreal, QC: J.E.L. Miller, 1844), 155; John M. Stanley, *Portraits of North American Indians* (Washington, DC: Smithsonian Institution, 1852), 10, 37, 45.

4. "Extract of a Letter from a Friend of Philadelphia, dated the 18th of the 8th Month, 1842," in *Further Information Respecting the Aborigines* (London: Edward Marsh, 1842), 14.

5. John Lang and Samuel Taylor, *Report of a Visit to Some of the Tribes of Indians, Located West of the Mississippi River* (New York: Press of M. Day and Co., 1843), 28.

6. *Laws of the Cherokee Nation Passed During the Years 1839–1867* (1868; St. Louis, MO: Missouri Democrat Print, 1973), 59–61; Gary E. Moulton, *John Ross: Cherokee Chief* (Athens, GA: University of Georgia Press, 1978), 22, 132; Gary E. Moulton, ed., *The Papers of Chief John Ross, 1807–1839*, 2 vols. (Norman: University of Oklahoma Press, 1985), 2: 338–39; William P. Ross, "Public Education among the Cherokee Indians," *American Journal of Education and College Review* 1, no. 1 (August 1855): 120–22; William G. McLoughlin, *Cherokee Ghost Dance: Essays on the Southeastern Indians, 1789–1861* (Macon, GA: Mercer University Press, 1984), 482–83; William G. McLoughlin, *After the Trail of Tears: The Cherokee Struggle for Sovereignty, 1839–1880* (Chapel Hill: University of North Carolina Press, 1993), 92, 240, 317; Jill Norgren, *The Cherokee Cases: Two Landmark Federal Decisions in the Fight for Sovereignty* (Norman: University of Oklahoma Press, 2004), 143–44; Andrew Denson, *Demanding the Cherokee Nation: Indian Autonomy and American Culture, 1830–1900* (Lincoln: University of Nebraska Press, 2004), 18, 32, 55; Dwight Mission, Folder 8, Box 57, Federal Writers Project, 81.105; Fairfield-Mulberry Mission, Folder 10, Box 57, Federal Writers Project, 81.105; Annual Message of DW Bushyhead, Folder 162, Box 4, Dennis Wolfe Bushyhead Collection, WHC; John B. Davis, "Public Education among the Cherokee Indians," *Peabody Journal of Education* 7, no. 3 (November 1929): 168–69; Carolyn T. Foreman, "The Cherokee Gospel Tidings of the Dwight Mission," *CO* 12 (December 1934): 454; Meg Devlin O'Sullivan, "Missionary and Mother: Jerusha Swain's Transformation in the Cherokee Nation, 1852–1861," *CO* 83 (Winter 2005–06): 452–65; "Education: Cherokee Nation," Folder 6, Box 57, Federal Writers Project 81.105, 2–4, WHC; Davis, "Public Education among the Cherokee Indians," 171–72; Izumi Ishii, *Bad Fruits of the Civilized Tree: Alcohol and the Sovereignty of the Cherokee Nation* (Lincoln: University of Nebraska Press, 2008).

7. John R. Finger, "The Abortive Second Cherokee Removal, 1841–1844," *JSH* 47, no. 2 (May 1981): 207–26.

8. Grant Foreman, *The Five Civilized Tribes: Cherokee, Chickasaw, Choctaw, Creek, Seminole* (Norman: University of Oklahoma Press, 1934), 301–5; Grace Steele Woodward, *The Cherokees* (Norman: University of Oklahoma Press, 1963), 195.

9. Delegates of the Cherokee Nation to the Senate and House of Representatives in Congress, Undated, John Ross Papers, TGM.

10. McLoughlin, *After the Trail of Tears*, ch. 2; Denson, *Demanding the Cherokee Nation*, esp. ch. 1; Theda Perdue and Michael Green, *The Cherokee Nation and the Trail of Tears* (New York: Viking, 2007), ch. 7.

11. *Ross Papers*, 1: 729; Francis P. Prucha, *The Great Father: The United States and the American Indians* (Lincoln: University of Nebraska, 1984), 273.

12. Kevin Mulroy, *Freedom on the Border: The Seminole Maroons in Florida, the Indian Territory, Coahuila, and Texas* (Lubbock, TX: Texas Tech University Press, 1993), 52; Jane F. Lancaster, *Removal Aftershock: Seminoles Struggles Survive the West, 1836–1866* (Knoxville: University of Tennessee Press, 1994), 1–3

13. Fred Eggan, "Historical Changes in the Choctaw Kinship System," *American Anthropologist* 39, no. 1 (January-March 1939): 34–52; Kenny A. Franks and William Tallack, "The California Overland Express through Indian Territory and Western Arkansas," *AHQ* 33, no. 1 (Spring 1974): 72; McLoughlin, *After the Trail of Tears*, 201; Gerard Reed, "Postremoval Factionalism in the Cherokee Nation" in *The Cherokee Indian Nation: A Troubled History*, ed. Duane King (Knoxville: University of Tennessee Press, 1979), 155–57.

14. Perdue and Green, *The Cherokee Nation*, 147.

15. "Notes on Cherokee History," Payne Papers, 1794–1841, Ayer Ms. 689, NL, 18; *Ross Papers*, 1: 720–21; McLoughlin, *After the Trail of Tears*, 11–14.

16. John Ehle, *Trail of Tears: The Rise and Fall of the Cherokee Nation* (New York: Anchor Books, 1988), 74–75.

17. Rennard Strickland, *Fire and the Spirits: Cherokee Law from Clan to Court* (Norman: University of Oklahoma Press, 1975), 27.

18. *Ross Papers*, 1: 717, 724, 737; Allen Ross, "The Murder of Elias Boudinot," *CO* 12, no. 1 (March 1934): 19–24; McLoughlin, *After the Trail of Tears*, 16; Perdue and Green, *The Cherokee Nation*, 150; Fay A. Yarbrough, *Race and the Cherokee Nation: Sovereignty in the Nineteenth Century* (Philadelphia: University of Pennsylvania Press, 2008), 19; Daniel Blake Smith, *An American Betrayal: Cherokee Patriots and the Trail of Tears* (New York: Henry Holt and Company, 2011), 263.

19. "Notes on Cherokee History," Payne Papers, 23, 37, 39–43, 49, 55; Stanley W. Hoig, *The Cherokees and Their Chiefs: In the Wake of Empire* (Fayetteville: The University of Arkansas Press, 1998), 194.

20. *Ross Papers*, 1: 714–15.

21. Moulton, *John Ross*, 117.

22. *Ross Papers*, 2: 137–38.

23. *Ross Papers*, 1: 726.

24. Ibid., 732, 735.

25. Ibid., 744.

26. Ibid., 747–49.

27. Ibid., 749, 761. See also *Annual Report of the Commissioner of Indian Affairs, 1839–40* (Washington, DC: J. Gideon, Jr., 1840), 37.

28. Robert J. Conley, *The Cherokee Nation: A History* (Albuquerque: University of New Mexico Press, 2005), 161; McLoughlin, *After the Trail of Tears*, ch. 1.

29. McLoughlin, *After the Trail of Tears*, 38.

30. Texas Travel Diary, 1838, Manuscripts Divisions, CL. See entries for January 18, 1838; January 19, 1838; January 22, 1838.

31. Sophia Sawyer to David Greene, January 4, 1842, ABC 18.3.1, V. 10, HL.

32. John Ross to "Dear Sir," February 7, 1840, *Ross Papers*, vol. 1.

33. James M. Payne to John Ross, April 20, 1842, Folder 854, TGM; Payne Papers, 6: 52, 77, 82; *Ross Papers*, 2: 76, 80.

34. *Ross Papers*, 2: 80, 115, 132.

35. "International Indian Council at Tahlequah, 1843," Thomas Lee Ballenger Papers, 1730–1968, Box 7, NL; Conley, *The Cherokee Nation*, 225.

36. "International Indian Council at Tahlequah, 1843," Ballenger Papers, Box 7, NL; Foreman, *The Five Civilized Tribes*, 367.

37. Woodward, *The Cherokees*, 235; Foreman, *The Five Civilized Tribes*, 301.

38. *Memorial of John Ross and Others, Representatives of the Cherokee Nation of Indians, on the Subject of the Existing Difficulties in that Nation, and Their Relations with the United States* (Washington, DC: Ritchie and Heiss, 1846), 1–2.

39. *Memorial of John Ross and Others*, 3.

40. Theda Perdue, *Slavery and the Evolution of Cherokee Society, 1540–1866* (Knoxville: University of Tennessee Press, 1987), ch. 1.

41. Thornton, *The Cherokees*, 52; McLoughlin, *After the Trail of Tears*, 127–28; Foreman, *The Emigration of the Five Civilized Tribes*, 142, 216–17, 231, 365–66; Barbara Krauthamer, *Black Slaves, Indian Masters: Slavery, Emancipation, and Citizenship in the Native American South* (Chapel Hill: University of North Carolina Press, 2013), 77.

42. Not all Cherokees owned slaves. See for example Edward Everett Dale and Gaston Litton, eds., *Cherokee Cavaliers: Forty Years of Cherokee History as Told in the Correspondence of the Ridge-Watie Family* (Norman: University of Oklahoma Press, 1939), xix.

43. R. Halliburton, Jr., *Red Over Black: Black Slavery Among the Cherokee Indians* (Westport, CT: Greenwood Press, 1977), 24–25. Historians disagree over just what type of slave master Vann was. See Perdue, "Cherokee Planters," 124; Ralph Henry Gabriel, *Elias Boudinot: Cherokee and His America* (Norman: University of Oklahoma Press, 1941), 25.

44. Halliburton, Jr., *Red Over Black*, 26.

45. Martin also maintained two homes for his two wives, demonstrating, perhaps, that the Cherokee elite did not always practice what they preached. See Halliburton, Jr., *Red Over Black*, 27

46. See for instance Folder 26, Box 7, Foreman Collection, OHS.

47. In comparison, the Choctaws owned 2,344 slaves, the Creeks 1,532, and the Chickasaws about 975. See Renate Bartl, "Native American Tribes and Their African Slaves" in *Slave Cultures and the Cultures of Slavery*, ed. Stephan Palmié (Knoxville: University of Tennessee Press, 1995), 167.

48. Runaways or stolen slaves see for example, Thomas Woodward to "the United States," November 16, 1840, TGM.

49. *LSA Daily World*, April 28, 1935, Item 3, Folder 14, Box 5, Grant Foreman Collection, 1900–1956. 83.229, OHS.

50. Payne Papers, 2: 72; Lynne Richards, "Dwelling Places: Log Homes in Oklahoma Indian Territory, 1850–1909," *Material Culture* 25, no. 2 (Summer 1993): 2; Tiya

Miles, *The House on Diamond Hill: A Cherokee Plantation Story* (Chapel Hill: University of North Carolina Press, 2010), 182; Jennifer Elliot, "Ga-ne-tli-yv-s-di (Change) in the Cherokee Nation: The Van and Ridge Houses in Northwest Georgia," *Buildings and Landscapes* 18, no. 1 (Spring 2011): 43–63.

51. Tiya Miles, "Showplace of the Cherokee Nation: Race and the Making of a Southern House Museum," *The Public Historian* 33, no. 4 (November 2011): 15.

52. "Report of Indian Affairs, 1888," Folder 1, Box 57, Federal Writers Project, 81.105, OHS.

53. James F. Brooks, *Captives and Cousins: Slavery, Kinship, and Community in the Southwestern Borderlands* (Chapel Hill: University of North Carolina Press, 2002), 16, 62, 141.

54. The following account is based on James Henry Carleton to Richard Barnes Mason, November 14, 1841, FAC 1951, Richard Barnes Mason, Correspondence Regard Texas Indians, 1841–1863. FAC 1951–1961, HHL.

55. Statements on the Stolen Slaves in Texas, April 8, 1842, FAC 1960, Mason Papers, HHL.

56. William G. McLoughlin, "Cherokee Slaveholders and Baptist Missionaries, 1845–1860," *The Historian* 45, no. 2 (February 1983): 162; Celia Naylor, *African Cherokees in Indian Territory: From Chattel to Citizens* (Chapel Hill: University of North Carolina Press, 2008), 136.

57. "History of the Keetoowahs," *Indian School Journal* 14, no. 1 (September 1913): 27.

58. "Report of Indian Affairs, 1888," Folder 1, Box 57, Federal Writers Project, 81.105, OHS; Duncan James, "The Keetoowah Society," *CO* 4 (1926): 251–55; Perdue, *Slavery and the Evolution of Cherokee Society*, 123–25; McLoughlin, "Cherokee Slaveholders," 147–63; McLoughlin, *After the Trail of Tears*, chs. 5 and 6; McLoughlin, *Cherokees and Christianity*, 221; Minges, *Slavery and the Cherokee Nation*, 72–73, 96; Moulton, *John Ross*, 163.

59. Dale and Litton, *Cherokee Cavaliers*, xix; Kenny A. Frank, *Stand Watie and the Agony of the Cherokee Nation* (Memphis, TN: Memphis State University Press, 1979), 114–15; Perdue, *Slavery and the Evolution of Cherokee Society*, 129–30; Moulton, *John Ross*, 163; McLoughlin , *Cherokees and Christianity*, 257–62; Minges, *Slavery and the Cherokee Nation*, 72–73; Anne J. Bailey, *Invisible Southerners: Ethnicity in the Civil War* (Athens, GA: University of Georgia Press, 2006), 32; Conley, *The Cherokee Nation*, 173.

60. Mulroy, *Freedom on the Border*, 54, 62; Naylor, *African Cherokees*, 67.

61. Resolution of the National Council Regarding the Negroes Mentioned in F88, November 18, 1842, Folder 883, TGM; Daniel F. Littlefield and Lonnie E. Underhill, "Slave 'Revolt' in the Cherokee Nation, 1842," *AIQ* 3 (Summer 1977): 121–31; R. Halliburton, Jr., "Black Slave Control in the Cherokee Nation," *JES* 3 (Summer 1975): 23–35; Perdue, *Slavery and the Evolution of Cherokee Society*, 83; Linda Reese, "Cherokee Freedwomen in Indian Territory, 1863–1890," *WHQ* 33, no. 3 (Autumn 2002): 278–79.

62. Krauthamer, *Black Slaves, Indian Masters*, 7, 83, 89.

63. Resolution of the National Council Regarding the Negroes Mentioned in F88, November 18, 1842, Folder 883, TGM.

64. Thomas H. Crawford to Joel R Poinsett, June 25, 1839, Correspondence 1814–1842, Box 1, William Holland Thomas Papers, DRML; Historian John Finger calculates that roughly 1,400 Cherokees remained in the East following the removal of 1838–39. See John R. Finger, *The Eastern Band of Cherokees, 1819–1900* (Knoxville: University of Tennessee Press, 1984), 29.

65. Finger, *The Eastern Band of Cherokees*, 31, 48–50, 61–62, 73.

66. Ibid., 42–44.

67. Census of the North Carolina Cherokees, 1840, Box 1, Thomas Papers.

68. Ibid.

69. Ibid.

70. Ibid.

71. Ibid. For further examples similar to those discussed above see A List of Names of Cherokees Supposed not to be Included in the Census being Made of the NC Cherokees under the Late Act of Congress, 1846, Box 2, Thomas Papers.

72. C. D. Barnitz to Commissioner Indian Affairs Baltimore, MD, 12 May 1851, Microfilm Roll 1, M1059, Selected Letters Received by the Office of Indian Affairs Relating to the Cherokees of North Carolina, NARA, Washington, DC.

73. Ibid.

74. Felix Axly to Charles E. Mix, Commissioner of Indian Affairs, 28 January 1858, Microfilm Roll 1, M1059, Selected Letters Received by the Office of Indian Affairs Relating to the Cherokees of North Carolina, NARA, Washington, DC.

75. Thomas H. Crawford to Joel R Poinsett, February 7, 1840, Correspondence 1814–1842, Box 1, Thomas Papers.

76. Frederick W. Hodge, ed., *Handbook of American Indians North of Mexico* (Part I, Washington, DC: Government Printing Office, 1912), 247; John R. Swanton, *The Indian Tribes of North America* (Baltimore: Genealogical Publishing Company, 1952), 223.

77. Finger, *The Eastern Band of Cherokees*, 39; Finger, "The Abortive Second Cherokee Removal," 207–26.

78. Resolution of the Senate of 1st February Instant, in "Extract from the Report of the Commission of Indian Affairs to the Secretary of War, 22nd February 1844," Box 2, Thomas Papers.

79. Resolution of the Senate of 1st February Instant, in "Extract from the Report of the Commission of Indian Affairs to the Secretary of War, 22nd February 1844," Box 2, Thomas Papers; Finger, *The Eastern Band of Cherokees*, 17; Brett H. Riggs, *Removal Period Cherokee Households and Communities in Southwestern North Carolina, 1835–1838* (Raleigh, NC: North Carolina State Historic Preservation Office, 1996).

80. Finger, *The Eastern Band of Cherokees*, 41–42.

81. James Taylor to Jacob Tompson, April 17, 1857, Microfilm Roll 2, M1059, Selected Letters Received by the Office of Indian Affairs Relating to the Cherokees of North; Joint Resolution in the Senate of the United States, July 8, Box 2, Thomas Papers.

82. PL Clayton to William Meredith, January 9, 1850, Box 2, Thomas Papers; Finger, *The Eastern Band of Cherokees*, 51, 71–73; E. Stanly Godbold, Jr., and Mattie U. Russell, *Confederate Colonel and Cherokee Chief: The Life of William Holland Thomas* (Knoxville: University of Tennessee Press, 1990), 67.

83. James Taylor to Jacob Tompson (Sec of Interior), April 17, 1857, Microfilm Roll 2, M1059, Selected Letters Received by the Office of Indian Affairs Relating to the Cherokees of North Carolina.

84. James Taylor to Jacob Tompson, April 17, 1857.

85. Strickland, *Fire and the Spirits*, 6; Conley, *Cherokee Nation*, 167–69; Denson, *Demanding the Cherokee Nation*, 55; Miles, *Ties that Bind*, 186.

86. Carolyn T. Foreman, "Edward W. Bushyhead and John Rollin Ridge: Cherokee Editors in California," Box 6, Item 1, p. 1, Grant Foreman Collection, 83.229, OHS; Henry Stevens, *Catalogue of the American Books in the Library of the British Museum* (London: Charles Whittingham, 1856), 113; George E. Foster, *The Story of the Cherokee Bible: An Address, with Additional and Explanatory Notes*, 2nd ed. (Ithaca, NY: Democrat Press, 1899), 79; "Journalistic Ventures of the Cherokees," *The Indian School Journal* 14, no. 5 (January 1914): 198.

87. "Dennis Wolfe Bushyhead, 1826–1898," *Encyclopedia of Oklahoma History and Culture*, accessed August 2, 2011, http://digital.library.okstate.edu/encyclopedia/entries/B/BU015.html; Foreman, "Edward W. Bushyhead and John Rollin Ridge," 2–3.

88. Emmet Starr, *History of the Cherokee Indians and Their Legends and Folk Lore* (Oklahoma City, OK: The Warden Company, 1921), 509, 665.

89. J. S. Holliday, *Rush for Riches: Gold Fever and the Making of California* (Berkeley: University of California Press, 1999); Madeline Y. Hsu, *Dreaming of Gold, Dreaming of Home: Transnationalism and Migration Between the United States and South China, 1882–1943* (Stanford, CA: Stanford University Press, 2000); Robert J. Willoughby, *The Great Western Migration to the Gold Fields of California, 1849–1850* (Jefferson, NC: McFarland and Company, 2003); Kenneth N. Owens, *Gold Rush Saints: California Mormons and the Great Rush for Riches* (Norman: University of Oklahoma Press, 2005).

90. Franks and Tallack, "The California Overland Express," 72; Deborah L. Duvall, *An Oral History of Tahlequah and the Cherokee Nation* (Chicago: Arcadia Publishing, 2000), 83; Will Bagley, *Blood of the Prophets: Brigham Young and the Massacre at Mountain Meadows* (Norman: University of Oklahoma Press, 2002), 58.

91. C. Rudston Read, *What I Heard, Saw and Did at the Australian Gold Fields* (London: T. and W. Boone, 1853), 191; L. G. Churchwarrd, "Americans and Other Foreigners at Eureka," *Australian Historical Studies* 6, no. 1 (1953): 43–49; E. Daniel Potts and Annette Potts, *Young America and Australian Gold: Americans and the Gold Rush of the 1850s* (St. Lucia, QLD: University of Queensland Press, 1974).

92. Murial H. Wright, "The Journal of John Lowery Brown, of the Cherokee Nation En Route to California in 1850," *CO* 12, no. 2 (June 1934): 177, 196–98; Annie Proulx, "Traversing the Desert" in *Red Desert: History of a Place*, ed. Annie Proulx (Austin: University of Texas Press, 2008), 257.

93. John W. Caughey, *The California Gold Rush* (Berkeley: University of California Press, 1948), 78–79; J.S. Holliday, *The World Rushed In: The California Gold Rush Experience* (1981; repr. Norman: University of Oklahoma Press, 2002), 50; Aims McGuinness, *Path of Empire: Panama and the California Gold Rush* (Ithaca, NY: Cornell University Press, 2008), 32; James P. Delgado, *Gold Rush Port: The Maritime Archeology of San Francisco's Waterfront* (Berkeley: University of California Press, 2009), 170–74.

94. Department of the Interior, *Bulletin of the United States Geological Survey*, No. 172 (Washington, DC: Government Printing Office, 1900), 66.

95. James W. Parins, *John Rollin Ridge: His Life and Works* (Lincoln, University of Nebraska Press, 1991), 26–32.

96. Thurman Wilkins, *Cherokee Tragedy: The Ridge Family and the Decimation of a People* (Norman: University of Oklahoma Press, 1970), 335–36; Parins, *John Rollin Ridge*, 31–32; Parins, *Elias Cornelius Boudinot: A Life on the Cherokee Border* (Lincoln: University of Nebraska Press, 2006), 21.

97. Reed, "Postremoval Factionalism in the Cherokee Nation," 157; Richard L. Trotter, "For the Defense of the Western Border: Arkansas Volunteers on the Indian Frontier, 1846–1847," *AHQ* 60, no. 4 (Winter 2001): 394, 396–98.

98. Edward B. Dale, "Arkansas and the Cherokees," *AHQ* 8, no. 2 (Summer 1949): 95–114, esp. 100–101. Cherokee families with connections to the Treaty Party also sought refuge at federal forts, such as Fort Gibson. See Daniel F. Littlefield, Jr. and Lonnie E. Underhill, "Fort Wayne and the Arkansas Frontier, 1838–1840," *AHQ* 35, no. 4 (Winter 1976): 334–59, esp. 348

99. Parins, *John Rollin Ridge*, 52–62.

100. John Rollin Ridge, "The Cherokees: Their History—Present Condition and Future Prospects," in *A Trumpet of Our Own: Yellow Bird's Essays on the North American Indian; Selections from the Writings of the Noted Cherokee Author, John Rollin Ridge*, ed. Davic Farmer and Rennard Strickland (San Francisco: Book Club of California, 1981), 49.

101. Ridge, "The Cherokees," 49–50.

102. Ridge, "The Cherokees," 51; Parins, *John Rollin Ridge*, 51, 188.

103. John Rollin Ridge to Stand Watie, September 23, 1853, FAC 1676, HHL.

104. James Parins argues that following the incident with David Kell, Ridge "saw his life as controlled by forces outside himself, by history and fate." Parins, *John Rollin Ridge*, 81. As I suggest below, Ridge's desire to connect to his family, and the Cherokee people more generally, through his writing and journalism reflected a determination to gain some control over those forces.

105. John Rollin Ridge to Stand Watie, September 23, 1853, FAC 1676, HHL.

106. John Rollin Ridge to Stand Watie, October 9, 1854, FAC 1677, HHL.

107. Parins, *John Rollin Ridge*, 114.

108. John Rollin Ridge to Stand Watie, October 9, 1854, FAC 1677, HHL.

109. John Rollin Ridge to Sarah B.N. Bird, October 5, 1855, FAC 1678, HHL. See also Parins, *John Rollin Ridge*, 115.

110. David E. Gordon, "Early California Journalism," *Overland Magazine* 44, no. 2 (August 1904): 128

111. John Caldwell Guilds, "Arkansas Backwards: Territory, Statehood, and Beyond the Civil War, 1804–1884" in *Arkansas, Arkansas: Writers and Writings from the Delta to the Ozarks, 1541–1969*, ed. John Caldwell Guilds (Fayetteville: University of Arkansas Press, 1999), 139.

112. Sean K. Teuton, "The Native American Tradition" in *The Cambridge History of the American Novel*, eds. Leonard Cassuto, Clare Virginia Eby, and Benjamin Reiss (Cambridge, UK: Cambridge University Press, 2001), 1109.

113. David Wyatt, *Five Fires: Race, Catastrophe, and the Shaping of California* (New York: Oxford University Press, 1997), 69; Lori Lee Wilson, *The Joaquin Band: The History Behind the Legend* (Lincoln: University of Nebraska Press, 2011), xi, 1–3.

114. John Lowe, "'I am Joaquin!': Space and Freedom in Yellow Bird's *The Life and Adventures of Joaquin Murieta, the Celebrated California Bandit*" in *Early Native American Writing: New Critical Essays*, ed. Helen Jaskoski (Cambridge, UK: Cambridge University Press, 1996), 104–21; David Moore, "Cycles of Selfhood, Cycles of Nationhood: Authenticity, Identity, Community, Sovereignty" in *Native Authenticity: Transnational Perspectives on Native American Literary Studies*, ed. Deborah L. Madsen (Albany: State University of New York Press, 2010), 56.

115. "Elias Cornelius Boudinot," Vertical File, Research Division, OHS; Thomas Burnell Colbert, "Visionary or Rogue?: The Life and Legacy of Elias Cornelius Boudinot," *CO* 65 (Fall 1987): 268–81.

116. US Federal Census, *Free Inhabitants in 7th district of San Francisco*, 26 June 1860

117. According to Emmet Starr, Barbara Longknife, nee Hildebrand, had been married once before, also to a Cherokee man. See Starr, *History of the Cherokee Indians*, 665 (see also n. 99 above); Dale and Litton, *Cherokee Cavaliers*, 91–92.

118. Robert W. Redsteer, "An Open Epistle to Dr. Traditional Cherokee of the Nonexistent Bear Clan," *AIQ* 27, nos. 1–2 (Winter 2003): 376–80.

119. Gavan Daws, *Shoal of Time: A History of the Hawaiian Islands* (Honolulu: University of Hawaii Press, 1968), 89; Laura Ruby and Ross W. Stephenson, *Honolulu Town* (Charleston, SC: Arcadia Publishing, 2012), 32, 52; *Congressional Record: Proceedings and Debates of the 111th Congress, First Session* (Washington, DC: Government Printing Office, 2009), 3185–86.

120. Norman Meller, "Missionaries to Hawaii: Shapers of the Islands' Government," *Western Political Quarterly* 11, no. 4 (December 1958): 188–99; Chester R. Young, "American Missionary Influence on the Union of Church and State in Hawaii During the Regency of Kaahumanu," *Journal of Church and State* 9, no. 2 (1967): 165–75; Daws, *Shoal of Time*, 97–98, 105, 221.

121. Patricia Grimshaw, "'Christian Woman, Pious Wife, Faithful Mother, Devoted Missionary': Conflicts in Roles of American Missionary Women in Nineteenth-Century Hawaii," *Feminist Studies* 9, no. 3 (Autumn 1983): 489–521; Patricia Grimshaw,

Path of Duty: American Missionary Wives in Nineteenth-Century Hawaii (Honolulu: University of Hawaii Press, 1989).

122. Reginald Yzendoom, *History of the Catholic Mission in the Hawaii Islands* (Honolulu, HI: Honolulu Star-Bulletin, 1927), 245–46; Adele Marie Lemon, *Hawaii, Lei of Islands: A History of Catholic Hawaii* (Honolulu, HI: Tongg Publishing Company, 1956), 51; Angelyn Dries, *The Missionary Movement in American Catholic History* (Maryknoll, NY: Orbis Books, 1998), 52.

FIVE   War, Division, and Refugees

1. Clarissa W. Confer, *The Cherokee Nation in the Civil War* (Norman: University of Oklahoma Press, 2007).

2. John C. Inscoe and Gordon B. McKinney, *The Heart of Confederate Appalachia: Western North Carolina in the Civil War* (Chapel Hill: University of North Carolina Press, 2000), 16.

3. John R. Finger, *The Eastern Band of Cherokees, 1819–1900* (Knoxville: University of Tennessee Press, 1984), 82.

4. Thomas quoted in Daniel E. Sutherland, *A Savage Conflict: The Decisive Role of Guerrillas in the American Civil War* (Chapel Hill: University of North Carolina Press, 2009), 189.

5. Andrew Denson, *Demanding the Cherokee Nation: Indian Autonomy and American Culture, 1830–1900* (Lincoln: University of Nebraska Press, 2004), 57.

6. William R. Dupree Interview, IPP 26: 350; Susie Blackwood Interview, IPP 8: 344; Rebecca M. Swain Interview, IPP 88: 476–77; Timothy Barnett, Jr. Interview, IPP 5: 411–14; Ada Smith Interview, IPP 84: 302.

7. William Wayne Interview, IPP 45: 154.

8. Patrick N. Minges, *Slavery in the Cherokee Nation: The Keetoowah Society and the Defining of a People, 1855–1867* (New York: Routledge, 2003), 175–76.

9. William H. Walker Interview, IPP 94: 467.

10. Duane Champagne, "Cherokee Social Movements: A Response to Thornton," *ASR* 50, no. 1 (February 1985): 128; Minges, *Slavery in the Cherokee Nation*, 71, 78.

11. William Potter Ross to John Ross, November 27, 1863, TGM, Folder 1201.

12. John Ross and Evan Jones, *The Cherokees: Their Loyalty and Sufferings* (n.p., 1864), 2. See also "Appeal in Behalf of the Loyal Cherokees," *The Missionary Herald of the American Board* 60, no. 4 (April 1864): 101.

13. North Carolina Convention, *Ordinances and Resolutions Passed by the State Convention of North Carolina, First Session in May and June, 1861* (Raleigh, NC: John W. Syme, 1862).

14. Ronald N. Satz, "The Mississippi Choctaw: From the Removal Treaty to the Federal Agency" in *After Removal: The Choctaw in Mississippi*, ed. Samuel J. Wells and Roseanna Tubby (Jackson: University of Mississippi Press, 1986), 17–18. See also Walter L. Williams, ed., *Southeastern Indians Since the Removal Era* (Athens: University of Georgia Press, 1979).

15. Francis P. Prucha, *The Great Father: The United States Government and the American Indians* (Lincoln: University of Nebraska Press, 1984), 421; Denson, *Demanding the Cherokee Nation*, 58.

16. Pike quoted in Moulton, *John Ross*, 168.

17. *The War of Rebellion: A Compilation of the Official Records of the Union and Confederate Armies*, ser. I (Washington, DC: Government Printing Office, 1881), 13: 493.

18. Quote is from Hubbard at *War of Rebellion*, 13:498. See also p. 495–96; Mark Bean, W. B. Welch, E. N. MacClare, John Spencer, J. A. McCulloch, J. M. Lacy, J. P. Carnahan, and many others, to John Ross, May 9, 1861, TGM, Folder 1099; Lt. Col. J. R. Kennedy to Ross, May 15, 1861, TGM, Folder 1101; Moulton, *John Ross*, 167–68; William H. Graves, "The Five Civilized Tribes and the Beginning of the Civil War," *JCS* 10, no. 2 (Fall 1985): 205–11.

19. J. P. Evans to Ross, July 2, 1861, TGM, Folder 1111.

20. David Hubbard to Ross, June 12, 1861, TGM, Folder 1107.

21. *The War of Rebellion*, 3: 675; See also Annie Heloise Abel, *The American Indian as Slaveholder and Secessionist: An Omitted Chapter in the Diplomatic History of the Southern Confederacy* (Cleveland, OH: The Arthur H. Clark Company, 1915), 223; Moulton, *John Ross*, 170; McLoughlin, *After the Trail of Tears*, 183; Gaines, *Confederate Cherokees*, 12.

22. *War of Rebellion*, 3: 674

23. *Treaty with the Cherokees, October 7th, 1861* (Richmond, s.n., 1861), 2.

24. W. Craig Gaines, *The Confederate Cherokees: John Drew's Regiment of Mounted Rifles*, Baton Rouge: LSU Press, 1988); *Treaty with the Cherokees*, 5.

25. Denson, *Demanding the Cherokee Nation*, 56.

26. *War of the Rebellion*, 13: 504.

27. Emmet Starr, *History of the Cherokee Indians and Their Legends and Folk Lore* (Oklahoma City, OK: The Warden Company, 1921), 155–56.

28. Abel, *The American Indian in the Civil War*, 25, 32; Confer, *Cherokee Nation in the Civil War*, 57; Dale and Litton, *Cherokee Cavaliers*, 113; Clara Sue Kidwell, *The Choctaws in Oklahoma: From Tribe to Nation, 1855–1970* (Norman: University of Oklahoma Press, 2007), 63; Minges, *Slavery in the Cherokee Nation*, 2003; Stephen B. Oates, *Confederate Cavalry West of the River* (Austin: University of Texas Press, 1961), 19; Gaines, *The Confederate Cherokees*, 34.

29. Roy Bird, *Civil War and the Indian Wars* (Gretna, LA: Pelican Publishing Company, 2007), 34; Confer, *Cherokee Nation in the Civil War*, 57–58.

30. Parker, *Cherokee Indians*, 80; Moulton, *John Ross*, 174; Denson, *Demanding the Cherokee Nation*, 61; Clarissa W. Confer, *Daily Life During the Indian Wars* (Santa Barbara, CA: Greenwood Publishing, 2011), 164

31. Minges, *Slavery in the Cherokee Nation*, 143.

32. Abel, *The Slaveholding Indians*, 135.

33. John Edwards, *Shelby and His Men: Or, The War in the West* (Cincinnati: Miami Printing and Publishing, 1867), 85; Whit Edwards, *The Prairie Was on Fire: Eyewitness Accounts of the Civil War in the Indian Territory* (Norman: Oklahoma Historical

Society, 2001), 106; Dale Cox, *The Battle of Massard Prairie: The 1864 Confederate Attacks on Fort Smith, Arkansas* (Bascom, FL: William Cox, 2008), 55.

34. John N. Edwards, *Shelby and His Men: Or; the War in the West* (Cincinnati, OH: Miami Printing and Publishing Company, 1867), 85; Thomas V. Parker, *The Cherokee Indians* (New York: The Grafton Press, 1907), 79.

35. Wardell, *A Political History of the Cherokee Nation*, 7; Joseph B. Thoburn, "The Cherokee Question," *CO* 2, no. 2 (June 1924): 177.

36. Wardell, *A Political History of the Cherokee Nation*, 12.

37. Undated Resolution by Cherokee Citizens, Folder 6722, Microfilm Roll No. 47, Cherokee Nation Papers, WHC.

38. Ibid.

39. Wardell, *A Political History of the Cherokee Nation*, 19; Thoburn, "The Cherokee Question," 177; James W. Parins, *Elias Cornelius Boudinot: A Life on the Cherokee Border* (Lincoln: University of Nebraska Press, 2006), 37–38

40. "Stand Watie's Regiment," Ca. 1861, TGM, Folder 1265.

41. James W. Parins, *John Rollins Ridge: His Life and Works* (Lincoln: University of Nebraska Press, 2004), 199.

42. Quintard Taylor, *In Search of the Racial Frontier: African Americans in the American West, 1528–1990* (New York: W.W. Norton and Company, 1998), 69.

43. William G. McLoughlin, *After the Trail of Tears: The Cherokees' Struggle for Sovereignty, 1839–1880* (Chapel Hill: University of North Carolina Press, 1993), 209.

44. Muriel H. Wright, "General Douglas H. Cooper, C.S.A.," *CO* 32 (Summer 1954): 166–67.

45. William S. Burns to Charles Burns, April 1, 1862, William S. Burns Papers, CL.

46. William S. Burns to Charles Burns, April 14, 1862, William S. Burns Papers, CL.

47. Thomas A. Aplin to Sarah L. Aplin, March 15, 1862, Aplin Family Papers, CL.

48. Samuel M. Schmucker, *A History of the Civil War in the United States* (Part II, Philadelphia: Bradley and Co., 1865), 118.

49. Frank Moore, ed., *The Rebellion Record: A Diary of American Events, with Documents, Narratives, Illustrative Incidents, Poetry, Etc.* (New York: G.P. Putnam, 1862), 100; Walter Lee Brown, *A Life of Albert Pike* (Fayetteville: University of Arkansas Press, 1997), 397.

50. Frank Cunningham, *General Stand Watie's Confederate Indians* (1959; repr. Norman: University of Oklahoma Press, 1998), 60.

51. William L. Shea and Earl J. Hess, *Pea Ridge: Civil War Campaign in the West* (Chapel Hill: University of North Carolina Press, 1992), 320.

52. Octavius A. Leland Dairy, October 6, 1863–September 12, 1864, CL.

53. "The War in Missouri; The First Fight at Newtonia," *NYT*, October 16, 1862; Larry Wood, *The Two Civil War Battles of Newtonia: Fierce and Furious* (Charleston, SC: The History Press, 2010), 77–91.

54. "Re. Mounting Indian Home Guards," Undated, Folder 1162, TGM; Request of Delegation to Congress re. Organization of Cherokee Regiment and Home Guards, Undated, Folder 1163, TGM.

55. Michael Fellman, *Inside War: The Guerrilla Conflict in Missouri during the Civil War* (New York: Oxford University Press, 1989), 189, n. 41, 301. On the significance of human mutilation see Richard Slotkin, *Regeneration through Violence: The Mythology of the American Frontier, 1600–1860* (Norman: University of Oklahoma Press, 1973).

56. Richard S. Brownlee, *Gray Ghosts of the Confederacy: Guerrilla Warfare in the West 1861–1865* (Baton Rouge: Louisiana State University Press, 1984), 6.

57. "Indian Troubles in Northern Iowa," Undated Newspaper Clipping, Octavius A. Leland Dairy, October 6, 1863–September 12, 1864, CL.

58. *The Reports of the Committees of the House of Representatives, Made During the First Session, Thirty-Ninth Congress, 1865–66* (Washington, DC: Government Printing Office, 1866), 164.

59. *War of Rebellion*, 53: 572; *Condensed Chronological History of the Great Rebellion, in the United States, from November 8th, 1860 to May 10th, 1865* (San Francisco: Deffebach and Co., 1867), 60; Charles R. Freeman, "The Battle of Honey Springs," *CO* 13 (1935): 154–68; Confer, *Cherokee Nation in the Civil War*, 88; Arrell M. Ginson, *Oklahoma, A History of Five Centuries* (Norman: University of Oklahoma Press, 1981), 124; Frank Arey, "The First Kansas Colored at Honey Springs" in *"All Cut to Pieces and Gone to Hell": The Civil War, Race Relations, and the Battle of Poison Spring*, ed. Mark K. Christ (Little Rock, AK: The Butler Center for Arkansas Studies, 2003), 79–81.

60. *War of Rebellion* 22: 457–61; Naylor, *African Cherokees in Indian Territory*, 150.

61. T. Lindsay Baker and Julie P. Baker, eds., *The WPA Oklahoma Slave Narratives* (Norman: University of Oklahoma Press, 1996), 83, 195.

62. On the impact of the Battle of Webbers Falls on Native Americans see Gaines, *The Confederate Cherokees*, 14–17; *Ross Papers*, 2: 271; McLoughlin, *After the Trail of Tears*, 181; Confer, *Cherokee Nation in the Civil War*, 89; Naylor, *African Cherokees in Indian territory*, 45.

63. Brad Agnew, "Indian Territory" in *Abraham Lincoln and the Western Territories*, ed. Ralph Y. McGinnis and Calvin N. Smith (Chicago: Nelson-Hall, Inc., 1994), 197.

64. Abel, *American Indian as Participant in the Civil War*, 86, 257; Bernice N. Crockett, "Health Conditions in the Indian Territory from the Civil War to 1890," *CO* 36 (1958): 34–37; Laurence M. Hauptman, *Between Two Fires: American Indians in the Civil War* (New York: Simon and Schuster, 1995), 18; Frank, "The Longhouse Divided," 128; Russell Thornton, *The Cherokees: A Population History* (Lincoln: University of Nebraska Press, 1990), 94.

65. Confer, *Cherokee Nation in the Civil War*, 41.

66. William A. Phillips to John P. Usher, May 15, 1863, Folder 1184, TGM.

67. Ross to "Dear Sir," December 9, 1861, Folder 1147, TGM; Gary Zeller, "Occupying the Middle Ground: African Creeks in the First Indian Home Guard Regiment, 1862–1865," *CO* 76, no. 1 (Spring 1998): 48–71.

68. Thoburn, "The Cherokee Question," n. 12, 233; Confer, *Cherokee Nation in the Civil War*, 59–62.

69. Baker and Baker, *The WPA Oklahoma Slave Narratives*, 356.

70. Francis P. Prucha, *The Great Father: The United States Government and the American Indians* (Lincoln: University of Nebraska Press, 1984), 424; Daniel F. Littlefield, Jr., *Alex Posey: Creek Poet, Journalist, and Humorist* (Lincoln: University of Nebraska Press, 1992), 15.

71. *War of Rebellion*, 13: 732, 762.

72. Quoted in Ross and Jones, *The Cherokees*, 5.

73. Tiya Miles, *Ties that Bind: The Story of an Afro-Cherokee Family in Slavery and Freedom* (Berkeley: University of California Press, 2005), 171; Steve Cottrell, *Civil War in the Indian Territory* (Gretna, LA: Pelican Publishing Company, 1998), 10, 87.

74. *War of Rebellion*, ser. I, vol. 13, 630, 697.

75. Laurence M. Hauptman, *The Iroquois in the Civil War: From Battlefield to Reservation* (Syracuse, NY: Syracuse University Press, 1993), 94.

76. *War of Rebellion*, 13: 93; Abel, *The American Indian as Participant in the Civil War*, 79–80, 86–88; Edward E. Dale and Gaston Litton, eds., *Cherokee Cavaliers: Forty Years of Cherokee History as Told in the Correspondence of the Ridge-Watie-Boudinot Family* (Norman: University of Oklahoma, 1939), 102; William G. McLoughlin, *The Cherokees and Christianity, 1794–1870: Essays on Acculturation and Cultural Persistence*, ed. Walter H. Conser, Jr. (Athens: University of Georgia Press, 1994), 272.

77. John F. Bradbury, "'Buckwheat Cake Philanthropy': Refugees and the Union Army in the Ozarks," *AHQ* 57 (Autumn 1998): 233–54; Anne J. Bailey and Daniel E. Sutherland, "Introduction: The History and Historians of Arkansas's Civil War" in *Civil War Arkansas: Beyond Battles and Leaders*, ed. Anne J. Bailey and Daniel E. Sutherland (Fayetteville: University of Arkansas Press, 2002), 7–8.

78. *War of Rebellion*, 13: 427, 785.

79. *War of Rebellion*, 13: 801.

80. Dale and Litton, *Cherokee Cavaliers*, 101, 182; David A. Nichols, *Lincoln and the Indians: Civil War Policy and Politics* (Columbia: University of Missouri Press, 1978), 58.

81. Nichols, *Lincoln and the Indians*, 59–60.

82. Dale and Litton, *Cherokee Cavaliers*, 134

83. Hauptman, *Between Two Fires*, 50.

84. Richard Harnage Interview, 15, M-27; Saugee R. Grigsby Interview, 14, T-426–2; Charles E. Vandergriff Interview, 46, T-128, Doris Duke Collection, WHC.

85. Dale and Litton, *Cherokee Cavaliers*, xxii, 148; Jack Gregory Interview, 43, T-503, Doris Duke Collection; Baker and Baker, *The WPA Oklahoma Slave Narratives*, 375.

86. Morris L. Wardell, *A Political History of the Cherokee Nation, 1838–1907* (Norman: University of Oklahoma Press, 1938), 48–49.

87. Wardell, *A Political History of the Cherokee Nation*, 49.

88. Wardell, *A Political History of the Cherokee Nation*, 50.

89. Ella Coody Robinson Interview, IPP 77: 22–23.

90. Hauptman, *Between Two Fires*, 108.

91. Sharlotte Neely, *Snowbird Cherokees: People of Persistence* (Athens: University of Georgia Press, 1991), 24.

92. Hauptman, *Between Two Fires*, 109–10.

93. War Department Collection of Confederate Records, Compiled Service Records of Confederate Soldiers Who Served in Organizations from the State of North Carolina, Record Group 109, M270, Roll 569, NARA, Washington, DC; John R. Finger, *The Eastern Band of Cherokees, 1819–1900* (Knoxville: University of Tennessee Press, 1984), 64, 84; E. Stanly Godbold, Jr. and Mattie U. Russell, *Confederate Colonel and Cherokee Chief: The Life of William Holland Thomas* (Knoxville: University of Tennessee Press, 1990), 178.

94. James Mooney, "Myths of the Cherokee," *Nineteenth Annual Report of the Bureau of American Ethnology to the Secretary of the Smithsonian Institution, 1897–98* (Washington, DC: Government Printing Office, 1900), 170.

95. The Cherokees, like African American soldiers, encountered suspicions from many whites that they were naturally predisposed to cowardice, lacked the discipline for "civilized" warfare, and tended to become deserters. See Hauptman, *Between Two Fires*, 109.

96. Quoted in Brian D. McKnight, *Contested Borderland: The Civil War in Appalachian Kentucky and Virginia* (Knoxville: University of Kentucky Press, 2012), 85. On allegations of scalping at Baptist Gap see also Hauptman, *Between Two Fires*, 113; Earl J. Hess, *Banners to the Breeze: The Kentucky Campaign, Corinth, and Stones River* (Lincoln: University of Nebraska Press, 2000), 48. Hess asserts there were "four documented incidents of scalping by Indian troops wearing the gray." The figure of four hundred scalps can be found in William R. Trotter, *Bushwhackers: The Civil War in North Carolina* (Winston-Salem, NC: John F. Blair, 1988), 74.

97. Trotter, *Bushwhackers*, 74. E. Stanly Godbold and Mattie Russell contend that the "scalping at Baptist Ridge was at most an isolated episode." See Godbold and Russell, *Confederate Colonel*, 107. See similarly Vernon H. Crow, *Storm in the Mountains: Thomas' Confederate Legion of Cherokee Indians and Mountaineers* (Cherokee, NC: Museum of the Cherokee Indian, 1982), 16, n. 32, p. 240; Finger, *Eastern Band of Cherokees*, 91.

98. Quoted in Louis H. Manarin, ed., *North Carolina Troops, 1861–1865: A Roster*, vol. 16 (Raleigh: North Carolina Office of Archives and History, 2008), 31.

99. Finger, *The Eastern Band of Cherokees*, 89; Hauptman, *Between Two Fires*, 115–16;

100. James B. Jones, Jr., *Tennessee in the Civil War: Selected Contemporary Accounts of Military and other Events, Month by Month* (Jefferson, NC: McFarland and Company, 2011), 184; Hauptman, *Between Two Fires*, 115–16.

101. Hauptman, *Between Two Fires*, 118. Compounding Cherokee anxieties, Thomas, their longtime patron, was court-martialed and found guilty of harboring deserters.

102. Ross to W. P. Dole, August 7, 1864, Folder 1254, TGM.

103. Andrew W. Frank, "The Longhouse Divided: Native Americans During the American Civil War" in *Civil War: People and Perspectives*, ed. Lisa T. Frank (Santa Barbara, CA: ABC-CLIO, 2009), 122.

104. Donald Ricky, *Indians of North Carolina* (Minneapolis, MN: Somerset Publishers, Inc., 1999), 97; Laurence M. Hauptman, *Tribes and Tribulations: Misconceptions about American Indians and Their Histories* (Albuquerque: University of New Mexico Press, 1995), 59.

105. Godbold, Jr., and Russell, *Confederate Colonel*, 188; Russell Thornton, *The Cherokees: A Population History* (Lincoln: University of Nebraska Press, 1990), 97.

106. *Ross Papers*, 2: 729; Grant Foreman, *The Five Civilized Tribes: Cherokee, Chickasaw, Choctaw, Creek, Seminole* (Norman: University of Oklahoma Press, 1934), 382; Moulton, *Ross*, 182.

107. Smith Christie to Brig. Gen. Thayer, Undated, Folder 1234, TGM; *Report of the Commissioner of Indian Affairs for the Year 1865* (Washington, DC: Government Printing Office, 1865), 36, 255, 271, 282; US Congress, *Index to the Executive Documents of the House of Representatives for the Second Session of the Forty-Fourth Congress, 1876–77* (Washington, DC: Government Printing Office, 1877), xvi; Richard J. Hinton, *Rebel Invasion of Missouri and Kansas* (Chicago: Church and Goodman, 1865), 10, 141, 307; John T. Trowbridge, *The South: A Tour of its Battlefields and Ruined Cities* (Hartford, CT: L. Stebbins, 1866), 251, 393, 445–46.

108. Wiley Britton, "Some Reminiscences of the Cherokee People Returning to Their Homes, the Exiles of a Nation," *CO* 6 (1928): 163–77; Dale Banks, "Civil War Refugees from Indian Territory in the North, 1861–1864," *CO* 41 (Autumn 1963): 286–93; Angie Debo, "Southern Refugees of the Cherokee Nation," *SHQ* 35 (1932): 255–66; Edmund J. Danziger, Jr., "The Office of Indian Affairs and the Problem of Civil War Refugees in Kansas," *KHQ* 35 (1969): 257–75.

SIX   The "Refugee Business"

1. "Treaty with the Cherokee, 1866" in *Indian Affairs: Laws and Treaties*, vol. 2, ed. Charles J. Kappler (Washington, DC: Government Printing Office, 1904), 942–50; Lulu L. Brown, *Cherokee Neutral Lands Controversy* (Girard, KS: Girard Press, 1931), 7; William G. McLoughlin, *After the Trail of Tears: The Cherokees Struggle for Sovereignty, 1839–1880* (Chapel Hill: University of North Carolina Press, 1993), 223–27; Gary L. Cheatham, "Divided Loyalties in Civil War Kansas," *KH* 11 (Summer 1988): 98. Ely Parker, the Seneca Indian leader and Civil War veteran, believed that all Native Americans with land claims in Kansas must unite, lest their claims fail. See Ely Parker to NH Parker, March 31, 1888, Ely S. Parker Papers, 497.3, P223, APS.

2. William J. Harsha, "Law for the Indians," *North American Review* 134, no. 304 (March 1882): 274; James W. Parins, *Elias Cornelius Boudinot: A Life on the Cherokee Border* (Lincoln: University of Nebraska Press, 2006).

3. Luther B. Hill, *A History of the State of Oklahoma*, vol. 2 (Chicago: The Lewis Publishing Company, 1910), 7; Vine Deloria, Jr., *Behind the Broken Trail of*

Treaties: An Indian Declaration of Independence (Austin: University of Texas Press, 1974), 188–89; Ray Allen Billington and Martin Ridge, *Westward Expansion: A History of the American Frontier* (Albuquerque: University of New Mexico Press, 2001), 373–75; Richard W. Etulain, "Abraham Lincoln and the Trans-Mississippi American West: An Introductory Overview" in *Lincoln Looks West: From the Mississippi to the Pacific*, ed. Richard W. Etulain (Carbondale: Southern Illinois University Press, 2010), 27–28.

4. "Introduction" in *The Papers of Will Rogers: Volume One, November 1879-April 1904*, ed. Arthur F. Wertheim and Barbara Bair (Norman: University of Oklahoma Press, 1996), 149.

5. A. V. Travis, "Life in the Cherokee Nation a Decade after the Civil War," *CO* 4, no. 1 (Mach 1926): 18.

6. WP Adair to Joseph L. Martin, August 4, 1864, Folder 6883, Microfilm Roll No. 47, Cherokee Nation Papers, WHC.

7. John B. Meserve, "Chief William Potter Ross," *CO* 15, no. 1 (March 1937): 26; Message of William P. Ross, October 19, 1866, Folder 1, Box 1, William Potter Ross Collection, WHC. See also William Potter Ross, *The Life and Times of the Hon. William P. Ross* (Fort Smith: Weldon and Williams Printers, 1893), 113.

8. Message of William P. Ross, October 19, 1866; Arrell M. Gibson, *The History of Oklahoma* (Norman: University of Oklahoma Press, 1972), 96–98.

9. See for example Emmiline Goodwin vs. Cherokee Nation, Cause Pending Before the Commission on Citizenship, June 11, 1878; Annie Kesterson vs. Cherokee Nation, Office Commission on Citizenship, October 5, 1887, RG 75, Demurer and Answers of the Cherokee Nation, 1896–1897, NARA, Ft. Worth, Texas.

10. George Roth, "Federal Tribal Recognition in the South" in *Anthropologists and Indians in the New South*, ed. Rachel A. Bonney and J. Anthony Paredes (Tuscaloosa: University of Alabama Press, 2001), 60; Susan L. Yarnell, *The Southern Appalachians: A History of the Landscape* (Durham, NC: Forest History Society, 1998), 17.

11. John R. Ridge, "The North American Indians: What they Have Been and What they Are," *The Hesperian* 8, no. 1 (March 1862), in *A Trumpet of Our Own: Yellow Bird's Essays on the North American Indian*, eds. David Farmer and Rennard Strickland (San Francisco: The Book Club of California, 1981), 77.

12. F. Seebohm, *The Crisis of Emancipation in America* (London: Alfred W. Bennett, 1865), 32; *Memorial Testimony, and Letters of Federal Prisoners, on the Claim of P. F. Frazee, a Loyal Citizen of New Jersey, for Property Destroyed at Columbia, S.C.* (Washington, DC: McGill and Witherow, 1866), 6; *Circulars, Etc., Issued by the Bureau of Refugees, Freedmen, and Abandoned Lands, from the Organization of Said Bureau to December 31, 1867* (Washington, DC: Government Printing Office, 1867), Circular No. 15, September 12, 1865; J.W. Ingalls to E.P. Smith, August 7, 1875, 1877-I348, Box 1, RG 75, Letters Received Relating to Cherokee Citizenship, 1875–89, Records of the BIA, Land Division, NARA, Washington, DC.

13. *Circulars, Etc.*, Circular No. 11, April 3, 1867.

14. Horace James, *Annual Report of the Superintendent of Negro Affairs in North Carolina, 1864* (Boston: W.F. Brown and Co., 1865), 63; Charles S. Greene, *Thrilling*

Stories of the Great Rebellion (Philadelphia: John E. Potter and Co., 1866), 229; South Carolina General Assembly, *Report of the Special Joint Committee, in Regard to Certain Public Property on Hand at the Evacuation of Columbia, and the Surrender of Gen. Johnston's Army* (Columbia: F.G. Fontaine, State Printer, 1866), 25; Whitelaw Reid, *After the War: A Southern Tour* (London: Sampson Low, Son, and Marston, 1866), 29; Mary S. Robinson, *A Household Story of the American Conflict: The Great Battle Year* (New York: N. Tibbals and Son, 1871), 233; "Haste to the Rescue! The Kansas Refugees!" February 28, 1881, Box 1, Folder 38, Elizabeth Comstock Papers, 1740–1829, CL; John F. Cameron, "Camps; Depopulation of Memphis; Epidemics of 1878 and 1879," *Public Health* 5 (1879): 152–53; LaWanda Cox, "The Promised Land for the Freedmen," *MVHR* 45, no. 3 (December 1958): 413–40; Nell Irvin Painter, *Exodusters: Black Migration to Kansas after Reconstruction* (New York: W.W. Norton and Company, 1976); Jane Baker, "From Egypt to Canaan: Why African American Exodusters Left Mississippi for Kansas in 1879," *Chrestomathy* 5 (2006): 44–64; Jim Downs, *Sick from Freedom: African-American Illness and Suffering during the Civil War and Reconstruction* (New York: Oxford University Press, 2012); Dale Banks, "Civil War Refugees from Indian Territory in the North, 1861–1864," *CO* 41 (Autumn 1963): 286–93.

15. Raymond D. Fogleson, "Perspectives on Native American Identity" in *Studying Native America: Problems and Perspectives*, ed. Russell Thornton (Madison: University of Wisconsin Press, 1998), 40–59; Melissa L. Meyer, "American Indian Blood Quantum Requirements: Blood is Thicker than Family" in *Over the Edge: Remapping the American West*, ed. Valerie J. Matsumoto and Blake Allmendinger (Berkeley: University of California Press, 1999), 231–50; Circe Sturm, *Blood Politics: Race, Culture, and Identity in the Cherokee Nation of Oklahoma* (Berkeley: University of California Press, 2002), 79–88; David A Chang, "Enclosures of Land and Sovereignty: The Allotment of American Indian Lands," *Radical History Review* 109 (Winter 2011): 108–19.

16. The challenge was made all the more daunting by the rise of "nativist" movements in the Cherokee Nation. These movements are famous for expressing an adherence to "traditional" cultural beliefs and practices, and expressing hostility toward white "intruders." Theda Perdue, ed., *Nations Remembered: An Oral History of the Cherokees, Chickasaws, Choctaws, Creeks, and Seminoles in Oklahoma, 1865–1907* (Norman: University of Oklahoma Press, 1993), 99–100.

17. Moulton, *John Ross*, 182, 195; Joan Gilbert, *The Trail of Tears Across Missouri* (Columbia: University of Missouri Press, 1996), 46.

18. Weston A. Goodspeed, *The Province and the States: Louisiana, Arkansas, Oklahoma, Indian Territory*, vol. 3 (Madison, WI: The Western Historical Association, 1904), 501; Nancy Cohen, *The Reconstruction of American Liberalism, 1865–1914* (Chapel Hill: University of North Carolina Press, 2002), 81; Clarissa W. Confer, *Cherokee Nation and the Civil War* (Norman: University of Oklahoma Press, 2007), 8; Naylor, *African Cherokees*, 188. So emotive were post-war elections in the Cherokee Nation that it was not uncommon for men to be "killed at the precincts." John Livers, IPP54: 328; Stanley A. Clark, IPP 18: 138–39; Thomas Buffington, IPP13: 65; Hattie Turner, IPP 78: 387; Frank Cunningham, *General Stand Watie's Confederate Indians* (Norman: University of Oklahoma Press, 1959), 210.

19. John B. Meserve, "Chief Lewis Downing and Chief Charles Thompson," *CO* 16, no. 3 (September 1938): 316–18.

20. Lewis Downing, *Cherokee Nation: Letter from Lewis Downing, Principal Chief of the Cherokee Nation* (Washington, DC: Government Printing Office, 1870), 2–15.

21. Thomas M. N. Lewis and Madeline Kneberg, *Tribes that Slumber: Indians of the Tennessee Region* (Knoxville: University of Tennessee Press, 1958), 156.

22. S. H. Mitchell, *The Indian Chief, Journeycake* (Philadelphia: American Baptist Publication Society, 1895), 69, 77; Claudia Haake, "Identity, Sovereignty, and Power: The Cherokee-Delaware Agreement of 1867, Past and Present," *AIQ* 26, no. 3 (Summer 2002): 418–35.

23. William M. Osborn, *The Wild Frontier: Atrocities During the American-Indian War from Jamestown Colony to Wounded Knee* (New York: Random House, 2000).

24. Dale F. Giese, ed., *My Life with the Army in the West: The Memoirs of James E. Farmer* (Santa Fe, NM: Stagecoach Press, 1967), 63.

25. On the long history of violence between European colonizers and Native Americans see Clare V. McKanna, Jr., *Homicide, Race, and Justice in the American West, 1880–1920* (Tempe: University of Arizona Press, 1997); Ned Blackhawk, *Violence over the Land: Indians and Empires in the Early American West* (Cambridge, MA: Harvard University Press, 2006); Brian DeLay, *War of a Thousand Deserts: Indian Raids and the U.S.-Mexican War* (New Haven, CT: Yale University Press, 2008).

26. Lewis Downing to Captain Sarcoxie, November 14, 1868, folder 198, Cherokee Nation Papers.

27. Tom Willard, *Buffalo Soldiers* (New York: Tom Doherty Associates, 1996), 7–8; William H. Leckie and Shirley A. Leckie, *The Buffalo Soldiers: A Narrative of the Black Cavalry in the West* (Norman: University of Oklahoma Press, 2003), 144; Kevin Mulroy, *The Seminole Freedmen: A History* (Norman: University of Oklahoma Press, 2007), 217–19; Alwyn Barr, "The Black Militia of the New South: Texas as a Case Study" in *Brothers to the Buffalo Soldiers: Perspectives on the African American Militia and Volunteers, 1865–1917*, ed. Bruce A. Glasrud (Columbia: University of Missouri Press, 2011), 34–71.

28. Lenard B. Brown, "John Benjamin Townsend: The Arizona Cherokee," *Arizoniana* (Fall 1961): 31.

29. *The Weekly Arizona Miner*, September 27, 1873, 2.

30. Ignatius Caleb and Lewis Daugherty to the National Council of the Cherokee Nation, November 30, 1867, Folder 197, Roll 3, Cherokee Nation Papers. Downing's reply and agreement with the Munsee delegates is contained in the same folder and dated December 6, 1867.

31. Choah Council Ground, NC, October 4, 1877, Folder 209, Roll 3, Cherokee Nation Papers.

32. John R. Finger, "The North Carolina Cherokees, 1838–1866: Traditionalism, Progressivism, and the Affirmation of State Citizenship," *JCS* 5 (Spring 1980): 17; John R. Finger, *The Eastern Band of Cherokees, 1819–1900* (Knoxville: University of Tennessee Press, 1984), 101–2; Catherine L. Albanese, "Exploring Regional Religion: A Case Study

of the Eastern Cherokee," *History of Religion* 23, no. 4 (May 1984): 360–61; Sharlotte Neely, *Snowbird Cherokees: People of Persistence* (Athens: University of Georgia Press, 1991), 27.

33. A. N. Colvard vs. Monroe, *North Carolina Reports* 63 (1869): 287–88; John R. Finger, "The Impact of Removal on the North Carolina Cherokees" in *Cherokee Removal: Before and After*, ed. William L. Anderson (Athens: University of Georgia Press, 1991), 98–99.

34. John Gulick, "The Acculturation of the Eastern Cherokee Community Organization," *Social Forces* 36, no. 3 (March 1958): 246–50; Finger, *The Eastern Band of Cherokees*, 107. See also the various "Letters Received, 1824–1907," RG 75, Microfilm 234, General Records of the BIA, 1801–1952, NARA, Washington, DC.

35. Finger, *The Eastern Band of Cherokees*, 109.

36. Petition for citizenship of Lewis, Sarah, Franklin, and Orna Lafalin.

September 25 1880, Folder 227, Roll 3, Cherokee Nation Papers; Smithers, *Science, Sexuality, and Race*, 144.

37. "An Act Admitting Lucy a Creek Indian to the rights of Citizenship," October 20, 1856, Folder 196, Roll 3, Cherokee Nation Papers.

38. Charles Thompson to S. W. Marston, August 30, 1877, vol. 208, Box 1, Letters Received Relating to Cherokee Citizenship, 1875–89.

39. Cherokee Nation, *Constitution and Laws of the Cherokee Nation* (St. Louis, MO: R and T.A. Ennis, 1875), 5, 9.

40. On the "ad Hoc" migrations of North Carolina Cherokees to the Cherokee Nation in 1871 and 1872, see Finger, *The Eastern Band of Cherokees*, 117.

41. Charles Thompson to S. W. Marston, August 30, 1877, vol. 208, Box 1, Letters Received Relating to Cherokee Citizenship, 1875–89.

42. See for example W. W. Hastings and Charles Pierce to the Honorable United States Commission, August 23, 1897, Demurer and Answers of the Cherokee Nation, 1896–1897, RG 75, NARA Ft. Worth, TX; W. P. Adair to Joseph L. Martin, August 4, 1864, Folder 6833, Roll 3, Cherokee Nation Papers; Morris L. Wardell, *A Political History of the Cherokee Nation, 1838–1907* (Norman: University of Oklahoma Press, 1938), 227; "Intruders and Disputed Citizenship in Indian Territory" in Folder 1883, 12339, Box 3, Letters Received Relating to Cherokee Citizenship; Rennard Strickland, *Fire and Spirits: Cherokee Law from Clan to Court* (Norman: University of Oklahoma Press, 1975), 209; Kerry K. Wynn, "The Embodiment of Citizenship: Sovereignty and Colonialism in the Cherokee Nation, 1880–1920" (Ph.D. diss., University of Illinois, Urbana-Champagne, 2006), 36.

43. Will P. Ross and H. J. Landman, February 19, 1877, vol. 208, Box 1, Letters Received Relating to Cherokee Citizenship, 1875–89; Travis, "The Cherokee Nation a Decade after the Civil War," 28.

44. Eugene F. Ware, *The Neutral Lands*. Before the Kansas State Historical Society, 24th Annual Meeting, January 16, 1900, in *Transactions of the Kansas State Historical Society, 1897–1900*, vol. 6, KHS, SS 1.8: vol. 6: 147; Elias C. Boudinot, *Speech of Elias C. Boudinot, of the Cherokee Nation, Delivered Before the House Committee on Territories,*

March 5, 1872, on the Question of a Territorial Government for the Indian Territory, in Reply to the Second Argument of the Indian Delegations in Opposition to Such Proposed Government (Washington, DC: M'Gill and Witherow, Printers, 1872), 4.

45. Johnson quoted in *Manifesto of the People of the Cherokee Neutral Lands, Kansas* (n.p., 1869), 3.

46. *Manifesto of the People of the Cherokee Neutral Lands*, 2–3; Ware, *The Neutral Lands*, 153–54, 168; "Records Relating to the Disposal of the Cherokee Neutral Lands, 1866–1872," RG 75, Records of the BIA, NARA, Washington, DC.; *The Settlers True Guide: A Descriptive Hand-Book of the Cherokee Strip and Oklahoma Territory* (Wichita, KS: Harding, Flora and Co., Publishers, 1893), 6–10; Leon Charles Fouquet (French Immigrant), Cherokee Outlet, 1893, Micro., Box 921, Indians Collection, 1855–1908, MS. Coll. Indians, KHS; William Walker Gear, "The Strip": Memory's Record of an Eventful Journey that Transpired Forty-Five Years Ago (1938), Misc. Gear., Ibid.

47. On the concept of "racial sovereignty" see J. Kehaulani Kauanui, *Hawaiian Blood: Colonialism and the Politics of Sovereignty and Indigeneity* (Durham, NC: Duke University Press, 2008), 11, 32; David Theo Goldberg, *The Threat of Race: Reflections on Racial Neoliberalism* (Malden, MA: Wiley-Blackwell, 2008), 3–4.

48. *Manifesto of the People of the Cherokee Neutral Lands*, 1

49. Emmet Starr, *History of the Cherokee Indians and Their Legends and Folk Lore* (Oklahoma City, OK: The Walden Company, 1921), 382; Parins, *Elias Cornelius Boudinot*, 17–18.

50. Alexandra Harmon, "American Indians and Land Monopolies in the Gilded Age," *JAH* 90, no. 1 (June 2003): 106–33.

51. Boudinot, *Speech of Elias C. Boudinot*, 16; Elias C. Boudinot, *Oklahoma: Argument of Col. E.C. Boudinot, January 29, 1878, the Committee Having Under Consideration H.R. Bill No. 1596* (Alexandria, VA: G.H. Ramey and Sons, Printers, 1878), 1; Khaled J. Bloom, "An American Tragedy of the Commons: Land and Labor in the Cherokee Nation, 1870–1900," *Agricultural History* 76, no. 3 (Summer 2002): 512.

52. Boudinot, *Oklahoma*, 13; K. Tsianina Lomawaima, "The Mutuality of *Citizenship* and *Sovereignty*: The Society of American Indians and the Battle to Inherit America," *Studies in American Indian Literatures* 25, no. 2 (2013): 333–52; Gregory D. Smithers, "The Soul of Unity: *The Quarterly Journal of the Society of American Indians*," *Studies in American Indian Literature*, 25, no. 2 (2013): 263–89, and *American Indian Quarterly* 37, no. 3 (Summer 2013), ed. Chadwick Allen and Beth H. Piatote.

53. Adair and Ross to E. A. Hayt, Box 1, 1878 — C1235, Letters Received Relating to Cherokee Citizenship, 1875–89.

54. On this point see Maureen Konkle, *Writing Indian Nations: Native Intellectuals and the Politics of Historiography, 1827–1863* (Chapel Hill: University of North Carolina Press, 2004); Jean O'Brien, *First and Lasting: Writing Indians out of Existence in New England* (Minneapolis: University of Minnesota Press, 2010).

55. *Annual Report of the Commissioner of Indian Affairs* (Washington, DC: Government Printing Office, 1896), 430; *Transactions of the Kansas State Historical Society*, vol. 6 (Topeka, KS: W.Y. Morgan, 1900), 165–66.

56. Paul W. Gates, *Fifty Million Acres* (1954; repr. New York: Arno Press, Inc., 1979), 171–73.

57. Leslie Hewes, "Making a Pioneer Landscape in the Oklahoma Territory," *Geographical Review* 86, no. 1 (October 1996): 588–603; Bloom, "An American Tragedy," 497–523; Chang, "Enclosures of Land and Sovereignty,"108–11.

58. C. W. Holcomb to the Department of the Interior, February 18, 1878, Folder 6, Box 0–21; Charles Thompson to Carl Schurz, August 24, 1878, Folder 14, Box 0–21; Charles Thompson to the National Council, November 27, 1878, Folder 32, Box 0–21, WHC.

59. E. A. Hayt, commissioner of Indian Affairs, April 4, 1879, Folder 223, Roll 3, Cherokee Nation Papers.

60. W. G. Rice, "The Position of the American Indian in the Law of the United States," *Journal of Comparative Legislation and International Law* 3rd Series, 16, no. 1 (1934): 88; Peggy Pascoe, *What Comes Naturally: Miscegenation Law and the Making of Race in America* (New York: Oxford University Press, 2009).

61. E. A. Hayt, commissioner of Indian Affairs, April 4, 1879, Folder 223, Roll 3, Cherokee Nation Papers. The federal government also maintained that by an act of Congress in 1868, the Cherokee Nation had "no right to expatriate its own citizens."

62. Thompson's appointments are dated January 7, 1878, Folder 214, Roll 3, Cherokee Nation Papers.

63. John Chambers to Chief Thompson, November 16, 1878, Folder 219, Roll 3, Cherokee Nation Papers.

64. Strickland, *Fire and the Spirits*, 209, 243.

65. D. B. to Senate and Council Branches of the National Council, April 26, 1886, Folder 143, Bushyhead Collection.

66. Quoted in Travis, "Life in the Cherokee Nation a Decade after the Civil War," 20.

67. Ellen Dean to Secretary of Interior, February 20, 1886, Folder 1886, 6283, Box 4, Letters Received Relating to Cherokee Citizenship, 1875–79.

68. See Folders 1886, 6284; 1886, 7587; 1886, 22379; 1886, 22514; 1886, 22670; 1886, 22980; 1886, 22981, Box 4, Letters Received Relating to Cherokee Citizenship, 1875–79.

69. William Adair and William P. Ross to Commissioner of Indian Affairs, 1878, C1235, Box 1, Letters Received Relating to Cherokee Citizenship.

70. Jeff Bowen, ed., *Cherokee Citizenship Commission Dockets: Volume I, 1880–1884 and 1887–1889* (Baltimore: Clearfield Company, 2011), 16.

71. *Constitution and Laws of the Cherokee Nation* (1875), 11; *Compiled Laws of the Cherokee Nation, Published by Authority of the National Council* (Tahlequah, CN: National Advocate Print, 1881), 13.

72. See the five volumes of CCC transcriptions by Bowen, *Cherokee Citizenship Commission Dockets*.

73. Wynn, "The Embodiment of Citizenship," 36.

74. For a comparative perspective from within Indian Territory see Jesse T. Schreier, "Indian or Freedman?: Enrollment, Race, and Identity in the Choctaw Nation, 1896–1907," *WHQ* 42, no. 4 (Winter 2001): 458–79.

75. First Annual Message of Dennis Bushyhead, November 10, 1879, Folder 160, Box 4, Dennis Wolfe Bushyhead Collection; Citizenship Commission Report 1880, Folder 229, Roll 3, Cherokee Citizenship Commission.

76. *Letter from the Secretary of the Interior, Transmitting Report of Commissioner of Indian Affairs relative to the Amount Appropriated March 3, 1883, for Cherokee Nation, and Legislation to Protect the Rights of Adopted Citizens of Said Act* (48th Congress, 1st Session, Senate Ex. Doc. No. 86), Library of Congress, Microfilm 58206, 4.

77. Charles Thompson to S. W. Marston, August 30, 1877, Box 1. 1877, vol. 208, Letters Received Relating to Cherokee Citizenship, 1875–89.

78. For example, Principal Chief Thompson requested that President Grant provide military assistance in dealing with "intruders." In a letter dated October 5, 1876, Thompson wrote: ". . . I respectfully beg have to insist upon you, as our protector, to cause the proper authorities of your Government, to not only remove the intruders complained of, but also to cause all *other* intruders to be promptly removed. These intruders are a source of great annoyance, since they are beyond our jurisdiction and many of them are bad men and are continually perpetrating crimes and wrong upon our people for which we cannot punish them. Furthermore the evil conduct of these *intruders* furnish a pretext to our enemies to continuously harrass [sic] Congress with the *false* idea, that the U.S. Territorial Government, is necessary to cure the evil." Charles Thompson to U. S. Grant, October 5, 1876, Box 1, Letters Received Relating to Cherokee Citizenship, 1875–89.

79. Charles Thompson to U. S. Grant, October 5, 1876, Box 1, Letters Received Relating to Cherokee Citizenship, 1875–89; *The Cherokee Advocate*, September 7, 1878 reproduced in Charles Thompson to Carl Schurz, August 24, 1878, folder 14, William P. Ross Collection.

80. See for example "Intruders Cooweeskoowee District 1876," 1877, vol. 208, Box 1, Letters Received Relating to Cherokee Citizenship, 1875–89.

81. McLoughlin, *After the Trail of Tears*, 298.

82. James N. Gregory, *The Southern Diaspora: How the Great Migrations of Black and White Southerners Transformed America* (Chapel Hill: University of North Carolina Press, 2005), 13.

83. D. W. Bushyhead to "the Honorable Senate and Council, November 24, 1879, Folder 5, Bushyhead Collection.

84. J. A. Walker to Columbus Delano, March 28, 1872, Folder 592, Roll 6; Cherokee Delegation to B. R. Cowen, September 30, 1875, Folder 596, Roll 6, Cherokee Nation Papers.

85. Cherokee Delegation to B. R. Cowen, September 30, 1875, Cherokee Nation Papers.

86. An Act Relating to the North Carolina Cherokees, Senate Bill No. 6, November 17, 1870, Folder 11, Oochalata (Charles Thompson) Collection.

87. *The Cherokee Advocate*, April 22, 1876, Folder 7, Oochalata (Charles Thompson) Collection.

88. Chief Thompson to JQ Smith, Commissioner of Indian Affairs, Reprinted in *The Cherokee Advocate*, September 5, 1877, Folder 20, Oochalata (Charles Thompson) Collection.

89. See *The Cherokee Advocate*, September 12, 1877; September 19, 1877; September 26, 1877; October 17, 1877, Folders 21–26, Oochalata (Charles Thompson) Collection.

90. Charles Thompson to National Council, November 27, 1876, Folder 16, Oochalata (Charles Thompson) Collection.

91. Cherokee Delegation re. Eastern Cherokee Claim, January 5, 1876, Folder 597, Roll 6, Cherokee Nation Papers. See also Cherokee Delegation to B. R. Cowen, September 3, 1875, Folder 596, Roll 6, Cherokee Nation Papers.

92. Chief Thompson to J. Q. Smith, reprinted in *The Cherokee Advocate*, November 7, 1877, Folder 26, Oochalata (Charles Thompson) Collection.

93. "Remonstrance of the Principal Chief and Delegates of the Cherokee Nation of Indians against the Passage of any Bill to allow the Eastern Band of Cherokees to Sue the Cherokee Nation, January 27, 1879," in *Index of Miscellaneous Documents of the House of Representatives for the Third Session of the Forty-Forth Congress, 1878–79*, vol. 1 (Washington, DC: Government Printing Office, 1879).

94. Dennis Bushyhead to the Senate and Council, December 3, 1881, Folder 51 Bushyhead Collection. See similarly Folder 54, 55, 59

95. Will P. Ross and H. J. Landman, February 19, 1877, 1877, vol. 208, Box 1, RG 75, Letters Received Relating to Cherokee Citizenship, 1875–89.

96. *The Cherokee Advocate*, September 26, 1877, Folder 23, Oochalata (Charles Thompson) Collection.

97. *The Cherokee Advocate*, September 26, 1877.

98. *The Cherokee Advocate*, October 24, 1877, Folder 25, Oochalata (Charles Thompson) Collection.

99. Abbott quoted in *Atlanta Constitution*, November 12, 1889, "Cherokee Indians in Georgia," Manuscript 4649, Smithsonian Institution, NAA.

100. Dennis Bushyhead to the National Council, December 1, 1885, Folder 119, Bushyhead Collection.

101. Petition of James Obediah, n.d., 1877-I348, Box 1, Letters Received Relating to Cherokee Citizenship, 1875–89.

102. B. C. Hobbs to Sec. of Interior, 12 May 1884, 1884, 9444, Box 4, Letters Received Relating to Cherokee Citizenship, 1875–89. See similarly Bowen, *Cherokee Citizenship Commission Dockets*1: 134, 136.

103. Bowen, *Cherokee Citizenship Commission Dockets* 1: 207–9, 296.

104. J. M. W. Smith to Sec of Interior, August 16, 1886, 1886, 22379, Box 4, Letters Received Relating to Cherokee Citizenship, 1875–89.

105. Bowen, *Cherokee Citizenship Commission Dockets*, 1: 24, 204–5, 272.

106. Bowen, *Cherokee Citizenship Commission Dockets*, 4: 294–95. See similarly Folder 1880, K133, Box 3, Letters Received Relating to Cherokee Citizenship, 1875–89.

107. Bowen, *Cherokee Citizenship Commission Dockets*4: 295.

108. Ibid., 296–97.

109. Ibid., 296–97.

110. See for example, Bowen, *Cherokee Citizenship Commission Dockets* 2: 65.

111. See Bowen, *Cherokee Citizenship Commission Dockets* 1: 24, 124, 138–39, 264, 326; 2: 36–7, 101–2, 249; 4: 100–102, 110–11, 174–76; 5: 16–17, 19, 36–7, 53, 90, 331–33.

112. Bowen, *Cherokee Citizenship Commission Dockets*, 1: 264–65.

113. Ibid., 265–66.

114. Ibid., 267–68.

SEVEN   Cherokee Freedmen

1. One observer claimed in 1879 that Former Indian masters and their slaves retained "the friendliest relations." See Theodora R. Jenness, "The Indian Territory," *The Atlantic Monthly* 42 (April 1879): 447. Since the 1970s, historians have taken a variety of perspectives on the treatment of slaves by Cherokee masters. See for example, Theda Perdue, *Slavery and the Evolution of Cherokee Society, 1540–1866* (Knoxville: University of Tennessee Press, 1979), 98; Celia E. Naylor, *African Cherokees in Indian Territory: From Chattel to Citizens* (Chapel Hill: University of North Carolina Press, 2008), 21, 49; Tiya Miles, *The House on Diamond Hill: A Cherokee Plantation Story* (Chapel Hill: University of North Carolina Press, 2010), 29; Mia Bay, *The White Image in the Black Mind: African-American Ideas about White People, 1830–1925* (New York: Oxford University Press, 2000), 172–73.

2. Gary E. Moulton, ed., *The Papers of Chief John Ross, 1840–1866*, 2 vols. (Norman: University of Oklahoma Press, 1985), 2: 526, 535; Laura S. Haviland, *A Woman's Life-Work: Labors and Experiences* 4th ed. (Chicago: Publishing Association of Friends, 1889), 383, 420, 424; Thomas Cox, *Blacks in Topeka, Kansas, 1865–1915: A Social History* (Baton Rouge: Louisiana State University Press, 1982), 40–41; Joseph V. Hickey, "'Pap' Singleton's Dunlap Colony: Relief Agencies and the Failure of a Black Settlement in Eastern Kansas," *Great Plains Quarterly* 11 (Winter 1991): 25. The Chickasaw Nation and the Seminole Nation had as a proportion of their total population a larger slave population. In the Chickasaw Nation, 18 percent of the total population of 5,235 were slaves. In the Seminole Nation, 29 percent of the total population of 3,630 were slaves. See Michael F. Doran, "Population Statistics of Nineteenth-Century Indian Territory," *CO* 53, no. 4 (1975–1976): 501; Barbara Krauthamer, *Black Slaves, Indian Masters: Slavery, Emancipation, and Citizenship in the Native American South* (Chapel Hill: University of North Carolina Press, 2013), 39–40.

3. Patrick N. Minges, *Slavery in the Cherokee Nation: The Keetoowah Society and the Defining of a People, 1855–1867* (New York and London: Routledge, 2003), 152; Hickey, "'Pap' Singleton's Dunlap Colony," 23–36; Nell Irvin Painter, *Exodusters: Black Migration to Kansas after Reconstruction* (New York: W.W. Norton and Company, 1976), 116. See also Leslie A. Schwalm, *Emancipation's Diaspora: Race and Reconstruction in the Upper Midwest* (Chapel Hill: University of North Carolina Press, 2009).

4. Folder 1879, W222, Box 2, RG 75, Letters Received Relating to Cherokee Citizenship, 1875–89, Records of the BIA, Land Division, NARA, Washington, DC.

5. *Journal of the General Council of the Indian Territory* (Lawrence, KS: Excelsior Book and Job Printing office, 1871), 59.

6. Cherokee officials sometimes willfully created archival gaps that made proving the legality of mixed marriages impossible. See Andrew Jolivétte, *Louisiana Creoles: Cultural Recovery and Mixed-Race Native American Identity* (Lanham, MD: Lexington Books, 2007), 44.

7. Annie H. Abel, *The American Indian Under Reconstruction* (Cleveland, OH: Arthur H. Clark, Company, 1925), 269–72; Gary E. Moulton, *John Ross: Cherokee Chief* (Athens, GA: University of Georgia Press, 1978), 113; William G. McLoughlin, *After the Trail of Tears: The Cherokees Struggle for Sovereignty, 1839–1880* (Chapel Hill: University of North Carolina Press, 1993), 228–29.

8. Tim Gannon, "Black Freedmen and the Cherokee Nation," *JAS* 11, no. 3 (December 1977): 357–64.

9. Duane Champagne, *Notes from the Center of Turtle Island* (Lanham, MD: Rowman and Littlefield Publishers, 2010), 68; Andrew Denson, *Demanding the Cherokee Nation: Indian Autonomy and American Culture, 1839–1900* (Lincoln: University of Nebraska Press, 2004), 81–86. See also *Laws and Joint Resolutions of the Cherokee Nation, Enacted by the National Council during the Regular and Extra Session of 1884–5-6* (Tahlequah, CN: E.C. Boudinot, Jr., Printer, 1887), 84.

10. Circe Sturm, "Blood Politics, Racial Classification, and Cherokee National Identity: The Trials and Tribulations of the Cherokee Freedmen," *AIQ* 22, no.1–2 (Winter-Spring 1998): 233–34; *The Correspondence of 1889, between the United States Commission and Cherokee National Authorities, and a Cherokee Memorial* (Washington, DC: Gibson Bros., Printers and Bookbinders, 1890), 23; Daniel F. Littlefield, Jr., *The Cherokee Freedmen: From Emancipation to American Citizenship* (Westport, CT: Greenwood Press, 1978), 405; McLoughlin, *After the Trail of Tears*, 239, 249–54, 294.

11. Committee on Indian Affairs, *Cherokee Freedmen and Others*, United States House of Representatives, Report No. 844, 50th Congress, 1st Session (1888).

12. McLoughlin, *After the Trail of Tears*, 293. Tensions between Cherokee leaders and Delawares and Shawnees continued into the 1890s. See for example "Decision of the United States Supreme Court on Rights of Delawares and Shawnees in Cherokee Nation, and on Claim of Shawnees vs. United States," November 19, 1894, *Annual Report of the Commissioner of Indian Affairs, 1894* (Washington, DC: Government Printing Office, 1895), 604–11.

13. Folder 1883, 6601, Box 3, Letters Received Relating to Cherokee Citizenship, 1875–89.

14. For data see the "Moses Ross" file, Case No. 880–882, Box 3, Records Related to Cherokee Citizenship, Affidavits, 1891–92, p. 17. In 1878, the federal government angered Cherokee officials when it unilaterally began issuing "certificates" permitting freedpeople to settle in the Cherokee Nation. V. O. King, "The Cherokee Nation of

Indians," *The Quarterly of the Texas State Historical Association* 2, no. 1 (July 1898): 69; McLoughlin, *After the Trail of Tears*, 294.

15. The Delaware District, located in the northeastern corner of the Nation, also seems to have been a popular destination for freedpeople.

16. In comparison, twenty-two whites applied, and were rejected, for Cherokee citizenship from the Cooweescoowee District in 1876. "Intruders, Cooweescoowee District, 1876," Folder 1877, 208, Box 1, Letters Received Related to Cherokee Citizenship, 1875–79.

17. Department of the Interior, *The Five Civilized Tribes in Indian Territory: The Cherokee, Chickasaw, Choctaw, Creek, and Seminole Nations* (Washington, DC: United States Census Printing Office, 1894), 8. McLoughlin, *After the Trail of Tears*, 291, 303; "Intruders," 1877, vol. 208, Box 1, Letters Received Relating to Cherokee Citizenship, 1875–89; Katja May, *African Americans and Native Americans in the Cherokee and Creek Nations* (New York: Garland, 1996), 69. Naylor, *African Cherokees in Indian Territory*, 158.

18. T. Lindsay Baker and Julie P. Baker, eds., *The WPA Oklahoma Slave Narratives* (Norman: University of Oklahoma Press, 1996), 465.

19. S. Alan Ray, "A Race or a Nation? Cherokee National Identity and the Status of Freedmen's Descendants," *Michigan Journal of Race and Law* 12 (2007): 387.

20. Circe Sturm, "Blood Politics, Racial Classification, and Cherokee National Identity: The Trials and Tribulations of the Cherokee Freedmen," *AIQ* 22, no. 1–2 (Winter-Spring, 1998): 230–58; Ray, "A Race or a Nation?" 387–463; Circe Sturm, *Becoming Indian: The Struggle Over Cherokee Identity in the Twenty-First Century* (Santa Fe, NM: School for Advanced Research Press, 2010).

21. Naylor, *African Cherokees in Indian Territory*, 1–2, 4, 25.

22. Ibid., 28–29.

23. Fourth Annual Message of Dennis Bushyhead, Reprinted in *The Cherokee Advocate*, November 10, 1882, Folder 165, Box 4, Bushyhead Collection.

24. It should be noted, however, that the "colored populations" of the states and territories surrounding the Cherokee Nation were not exactly clamoring at the Nation's borders. In Missouri, for example, the vast majority of that state's black population resided in and around St. Louis. In Arkansas, African American populations remained concentrated in the southern, central, and eastern portions of the state. And in Texas, most African Americans lived in the eastern half of the state, although a significant population of "colored" people made their homes in north Texas, in the counties of Red River and Lamar, which abutted the southern border with Indian Territory.

25. Bureau of the Census, *Population of Oklahoma and Indian Territory, 1907* (Washington, DC: Government Printing Office, 1907), 9.

26. Russell Thornton, *The Cherokees: A Population History* (Lincoln: University of Nebraska, 1990), 105.

27. Ibid., 112.

28. Thornton, *The Cherokees*, 112.

29. Eric Foner, *Forever Free: The Story of Emancipation and Reconstruction* (New York: Random House, 2006), 109; Nell Irvin Painter, *Exodusters: Black Migration to*

Kansas after Reconstruction (New York: Alfred A. Knopf, 1976), 170; Quintard Taylor, *In Search of the Racial Frontier: African Americans in the West, 1528–1990* (New York: W.W. Norton and Company, 1998), 141.

30. Painter, *Exodusters*, 147.

31. Roy Garvin, "Benjamin, or 'Pap, Singleton and His Followers," *JNH* 33, no 1 (January 1948): 7–23; Robert G. Atheam, *In Search of Canaan: Black Migration to Kansas, 1879–80* (Lawrence, KS: Regents Press of Kansas, 1978); Gary L. Cheatham, "Divided Loyalties in Civil War Kansas," *KH* 11 (Summer 1988): 96; Painter, *Exodusters*, 147.

32. Cheatham, "Divided Loyalties in Civil War Kansas," 96; Taylor, *In Search of the Racial Frontier*, 115–16.

33. Cheatham, "Divided Loyalties in Civil War Kansas," 97–98.

34. Walter P. Fleming, "'Pap' Singleton: The Moses of the Colored Exodus," *American Journal of Sociology* 15 (July 1909): 61–82; Orval L. McDaniel, "A History of Nicodemus," unpublished typescript, 1950, KHS, 41–42; Nell B. Waldren, "Colonization in Kansas, 1861–1890," unpublished typescript, n.d., KHS, 120–25; Taylor, *In Search of the Racial Frontier*, 116.

35. Re. Cherokee Intermarriage, Folder 6459, Roll 46, Cases re. Board of Commissioners appointed to adjudicate claims upon the Treaty Party, Cherokee Nation Papers; Yarbrough, *Race and the Cherokee Nation*, 73.

36. Folder 1880, B404, Box 3, Letters Received Relating to Cherokee Citizenship, 1875–89.

37. Jane Hubbard, Folder 1881, 9494, Box 3, Letters Received Relating to Cherokee Citizenship, 1875–89.

38. On federal government intervention in citizenship cases pertaining to Cherokee freedpeople see William A. Phillips to H. M. Teller, November 5, 1883, Folder 1883, 21353, Box 3, Letters Relating to Cherokee Citizenship, 1875–89; J. J. Ingalls, Report, July 3, 1878, 1878-I1170, Box 2, Letters Received Relating to Cherokee Citizenship, 1875–89; James W. Parins, *Elias Cornelius Boudinot: A Life on the Cherokee Border* (Lincoln: University of Nebraska Press, 2006), 205–7.

39. For recollections on how railroads connected Indian Territory to Kansas see for example Andrew W. Little, Questionnaire, IPP 116: 304.

40. Mrs. Flora Lane, April 4, 1883, Box 3, 1883, 6601, Letters Received Relating to Cherokee Citizenship, 1875–89.

41. Naylor, *African Cherokees in Indian Territory*, 166, 176.

42. Records of the Bureau of the Census, *Township 1 Range 6, Limestone, Alabama, Ninth Census of the United States*, RG29, M593, Roll: M593_24, p. 154A, NARA, Washington, DC.

43. Records of the Bureau of the Census, *Beat 8, Limestone, Alabama, Ninth Census of the United States*, RG 29, T 9, Microfilm Roll: 20, p. 382B, NARA, Washington, DC.

44. Darlene Clark Hine, "Rape and the Inner Lives of Black Women in the Middle West," *Signs* 14, no. 4 (summer 1989): 912–20; Michele Mitchell, *Righteous Propagation:*

African Americans and the Politics of Racial Destiny after Reconstruction (Chapel Hill: University of North Carolina Press, 2004), 13.

45. Folder 1888, 1336, Box 6, Letters Relating to Cherokee Citizenship, 1875–89.

46. Yarbrough, *Race and the Cherokee Nation*, 123.

47. See for example Box 1, RG 75, Records of the BIA, Land Division, Records Relating to Cherokee Citizenship, 1889–91, NARA, Washington, DC.

48. Dennis Bushyhead to National Council, December 9, 1880, Folder 34, Box 1, Dennis Wolfe Bushyhead Collection; *Constitution and Laws of the Cherokee Nation, Published by Authority of the National Council* (St. Louis, MO: R. and T. Ennis, 1875), 11; *Compiled Laws of the Cherokee Nation, Published by Authority of the National Council* (Tahlequah, CN: National Advocate Print, 1881), 13.

49. Ibid.

50. Eric Foner, *Reconstruction: America's Unfinished Revolution, 1863–1877* (New York: Harper Collins Publishers, 1988), 507–9; 77, 149.

51. Fourth Annual Message of Dennis Bushyhead, Reprinted in *The Cherokee Advocate*, November 10, 1882, Folder 165, Bushyhead Collection.

52. Yarbrough, *Race and the Cherokee Nation*, 94–95; May, *African Americans and Native Americans*, 73–74; Taylor, *In Search of the Racial Frontier*, 118.

53. Angie Debo, *The Road to Disappearance* (Norman: University of Oklahoma Press, 1938), 126–27.

54. Yarbrough, *Race and the Cherokee Nation*, 75–77. See also Kevin Mulroy, *The Seminole Freedmen: A History* (Norman: University of Oklahoma Press, 2007), 226–27; Peter Wallenstein, "Native Americans are White, African Americans are Not: Racial Identity, Marriage, Inheritance, and the Law in Oklahoma, 1907–1967," *Journal of the West* 39, no. 1 (2000): 55–63, esp. 57.

55. Dennis Bushyhead to National Council, December 9, 1880, Folder 34, Box 1, Bushyhead Collection; Rennard Strickland, *Fire and the Spirits: Cherokee Law from Clan to Court* (Norman: University of Oklahoma Press, 1975), 161; *Hearings Before the Senate Committee on Indian Affairs on Matters Relating to the Osage Tribe of Indians* (Washington, DC: Government Printing Office, 1909), 71, re. "Joint Resolution for the Enrollment of Certain Persons as Members of the Osage Tribe of Indians;" Perdue, *Slavery and the Evolution of Cherokee Society*, 36; Halliburton, *Red Over Black*; Minges, *Slavery and the Cherokee Nation*, 2–4, 183–84; Yarbrough, *Race and the Cherokee Nation*, 89–90; Mulroy, *The Seminole*, 226; May, *African Americans and Native Americans*, 102.

56. Halliburton, *Red over Black*, 136, 179; McLoughlin, *After the Trail of Tears*, 282–83.

57. *The Executive Documents Printed by order of the House of Representatives during the Second Session of the Forty-Second Congress, 1871–72* (Washington, DC: Government Printing Office, 1872), 984; Minges, *Slavery in the Cherokee Nation*, 199.

58. Folder 1879, B684, Box 2, Letters Received Relating to Cherokee Citizenship, 1875–89.

59. Painter, *Exodusters*, 113.

60. List of Intruders, August 21, 1877, vol. 208, Box 1, Letters Received Relating to Cherokee Citizenship, 1875–89. See similarly Louis Carter to the Commissioner of Indian Affairs, July 18, 1878, C455, Box 1, Letters Received Relating to Cherokee Citizenship, 1875–89. See also "Response of the Commission," June 19, 1878, C455, Box 1, Letters Received Relating to Cherokee Citizenship, 1875–89.

61. S. D. Barclay to Principal Chief, July 19, 1878, Folder 10, Box O-21, Oochalata (Charles Thompson) Collection, WHC; American Sunday-School Union, *The Fiftieth Annual Report of the American Sunday-School Union, 1874* (Philadelphia: American Sunday-School Union, 1874), 93; Painter, *Exodusters*, 113–115; Bryan M. Jack, *Saint Louis African American Community and the Exodusters* (Columbia: University of Missouri Press, 2007), 95.

62. Bowen, *Cherokee Citizenship Commission Dockets* 1: 65, 66, 104; Jerry W. Jordan, ed., *Cherokee by Blood: Applications 1 to 1550* (Berwyn Heights, MD: Heritage Books, 1997), 297–98.

63. "Subject: "Colored Cherokees claiming treaty rights," November 22, 1875, Box 1, Letters Received Relating to Cherokee Citizenship, 1875–89.

64. Bowen, *Cherokee Citizenship Commission Dockets* 1: 16; *Tenth United States Census, Tyler, Texas,* T9, Microfilm 1330, 369B, NARA, Washington, DC.

65. Bowen, *Cherokee Citizenship Commission Dockets* 1: 52.

66. Louis Carter to the Commissioner of Indian Affairs, July 18, 1878, 1878-C455, Box 2, Letters Received Relating to Cherokee Citizenship, 1875–89. See similarly 1878—C745; 1878-G526; Box 2, Letters Received Relating to Cherokee Citizenship, 1875–89.

67. 1878, P131, Box 2, Letters Received Relating to Cherokee Citizenship, 1875–89.

68. The following analysis of William Hudson's case comes from 1878-H-1187, Box 2, Letters Received Relating to Cherokee Citizenship, 1875–89.

69. See the "Response of Commission to William Hudson," June 9, 1878, 1878-H-1187, Box 2, Letters Received Relating to Cherokee Citizenship, 1875–89. For similar cases see 1878, L475; L1088; 1879, W1490; B320, Box 2, Letters Received Relating to Cherokee Citizenship, 1875–89.

70. Folder 1880, C602, Box 3, Letters Received Relating to Cherokee Citizenship, 1875–89.

71. J. J. Ingalls, Report, July 3, 1878, 1878, I1170, Box 2, Letters Received Relating to Cherokee Citizenship, 1875–89; See also 1878, P131, Box 2, Letters Received Relating to Cherokee Citizenship, 1875–89; 1879, B134, Box 2, Letters Received Relating to Cherokee Citizenship, 1875–89. See similarly Folder 1879, V21.

72. "Undated Resolution by Cherokee Citizens," Folder 6722, Cherokee Nation Papers. On the ways in which institutional memory operates to create narratives of exclusion and inclusion see Charlotte Linde, *Working the Past: Narrative and Institutional Memory* (New York: Oxford University Press, 2008), 3.

73. Statement Regarding the Afro-American Cherokees, undated, Folder 6478, Microfilm Roll 46, Cherokee Nation Papers.

EIGHT Diasporic Horizons

1. Dernoral Davis, "Toward a Socio-Historical and Demographic Portrait of Twentieth-Century African-Americans" in *Black Exodus: The Great Migration from the American South*, ed. Alferdteen Harrison (Jackson: University Press of Mississippi, 1991), 1; W. Michael Byrd and Linda A. Clayton, *An American Health Dilemma: A Medical History of African Americans and the Problem of Race, Beginnings to 1900* (New York and London: Routledge, 2000), 410.

2. L. J. Lacey, "White Man's Law and the American Indian Family in the Assimilation Era," *Arkansas Law Review* (1986–1987): 328–64; Judith Royster, "The Legacy of Allotment," *Arizona State Law Journal* 27 (1995): 2–78.

3. Whites in Oklahoma and Indian Territories referred to "Those Indians disaffected [by allotment as] 'Snakes.'" Such labels were likely references to the Creek orator Chitto Harjo, an opponent of Oklahoma statehood whose name whites mistranslated as "Crazy Snake." See Records of the BIA, Indian Agent, Muskogee, to Commissioner of Indian Affairs, February 16, 1905, Folder 1, Box 1, HM2007 E.41, NARA, Ft. Worth, Texas.

4. *The Cherokee Advocate*, January 3, 1894, Folder 37, Box H-55, C. Johnson Harris Collection, WHC; Angie Debo, *And Still the Waters Run: The Betrayal of the Five Civilized Tribes* (1940; repr. Princeton, NJ: Princeton University Press, 1991), 84–99; Wilcomb E. Washburn, *The Assault on Indian Tribalism: The General Allotment Law (Dawes Act) of 1887* (Philadelphia: Lippincott, 1975); Tom Holm, "Indian Lobbyists: Cherokee Opposition to the Allotment of Tribal Lands," *AIQ* 5, no. 2 (May 1979): 115–34; Frederick E. Hoxie, *A Final Promise: The Campaign to Assimilate the Indians, 1880–1920* (Lincoln: University of Nebraska Press, 1984), 154–55; Tom Holm, *The Great Confusion in Indian Affairs: Native Americans and Whites in the Progressive Era* (Austin: University of Texas Press, 2005), 13; Rose Stremlau, *Sustaining the Cherokee Family: Kinship and the Allotment of an Indigenous Nation* (Chapel Hill: University of North Carolina Press, 2011), 154–55.

5. "Termination" referred to the federal government's policy of "terminating" government trusteeships of Indian lands, while "relocation" involved attempts to assimilate Native Americans into the social and economic fabric of American towns and cities. See Donald Fixico, *Termination and Relocation: Federal Indian Policy, 1945–1960* (Albuquerque: University of New Mexico Press, 1986); Jere B. Franco, *Crossing the Pond: The Native American Effort in World War II* (Denton, TX: University of North Texas Press, 1999).

6. In 1880, the United States Census Bureau estimated the total Native American population—excluding Indigenous Alaskans—at 306,543. By 1900, the American Indian population had declined to 237,196. Carroll D. Wright, *The History and Growth of the United States* (Washington, DC: Government Printing Office, 1900), 128–29.

7. The statistics in this paragraph come from Russell Thornton, *The Cherokees: A Population History* (Lincoln: University of Nebraska Press, 1990), 116, 125–26.

8. The Cherokee diaspora was also a place of varying legal identities. See Opinion of the Assistant Attorney General to Sec of Interior, March 14 1894, "Selected Letters Received by the Office of Indian Affairs Relating to the Cherokees of North Carolina," Roll 6, M1059, NARA, Ft. Worth, Texas.

9. "Commission of the Five Civilized Tribes (Dawes Commission), March 3, 1893" in *Documents of United States Indian Policy*, 3rd ed., ed. Francis Paul Prucha (Lincoln: University of Nebraska Press, 2000), 187–89; Loren N. Brown, "The Dawes Commission," *CO* 9, no. 1 (1931): 71–105; Loren N. Brown, "The Establishment of the Dawes Commission for Indian Territory," *CO* 18, no. 2 (1940): 171–81.

10. Debo, *And Still the Waters Run*, 65, 86, 120–21.

11. It was not until 1906 that the Dawes Commissioners finalized what they believed was an accurate census of Native American populations—including freed-people—and of those individuals eligible for allotment. Circe Sturm, *Blood Politics: Race, Culture, and Identity in the Cherokee Nation of Oklahoma* (Berkeley: University of California Press, 2002), 78–79, 171.

12. Charles J. Kappler, *Indian Affairs: Laws and Treaties*, vol. 1 (Washington, DC: Government Printing Office, 1904), 787–98; Brad A. Bays, *Townsite Settlement and Dispossession in the Cherokee Nation, 1866–1907* (New York and London, 1998), 184–85; Rose Stremlau, "In Defense of 'This Great Family Government Estate': Cherokee Masculinity and the Opposition to Allotment" in *Southern Masculinity: Perspectives on Manhood in the South since Reconstruction*, ed. Craig Thompson Friend (Athens, GA: University of Georgia Press, 2009), 78.

13. David Wallace Adams, *Education for Extinction: American Indians and the Boarding School Experience, 1875–1928* (Lawrence, KS: University Press of Kansas, 1995), 143.

14. Stremlau, *Sustaining the Cherokee Family*, 4–5. Native American landholdings fell from 1140 million acres in 1887 to 48 million by 1934. See James S. Olson and Raymond Wilson, *Native Americans in the Twentieth Century* (Urbana: University of Illinois Press, 1984), 81.

15. *Reply of the Cherokee National Committee to the Proposition of the Dawes Commission in Regard to Change of Government for the Cherokee Nation* (Washington, DC: Gibson Bros., 1894), 6; Eva Marie Garroutte, *Real Indians: Identity and the Survival of Native America* (Berkeley: University of California Press, 2003), 14–15. Allotment applications in the Cherokee Nation in Indian Territory came from individuals possessing as little as 1/256 parts Cherokee blood. See John R. Finger, *Cherokee Americans: The Eastern Band of Cherokees in the Twentieth Century* (Lincoln: University of Nebraska Press, 1991), 48.

16. David A. Chang, "Enclosures of Land and Sovereignty: The Allotment of American Indian Lands," *RHR* 109 (2011): 116. With the exception of the "$5 Indians"—whites who paid a $5 fee to have their name listed on the Guion Miller roll of Eastern Cherokees—one-sixteenth Cherokee blood was required to acquire allotted land. Finger, *Cherokee Americans*, 48, 135.

17. Ibid., 9, 22, 44, 51.

18. Jennie M. Bard and Anna F. Graham, *Cherokee Recollections: The Story of the Indian Women's Pocahontas Club and its Members in the Cherokee Nation and Oklahoma, beginning in 1899* (Stillwater, OK: Thales Microuniversity Press, 1976), 4, 9. See also Cherokee Nation vs. Martha Payne, February 13, 1888, in Supreme Court of the United States, *Transcript of Record* (Washington, DC: Judd and Detweiler, 1898), 53.

19. C. C. Lipe to G. B. Foreman, August 14, 1886, Item 23; February 21, 1887, Item 27, Box 6, Grant Foreman Collection, 1900–1956. 83.229; *Congressional Record*, 59th Congress, 2nd Session, December 3, 1906-March 4, 1907, 36 vols. (Washington, DC: Government Printing Office, 1907), 5: 29–30; Jeff Bowen, *Eastern Cherokee by Blood, 1906–1910*, vol. 4 (Baltimore, MD: Clearfield Company, 2007), 120.

20. C. C. Lipe to G. B. Foreman, August 10, 1887, Item 31, Box 6.

21. Speech of Hon. George W. Benge made at Bluejacket on June 10, 1891, Folder 6697, Microfilm Roll 46, Cherokee Nation Papers; D. C. Gideon, *Indian Territory, Descriptive, Biographical, and Genealogical* (New York: Lewis Publishing Company, 1901), 384–85; *Fairland News*, July 5, 1895, Folder 19, Box M-50; *South McAlester Capital*, September 23, 1897, Folder 53, Box M-50, S. H. Mayes Collection, WHC.

22. Marquis James, *The Raven: A Biography of Sam Houston* (Austin: University of Texas Press, 2004), 150–51.

23. Georgia Rae Leeds, *The United Keetoowah Band of Cherokee Indians in Oklahoma* (New York: Peter Lang, 1996), 10.

24. John B. Meserve, "Chief Thomas Mitchell Buffington and Chief William Charles Rogers," *CO* 17, no. 2 (June 1939): 145.

25. Robert J. Conley, *The Cherokee Nation: A History* (Albuquerque: University of New Mexico Press, 2005), 198–99.

26. James, *The Raven*, 48, 150–51; Jack Gregory and Rennard Strickland, *Sam Houston with the Cherokees, 1829–1833* (Norman: University of Oklahoma Press, 1967), 36, 40–1; Jack F. Kilpatrick and Anna G. Kilpatrick, *Friends of Thunder: Folktales of the Oklahoma Cherokees* (Norman: University of Oklahoma Press, 1964), xii; Kilpatrick, "Folk Formulas of the Oklahoma Cherokees," *Journal of the Folklore Institute* vol. 1, no. 3 (1964): 214–15; Janey B. Hendrix, "Redbird Smith and the Nighthawk Keetoowahs," *JCS* 8, no. 2 (Fall 1983): 74

27. Leeds, *United Keetoowah Band*, 9; Hendrix, "Redbird Smith," 9–10; Theda Perdue, ed., *Nation's Remembered: An Oral History of the Cherokee, Chickasaw, Choctaws, and Seminoles in Oklahoma, 1865–1907* (Norman: University of Oklahoma Press, 1993), 97–102.

28. Hendrix, "Redbird Smith," 22.

29. Raymond D. Fogelson, "Who Were the Ani-Kutani? An Excursion into Cherokee Historical Thought," *Ethnohistory* 31, no. 4 (Autumn 1984): 255–63; Leeds, *United Keetoowah Band*, 2–3.

30. Leeds, *United Keetoowah Band*, 9.

31. Ibid., 3–5; Janey B. Hendrix, "Redbird Smith," 22–32.

32. Emmet Starr, *History of the Cherokee Indians and Their Legends and Folk Lore* (Oklahoma City, OK: The Warden Company, 1921), 481–82.

33. *Muskogee Daily Phoenix*, July 20, 1931, Item 1, Folder 24; *Muskogee Times Democrat*, July 20, 1931, Item 1, Folder 24, OHS; Conley, *The Cherokee Nation*, 198.

34. Application of Robert L. Carter and Rebecca Sam Carter, 3 September 1896, Demurer and Answers of the Cherokee Nation, 1896–1897, NARA, Ft. Worth, Texas; See similarly Application for enrollment to Cherokee citizenship by Allen Bradshaw, 20 November 1897, Demurer and Answers of the Cherokee Nation, 1896–1897; Application for enrollment to Cherokee citizenship by John W. Jordan and family 20 September 1897, Demurer and Answers of the Cherokee Nation, 1896–1897; R. R. Keys et.al., September 1, 1897, NARA, Ft. Worth, Texas.

35. Petition of William T. Taylor to the U. of America, Western District of Indian Territory, March 9, 1905, Item 12, Folder 1, Box 7, NC Cherokees Migrate West, OHS.

36. Application for enrollment to Cherokee citizenship by Manuel Taylor, 1 September 1897; Louis Vanderford, 20 September 1897; Charles E. Daugherty et al., 20 September 1897; Mary A. Hulsey (20 September 1897); Sarah M. Hulsey (20 September 1897); Julia A. Rogers (20 September 1897), William Russell and family, Webber Falls, 31 May 1887; Verda A. Kerr, et al., 20 September 1897, Pa-ti-a-can (Guardian), September 1, 1897, Demurer and Answers of the Cherokee Nation, 1896–1897, NARA, Ft. Worth, Texas; Department of the Interior, Commission to the Five Civilized Tribes, Statement of A. B. Person, attorney, June 25, 1900, Folder 2, Box 1, Records of the Five Civilized Tribes Agency, Reference Documents (Misc. Docs.), HM2007 E.41.

37. Ben Yagoda, *Will Rogers: A Biography* (Norman: University of Oklahoma Press, 1993), 36.

38. Thomas A. Britten, *American Indians in World War I: At Home and at War* (Albuquerque: University of New Mexico Press, 1998); Donald L. Fixico, *American Indians in a Modern World* (Lanham, MD: Rowman and Littlefield, 2006), 82; Russel L. Barsh, "American Indians in the Great War," *Ethnohistory* 38 (Summer 1991): 276–303.

39. "Record of the Cherokees," *The Seamen's Journal*, April 23, 1919: 11.

40. Susan A. Krouse, *North American Indians in the Great War* (Lincoln: University of Nebraska Press, 2007), 27. See also "Biography of Frank J. Boudinot, Jr., March 23, 1937, IPP 62, 82–85; Starr, *History of the Cherokee Indians*, 644. In North Carolina, seventy Cherokees served during World War I, half of these being draftees. Britten, *American Indians in World War I*, 67; Gary C. Stein, "The Indian Citizenship Act of 1924," *New Mexico Historical Review* 47, no. 3 (July 1972): 266–70.

41. Jennifer D. Keene, *World War I* (Westport, CT: Greenwood Press, 2006), 46–47. See also David M. Kennedy, *Over Here: The First World War and American Society* (New York: Oxford University Press, 1980), 187–88.

42. Britten, *American Indians in World War I*, 110.

43. Ibid., 113.

44. US Selective Service System, *World War I Selective Service System Draft Registration Cards, 1917–1918*, Draft Board 10, M1509, NARA, Washington, DC.

45. US Selective Service System, *World War I Selective Service System Draft Registration Cards, 1917–1918*, Draft Board 10, M1509, NARA, Washington, DC; Britten, *American Indians in World War I*, 112.

46. US Selective Service System, *Selective Service Registration Cards, World War II: Fourth Registration*, NARA, Chicago.

47. Bureau of the Census. *Fifteenth Census of the United States, 1930, T626, Braddock, Allegheny, Pennsylvania*, Roll: 1960, Enumeration District: 518, p. 5B, NARA, Washington, DC.

48. *Crew Lists of Vessels Arriving at New Orleans, Louisiana, 1910–1945*, Series: T939, Roll No. 287, NARA, New Orleans.

49. Fixico, *American Indians in the Modern World*, xv; Britten, *American Indians in World War I*, 107; Deanne Durrett, *Unsung Heroes of World War II: The Story of the Navajo Code Talkers* (Lincoln: University of Nebraska Press, 1998), 18.

50. House Select Committee, *Interstate Migration: Hearings on H.R. 63 and 491, 76th Cong., 3rd sess., 1940* (Washington, DC: Government Printing Office, 1941); James N. Gregory, *American Exodus: The Dust Bowl Migration and Okie Culture in California* (New York, NY: Oxford University Press, 1989); Greg Hise, *Magnetic Los Angeles: Planning the Twentieth-Century Metropolis* (Baltimore, MD: Johns Hopkins University Press, 1999), 96, n. 21, 232; James N. Gregory, *The Southern Diaspora: How the Great Migrations of Black and White Southerners Transformed America* (Chapel Hill: University of North Carolina Press, 2005).

51. Sean Kicummah Teuton, *Red Land, Red Power: Grounding Knowledge in the American Indian Novel* (Durham, NC: Duke University Press, 2008), xiv.

52. Records of the BIA, Enrollment Cards for the Five Civilized Tribes, 1898–1914, RG 75, Census Card 4008, NARA, Washington, DC. Federal bureaucrats also appear to have made attempts to redefine McGhee's identity for him. In 1910, Census Bureau demographers enumerated McGhee and his family as Indian. In all subsequent censuses, the McGhee family was categorized as "white." Bureau of the Census, *Thirteenth Census of the United States, 1910*, RG 29, T624, Roll 1267, 11B, NARA, Washington, DC; Bureau of the Census. *Fifteenth Census of the United States, 1930*, RG 29, T626, Roll 1198, 20B, NARA, Washington, DC; Bureau of the Census. *Sixteenth Census of the United States, 1940*, RG 29, T627_2173, 6B, NARA, Washington, DC.

53. Finger, *Cherokee Americans*, 50–51.

54. It should be remembered that for migrants from Mexico, the migratory trajectory was not east to west, but south to north. Alternatively, migration from China and Japan, despite the implementation of restrictive immigration laws, occurred along a west to east trajectory. As a result, the American West became a crossroads for a cosmopolitan mixture of diasporic populations during the inter-war decades. See Ronald Takaki, *A Different Mirror: A History of Multiculturalism America* (New York: Little, Brown, and Company, 1993), 76.

55. Immigration Correspondence Files, Cherokee Indians, 1920, A2 CA12, NAAA.

56. James Mooney, "The Sacred Formulas of the Cherokees," *Seventeenth Annual Report of the Bureau of Ethnology to the Secretary of the Smithsonian Institution, 1885–86* (Washington, DC: Government Printing Office, 1891); G. Moses, *The Indian Man: A Biography of James Mooney* (Lincoln: University of Nebraska Press, 1984), 19–22.

57. Epeli Hauʻofa, "Our Sea of Islands" in *Inside Out: Literature, Cultural Politics, and Identity in the New Pacific*, ed. Vilsoni Hereniko and Rob Wilson (Lanham, MD: Rowman and Littlefield Publishers, Inc., 1999), 27–38. See also Hauʻofa's *We are the Ocean: Selected Works* (Honolulu: University of Hawaii Press, 2008); Malama Meleisea, *The Cambridge History of the Pacific Islanders*, (Cambridge, UK: Cambridge University Press, 1997), 441.

58. The Sherman Institute remains understudied; however, historians are beginning to develop a detailed historical portrait of life at Sherman. See for example Leleua Laurite Loupe, "Unhappy and Unhealthy: Student Bodies at Perris Indian School and Sherman Institute, 1897–1910" (Ph.D. diss., University of California, Riverside, 2005); Matthew Thomas Gilbert, "Education Beyond the Mesas: Hopi Student Involvement at the Sherman Institute, 1902–1929" (Ph.D. diss., University of California, Riverside, 2006).

59. *Sherman Institute* (n.p., 1909), 1; Records of the BIA, Annual Reports (1909), Box 6, p. 1; Annual Reports (1918–1919), Box 5, p. 2, (1922), Box 5, p. 6; Annual Reports (1926), Box 7, p. 3; Annual Reports (1936), Box 7, p. 9, NARA, Laguna Niguel, California; "Bishop Cantwell at Sherman Institute," *The Indian Sentinel*, II, 10 (April 1922): 472; Richard Henry Pratt, *Battlefield and Classroom: An Autobiography*, ed. Robert M. Utley (Norman: University of Oklahoma Press, 2003), xii; James Boyd, *History of San Bernardino and Riverside Counties*, vol. 1 (Chicago: The Lewis Publishing Company, 1922), 599; James J. Rawls, *Indians of California: The Changing Image* (Norman: University of Oklahoma Press, 1986), 211; Graham D. Taylor, *The New Deal and American Indian Tribalism: The Administration of the Indian Reorganization Act, 1934–45* (Lincoln: University of Nebraska Press, 1980), 17; Jacqueline Fear-Segal, *White Man's Club: Schools, Race, and the Struggle of Indian Acculturation* (Lincoln: University of Nebraska Press, 2007), xviii, 87, 215; Adams, *Education for Extinction*, 58; Clifford E. Trafzer and Leleua Loupe, "From Perris Indian School to Sherman Institute" in *The Indian School on Magnolia Avenue: Voices and Images from Sherman Institute*, eds. Clifford E. Trafzer, Matthew Sakiestewa Gilbert, and Lorene Sisquoc (Corvallis: Oregon State University Press, 2012), 19–34.

60. Records of the BIA, Annual Reports (1912), Box 6, p. 1; Annual Reports (1917), Box 5, pp. 1, 4; Annual Reports (1918–1919), Box 6, p. 2; Annual Reports (1922), Box 5, p. 1, NARA, Laguna Niguel, California.

61. "Education: Cherokee Nation," Folder 6, Box 57, Federal Writers Project, 81.105, OHS; Cherokee Orphan Asylum, *To the Men and Women of the Cherokee Nation* (Tahlequah, CN: Cherokee Orphan Asylum Press, 1881); *The Carlisle Arrow*, October 25, 1912, 4; February 6, 1914, 8; March 6, 1914, 2; Thomas Donaldson, *Eastern Band of Cherokees of North Carolina* (Washington, DC: United States Census Printing Office, 1892), 9; Sharlotte Neely, "The Quaker Era of Cherokee Indian Education, 1880–1892," *Appalachian Journal* 2, no. 4 (Summer 1975): 316–18; Finger, *Cherokee Americans*, 28, 162, 169, 178; Katja May, *African Americans and Native Americans in the Creek and Cherokee Nations, 1830s–1920s: Collision and Collusion* (New York and London, Routledge, 1996), 208; Marilyn Irvin Holt, *Indian Orphanages* (Lawrenceville: University of Kansas Press, 2001), 85; Brad Agnew, "Legacy of Education: The History of the Cherokee Seminaries,"

CO 63 (Summer 1985), 128–47; Devon I. Abbott, "Medicine for the Rosebuds: Health Care at the Cherokee Female Seminary," *AICRJ* 12, no. 1 (1988): 59–60; Devon A. Mihesuah, *Cultivating the Rosebuds: The Education of Women at the Cherokee Female Seminary, 1851–1909* (Urbana: University of Illinois Press, 1998), 1–2.; Devon A. Mihesuah, "Out of the 'Graves of the Polluted Debauches': The Boys of the Cherokee Male Seminary," *AIQ* 15, no. 4 (Fall 1991): 503–5.

62. The recent collection by Clifford Trafzer, Matthew Sakiestewa Gilbert, and Lorene Sisquoc detailing life at Sherman does not mention Cherokee children at that institution. Trafzer, Gilbert, and Sisquoc, *The Indian School on Magnolia Avenue.* For contemporary perceptions of the mixed-race student body at the Sherman Institute see Margaret E. Dunbar, *Towards the Sunset: Some Impressions of California and the West in 1915* (New York: n.p., 1915), 21.

63. Charles Starr, Box 343, Records of the Superintendent, Central Classified Files, 1907–1939, Sherman Institute, NARA, Laguna Niguel.

64. Box 7, Records of the Superintendent, Central Classified Files, 1907–1939, Sherman Institute, Annual Reports (1926), NARA, Laguna Niguel, California; "A New Indian School," *Friends' Intelligencer and Journal,* September 1901, 627; "The Education of the Indian," *Public Opinion,* 33, no. 17 (October 1902): 524. Indigenous people throughout North America and into the Pacific recall settler colonial efforts to inculcate their children "in the ways of the white people." See Luther Standing Bear and William S. Hart, *My People the Sioux* (1928; repr. Lincoln: University of Nebraska Press, 2006), 140; Thomas C. Moffett, "The Bible in the Life of the Indians," *The Southern Workman,* 45 (1916): 238; Trafzer, Gilbert, and Sisquoc, "Introduction" in *The Indian School,* 5–6.

65. Charles Starr, Box 343, Records of the Superintendent, Central Classified Files, 1907–1939, Sherman Institute.

66. *Reports of the U.S. Department of the Interior for the Fiscal Year Ended June 30, 1916,* vol. 2 (Washington, DC: Government Printing Office, 1917), 354.

67. Kevin Whalen, "Labored Learning: The Outing Program at Sherman Institute" in Trafzer, Sakiestewa, Gilbert, and Sisquoc, *The Indian School,* 107–36; Sherman Institute, Riverside, CA, Vocational Education Reports, 1936–1941, Box 112.

68. Charles Coleman to Superintendent Conser, June 22, 1929, Josephine Coleman, Student Case Files, 1903–1939, Sherman Institute, Box 72, NARA, Laguna Niguel, California.

69. Frank Watson, Student Case Files, 1903–1939, Sherman Institute, Box 379, NARA, Laguna Niguel, California.

70. Lucille May Woodall, Student Case Files, 1903–1939, Sherman Institute, Box 397; David J. Wishart, *An Unspeakable Sadness: The Dispossession of the Nebraska Indians* (Lincoln: University of Nebraska Press, 1995), 96; Paul Stuart, *Nations Within Nations: Historical Statistics of American Indians* (Santa Barbara, CA: Greenwood Press, 1987), 73–75.

71. Elizabeth Hobbs, Student Case Files, 1903–1939, Sherman Institute, Box 151, NARA, Laguna Niguel.

72. Elizabeth Hobbs, Student Case Files, 1903–1939, Box 151, Ibid.

73. William Tanner, Student Case Files, 1903–1939, Box 352, Ibid.

74. Kevin Starr, *Endangered Dreams: The Great Depression in California* (New York: Oxford University Press, 1996); Emma Ann Rice, Student Case Files, 1903–1939, Sherman Institute, Box 305.

75. Georgia Tanner, Student Case Files, 1903–1939, Box 352, Sherman Institute, NARA, NARA, Laguna Niguel.

76. Marilyn Irvin Holt, *The Orphan Trains: Placing Out in America* (Lincoln: University of Nebraska Press, 1992), 23–26; Timothy Hacsi, *Second Home: Orphan Asylums and Poor Families in America* (Cambridge, MA: Harvard University Press, 1997), 1–4, 6–7.

77. Holt, *Indian Orphanages*, 85–87, 100.

78. Ruth Whitley, Student Case Files, 1903–1939, Box 387, Sherman Institute. See also Perry Smith, Student Case Files, 1903–1939, Box 338; Sammie Thompson, Student Case Files, 1903–1939, Box 358, Sherman Institute.

79. Richard Cooper, Student Case Files, 1903–1939, Box 76, Sherman Institute. Parents of non-Cherokee students also lamented the "bad influences" their children had become entangled in and viewed the Sherman Institute as the best hope of saving future generations of indigenous Americans from a life of poverty and crime. See for example, Lola Aguilor, Student Case Files, 1903–1939, Box 2, Sherman Institute.

80. Margaret Duncan, Student Case Files, 1903–1939, Box 102, Sherman Institute.

81. William and Mary Slaughter, Student Case Files, 1903–1939, Box 335, Sherman Institute.

82. Margaret Duncan, Student Case Files, 1903–1939, Box 102; Delia Vieyra, Student Case Files, 1903–1939, Box 373, Sherman Institute.

83. Kay Knox Beldon and Robert Cliffton Beldon, Student Case Files, 1903–1939, Box 31, Sherman Institute.

84. Kay Beldon to Hazel Beldon, September 2, 1926, Robert Cliffton Beldon, Student Case Files, 1903–1939, Box 31, Sherman Institute.

85. Superintendent Conser, August 13, 1926, Robert Cliffton Beldon, Student Case Files, 1903–1939, Box 31, Sherman Institute. See similarly Brenda J. Child, *Boarding School Seasons: American Indian Families, 1900–1940* (Lincoln: University of Nebraska Press, 1998), 87–95.

86. Robert Beldon, Sr., to Superintendent Conser, September 21, 1926, Robert Cliffton Beldon, Student Case Files, 1903–1939, Box 31, Sherman Institute.

87. Hazel Wright to Robert Beldon, Sr., September 14, 1926, Robert Cliffton Beldon, Student Case Files, 1903–1939, Box 31, Sherman Institute.

88. Robert E. Johnson to Superintendent Conser, February 12, 1929, Robert Cliffton Beldon, Student Case Files, 1903–1939, Box 31, Sherman Institute.

89. See similarly Evart Woodrow Wilson Hobbs, Box 151; Jack J. Jones, Box 180; Charles Homer Hobbs, Box 151, Sherman Institute.

90. Raymond D. Fogelson, "The Ethnohistory of Events and Nonevents," *Ethnohistory* 36, no. 2 (Spring 1989): 133–47.

91. See for example William Henry Milburn's *The Rifle, Axe, and Saddle-Bags, and other Lectures* (Cincinnati, OH: Derby and Jackson, 1857), 26. Republished as *The Pioneer Preacher, Or, the Rifle, Axe, and Saddle-Bags, and other Lectures* (New York: Derby and Jackson, 1858).

92. Joseph B. Thoburn and Isaac M. Holcomb, *A History of Oklahoma* (San Francisco: Doub and Company, 1908), 51.

93. Rachel Caroline Eaton, *John Ross and the Cherokee Indians* (Menasha, WI: George Banta Publishing Company, 1914), 124.

94. Ibid., 124.

95. Deborah L. Duvall, *The Cherokee Nation and Tahlequah* (Charleston: Arcadia Publishing, 1999), 115; Daniel F. Littlefield, Jr., and James W. Parins, eds., *Encyclopedia of American Indian Removal*, vol. 2 (Santa Barbara, CA: ABC-CLIO, 2010), 240; Nicholas G. Rosenthal, *Reimagining Indian Country: Native American Migration and Identity in Twentieth-Century Los Angeles* (Chapel Hill: University of North Carolina Press, 2012), 40

96. Quoted in Robert Dale Parker, "American Indian Poetry at the Dawn of Modernism" in *The Oxford Handbook of Modern and Contemporary American Poetry*, ed. Cary Nelson (New York: Oxford University Press, 2012), 76.

97. *Encyclopedia of American Indian Removal*, 240–41; Lucinda Fleetwood, March 16, 1937, IPP 30: 215.

98. Muriel Wright, "Rachel Caroline Eaton," *CO* 16 (March/December 1938): 509–10; "Rachel Caroline Eaton" in *Native American Writing in the Southeast: An Anthology, 1875–1935*, ed. Daniel F. Littlefield, Jr. and James W. Parins (Jackson: University Press of Mississippi, 1995), 235

99. Ross, *Life and Times*, 194; Anderson, *Stand Watie*, 13.

100. Donald L. Fixico, *The American Indian Mind in a Linear World: American Indian Studies and Traditional Knowledge* (New York and London: Routledge, 2003), 144; James Hamill, *Going Indian* (Urbana: University of Illinois Press, 2006), x.

100. Dennis Bushyhead to the National Council, December 1, 1885, Folder 119, Bushyhead Collection.

101. Washington Lee, IPP 2 (August 20, 1937): 337. See similarly Rachel Dodge, IPP 25 (May 4, 1937): 63

102. Estella Stickle, "A Real American Tragedy," recorded by Elizabeth Ross, IPP 109 (June 21, 1937): 387.

103. Ibid., 387.

104. Ibid., 389.

105. If a "generation" is understood to be 20–25 years, than at a minimum the firsthand memories of children during the late 1830s would be four or five generations old.

106. Ella Robinson, IPP 70 (May 10, 1937): 72.

107. Jim McCurtain, IPP 57 (March 5, 1837): 505.

108. Amos Green, IPP 36 (October 10, 1937): 9.

109. See similarly Alice Jones Fulsom (Choctaw), IPP 32 (June 10, 1937): 447.

110. Rachel Dodge, IPP 25 (May 14, 1937): 63.

111. Siah Hicks, IPP 42 (November 17, 1838): 183.

112. W. R. Mulkey, IPP 65 (n.d.): 365–74; John M. Adair, IPP 1 (n.d.): 139–40; Joseph A. Scales, IPP 80 (n.d.): 357; Oliver H. P. Brewer, Jr., "Oliver Hazard Perry Brewer, Written for Miss Ella Robinson," IPP 101 (n.d.): 125; W. B. Morrison, IPP 65 (August 13, 1937): 151–52.

113. William C. Sturtevant, ed., "John Ridge on Cherokee Civilization in 1826," *JCS* 6, no. 2 (Fall 1981): 79–88; Claudio Saunt, "Telling Stories: The Political Uses of Myth and History in the Cherokee and Creek Nations," *JAH* 93, no. 3 (December 2006): 682.

114. Margaret Drew, IPP 26 (n.d.): 50.

115. Elizabeth Watts, IPP 95 (April 27, 1937): 526.

116. Stremlau, *Sustaining the Cherokee Family*.

117. Magnolia Adair Jones, IPP 49 (May 25, 1937): 200

118. Myrtle Emery, IPP 28 (March 20, 1937): 53; Narrative by Elizabeth Ross, IPP 108 (December 20, 1938): 353–54. See similarly IPP 109: 182–83; J. C. Star, "Early History of the Cherokees," IPP 103: 51.

119. See for example W. W. Harnage, IPP 39 (March 19, 1937): 102–4.

120. W. R. Mulkey, IPP 65 (n.d.): 386–87; Laura Chaney, IPP 17 (n.d.): 188; Felix Reece, IPP 75 (January 4, 1937): 2; Elmer Hill, IPP 42 (November 9, 1937): 314; Nancy Jane Rider, IPP 76 (November 17, 1937): 162; Elsie Edwards, IPP 27 (1937): 192; IPP 4: 84; IPP 84: 301–2; Perdue, *Nations Remembered*, 47.

121. Robert L. Cox, IPP 21 (April 4, 1938): 270.

122. Elizabeth Ross, IPP 109: 110–11.

123. Susan Colbert, IPP 19 (January 6, 1838): 135.

124. Jeff D. Randolph, IPP 74: 236.

125. T. Lindsay Baker and Julie P. Baker, eds., *The WPA Oklahoma Slave Narratives* (Norman: University of Oklahoma Press, 1996), 45.

126. Ibid., 170.

127. Ibid., 233–35.

128. Ibid., 241, 274, 376.

129. Ibid., 398.

130. Charley Lynch, IPP 56 (August 18, 1937): 293; Eliza Whitmire, IPP 97 (February 14, 1938): 398–99; George A. Butler, IPP 14: 98–99.

131. Baker and Baker, *The WPA Oklahoma Slave Narratives*, 276.

132. Ibid, 314.

133. Ibid., 316–21. See similarly O. C. Davidson, IPP 113 (n.d.): 187–88.

134. Baker and Baker, *The WPA Oklahoma Slave Narratives*, 347–51.

135. Ibid., 375–81.

136. Perdue, *Nations Remembered*, 181.

137. Tom Foster, IPP 31 (July 16, 1937): 335.

138. *Ross Papers* 2: 141, 149.

EPILOGUE

1. Russell Thornton, *The Cherokees: A Population History* (Lincoln: University of Nebraska Press, 1990), 147–48.

2. Donald L. Fixico, *Termination and Relocation: Federal Indian Policy, 1945–1960* (Albuquerque: University of New Mexico Press, 1986).

3. Wilma Mankiller and Michael Wallis, *Mankiller: A Chief and Her People* (New York: St. Martin's Press, 1993), 62.

4. Marjorie J. Lowe, "'Let's Make It Happen': W. W. Keeler and Cherokee Renewal," *CO* 74, no. 2 (Summer 1996): 116–29.

5. Russell Thornton, "Tribal Membership Requirements and the Demography of 'Old' and 'New' Native Americans," *Population Research and Policy Review* 16, nos. 1–2 (April 1997): 33–42.

6. James B. LaGrand, *Indian Metropolis: Native Americans in Chicago, 1945–75* (Urbana: University of Illinois Press, 2002), 78, 183, 199; Kendra B. Tabor, "Understanding Native American Perceptions of Sustainable Forest Management" (master's thesis, Michigan State University, 2009), 16; On the "ecological Indian" see the provocative Shepard Krech, *The Ecological Indian: Myth and History* (New York: W.W. Norton and Company, 1999).

7. During the 2012 senatorial election campaign in Massachusetts, Democratic contender Elizabeth Warren suggested that she had grown up with family stories of her Cherokee ancestors. See Josh Hicks, "Everything you Need to Know about Elizabeth Warren's Claim of Native American Heritage," *Washington Post*, September 28, 2012, accessed October 1, 2012, http://www.washingtonpost.com/blogs/fact-checker/post/everything -you-need-to-know-about-the-controversy-over-elizabeth-warrens-claimed-native -american-heritage/2012/09/27/d0b7f568–08a5–11e2-a10c-fa5a255a9258_blog.html. Cherokee writer Robert Conley reports that during his many travels over the years he has rarely gone anywhere without being told personal stories of Cherokee ancestry. See Robert Conley, *Cherokee Thoughts: Honest and Uncensored* (Norman: University of Oklahoma Press, 2008), 38.

8. Stella U. Ogunwole, *The American Indian and Alaska Native Population: 2000* (Washington, DC: US Census Bureau, 2002), 8–9; Stella U. Ogunwole, *We the People: American Indians and Alaska Natives in the United States* (Washington, DC: US Census Bureau, 2006).

9. Tina Norris, Paula L. Vines, and Elizabeth M. Hoeffel, *The American Indian and Alaska Native Population: 2010 Census Briefs* (Washington, DC: US Census Bureau, 2012), 17; Todd Crow, "Census Shows Increase in Cherokee Respondents," *Cherokee Phoenix*, February 21, 2012, accessed March 2, 2012, http://www.cherokeephoenix.org/Article/Index/5990.

10. Circe Sturm, *Becoming Indian: The Struggle Over Cherokee Identity in the Twenty-First Century* (Santa Fe, NM: School for Advanced Research Press, 2011), 32–33, 136–37. The Cherokee Nation of Oklahoma has no minimum "blood quantum" for

membership. The Eastern Band and the United Keetoowah require members to have proof of one-sixteenth Cherokee "blood."

11. Amy Harmon, "Seeking Ancestry in DNA Ties Uncovered by Tests," *New York Times*, April 12, 2006

12. Matthew Frye Jacobson, *Roots Too: White Ethnic Revival in Post-Civil Rights America* (Cambridge, MA: Harvard University Press, 2006).

13. Fay A. Yarbrough, *Race and the Cherokee Nation: Sovereignty in the Nineteenth Century* (Philadelphia: University of Pennsylvania Press, 2008), 130–31; Steve Russell, "Tsunami Warning from the Cherokee Nation," *Indian Country Today Media Network*, September 14, 2011, accessed December 22, 2014, http://indiancountrytodaymedianet work.com/2011/09/14/tsunami-warning-cherokee-nation; Paul Harris, "US government warns Cherokee nation not to exclude black freedmen," *The Guardian*, September 13, 2011, accessed December 22, 2014, http://www.theguardian.com/world/2011/sep/13/us -government-cherokee-nation-freedmen.

14. Scott Mckie, "Tribe Establishes Cherokee Identity Committee," *Cherokee One Feather*, October 14, 2011, accessed November 12, 2011, http://theonefeather.com/2011/10/ tribe-establishes-cherokee-identity-protection-committee/.

A Note about Sources

There exists a wealth of archival material throughout the world that sheds light on the Cherokee diaspora. Archival sources consulted in this book included:

American Philosophical Society
    Alfred I. Hallowell Papers, MS. Coll. 26
    A. Paul Wallace Papers, B W15p
    Ely S. Parker Papers, Mss. 497.3.P223
David M. Rubenstein Rare Book and Manuscript Library, Duke University
    Joel Roberts Poinsett Papers, 1825–1851
    John Ellis Wool Papers, 1837–1869
    John Howard Payne Papers, 1835–1836
    Jeremiah Evarts Papers, 1830
    William H. Thomas Papers
Southern Historical Collection, Wilson Library, University of North Carolina, Chapel Hill
    Alphonso Calhoun Avery Papers
    John R. Peacock Papers
    Willie Stewart White News clippings
Beinecke Rare Book and Manuscript Library, Yale University
    Herman Landon Vaill Collection, 1821–1952
Cornwall Historical Society, Cornwell, Connecticut
    Members of the Foreign Mission School, Nov 1st 1819, 2009.63.04
    Boudinot Wedding Record, 2009.57.06
    Ridge Wedding Record, 2009.57.05
Georgia Historical Society Manuscript Collection
    Cherokee Indians Relocation Papers, 1815–1838, MS 927

Huntington Library, San Marino, California
   Eldridge Collection
   Edward W. Bushyhead and Others, Articles and Argument Regarding Publica-
      tion of the *San Diego Union*, CT150
   Indian File, HM13240 A and B
   John Rollin Ridge, Letters to family, 1853–1855. mssFAC 1676–1678
   John Ridge, *The Cherokee Warpath, 1836–1840*, mssHM1730
   Letters to Stand Watie, 1850–1856-mssFAC 1789–1792
   Richard Barnes Mason, Correspondence Regard Texas Indians, 1841–1863. FAC
      1951–1961
   Robert Alonzo Brock Collection
Kansas Historical Society, Topeka, KS
   Indians Collection, 1855–1908, MS. Coll. Indians
Kenneth Spencer Research Library, University of Kansas, Lawrence
   Cherokee National Collection, High Sheriff Report
   James William Denver Papers, Kansas Collection, RH MS 19
   Brittendall Family Papers, Kansas Collection, RH MS 1120
Library of Congress
   *Letter from the Secretary of the Interior, Transmitting Report of Commissioner of
      Indian Affairs relative to the Amount Appropriated March 3, 1883, for Cherokee
      Nation, and Legislation to Protect the Rights of Adopted Citizens of Said Act*
      (48th Congress, 1st Session, Senate Ex. Doc. No. 86), Microfilm 58206
   *A Vindication of the Cherokee Claims, Addressed to the Town Meeting in Philadel-
      phia, on the 11th of January*, 1830, Microfilm 58206
McFarlin Library, University of Tulsa, Oklahoma
   Alice Robertson M. Collection
   Indians of North America Historical Manuscripts and Documents, 1724–1981
National Anthropological Archives, Smithsonian Institution
   Belle K. Abbott, "Cherokee Indians in Georgia," Manuscript 4649
   Benjamin Gold, Letter to his Brother, Cornwell, Connecticut, December 8, 1829.
      Manuscript 4747
   James Mooney Collection, Manuscript 1876
   _____, "Original Manuscript of Cherokee Stories Published in the 19th Annual
      Report of the Bureau of American Ethnology," Manuscript 1905
   John Howard Payne, Fragment of a Manuscript about the Cherokee, Manu-
      script 3710
   Frans M. Olbrechts Papers, Manuscript 4600
   Wahnenauhi, "Historical Sketches of the Cherokees: Together with Some of
      their Customs, Traditions, and Superstitions," Manuscript 2191
National Archives of Australia, Canberra
   Application for Entry for Residence, A12513
   Subject: Immigration, A2, 1920/509/5
National Archives Record Administration, Washington, DC

Records of the Bureau of Indian Affairs. Land Division. Letters Received Relating to Cherokee Citizenship, 1875–89. Record Group 75, Boxes 1–7

Records of the Bureau of Indian Affairs. Land Division. Records Relating to Cherokee Citizenship, Affidavits, Record Group 75, 1889–91

Records of the Bureau of Indian Affairs. Land Division. Records Relating to Cherokee Citizenship, Affidavits, 1891–92. Record Group 75, Boxes 1–5

War Department Collection of Confederate Records, Record Group 109, M270

National Archives Record Administration, Kansas City

Records of the Bureau of Indian Affairs, Pine Ridge Agency, Pine Ridge, South Dakota, Education Records, Descriptive Statements of Children Sent to Schools Off the Reservation, 1879–87, Record Group 75

National Archives Record Administration, Forth Worth, Texas

Selected Letter Received by the Office of Indian Affairs Relating to the Cherokees of North Carolina, M1059

Demurer and Answers of the Cherokee Nation, 1896–1897, Record Group 75

Records of the Bureau of Indian Affairs, Records of the Five Civilized Tribes Agency Reference Documents (Misc. Documents), HM2007 E.41

National Archives of the United Kingdom

CO 5/7, Original Correspondence, Secretary of State, 1755–1779

CO 5/67, Original Correspondence, Secretary of State, Indian Affairs, 1766–1767

CO 5/214, Entry Book of Letters and Dispatches, 1759–1763

T1/389/76–77, Treasury Board Papers and In-Letters

National Archives of Scotland, Edinburgh

Documents Relating to Royal Scots 1684–1855, RH 2/4/561

Papers of the Fergusson Family of Craigdarroch, Dumfriesshire, 1743–1925, GD 77/200/6

Papers of the Murray Family of Murraythwaite, Dumfriesshire, 1466–1903, GD 219/287

Newberry Library, Chicago

Thomas Lee Ballenger Papers, 1730–1968

William Bollaert, Cherokee Memos, VAULT Ayer MS 89

John Howard Payne Papers, 1794–1841, Ayer MS 689

John Ridge, ca. 1821–1835, Box Ayer MS 761

Oklahoma Historical Society, Oklahoma City

Cherokee Citizenship, 1871–1925. 85.65

Cherokee Orphan Asylum Press, 88.22

Cherokee Religion (Antiquities), 1884. 85.56

Federal Writers Project. 81.105

Grant Foreman Collection, 1900–1956. 83.229

Lewis Downing, 10 November, 1869. 85.07

Park Hill Seminary, 26 June, 1879. 90.75

T. L. Ballenger Papers, 1887–1936. 97.53

Thomas Gilcrease Museum, Tulsa, Oklahoma
    John Drew Papers
    John Ross Papers
Virginia Historical Society
    Preston Davie Papers, 1750–1967
    William Byrd Letterbook
Western Historical Collections, University of Oklahoma, Norman
    Cherokee Nation Papers
    S. H. Mayes Collection
    C. Johnson Harris Collection
    Dennis Wolfe Bushyhead Collection
    John D. Jordan Collection
    Oochalata (Charles Thompson) Collection
    William Charles Rogers Collection
    William Potter Ross Collection
William L. Clements Library, University of Michigan, Ann Arbor
    Aplin Family Papers
    Eaton-Shirley Family Papers, 1790–1939
    Elizabeth Comstock Papers, 1740–1929
    Israel Shreve Diary, M-4505.3
    Josiah Harmer Papers, 1681–1937
    John Love Papers, 1840–1853
    M. E. Mann Papers
    Native American History Collection, 1689–1921
    Octavius Leland Diary
    Robert McCallen Papers
    Texas Travel Diary, 1838
    William Henry Lyttelton Papers, 1730–1806
    William S. Burns Papers

Students wishing to explore Cherokee history in relation to print culture may wish to consult the following publications, all of which are cited throughout this book: *Americana; Atlantic Monthly; Baptist Missionary Magazine; Boston Quarterly; Botanico-Medical Recorder; Carlisle Arrow; Cherokee Advocate; Cherokee Almanac; Cherokee One Feather; Cherokee Phoenix; Christian Observer; Congressional Record; Ebony; Friends' Intelligencer and Journal; Humanity and Society; Indian Chieftain; Indian School Journal; Journal of American Indian Family Research; Journal of Education and College Review; Literary Gazette; LSA Daily World; Maryland Gazette; Missionary Herald of the American Board; Missionary Review of the World; New York Times; Niles' Weekly Register; North American Review; Orphans News; Overland Magazine; Peabody Journal of Education; Public Opinion; Science; Seamen's Journal; Southern Workman; The Indian School Journal; The People's Magazine; St. Louis Christian Advocate; United Daughters of the Confederacy Magazine; USA Today; Washington Post; Weekly Arizona Miner.*

There exists an enormous library of printed primary and secondary literature on virtually every aspect of Cherokee life since the eighteenth century. Much of this material is cited in the endnotes of this book and addresses issues as diverse as Cherokee origin narratives, political tracts, Church and missionary society pamphlets, and published literature, poetry, and history. These sources have helped me to shed light on the meaning of Cherokee identity in a diasporic context, but I believe many other original insights remain to be gleaned from these sources.

Acknowledgments

This book began its life at the beginning of the twenty-first century. In the time it has taken me to travel, research, and write it, I have accumulated many debts to friends and family who helped make the idea of this book a reality. My research was made possible by grants from the School of Humanities at The Australian National University; an Earhart Civil War Fellowship from Clements Library at the University of Michigan, Ann Arbor; and a grant from the School of Humanities at Virginia Commonwealth University. Special mention goes to Alan Gallay, then at the Ohio State University, and the Director of the Center for Historical Research, for granting me the opportunity to spend the 2010–2011 academic year thinking about, researching, and writing significant portions of this book. I would also like to acknowledge my gratitude to Sharon Harris and the Humanities Institute, University of Connecticut, who awarded me a residential fellowship for 2012–2013, which I was unable to accept.

No work of history, or any form of literary endeavor, is completed in isolation. This is certainly true of my own work. It is therefore incumbent upon me to acknowledge the friendship and the feedback I have received on various portions of this book from some brilliant scholars and incredibly generous people. To Brian Behnken, Steven Deyle, Carolyn Eastman, Alan Gallay, Karen Halttunen, Pekka Hämäläinen, Margaret D. Jacobs, Ann McGrath, Kathryn Meier, Randall Miller, Paul Spickard, Richard Godbeer, Emilie Raymond, James Roark, Carolyn Strange, Alan Taylor, Kathryn Tomasek, Clarence Walker, and Aram Yengoyan, thank you all for offering your insights and criticisms of this book as it came together over the past decade and a half. Special thanks also go to Seth Rockman for providing me with the opportunity to present a portion of my research at his Nineteenth-Century U.S. History Workshop at Brown University. My gratitude also to Scott Manning Stevens, then Director of the D'Arcy McNickle Center for American Indian and Indigenous Studies, who provided me with the opportunity to discuss my work in progress at the American Indian Studies Seminar Series at the Newberry Library. I am also grateful to the two anonymous readers for Yale University Press who showed themselves to be models of professionalism and generosity in helping me nurture this book, and to Margaret Otzel for her outstanding work as production editor of this book. In a similar vein, I am thankful to Laura Davulis, associate editor for history at the Yale University Press, who was a constant source of support, encouragement, and deadline reminders! Finally, I am grateful to all of the brilliant and hardworking archivists in numerous countries who have helped me over these many years, for sharing their expertise with me.

As I completed this book, my mother lost her long and brave fight with cancer. I owe my mother much, and recognize that it was never easy for her to watch her son leave Australia so many years ago to set out on his own diasporic journey. Through all the years, my mother was nurturing and supportive; she was also kind and generous, and just occasionally had an opinion or two about the world to share with me! Her passing has left a great void in my life, but I hope that wherever her spirit now resides she can look with pride on the work I am doing.

Finally, to my wife, Brooke Newman: I dedicate this book to you. You are a fine historian in your own right, but without you I could not have written this book—or anything else that I have written over the years. For your love, encouragement, and criticism of my work I owe you an enormous debt of gratitude. I am a lucky man to have you (and our two beautiful daughters, Gwyneth and Simone) in my life, and I hope you accept the dedication of this book as a small token of my appreciation for all that you bring to my life.

Index